FT Guide to Using and Interpreting Company Accounts

Fourth edition

Wendy McKenzie

**Financial Times
Prentice Hall
is an imprint of**

Harlow, England • London • New York • Boston • San Francisco • Toronto • Sydney • Singapore • Hong Kong
Tokyo • Seoul • Taipei • New Delhi • Cape Town • Madrid • Mexico City • Amsterdam • Munich • Paris • Milan

PEARSON EDUCATION LIMITED
Edinburgh Gate
Harlow
Essex CM20 2JE
England

and Associated Companies throughout the world

Visit us on the World Wide Web at:
www.pearson.co.uk

First published in Great Britain in 1994
Fourth edition published 2010

© Wendy McKenzie 1994, 2010

ISBN: 978-0-273-72396-7

British Library Cataloguing in Publication Data
A CIP catalogue record for this book can be obtained from the British Library

ARP Impression 98

Typeset by 9.5/14pt ITC Stone Serif by 30
Printed in Great Britain by Clays Ltd, St Ives plc

The Publishers' policy is to use paper manufactured from sustainable forests.

What's new in the fourth edition?

Just about everything!

Since the last edition the regulatory framework has changed with the enactment of the Companies Act 2006. Plus all companies in the European Union listed on a Stock Exchange have to prepare their accounts using the International Financial Reporting Standards (IFRS), which are now used in most countries. IFRS has changed the presentation, content and complexity of listed companies' financial statements. It also means that, in the UK, organisations use two different sets of accounting rules: IFRS that is largely used by listed companies, and UK GAAP (the UK's rules) that is used by most other organisations.

This edition is fully updated to reflect the changes in the Companies Act, the different accounting rules, and the presentation and content of the financial statements prepared using IFRS and UK GAAP. This enables you to understand and interpret the accounts prepared by both listed companies and other UK organisations. It uses illustrative examples from listed companies' accounts and a listed company's accounts as a worked example to illustrate ratio analysis and interpreting accounts.

Reading this book shows you how to calculate ratios and compare different businesses' performance and enables you to understand:

- The presentation and content of the financial statements using IFRS, both before and after the implementation of the revised IAS 1 during 2009. (For example the income statement and the statement of recognised income and expense can be combined in a new financial statement – the statement of comprehensive income.)

■ How this differs from the presentation used in UK GAAP.

■ The main differences between IFRS and UK GAAP.

■ The effect of financial derivatives and hedging on a business's reported profitability and its financial position.

■ The effect of final salary pension schemes on a business's reported profitability and its financial position.

Acknowledgement

Thanks to Douglas Hurt, IMI's Finance Director, for permission to use IMI's accounts.

Contents

part 3   How can I use my analysis?

Preface

Everyone prepares accounts in one form or another. If you ask yourself whether you can afford to buy a new house, change the car, or how much you're worth then you've prepared accounts. You're unlikely to have prepared them in a formal way, just done them mentally. They wouldn't look anything like published accounts. Company accounts are not really very different from the ones that we prepare for ourselves, but their presentation and the words used make them look more complicated than they really are. Although most people prepare accounts, they believe that understanding company accounts is difficult, if not impossible. This book shows that once you have cut through the jargon and understood the presentation, anyone can use published accounts to assess a business's performance.

All senior managers need to be able to understand and analyse company accounts. This book shows you how to do these. It shows you the information found in a set of accounts and how to analyse this information so that you understand how well the company is performing. Although I'm primarily covering the accounts prepared by companies that are listed on a European stock exchange, I'll also discuss some of the major differences that you'll find in other accounts, prepared by other organisations in the UK.

The book is in three sections, each designed to answer different questions.

The first section answers the question '*What information will I find in the accounts?*' This shows you:

- what the financial statements look like;
- what they tell you about a business;
- the way they are prepared;

- the judgements involved in preparing these statements;
- the main differences between listed companies' accounts and those prepared in the UK by other organisations.

The second section answers the question *'How do I analyse the accounts?'* and works through a set of published accounts, from the engineering company IMI, to show you:

- how to approach and structure your analysis;
- what ratios to use;
- what the ratios do and don't tell you.

The third section answers the question *'How can I use my analysis?'* by looking at four common uses for financial analysis:

- analysing suppliers' accounts;
- analysing customers' accounts;
- analysing competitors' accounts;
- identifying a companys' acquisition potential.

I shall be using the accounts of the international engineering company, IMI, to explain the financial statements and show you how to analyse accounts. You may not have heard of them, as they sell 'business to business', but you will have benefited from their products. So what does the company do? I'm pretty sure that you'll have had a cold drink on a hot day. Well the chances are it's been cooled and dispensed by one of its systems. Perhaps you've been in the new terminal at Madrid airport, or Terminal 5 in Heathrow? They use IMI's products to control the temperature and ventilate the buildings. Or perhaps you've looked at a product display in a car showroom or a cosmetic counter? IMI again. Some of its other products are a little more specialised, but still affect our quality of life. It makes valves to control critical processes in the power generation industry, valves that precisely dose your medication, and valves for commercial vehicle braking systems.

It has organised its business into 'Fluid Controls' and 'Retail Dispense'. The Fluid Controls business designs and produces valves for applications in pneumatics, severe service valves and indoor climate products and services. The

Retail Dispense business is concerned with beverage dispense and merchandising systems.

Let's consider these in more detail – firstly I'll tell you a bit about the Fluid Controls business. This is organised into three businesses: Fluid Power, Severe Service and Indoor Climate.

- The *Fluid Power* business develops and manufactures fluid control systems, principally pneumatic devices, for original equipment manufacturers in commercial vehicles, medical, print, packaging and other industries. These have wide applications and are used in factory automation, the ultrafine control of medical dosing valves and commercial vehicle braking systems.

- The *Severe Service* business develops valve actuation and control solutions that are used to control critical plant processes in power generation, oil and gas production, the petrochemical industry and pulp and paper facilities.

- The *Indoor Climate* business develops and produces valves that are used in heating and cooling commercial buildings and controlling temperatures in residential buildings.

Now let's look at the Retail Dispense business. It is organised into Beverage Dispense and Merchandising:

- The *Beverage Dispense* business develops systems to cool and deliver still and carbonated drinks, and 'point of purchase' displays for bars, restaurants and brand owners.

- The *Merchandising* business designs and develops 'point of purchase' displays and merchandising systems for retailers and brand owners.

part

1

What information will I find in the accounts?

1

Introduction to the accounts

Introduction

The amount of information that you'll find in the accounts and that is publicly available depends on the type of company and its size. All companies registered in the UK have to file their annual accounts at Companies House and, with the exception of small private companies, must have their accounts audited by an independent accountant. This means that, in the UK, company accounts are in the public arena. However, small private companies prepare their accounts using a simpler set of rules and file modified accounts. Medium-sized private companies prepare the full financial statements but can file a simpler set at Companies House. Public companies and large private companies have to file their full annual accounts at Companies House, and consequently all of their accounts are in the public domain.

As a general rule the amount of information found in a set of accounts increases as ownership separates from control. A sole trader gives very little external information, as he owns, controls and takes all the risks in his business. The other extreme is a public company listed on the stock exchange. Anyone can own a share in the business, and the directors of the company are unlikely to be its biggest shareholders. Consequently listed companies have to comply with the Companies Act, the accounting rules (International Financial Reporting Standards or IFRSs), and additional Stock Exchange listing requirements. They give a wide range of additional information enabling external investors to have a clearer assessment of the investment risk.

Consequently the amount of detail disclosed in the accounts is influenced by the interrelationship of four factors:

- the Companies Act;
- the accounting rules;
- a Stock Exchange listing;
- the company's size and ownership.

The Companies Act

All companies have a legal requirement to prepare accounts that are 'true and fair' and, with the exception of very small companies, have been audited by an independent accountant. Until the implementation of the Fourth and Seventh EU Directives, in 1981 and 1989, there were no detailed rules on either accounting presentation or measurement in British law. The Companies Act 2006 now identifies the minimum information that must be both disclosed in the accounts and subsequently filed at Companies House. It also requires that the accounts should include a director's report, a profit and loss account, a balance sheet, an auditor's report and that some additional disclosures are given in the notes to the accounts. The Act allows companies to prepare their accounts using either IFRS or UK GAAP (see below).

The accounting rules

The accounting rules, called accounting standards, clarify the way that profit should be measured, assets and liabilities should be valued, and require more information to be disclosed in the notes to the accounts. They also determine the language used in the financial statements. Whilst the accounting standards remain separate from the Companies Act, their legal position has been strengthened.

Within the UK the accounting rules used by companies depend on the companies' size and ownership. Small privately owned companies follow a simpler set of rules called the *Financial Reporting Standard for Smaller Enterprises*, or the *FRSSE*. Whilst other unlisted companies can use the international rules, most use the UK's accounting rules. UK accounting rules are called *Financial Reporting Standards* (*FRSs*) or, if they were issued before August 1990, *Statements of Standard Accounting Practice* (*SSAPs*). All listed companies within the EU use the international accounting rules which are called *International Financial Reporting Standards* (*IFRSs*) or, if they were issued before 2001, *International Accounting Standards* (*IASs*). The differences will be less important over time, as the UK aligns its rules to the international ones as part of the global harmonisation process. However, most of the EU member states have few, or no, plans to converge their national GAAP (**G**enerally **A**ccepted **A**ccounting **P**ractice) with IFRS. (GAAP represents the principles, rules, disclosure requirements and guidance statements used by companies to measure their profits, assets and liabilities.)

The US is currently engaged in a significant programme with the International Accounting Standards Board to converge IFRS and US GAAP. This programme is influencing the way in which IFRS is being developed for the rest of the world, as it is likely that within the foreseeable future the same set of accounting rules would be used by all listed companies. This convergence process has also changed, from 2009 both the presentation and terminology used in accounts prepared using IFRS are different. However, it is possible that the convergence process may be superseded, as in November 2008 the Securities and Exchange Commission issued a proposal that all US listed companies should use IFRS from 2014.

Whilst the Companies Act provides a framework for the presentation of accounts, the accounting rules require companies to publish additional financial statements and more information in their accounts.

A Stock Exchange listing

Companies listed on a Stock Exchange must disclose additional information concerned with the company's status, affairs and activities, directors, shares and shareholders, and loans and interest.

Company size and ownership

Until recently the accounts prepared by small and large companies were broadly similar, although smaller private companies were exempt from some accounting standards. Since 1992 smaller companies have been increasingly allowed to prepare simpler accounts, and most small private companies do not have to have their accounts audited. However, in practice, most small companies still continue to have their accounts audited, as lending bankers usually require audited accounts. (A private company's size is determined by its turnover, total assets and its average employees. It is currently regarded as 'small' if two out of the three following conditions are met. Its revenue, or turnover, must be less than £6.5 million, its total assets less than £3.26 million, and it has, on average, less than 50 employees. If it satisfies two of these conditions it qualifies for the Companies Act's small company disclosure exemptions, and its accounts may be based on the FRSSE.)

We are now seeing two different sets of generally accepted accounting practices evolving. Larger companies are required to comply with all statutory provisions and increasingly complex and detailed accounting standard requirements. Whereas smaller private companies comply with a shorter, restricted set of rules requiring fewer disclosures in the accounts.

The accounting principles

There are six accounting principles, or concepts, that influence the way that accounts are prepared, with the first two forming the basis for the way they are prepared:

- matching/accruals;
- going concern;
- prudence;
- consistency;
- substance over form;
- materiality.

These provide the foundation for the preparation of the accounts, and consequently it's important to understand them.

The matching, or the accruals, principle

This requires companies to match their costs to the period's revenues. This means that in the income statement (or *profit and loss account*) revenue is the sales that have been legally made in the period, and the costs are those that relate to these sales, regardless of when they are paid. This means that transactions are recognised when they occur and the income statement is unlikely to reflect the cash that has come in and gone out of the business.

Companies have to determine the costs that relate to the sales, and this means that judgements have to be made to identify the appropriate period. I'll discuss these judgements later in Chapter 2 – they are important as they can provide an opportunity for creative accounting.

The going concern principle

This assumes that the business will continue in existence for the foreseeable future. This is defined as at least 12 months into the future. However there is a significant difference between the international rules and UK GAAP. The international rule starts the 12 months from the latest balance sheet date, whereas the UK rules say that its should run from the date of signing the financial statements. (These can be very different dates. For example the unlisted XL travel group had its year end on 31 October and the accounts were signed off in May 2008. They went into administration four months later in September 2008.)

The prudence principle

This is the most important principle, as it ensures that income and asset values aren't overstated and costs and assets aren't understated.

The consistency principle

This requires items to be accounted for in a consistent manner, both within a period and from one period to the next, and ensures that the accounts are comparable.

Substance over form

This is one of the most important principles in European accounting, and has protected us from the worst excesses of creative accounting experienced in the US. This principle ensures that accounts reflect the commercial reality rather than the legal position. If a company has all the risks and rewards normally associated with owning something, it should be shown in the accounts in the same way as if the company owned it. The way that long-term leases (called *finance leases*) are treated in the accounts is a good example of this. The company leasing the assets, the lessee, has all the benefits and risks that are associated with owning the assets. So, although the leasing company legally owns the assets, they are shown in the lessee company's accounts as property, plant and equipment, and depreciated in the usual way. The amount owed to the leasing company over the life of the lease is included in debt.

Materiality

Accounts must disclose items that are considered to be material. But what is 'material'? Anyone reading accounts uses the accounts and their subsequent analysis to make 'economic decisions'. Maybe you're looking to make an investment. Or perhaps you're deciding whether this company should become one of your suppliers. Something is regarded as material if it would change a user's economic decision if it was not disclosed, or was misstated. Consequently, accountants tend to think something is material if there is a statutory requirement to disclose it accurately, or if knowing about it would influence your view about the company.

Now let's summarise: accounts are prepared using six accounting principles. The accounting principles ensure that the accounts reflect an accountant's view of reality as:

- Profitable businesses can fail, as cash transactions are not necessarily reflected in the current period's income statement.

- Companies have to make judgements to determine the costs that relate to the sales.

- The book value of a company is unlikely to be realised if it is liquidated.

- The accounts aren't totally accurate as they contain approximations, and they may not reflect the legal position.

The accounts

The accounts found in listed companies follow the same format and comprise:

- a chairman's statement;
- a directors' report;
- an income statement, or *profit and loss account*;
- a statement of recognised income and expense, or *statement of total recognised gains and losses*;
- a balance sheet;
- a cash flow statement;
- an auditor's report;
- some notes to the accounts.

They will also either have a financial and an operating review, or a detailed business review shown in the directors' report.

However, a change in IAS 1 (*Presentation of financial statements*) means that for accounting periods starting in 2009 the income statement and the statement of recognised income and expense may be combined in a 'Statement of comprehensive income'. (Under IAS 1 companies have the choice of showing either a combined statement, or an income statement followed by a statement of comprehensive income (recognised income and expense).) This is part of the convergence process, as it more closely aligns IFRS to US GAAP.

I'll talk about most of these in later chapters, but I'll summarise each of them here.

The chairman's statement

The chairman's statement is a marketing document shown in most companies' accounts. It usually presents the company's performance in the best light and usually contains information on:

- the company's strategy and business plans;
- the general trading performance of the company within the context of the economic and competitive climate;
- the company's prospects for the next year;

- the performance of specific businesses within the company;

- any items of special interest during the year (for example acquisitions).

The directors' report

This contains statutory information that may also be found elsewhere in the accounts. The Companies Act 2006 has increased the information that has to be disclosed in the directors' report where you'll find information about:

- The company's principal activities.

- Apart from small private companies, a review of the business's performance. The business review should comprise a comprehensive and balanced analysis of the business's development and performance during the year and its financial position at the end of the year. This means that the review now has to be quite detailed and should contain:

  - a description of the business and its business environment;
  - a discussion of the business's objectives and the strategies developed to achieve these objectives;
  - a review and analysis of the business's development and performance during the year;
  - the business's position at the end of the year;
  - a description of the major risks facing the company;
  - any financial and non financial key performance indicators (medium sized businesses don't have to disclose their non financial key performance indicators);
  - the resources that are available to the business, including any not reflected in the balance sheet.

As ownership separates from control, the information, detail and depth of the discussion increases. Listed companies also have to disclose:

  - the main trends and developments that would affect their future performance;

  - their policies on the employment of disabled persons, the health, safety and welfare of employees, and the involvement of employees in the management of the company;

  - Social and community issues.

While the Companies Act 2006 requires that this information should be in the directors' report, most large companies publish an 'Operating and financial review' detailing the same information. In this case, they may continue to disclose this information in their operating and financial review as long as they are published together and readers are referred to the appropriate pages.

- A summary of the company's results and dividends.
- The difference between the book value and the market value of land and buildings.
- If the company's use of financial instruments is material, it has to disclose its:
  - financial risk management objectives and policies;
  - exposure to price risk, credit risk, liquidity risk and cash flow risk.
- The directors, directors' interests and shareholdings, and any changes in the directors.
- An indication of the company's research and development activity (this may be shown in the business review).
- All limited companies in the UK must disclose the existence of any overseas branches.
- If a company has more than 250 employees it must disclose employees' involvement in the running of the company, and their employment policies on equal opportunities and the employment of disabled persons.
- Any political donations made during the year to non EU political parties and organisations and to EU parties and organisations that are over £200. Most donations to EU political parties and organisations now have to be approved by shareholders. The main exceptions are if they're for non political purposes, or the total donations in a 12-month period are below £5,000.
- Any charitable donations above £200 made during the year.
- The company's policy and the average payment days for the payment of suppliers. If the financial statements are for a group of companies, both the group's and the parent's/holding company's should be disclosed. (In practice you don't always see average payment days. For example, in its 2008 directors' report Tesco disclosed 'Tesco PLC [the parent/holding company] has no trade creditors on its Balance Sheet. The Group pays its creditors on a pay on time basis which varies according to the type of product and territory in which the suppliers operate'.

- Details of any important events that have occurred after the balance sheet date.

- Whether, or not, the directors believe that the business is a going concern.

- If the company has a qualifying directors indemnity provision for the benefit of one, or more, of the directors, it must be disclosed in the directors' report. (The Companies Act 2006 defines a qualifying third party indemnity provision as indemnity for a directors' liability that isn't related to:

  - any amounts due to the company, group company or associated company;
  - any fines imposed by criminal proceedings, or penalties payable to a regulatory authority for a breach of regulations;
  - the costs of criminal proceedings where the director has been convicted;
  - the costs involved in unsuccessfully defending civil proceedings brought by the company or group company;
  - The costs of any application where the courts refused the director relief.)

- A statement of the directors' responsibilities and a confirmation that the auditors have been provided with appropriate information and directors have not withheld any relevant information.

- The appointment of the auditors. Whilst this isn't a statutory requirement, you'll usually find at the end of the directors' report a note that a resolution will be put to the annual general meeting to reappoint the auditors.

Listed companies' directors' reports will also contain:

- Information about the structure of the company's capital, including any rights and obligations attached to the shares.

- Any share buy backs and treasury shares.

- Details of any shareholder, and their shareholding, who has more than 3% of the company's shares.

- Information about any transactions and contracts with a 'controlling shareholder'.

(A controlling shareholder is one who either:

- controls, or has the ability to control 30%, or more, of the voting power at company's meetings;

or

- can control the composition of the majority of the board's directors.)

▨ If any shareholder has agreed to waive its dividend, and the dividend represents 1%, or more, of the total dividend, the details of the arrangement must be disclosed.

The financial statements

The financial statements comprise:

IFRS		UK GAAP
Accounting periods starting before 1/1/2009	*Accounting periods starting after 1/1/2009*	
The following financial statements are shown in the accounts: ▨ A balance sheet ▨ An income statement ▨ A statement of changes in equity or ▨ A statement of recognised income and expense (SORIE), with the information shown in a statement of changes in equity disclosed in the notes ▨ A cash flow statement	The following financial statements are shown in the accounts: ▨ A statement of financial position (this is the revised name for the balance sheet, and doesn't have to be used) ▨ A single statement of comprehensive income (this combines the income statement and the SORIE) or ▨ An income statement immediately followed by a statement of comprehensive income (SORIE) ▨ A statement of changes in equity ▨ A statement of cash flows The financial statement's revised names do not have to be used	*The following financial statements are shown in the accounts:* ▨ *A balance sheet* ▨ *A profit and loss account* ▨ *A statement of total recognised gains and losses (STRGL)* *If a company revalues its assets, a note of historical cost profits and losses may follow the profit and loss account or the STRGL* *Most companies also include a cash flow statement in their financial statements*
Notes to these financial statements	Notes to these financial statements	*Notes to these financial statements*

Now I'd like to introduce you to these financial statements.

The balance sheet or the statement of financial position

This is a 'snapshot' of the business on a certain day, identifying the company's assets, the liabilities, and the shareholders' equity. It shows what the business was worth at the end of the year, given the set of assumptions and valuations that are detailed in the notes. From 2009, companies preparing their accounts using IFRS may describe this as 'a statement of financial position'.

The balance sheet represents a picture of the business on a certain day. Like any picture, there is a number of different views you can have of the company. A UK balance sheet usually identifies how much the business is worth to its shareholders, but you'll find that other countries look at the business from a different point of view, grouping the business's assets and liabilities and shareholders' equity.

This is a very important snapshot as it is used to determine things such as:

- the company's credit terms with its suppliers;
- the company's borrowing facilities;
- whether people are going to invest their life's savings in this company.

Like a snapshot of the business on a certain day, it can be 'managed'. Companies will pick the best day in their year to take the snapshot, and you should always remember that they have 364 days' notice of that day arriving! It may be as like the business for the rest of the year as your passport photographs represent true and fair views of you! Balance sheets should be read very carefully, and you should always remember to look for trends. Every year the company tries to show the best picture – is the best picture getting better or worse?

You'll find more information about the balance sheet in Chapter 3.

The income statement or the *profit* and *loss account*

I mentioned earlier that different accounting rules use different accounting terminology. Companies using IFRS prepare an 'income statement', whereas those using UK GAAP prepare a 'profit and loss account'. Whilst the terminology may be different, in essence an income statement is the same as a profit and loss account. As I'm focusing on analysing listed company accounts I shall always start with IFRS terminology, subsequently giving the UK GAAP's term in italics. In the chapters explaining each of the financial statements I shall discuss the different terminology, presentations and valuations used in IFRS and UK GAAP. Then, in Chapter 7, I shall tell you about the main differences between IFRS and UK GAAP.

Now let's look at the similarities. The income statement tells you whether the company sold its goods and services for more, or less, than it costs to deliver them to the customer. It takes the income from sales made in the period and then deducts the costs that relate to those sales.

When looking at any income statement you must remember three things:

It is historical. All income statements will tell you what has happened, not what is happening now – they're out of date when you see them. A UK company's accounts are usually published three months after the end of its financial year. To reinforce the fact that they're historical, income statements always say something such as 'for the year ending ... for the six months ending ... for the period ending'.

It does not include all of the capital expenditure. The income statement is concerned with the costs that relate to the period's sales. Businesses use property, plant and equipment over a long period and spread the cost of these assets over their life through the depreciation charge. The depreciation charge reflects a percentage of the money that has been spent on the fixed assets. Consequently, a business can be profitable but run out of cash because of a capital expenditure programme.

It is not concerned about whether the cash has been received from customers or paid to suppliers, just that the sale has been made and costs have been incurred. If I buy an apple for 5 and sell it for 8, the profit and loss account records a profit of 3. But I may have paid cash to buy the apple and sold it on credit. The profit remains the same even though my cash is now –5. Consequently a business can be profitable but run out of cash if its customers haven't paid for the sales in the period. Equally I'd report the same profit if I were a supermarket, where I buy the apple on credit and sell it for cash. In that case, I report a profit of 3 but have cash of 8.

This means that a business that is profitable in its latest accounts could be making losses today and profitable businesses can easily be bankrupt, as profitable businesses can still run out of cash.

The way an income statement is laid out varies from one company to another, as there are different ways you can look at costs. The costs of materials, labour and overheads used in sales (the operating costs) can be presented in two different ways:

*You can look at **what** you have spent the money on:*

materials

staff costs

overheads

or

*You can look at **why** you have incurred the cost:*

cost of sales

administration expenses

selling and distribution expenses.

You'll find more information about the income statement, and the differences in presentation between IFRS and UK GAAP, in Chapter 2.

The statement of recognised income and expense, or *the statement of total recognised gains and losses*

This statement combines all the gains and losses in the period regardless of whether they have been shown in the income statement or the balance sheet. This enables the shareholders to clearly identify any gains, or losses, that the company has chosen to recognise in the period.

These gains and losses are analysed into those arising from:

- profits;
- actuarial gains and losses arising from final salary pension schemes (I'll explain what these are in later chapters);
- revaluations of assets;

■ currency translation differences;

■ cash flow and net investment hedges (these aren't shown under UK GAAP and I'll explain what they are in Chapters 2 and 3).

It also discloses whether there have been any 'prior period adjustments' arising from changes in accounting policies or errors in the accounts.

You'll find more information about the statement of recognised income and expense in Chapter 4.

The statement of comprehensive income

This heading could reflect two different financial statements:

■ It could be the combination of the income statement with the other gains and losses that have been recognised in the period, enabling the readers of accounts to see all the gains and losses that have been recognised in the period on one page;

or

■ It could follow the income statement, and contain the information currently shown in the statement of recognised income and expense.

The statement of cash flows, or *the cash flow statement*

This shows the movement of cash in the business during the past year. It identifies where the company's money has come from and where it has spent this money. Looking at the cash flow statement helps you see whether the company is living within its means.

It is probably the most important document of all; profit can be created, but you can't create cash. You either have cash or you don't. You can always spot a business engaging in creative accounting, and one of the best indicators is when it is profitable but has no cash. Now this could happen quite legitimately if the company has had a major capital expenditure programme, has a credit control problem, or high stock levels and you'll see this on the cash flow statement.

You'll find more information about the cash flow statement in Chapter 5.

The auditors' report

With the exception of small private companies with turnover of not more than £6.5 million and whose balance sheet total is not more than £3.26 million, the accounts include a report from the auditors. The auditors are required to report to the shareholders whether, in their opinion, the financial statements:

- have been properly prepared in accordance with the Companies Act and the relevant accounting standards;
- give a true and fair view of the company's financial position and profit or loss.

To do this the auditor will check that proper accounting records have been kept and that the accounts reflect those accounting records.

The auditors' report is very important. Anyone looking at a set of accounts needs to be confident that those accounts are a true reflection of the company's performance. Auditors' reports must contain:

- a title specifying to whom the report is addressed;
- an introductory paragraph identifying the financial statements that have been audited;
- appropriately headed, separate sections discussing:
    - the respective responsibilities of the directors and the auditors;
    - the basis of the auditors' opinion;
    - the auditors' opinion on the financial statements.

The auditors' report should be signed and dated.

The auditors may offer an unequivocal opinion that the accounts are true and fair, or that they're not. They may even, in very rare cases, not offer an opinion. However it's not always that black and white. In some situations they may want to bring something to your attention, or qualify their opinion in some way. So let's look at some of the things you may find in an auditors' report and I'll start with items they wish to draw to your attention, as these don't affect the auditors' opinion.

▦ **Emphasis of matter** The auditors must draw attention to any inherent uncertainties that they believe to be fundamental to understanding the accounts, or to the company's ability to continue trading. For example, the auditors may be concerned about the continued support of the company's bankers, or the outcome of a major litigation. (I'm currently writing this in the 'credit crunch' and expect to see many of these, as there is a number of large highly indebted companies needing to refinance their debt in the next 12 months.)

The fundamental uncertainty may, or may not, lead to the accounts being qualified. If the uncertainty has been properly disclosed and accounted for within the accounts, there will be no reason for the accounts to be qualified. The auditors will show an 'emphasis of matter' paragraph immediately after the paragraph giving their opinion on the accounts.

▦ **Other matters** Occasionally auditors may feel it's necessary to communicate something that isn't disclosed elsewhere in the financial statements. In this case, they can disclose the 'other matters' after their opinion and any emphasis of matter.

Now let's look at how the auditors' opinion can be qualified in the report.

▦ **Disagreement** There are some situations where the auditors may disagree about the accounting treatment, or disclosure, of information contained in the accounts. For example, they may be unhappy about the bad debt provisions or inventory values. Or, they may believe that the company is not complying with the relevant GAAP. If there is some disagreement, the reason for the disagreement is disclosed in the auditor's report and the auditors' opinion starts with 'Except for ...'.

▦ **Limitation of scope** This occurs when there is inadequate, or insufficient, information available to the auditors; therefore they are unable to determine whether proper accounting records have been kept. This often happens in small companies, where sometimes there is insufficient information to support some of the items shown in the accounts. If there is a limitation of scope, the reason for the limitation of scope is disclosed in the auditors' report and the auditors' opinion starts with 'Except for ...'.

Then there are situations where the auditor is either unable to give an opinion or gives an adverse opinion:

▨ **Disclaimer of opinion** If an uncertainty, or lack of adequate information, could have a major impact on the accounts, the auditors will give a 'disclaimer of opinion'. This is given when the auditors have been unable to obtain sufficient evidence to support an opinion on the financial statements. (For example, this could happen if there is doubt about the company's ability to continue as a going concern, or the auditor were significantly limited in obtaining evidence and carrying out their auditing procedures.) The opinion in the auditors' report will start with 'We were unable to form an opinion on …'.

▨ **Adverse opinion** This is the report you don't want to find in the accounts! This is given when the auditors believe that the information in the accounts is seriously misleading. They will then state that in their opinion the accounts do not give a true and fair view.

The notes to the accounts

My advice is to read these first. They tell you the accounting policies used in the preparation of the accounts and how all the numbers in the accounts have been calculated. Careful reading of the notes is essential if you want to spot creative accounting or potential problems facing the company.

Summary

The accounts contain several financial statements, each showing different things about the company's performance:

▨ The income statement is an historical document that shows whether the company has been selling its goods and services for more, or less, than it cost it to deliver them to its customers. As it is not concerned with the cash that has been received and paid during the year, profitable businesses can fail.

▨ The balance sheet is a snapshot of the business at the year end, showing the company's assets, liabilities and equity.

▨ The statement of cash flows discloses the company's cash flows during the year, and helps you to understand whether the company is living within its means.

▨ The statement of recognised income and expense clearly identifies any gains and losses that the company has recognised during the year. If this is combined with the income statement in the statement of comprehensive income, all the gains and losses the company has recognised in the period are shown on one page.

These documents should be read in conjunction with the auditors' report. This report will disclose if, in the auditors' opinion, the accounts are true and fair, if there are any matters they want to bring to readers' attention and any qualifications to their opinion. The notes to the accounts will disclose the accounting policies and give additional information about the financial statements.

The terminology, content and presentation of accounts are determined by the accounting rules used. In this book I shall be primarily concerned with the international rules, IFRS, but will also show you accounts prepared using UK GAAP. You may be interested in one or the other, or both. To make it easier to find your way around the book, information on UK GAAP will be preceded by a Union Jack ▥ and followed by a line denoting the end of the section.

2

The income statement, or the
profit and loss account

Introduction

In this chapter I'll tell you all about the income statement, or the *profit and loss account,* showing you the profit the company has made in year. The income statement shows you whether the company is selling its products, or services, for more or less that it costs to deliver them to its customers. To do this, it starts with the income from sales that the company has made during the period, called revenue (or *turnover* in the UK's rules) and then deducts the costs relating to those sales. The income statement is not concerned with whether the company has received the cash for its sales or paid for its costs. This means that income statements rarely reflect a company's cash position.

In this chapter I'm looking at the income statement in detail and when you've finished this chapter you will understand:

▩ *the difference between capital and revenue costs;*

▩ *the judgements that must be made to determine a business's operating profit;*

▩ *the things you can expect to find in an income statement;*

▩ *the way the income statement is presented in the accounts.*

Capital costs and revenue costs

You need to understand the way a company classifies costs, as it affects a business's reported profits and its asset values. Costs are classified as:

- **Capital costs** These are the costs of buying, or improving, a business's assets. Consequently these costs are charged to property, plant and equipment.

- **Revenue costs** These costs relate to the period's sales and are charged to the income statement.

You might also think about costs in the following way. Putting in an extra bathroom is a capital cost, as you'd expect the extra bathroom to increase your house's value. Even if you hate DIY you can usually be talked into a capital project! On the other hand decorating a bedroom is a revenue cost that is unlikely to increase your property's value, even though it may speed up the sale.

The distinction is important in accounting, as only revenue costs are charged to the income statement. Any capital costs are charged to the balance sheet. This means that it is possible for companies to improve their profitability (and apparent net worth) by capitalising costs. This was how the US telecom business WorldCom overstated its profits by more than $7 billion in 2002 – by classifying operating expenses as capital expenditure. Both profits and asset values improved! The opportunity for creative accounting arises because it is not always easy to work out what costs should be capitalised, even though both the Companies Act and the accounting standards define what should be shown as part of an asset's cost:

- **Company purchases the asset** If the company buys the asset it is relatively straightforward; it is the purchase cost and any other costs incurred to make the property plant and equipment operational.

- **Company builds the asset** This is where the problems start, as the company has to calculate the cost of production. The Companies Act defines the production cost as the price of raw materials and consumables used, plus additional costs that are 'directly attributable to the production of the asset'. During the period of production, companies may also include 'a reasonable proportion of the costs … which are only indirectly attributable to the production of the asset'. This includes 'interest on capital borrowed to finance the production of the asset'. From 2009, as part of the convergence with US GAAP, companies that are using IFRS to prepare their accounts must also include any borrowing costs directly attributable to the asset's purchase.

The problem lies in the interpretation of – what is 'reasonable'? How do you calculate capitalised interest costs when the borrowings aren't necessarily specific to the construction of the asset? IAS 23 (*borrowing costs*) states that the borrowing costs that can be capitalised are those that 'would have been avoided had the expenditure … not been made'. Before 2009 companies could decide whether they capitalised interest costs, but now they **must** capitalise them if all the following conditions are met:

– The company spends money buying the asset.

– It incurs borrowing costs.

and

– It starts activities that are necessary to prepare the asset for either its use or its sale.

Once the asset is ready for use, or sale, the company can no longer capitalise any borrowing costs.

For example, Tesco's has always capitalised interest. In its 2008 accounts their accounting policies disclose:

Borrowing costs

Borrowing costs directly attributable to the acquisition or construction of qualifying assets are capitalised. Qualifying assets are those that necessarily take a substantial period of time to prepare for their intended use. All other borrowing costs are recognised in the Group Income Statement in the period in which they occur.

Their note on finance costs discloses that they capitalised £103 million interest in 2008, and the note on property, plant and equipment discloses:

(b) Includes £103m (2007 – £78m) in respect of interest capitalised, principally relating to land and building assets. The capitalisation rate used to determine the amount of finance costs capitalised during the year was 5.1% (2007 – 5.1%). Interest capitalised is deducted in determining taxable profit in the year in which it is incurred.

(c) Net carrying value includes:

(i) Capitalised interest at 23 February 2008 of £790m (2007 – £716m).

This means that, in 2008, of the £353 million interest payable on their loans, only £250 million was charged to the income statement, with the remaining £103 million included in their property, plant and equipment. The capitalisation of interest didn't affect its tax position, as it's still tax deductible.

 The UK's rule FRS 15 (*tangible fixed assets*) allows interest costs to be charged to tangible assets during the construction period if the interest is directly attributable and the company applies this accounting policy to all its tangible assets.

What does an income statement look like?

IAS 1 *(The presentation of financial statements)* requires that any material items of income and expense should be shown separately, and prescribes the minimum information that must be shown. However, companies can disclose more information as long as the terms are defined and are consistently used from one period to another.

This means that the income statement can be presented in different ways, but it broadly comprises a number of 'building blocks' that I've summarised below. The income statement starts with the business's 'revenue', and then deducts the costs in order to arrive at the profit for the period.

The building blocks of profit using IFRS

Revenue
Minus
▨ Operating costs
Plus
▨ Other operating income

= Operating profit

Plus/minus
▨ Finance income and expense
Plus
▨ Share of associate's and joint venture's after tax profits

= Profit before tax

Minus
▨ Tax

= Profit after tax

Plus/minus
▨ Profit, or loss, from any discontinued operations

= Profit for the financial year

Attributable to:
▨ Equity shareholders
▨ Minority interests (or non controlling interests)

Now let's see how a profit and loss account is constructed using the UK's rules.

 A UK profit and loss account is broadly similar, but has a different definition of operating profit, and some items show in different places, as you'll see in the next diagram.

The building blocks of profit using UK GAAP

Turnover
Minus
▨ Operating costs
Plus
▨ Other operating income

= Operating profit

Plus/minus
▨ Share of associated undertakings' profits
▨ Profits, or losses, on sale of fixed assets
▨ Profits, or losses, on sale of businesses
▨ Restructuring costs

= Profit before interest

Minus
▨ Net interest
▨ Other financial expenses
Plus
▨ Other financial income

= Profit before tax

Minus
▨ Tax

= Profit after tax

Minus
▨ Minority interests

=   Profit for the financial year

Up to profit before interest all entries are split between continuing and discontinued operations, and any acquisitions are separately disclosed within continuing operations.

You now know that income statements and profit and loss accounts are broadly similar, but there are some differences between IFRS and UK GAAP. I'm focusing on IFRS, but will discuss the main differences between the international rules and the UK's rules. So now I'd like to explain each of the items found on an income statement.

Revenue or *turnover*

This represents the company's total sales in the period, excluding any recoverable VAT or similar taxes. Group accounts show only the third party sales; any sales within the group are not shown on the income statement, although they may be disclosed in the notes to the accounts. Revenue can arise from the sale of goods or services, or from licence fees and royalties, and companies have to disclose the amount of revenue arising from each category in the notes to the accounts. Companies obtain their revenue from various sources and IAS 18 (*Revenue*) requires companies to disclose, in the notes to the accounts, any significant amounts of revenue arising from:

- the sale of goods;
- the rendering of services;
- interest;
- royalties;
- dividends.

Clearly most companies would not include the last three as part of their revenue. Companies also have to disclose any revenue arising from exchanges of goods, or services, which has been included in each significant category of revenue.

Revenue can't be recognised if the company still has any significant risks and rewards normally associated with ownership. (For example if the company retains an obligation for any unsatisfactory performance that isn't covered by any normal warranty provisions.)

Companies bring revenue into their income statement in a number of different ways that can be broadly divided into two categories based on:

- An event that transfers the ownership of the goods, for example raising the invoice or shipping the product to the customer.
- Time. This is used in long-term contracts, where the revenue shown in the income statement is based on the completed percentage of the contract.

Now let's consider what would happen if you bought a television and an extended warranty agreement. There are two elements to your purchase, the company would immediately 'recognise' revenue for the sale of the television. However, the extended warranty would be recognised over the warranty agreement's period. So if you paid £240 for a 24 month extended warranty, the company would report revenue from the warranty of £10 each month (which is partly offset by a provision for any work needed under the warranty). So you can see that revenue can only be shown in the income statement when it has been earned. Any advance payments for sales are not shown in the income statement until the sales are recognised as revenue. They are shown as *deferred income* and included in trade and other payables on the balance sheet, as the company has an obligation to provide the warranty in the future.

Now let's consider companies that have long-term contracts, as they have different rules for revenue and profit recognition.

Long-term contracts

Construction companies have different problems, as large construction contracts often span a number of years. Normally, revenue and profit can only be shown in the income statement once the full terms of the contract have been fulfilled. However, if a construction company waited until the project is finished before including a contract in the income statement, the accounts would not reflect a fair view of its financial performance. It might complete no contracts in one year and three in the following year. Consequently there is a different way of accounting for long-term contracts, and this is known as *the percentage of completion method*. This allows construction companies to include in their income statement an appropriate proportion of uncompleted profitable long-term contracts once the contract's outcome can be reliably estimated. If you're analysing a construction company you need to understand how they incorporate revenue and profit into their income statement.

IAS 11 *Construction contracts* applies to construction contracts, and contracts for services that are directly related to the construction of an asset. The first thing a company has to do when determining its revenue and costs for the period is to make a reliable estimate for the contract's total profit or loss, and IAS 11 offers guidance for estimating the outcome of both fixed price contracts and cost-plus contracts. Then it estimates the contract's stage, or percentage, of completion, which is then applied to the contract's total revenue and expenses to determine the revenue and expenses that are shown in the current period's income statement. The accounting standard provides detailed guidance on contract accounting including:

▪ *Bid costs* – Companies can incur significant costs bidding for contracts, and these costs are usually allocated to the contract from the date the contract is secured. All the contract's direct costs should be included in the contract's costs as soon as they can be measured reliably, and it's probable that the contract will be given to the company. (This happens when the company has been named the 'preferred bidder'.)

▪ *Contract losses* – If a company believes that a contract will make a loss, the full loss must be taken immediately in the income statement.

▪ *Inability to estimate the contract's outcome* – If a company can't reliably estimate a contract's outcome, no profit can be taken in the income statement. The revenue shown is the recoverable amount of the costs incurred, and the contract's costs are expensed as they're incurred.

▪ *Profitable contracts* – If the contract is almost certainly profitable, the value of work completed is shown as revenue and any costs relating to the work done are charged to cost of sales. Then the 'attributable profit' is shown in the income statement. (A lot of companies believe that profitability can be assessed with some certainty when more than 30% of the contract has been completed.)

Companies determine the stage of completion by:

▪ measuring the costs incurred for work performed to date as a percentage of the estimated total costs;

▪ surveys of the work performed to date – this is usually done by the main contractor, who hires an architect to certify the contract's progress;

▪ completing a physical proportion of the contract work.

The contract's billings are unlikely to follow the percentage of completion, and are more likely to be based on agreed milestones. Consequently, there will be assets, and possibly liabilities, on the balance sheet reflecting the amounts owed by, or to, the customer. The asset shows with trade and other receivables, and the liability shows with trade and other payables. The asset, or liability, is calculated by deducting the progress billings from the total of the reported profit plus the costs. I've illustrated this in the example below, showing a three-year contract.

Example 2.1

	Year 1	Year 2	Year 3
Cumulative costs to date	4,000	7,100	9,500
Cumulative profits	500	400	500
Cumulative billings	(4,000)	(8,000)	(9,000)
Receivable/(payable) shown on the balance sheet	500	(500)	1,000

The contracting and engineering group Costain's accounting policy is covered in two of its accounting policy notes, and I've extracted the part of the revenue note and the trade and other receivables note relating to construction contracts.

Construction contracts

Revenue arises from increases in valuations on contracts. Where the outcome of a construction contract can be estimated reliably and it is probable that the contract will be profitable, revenue and costs are recognised by reference to the stage of completion of the contract activity at the balance sheet date. Stage of completion is assessed by reference to the proportion of contract costs incurred for the work performed to date relative to the estimated total costs, except where this would not be representative of the stage of completion.

When it is probable that total contract costs will exceed total contract revenue, the expected loss is recognised as an expense immediately.

Variations and claims are included in revenue where it is probable that the amount, which can be measured reliably, will be recovered from the customer.

When the outcome of a construction contract cannot be estimated reliably, contract revenue is recognised to the extent of contract costs incurred where it is probable those costs will be recoverable.

Contract costs are recognised as expenses in the period in which they are incurred.

Bid costs

Costs associated with bidding for contracts are written off as incurred. When it is probable that a contract will be awarded, usually when the Group has secured preferred bidder status, costs incurred from that date to the date of financial close are carried forward in the balance sheet.

When financial close is achieved on PFI contracts, costs are recovered from the special purpose vehicle and pre-contract costs within this recovery that were not previously capitalised are credited to the income statement. When the Group retains an interest in the special purpose vehicle and accounts for its interest as an associate or joint venture, the credit is recognised over the life of the construction contract to which the costs relate.

Trade and other receivables

Construction work in progress is stated at cost plus profit recognised to date less a provision for foreseeable losses and less amounts billed and is included in amounts due from customers for contract work. Amounts valued and billed to customers are included in trade receivables. Cost includes all expenditure related directly to specific projects and an appropriate allocation of fixed and variable overheads incurred in the Group's contracting activities based on normal operating capacity. Where the cash received from customers exceeds the value of work performed, the balance is included in credit balances on long-term contracts.

In the notes to their 2007 balance sheet they disclosed:

▦ In the note on trade and other receivables – The amounts due from customers for contract work was £45.8 million. The total amount of contract costs incurred plus recognised profits, less recognised losses, at the balance sheet date was £1,796.2 million.

▦ In the note on trade and other payables – There were credit balances on long-term contracts of £7.2 million.

 The major difference between IAS 11 and SSAP 9 *Stocks and long term contracts* is the presentation on the balance sheet, as the UK has always included contract work in progress with stock. Consequently, long-term contract balances are analysed as:

• amounts recoverable on contracts (included in debtors);
• work in progress (included in stock);
• payments on account (which can be deducted from the debtor and stock, or shown as a creditor).

Operating costs

These are the costs of materials, labour and overheads used in sales. In the first chapter I told you that there are two different ways that these can be shown in the income statement, firstly I'd like to show you how they would normally be presented.

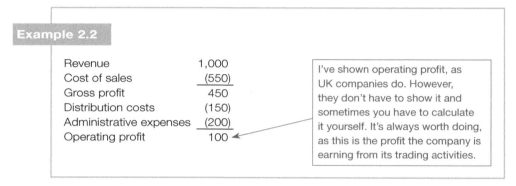

Example 2.2

Revenue	1,000
Cost of sales	(550)
Gross profit	450
Distribution costs	(150)
Administrative expenses	(200)
Operating profit	100

I've shown operating profit, as UK companies do. However, they don't have to show it and sometimes you have to calculate it yourself. It's always worth doing, as this is the profit the company is earning from its trading activities.

This is a 'functional' presentation with the materials, staff costs, overheads and depreciation shown under the respective headings. Unfortunately, the classifications into cost of sales, distribution costs and administrative expenses aren't defined and different companies include different costs under these headings. Whilst most manufacturing companies use their manufacturing costs as their cost of sales, not all do. This means that you can't compare different companies' gross profit, and gross profit margins.

Not every company presents their costs functionally, and here's the alternative presentation:

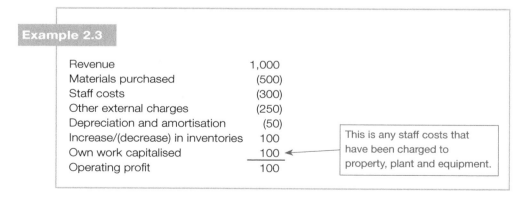

Example 2.3

Revenue	1,000
Materials purchased	(500)
Staff costs	(300)
Other external charges	(250)
Depreciation and amortisation	(50)
Increase/(decrease) in inventories	100
Own work capitalised	100
Operating profit	100

This is any staff costs that have been charged to property, plant and equipment.

Looking at this income statement, you probably have a few questions. Is it normal for 33% of the staff costs to be charged to property plant and equipment? What was the percentage of staff costs capitalised the previous year? Why have inventories increased? You can see that this presentation gives you enough information to be able to start to ask some sensible questions, but this is the least popular presentation of the income statement.

However, this presentation is popular in some European countries. For example Eon, the German power company, uses this presentation. Like all utilities, a significant percentage of its staff costs are capitalised (its 2007 annual report disclosed that €517 million of their 4,597 million staff costs were capitalised). If you look at its accounts you'll also see that a figure for operating profit is not shown.

It doesn't matter how they're presented – you need to remember that the calculation of the operating costs requires judgment, as companies have to match their costs to their revenues. I'll discuss these judgments, and how they're made, towards the end of this chapter.

Other operating income

This is income that doesn't arise from the company's normal trading activities, such as a rental income. For example Morrisons in its 2009 accounts discloses that its £30 million other operating income '... consists of income not directly related to the operating of supermarkets and mainly comprises rental income from investment properties. Other categories of income included within other operating income are backhaul income and credits earned from the recycling of waste and packaging material.'

Finance income and expense

When you looked at this heading, I expect that you thought of interest received and paid and you'd be right. Interest is included, but may only be a relatively small component. I'd like to start by discussing interest and then tell you about the other components of finance income and expense.

Interest

Companies show interest receivable, dividends receivable and similar income as interest receivable. Interest payable covers interest on loans and preference dividends. (Preference shares are usually classified as debt, as they have fixed dividends and often have a repayment date – called a *redemption date*.) Interest payable excludes any interest that has been capitalised (which means that it's charged to the balance sheet, not the income statement). From 2009 companies will be capitalising more interest, as IAS 23 *Borrowing costs* requires that all borrowing costs that are directly attributable to the acquisition, construction or production of property plant and equipment must be capitalised and included in the asset's cost.

When you're analysing a business's performance you need to remember that its cash position isn't affected by where the interest is charged. A company could be having difficulties with its bankers, but on the income statement the interest shown may be only a small proportion of the interest charge if most of the interest has been capitalised.

Other components of finance income and expense

Now we've looked at interest, let's return to finance income and expense which has a much broader definition, as it can also include:

- *Gains and losses on some financial instruments* – Financial instruments* (a term embracing most investments that are traded in the stock markets and money markets such as bonds and shares) and derivatives (spin-offs from a basic instrument, such as options and futures) are widely used by companies to manage their exposure to risks. Most of these have to be revalued to their market value at the end of the financial year, with any profit or loss shown in the income statement as part of other finance income or expense. I'll tell you more about derivatives, and the way that companies account for them, in the next chapter.

(*The accounting rules have a wider definition of financial instruments than the commonly used one that I've given above – they define them as 'a contract that gives rise to an asset in one entity and a financial liability or equity in another'. This means that it includes cash, receivables and payables. Receivables are shown net of any bad debt provisions; a *realisable* value rather than a market value.)

▨ *The financing income and costs of final salary pension schemes* – Whilst IAS 19 *(Employee benefits)* doesn't require these to be included in finance income and expense, it only states that they have to be charged to profit, most UK companies follow their previous practice under UK GAAP (covered by FRS 17 – *Retirement benefits*). I'll explain more details about pension accounting in Chapter 6, but the income and costs charged here effectively reflect the return on the fund's assets (shown as income) and a notional interest charge on the fund's liabilities (shown as expenses).

 Most companies using UK GAAP don't recognise financial instruments, so their gains and losses aren't included in other financial income and expense. The financing costs of final salary pension schemes must be shown as other financial income and expense.

IMI's note on financial income and expense

If you looked at IMI's income statement you would see that their financial income has increased from £81.1 million to £85.6 million, and their financial expenses have increased by almost 46% from £81.8 million to £119.4 million. When you look at this note you can see why they've changed, by looking at the individual items. Don't worry if you don't understand all the terminology, I'll be discussing it in detail in later chapters.

7 Net financial income and expense

	2008				2007			
	Interest	Financial instruments	Other	Total	Interest	Financial instruments	Other	Total
Recognised in the income statement	£m	£m	£m	£m	£m	£m	£m	£m
Interest income on bank deposits	10.2			10.2	7.4			7.4
Financial instruments at fair value through profit or loss:								
Designated hedges		3.1		3.1		0.8		0.8
Other economic hedges								
– future year transactions		–		–		3.3		3.3
Income from investments			0.7	0.7			–	–
Expected return on defined benefit pension plan assets			71.6	71.6			69.6	69.6
Financial income	10.2	3.1	72.3	85.6	7.4	4.1	69.6	81.1
Interest expense on financial liabilities measured at amortised cost	(26.3)			(26.3)	(20.2)			(20.2)
Financial instruments at fair value through profit or loss:		(3.2)		(3.2)		(0.9)		(0.9)
Designated hedges								
Other economic hedges		(2.6)		(2.6)		–		–
– current year trading		(17.2)		(17.2)		(1.6)		(1.6)
– future year transactions								
Impairment of available for sale financial assets		(2.3)		(2.3)		–		–
Financial cost of defined benefit pension scheme liabilities			(67.8)	(67.8)			(59.1)	(59.1)
Financial expense	(26.3)	(25.3)	(67.8)	(119.4)	(20.2)	(2.5)	(59.1)	(81.8)
Net financial (expense)/income	(16.1)	(22.2)	4.5	(33.8)	(12.8)	1.6	10.5	(0.7)

Included in financial instruments are current year trading gains and losses on economically effective transactions which for management reporting purposes (see note 3) are included in segmental operating profit. For statutory purposes these are required to be shown with in net financial income and expense above. Gains or losses for future year transactions are in respect of financial instruments held by the Group to provide stability of future trading cash flows.

Recognised directly in equity

	2008 £m	2007 £m
Foreign currency translation differences	73.4	(2.5)
Change in fair value of other financial assets	–	4.2
Change in fair value as effective portion of net investment hedges	(5.3)	(3.3)
Income tax on financial income/(expense) recognised directly in equity	(0.7)	2.5
Financial income/(expense) recognised directly in equity (net of tax)	67.4	0.9
Recognised in:		
Hedging reserve	(3.8)	1.9
Translation reserve	68.1	(1.0)
Minority interest	3.1	–
	67.4	0.9

Exceptional items

Exceptional items are things that you would expect to occur in the normal course of events, like bad debts but their size, or their frequency, is so unusual that companies disclose them. There isn't an international accounting standard covering exceptional items, however IAS 1 requires that material items of income and expenses are shown separately. It gives the following examples of circumstances that would require separate disclosure if they were material:

■ asset write-downs to net realisable value, or recoverable amount, and any reversals of these write-downs;

■ restructuring provisions and any reversals of these provisions;

■ profits or losses arising from disposals of property plant and equipment;

- profits or losses arising from disposal of investments;

- discontinued operations;

- litigation settlements;

- other reversals of provisions.

Some of these would obviously be exceptional items. They can either be shown in the income statement itself or disclosed in the notes.

 Exceptional items are covered by FRS 3 (*Reporting financial performance*). It requires that most exceptional items are included in the relevant operating cost heading, with the details disclosed in the notes to the accounts. The only exceptional items disclosed separately on the income statement itself, after operating profit, are:

- profits, or losses, on sale of fixed assets;
- profits, or losses, on sale or termination of subsidiaries;
- the costs of a major restructuring, or reorganisation, having a material effect on the business.

UK GAAP's treatment of these exceptional items has continued to influence their presentation in listed companies accounts in the UK. Even though they are using IFRS, most listed companies still show the UK GAAP exceptional items shown above in their income statement. These are usually shown separately with companies showing two operating profit figures: one before exceptional items, and the other after exceptional items.

As most exceptional items don't have to be disclosed on the income statement itself, you really have to read the notes if you want to understand the underlying trends in the company's profitability. This is particularly important if you are looking at overseas accounts, where historically exceptional items have been shown in the notes rather than in the income statement.

I'd now like to explain how to calculate profits and losses on sale of property, plant and equipment and businesses.

Property, plant and equipment are things the business means to keep. But all businesses sell assets when they reach the end of their useful life. The sale of assets affects profitability if the company receives more or less than the asset's value in the accounts.

I'll illustrate this with an example. A company buys a machine for £15,000 and depreciates it by £10,000, so it's worth £5,000 in its books. If it then sells the asset for £6,000, it has made £1,000 profit on the sale of the machine. This is shown as a profit because the machine is over depreciated. If it only sold the machine for £3,000, it reported a loss of £2,000 in its income statement. All assets have a value in the company's books. If they're sold for more than their book value the company reports the difference as a profit, if they're sold for less the difference shows as a loss. This means that profits, or losses, on sale of assets are determined by the asset's value in the accounts.

Profits, or losses, on sale or termination of subsidiaries is just an extension of this. Companies have assets and liabilities. Their liabilities are deducted from their assets to arrive at their net assets. If a company is sold for more than its net assets, the seller reports a profit. If it's sold for less, the seller reports a loss. Companies using the international rules don't show them separately on the income statement, they are combined with the subsidiary's after tax profits and shown after tax. However, they are disclosed in the notes.

Share of associates and joint ventures profits

Both associates and joint ventures are long-term investments, but the accounting treatment of their profits in the group's income statement can be slightly different. Both should have year ends within three months of the investor's year end, and their results may be adjusted to reflect the investor's accounting policies and any significant transactions between the reporting date of the associate/joint venture and that of the investor.

The notes to the accounts list all of the significant associates and jointly controlled businesses detailing:

▓ their name;

▓ the country of incorporation or residence;

▓ the company's proportion of ownership (and the voting power it has if this is different from the proportion of ownership);

▓ the method used to account for the investments.

Now let's look at how we account for associates and joint ventures.

Associates

An associate is an investment where the investor has the power to participate in the business's financial and operating policies, but doesn't control the business. IAS 28 (*Associates*) refers to this as 'significant influence' and presumes that it arises when the investor has 20%, or more, shareholding in a business. (I've deliberately used the word 'business', as it doesn't have to be a company – it can be any business that trades, regardless of its legal structure. The international rules call this an *entity*, whereas the UK rules calls this an *undertaking*.) When investors have significant influence they usually have a seat on the board of directors, or the equivalent governing body.

Once the investment is classed as an associate, the investing company brings its share of the associate's profit into its consolidated income statement. This is called *the equity method* of accounting. (If the investment is not classed as an associate, or a subsidiary, only the income received from the investment will be shown in the income statement as part of interest receivable and similar income.)

The international rules interpret the equity method in a different way from the UK rules. IAS 28 (*Associates*) requires the investing company to show its share of the associate's *after* tax profit before profit before tax. (This doesn't mean it's taxed twice, the investor's tax charge is only affected by any dividends it receives from the associate not the associate's profits.)

 There is an important difference in the definition of an associate under UK GAAP. To classify an investment as an associate, the international rule only requires the investor to have the *power* to participate, whereas the UK accounting standard, FRS 9 (*Associates and joint ventures*), requires the investor to actually *participate* in the decision making. FRS 9 requires more disclosure about associate's costs, as the investor must show the associate's operating profit, and all subsequent profit and loss account items in its consolidated profit and loss account. This means that the investing company includes its share of the associate's following items in its profit and loss account:

- operating profit;
- profits, or losses, on sale of fixed assets;
- profits, or losses, on sale or termination of subsidiaries;

- major restructuring and reorganisation costs;
- interest;
- tax.

As these aren't cash flows in the investing company, they have to be disclosed to enable you to understand the business's performance. Any material exceptional items and interest are separately disclosed on the income statement itself, immaterial amounts are disclosed in the notes. The investor's share of the associate's tax charge is disclosed in the notes to the accounts.

You can see that the UK's approach is more complicated. I'll show you the effect that the different approaches have on reported profitability in Example 2.4.

Example 2.4

Company A buys a 30% stake in Company B, and the investment is classed as an associate under the accounting rules. Before Company B's results are included in Company A's results, the two companies' income statements were as follows:

	Company A (the investor) £m	Company B (the associate) £m
Revenue	1,000	700
Operating costs	(750)	(520)
Operating profit	250	180
Interest payable	(50)	(30)
Profit before tax	200	150
Tax	(60)	(30)
Profit for the financial year	140	120

Firstly let's look at how Company A's associate is shown in the income statement if the accounts were prepared using the international rules:

IFRS	Company A £m
Revenue	1,000
Operating costs	(750)
Operating profit	250
Interest payable	(50)
Share of associates' profits	36
Profit before tax	236
Tax	(60)
Profit for the financial year	176

2.4 *continued*

Now let's see how the profit and loss account would look when it's prepared under the UK's rules. Company A has to *consolidate* its investment in Company B. This means that it includes its 30% share of Company B's operating profits (£54,000), interest (£9,000), and tax charge (£9,000) into its consolidated profit and loss account:

UK GAAP	£m	Company A £m
Turnover		1,000
Operating costs		(750)
Operating profit		250
Share of associate's operating profits		54
Interest payable		
Group	(50)	
Associate	(9)	(59)
Profit on ordinary activities before tax		245
Tax on profit on ordinary activities[1]		(69)
Profit for the financial year		176

The notes would disclose the associate's charge:

1 Tax
Group	(60)
Associate	(9)
	(69)

You can see that associates only affect the after tax profits if the company is using the international rules, whereas the UK's rules affect reported profit before and after tax. Whichever rules are used, Company A's after tax profits have grown by over 25%, but their cash only increases if their associate pays a dividend. Associates can have a significant effect on reported profitability, but may have a minimal effect on cash flow.

Joint ventures

A joint venture is a business, an entity, in which a company has a long-term interest and is jointly controlled by the company and one or more other venturers under a contractual agreement. A joint venture could be a jointly controlled business (referred to as an *entity* in the international rules), jointly controlled operations, or jointly controlled assets. (Venture capitalists, mutual funds, unit trusts and similar organisations do not have to account for their jointly controlled businesses in the following way. These are shown at fair value, and are covered by a different accounting rule (IAS39 *Financial instruments: recognition and measurement*).)

A jointly controlled business is usually accounted for in the same way as associates, using the equity method, but currently IAS 31 (*Interests in joint ventures*) also allows proportional consolidation. (So if an investor controlled 40% of a joint venture, it would include 40% of the joint venture's revenue and costs into its income statement. The accounting standard allows companies to consolidate the joint venture's revenue and expenses into its income statement, or alternatively they can show separate line items for the joint venture's income and expenses. Proportional consolidation is unusual in the UK, but is common in other parts of Europe. It may not be allowed in the future, as the IAS has issued a discussion document that would remove this option.)

Jointly controlled operations use the venturers' resources and assets, instead of establishing a separate business. This means that each investor recognises its share of the joint venture's revenue and the expenses it occurs. A jointly controlled asset is one that is under the joint control, and often ownership, of assets used specifically in a joint venture. The revenue from the asset and the expenses incurred are incorporated into the income statement in accordance with the contractual arrangement.

 The UK's accounting rule, FRS 9 (*Associates and joint ventures*), only covers jointly controlled businesses and requires companies to use an expansion of the equity method, the *gross equity method*, to account for these joint ventures. This means that the investor's share of the joint venture's turnover is noted on the consolidated profit and loss account.

To show you how this works I'll use the same numbers I used in Example 2.4, but this time I'll assume that Company B is a joint venture and that Company A has a 30% stake in it.

Example 2.5

The consolidated profit and loss account for Company A would then be as follows:

	£m	£m
Turnover: group and share of joint venture		1,210
Less: share of joint venture's revenue		(210)
Group turnover		1,000
Operating costs		(750)
Operating profit		250
Share of joint venture's operating profits		54
Interest payable:		
Group	(50)	
Joint venture	(9)	(59)
Profit on ordinary activities before tax		245
Tax on profit on ordinary activities[1]		(69)
Profit after tax		176

The notes disclose:

1 Tax

Group	(60)
Joint venture	(9)
	(69)

Reporting significant associates and joint ventures using UK GAAP

You've seen that associates and joint ventures can have an important effect on the reported profits, but only affect the business's cash flow if they pay dividends. In some industries associates and joint ventures can be an important element of a company's trading activities. This often happens in the construction industry where major projects are managed through joint ventures. FRS 9 requires companies to give more information where the investor's total share in its associates or joint ventures exceed 15% of the infvesting group's:

- gross assets;

- gross liabilities;

- revenue;

◼ operating results (based on a three-year average).

The company then has to disclose an associate's revenue and give more information about some items on the balance sheet – I'll discuss these in the next chapter when I look at the balance sheet.

More information has to be given if an associate, or joint venture, exceeds 25% of any of the above. Then the investor's share of the following income statement items are also disclosed:

◼ profit before tax;

◼ tax;

◼ profit after tax.

There are also more disclosures of balance sheet items.

Taxation

This is shown on the income statement as a total and if you want to know the components of the tax charge you'll have to look at the notes to the accounts. It's often worth a look as one of the things that you'll notice is that the tax charge may not be the amount you would expect. (For example the UK's tax charge is currently 28% for large companies. Even if the company trades exclusively in the UK, its tax charge isn't always 28% of its pre-tax profit.) This is because the way that the accounting rules recognise income and expenses is often different from the tax rules. (This means that most companies prepare three sets of accounts, the statutory published accounts, the tax accounts and their detailed management accounts.)

The note on taxation discloses:

◼ the income statement's tax charge, analysed between *current tax* and *deferred tax*;

◼ a reconciliation of the *effective tax charge*;

◼ the tax relating to items that have been charged to the shareholders' equity;

- the main deferred tax assets and liabilities and how they have changed during the year;

- any unrecognised deferred tax assets and liabilities.

Firstly let's have a look at the difference between current tax and deferred tax. The current tax is a tax that relates to this year's financial performance. It is the amount that will be shown on the company's tax return for the year. So this is the tax charge that you would expect. Now let me explain deferred tax.

Deferred taxation

I've already explained that in many countries taxable profits aren't the same as the reported profit before tax. So you can't take the pre tax profits, multiply them by the tax rate and arrive at the tax charge. Some things that are charged to the published income statement (in the UK a good example is entertaining clients) aren't allowed for tax purposes. Other things have different values in the tax accounts and the published accounts.

These differences between the two sets of accounts are called *timing differences*. They can either be permanent, where they appear in one set of accounts but not the other. Or, they could show in the published accounts in a different year than they show in the tax accounts. Accountants talk about these differences being either 'permanent' or 'timing'. Perhaps the best example of a timing difference is the different property, plant and equipment values that are found in the two sets of accounts. Each company determines its depreciation charge, and the depreciation charged on the same asset is often different in one company to another. The tax authorities in the UK ignore the depreciation charge, as it varies from one company to another, and gives companies a standard tax allowance. This is called a *capital allowance*. (Company tax allowances work essentially the same way as personal tax allowances, reducing the taxable profit.) Because the depreciation charge is different from the tax allowance, the asset's value is not the same in the tax accounts as the published accounts. There's usually a temporary difference between an asset's book value, shown at cost or valuation less depreciation to date, and its tax value. These differences could either be taxable (the book value is higher than the tax value) or deductible (the book value is lower than the tax value). If the asset's book value is higher than its tax value, and the asset is sold at its book value, the company will have a taxable profit.

I'll explain this in the next example.

Firstly let's look at the published accounts.

A company buys a machine for £5,000 and plans to keep it for five years. At the end of the five years it believes that the machine will be worth nothing. To the company, depreciation is a matter of simple arithmetic – it has £5,000 to write off over five years – £1,000 a year. (Most companies make an equal charge over the life of the asset, using a method of depreciation called the *straight line method*, and I'll discuss the different depreciation methods later in this chapter.) The depreciation charge is part of the operating costs in the income statement.

Now let's consider the tax accounts. I'll assume that the machine qualifies for a 25% tax allowance. Most UK companies use the straight line method to calculate their depreciation charge, but tax allowances in the UK are calculated using a different method. In the first year the allowance would be 25% of £5,000 = £1,250, giving an asset value of £3,750. In the second it would be 25% of £3,750 (£5,000 – £1,250) = £938. The tax allowance is given on a *reducing balance* basis. (Some companies, largely overseas and small UK companies, use this method to calculate their depreciation charge.)

You can see that that the tax value of the asset is very different from the book value of the asset when assets are depreciated on a straight line basis and tax allowances are given on a reducing balance basis. I've graphed the different values in the figure below:

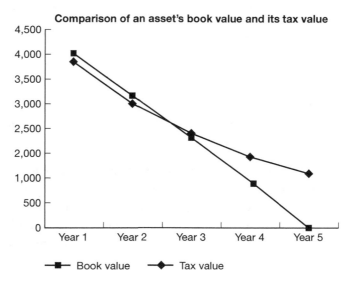

Comparison of an asset's book value and its tax value

You can see that the machine's value is different in the two sets of accounts. In the early years it is worth more in the published accounts, but from the third year onwards it is worth more in the tax accounts. At the end of the fifth year the asset has a zero book value, but is still worth over £1,186 in the tax accounts. In the first two years there would be a deferred tax liability (a future tax payment) and from year three onwards there would be a deductible difference, a deferred tax asset (a future tax repayment or credit note). You'll see these deferred tax assets and liabilities shown on the balance sheet. Deferred tax assets may be small, unless the company has a large pension deficit and, or, has made large acquisitions, as they can only be shown if they are recoverable.

I'll use my previous example to illustrate the deferred tax charge and the resulting deferred tax liability. In the first year the machine was worth £4,000 in the company's published accounts and £3,750 in its tax accounts. Assuming a tax rate of 28% there is a deferred tax charge of £70 (£250 x 28%), which would show as a deferred tax liability on the company's balance sheet. Deferred tax has the effect of aligning the tax charge with the country's tax rate, and I'll show you what I mean by continuing my previous example and assuming that the company makes £11,000 profit before the depreciation charge of £1,000, so its reported profit before tax is £10,000.

Tax accounts:	£	Published accounts:	£
Reported profit	10,000	Profit before tax	10,000
Depreciation	1,000	Tax charge:	
Profit for tax purposes	11,000	Current tax	(2,730)
Less capital allowance	1,250	Deferred tax	(70)
Taxable profit	9,750	Profit after tax	7,200
Tax @ 28%	(2,730)		

The total tax charge is £2,800, 28% of the profit before tax. If only the current tax had been charged the effective tax rate would have been 27.3%, lower than the country's corporation tax rate.

Deferred tax just follows normal accounting practice – a deferred tax liability is effectively an accrual for tax, and a deferred tax asset is a tax prepayment. Deferred tax brings the tax accounts and the published accounts into line. It adjusts the tax charge to reflect the tax that would be payable if the asset's book value was the same as its tax value. This means that the tax charge now reflects the total possible tax charge, including tax that might never have to be paid.

Deferred tax must be provided for in full for all temporary differences between the tax value of the assets and liabilities and their book value in the financial statements unless the temporary difference arises from:

■ the initial recognition of goodwill (this only applies to a potential deferred tax liability);

■ the initial recognition of an asset or a liability in a transaction that is not a business combination and that affects neither accounting profit nor taxable profit;

■ investments in subsidiaries, branches, associates and joint ventures but only where certain criteria apply.

Reconciling the tax charge to the profit before tax in the income statement

There will be a note to the accounts that reconciles the tax charge with the reported operating profit before tax. It starts with a profit before tax and I've illustrated it with Example 2.6:

Example 2.6

Profit before tax	1,000
Effective tax charge at 28%	(280)
Effect of:	
Non-deductible expenses	(22)
Differences in overseas taxation rates	5
Adjustments in respect of prior years	7
Share of results of joint ventures and associates	(3)
Other	2
Total income tax charge for the year from continuing operations	(291)
Effective tax rate	29.1%

In the UK's accounting rules deferred tax is covered by FRS 19 *Deferred tax*. It's calculated in a slightly different way. Instead of looking at the difference between the asset's book value and its tax value, it looks at the difference between the capital allowance and the depreciation charge. So, using my earlier example, in the first year the depreciation charge is £1,000 compared with a capital allowance of £1,250. Assuming the same tax rate of 28% there is a deferred tax charge of £70 (£250 × 28%), shown as a deferred tax liability on the company's balance sheet.

Apart from small companies, the notes will show you how the tax charge has been calculated. (Small companies only show the total tax charge, and don't have to disclose the components.)

Profit for the period from discontinued operations

A single number is usually disclosed on the income statement, representing the total of the discontinued operation's profit or loss after tax and any profits, or losses, arising from its disposal. This is the minimum presentation and more information can be shown on the income statement. In the notes to the accounts this single number is analysed, disclosing the discontinued operation's:

- revenue;
- expenses;
- pre-tax profit, or loss;
- tax charge;
- a profit, or loss, on disposal of the discontinued operation;
- the related tax charge.

Companies using UK rules must show all line items for discontinued operations. FRS 3 (*Reporting financial performance*) requires acquisitive companies to show a more detailed profit and loss account, analysing profits between discontinued and continuing operations and clearly identifying, on the profit and loss account, the contribution arising from acquisitions. (Companies preparing their accounts using the international rules provide less information in their income statements. They must disclose in the notes the acquisition's revenue and profit since its acquisition date and, unless it's impractible, the combined business's revenue and profit for the whole period. This enables you to see what the revenue and profit would have been if the business had been acquired at the beginning of the period.)

This means that a UK profit and loss account often appears more complicated than the income statements prepared under IFRS (as in Example 2.7):

Example 2.7

	Continuing Operations	Acquisitions	Discontinued	Total
	£000	£000	£000	£000
Revenue	500	300	200	1,000
Cost of sales	(280)	(160)	(160)	(600)
Gross profit	220	140	40	400
Distribution costs	(70)	(40)	(30)	(140)
Administrative expenses	(35)	(15)	(20)	(70)
Other operating income	10			10
Operating profit	125	85	(10)	200
Share of associate's operating profits	20			20
Profit on sale of fixed assets	5	2	3	10
Profit before interest	150	87	(7)	230
Interest receivable – group				10
Interest payable:				
Group				(50)
Associate				(10)
Profit on ordinary activities before taxation				180
Taxation				(40)
Profit on ordinary activities after taxation				140
Minority interests				(10)
Profit for the financial year				130

Minority interests or non-controlling interests

You'll find minority interests when the group doesn't own all the shares in its subsidiaries. I'd like to tell you how a subsidiary is defined and how minority interests are shown on the income statement.

IAS 27 (*Consolidation*) requires companies to consolidate any businesses that they control. Usually, but not always, control and ownership are the same. A subsidiary is a business that is controlled by another, which is called the 'parent'. Control is defined as the power to govern the operating and financial policies of a business to obtain benefits from its activities. Control is presumed to exist when a company has the majority of the votes in another business, but can also arise when:

- a company has an agreement with other investors effectively giving it the majority of the voting rights;
- it has the power to govern the financial and operating policies of another business under a statute or an agreement;
- it has the power to appoint, or remove, the majority of the board of directors;
- it has the power to cast the majority of the votes at a board meeting.

This means that effectively there can be large minority interests where the company has been forced to consolidate because it has the power to control the subsidiary. It can have the control, but does not own all of the shares. Whilst I've talked about companies, in fact the term you'll find is *entities* and you'll recall it is a much wider term. This effectively makes *off-balance sheet funding* much more difficult. Enron held some of its debt (and some of its loss making businesses) in partnerships where it effectively controlled them. The fact that these were partnerships where it had limited ownership would have been regarded as irrelevant under both the international and UK's accounting rules and it would have had to consolidate them into the group accounts.

Where one company controls another it must prepare *consolidated accounts* showing the results and financial position of both companies even if it doesn't own all of the shares in the company. If a company's results are consolidated, all its sales and costs will be taken into the group's income statement and all its assets and liabilities will be taken into the group's balance sheet. And all its cash flows will be taken into the cash flow statement. Any of the profits, or net assets, that do not belong to the parent company's shareholders are shown as minority interests.

I'll show you how the consolidation process works in Example 2.8.

Example 2.8

I'll use the same income statements I used in Example 2.4 to illustrate accounting for associates, but I'll assume that Company A now owns 60% of Company B. The two companies' income statements before consolidation are:

	Company A (the parent)	Company B (the subsidiary)
	£m	£m
Revenue	1,000	700
Operating costs	(750)	(520)
Operating profit	250	180
Interest payable	(50)	(30)
Profit before tax	200	150
Tax	(60)	(40)
Profit after tax	140	110

The consolidated income statement would then be:

	£m	
Revenue	1,700	
Operating costs	(1,270)	
Operating profit	430	
Interest payable	(80)	
Profit on ordinary activities before tax	350	
Tax on profit on ordinary activities	(100)	
Profit for the year	250	
Attributable to:		
Equity shareholders of the parent	206	
Minority interests	44	(110 × 40%)

The £44 million in my example represents the profit that has to be deducted from the consolidated income statement to arrive at the profit available to the group's shareholders. Unfortunately, not all subsidiaries are profitable. If the subsidiary is making a loss, the minority interest's share of the subsidiary's loss would be *added* to the profit for the year.

As part of the convergence process of IFRS with US GAAP, minority interests will be referred to as 'non-controlling interests' in accounting periods starting after 1 July 2009.

 The requirements of the UK's accounting rule, FRS 2 (*Accounting for subsidiary undertakings*), are broadly similar to the IAS 27. The main difference is that the minority interests are deducted from the after tax profits to show the profit for the financial year:

	£m	
Revenue	1,700	
Operating costs	(1,270)	
Operating profit	430	
Interest payable	(80)	
Profit on ordinary activities before tax	350	
Tax on profit on ordinary activities	(100)	
Profit after tax	250	
Minority interests	(44)	(110 × 40%)
Profit for the financial year	206	

Dividends

I'd like to talk to you about dividends, even though they are no longer shown on income statements and profit and loss accounts. Dividends that are proposed, or declared after the balance sheet date but before the financial statements have been issued are disclosed, but not recognised as a liability.

There are legal restrictions on the amount of dividends that companies are allowed to pay. All companies can only pay dividends if they have accumulated sufficient profits. This means that it is possible for companies to pay dividends when they have made a loss, but only if they have accumulated sufficient profits in the past to cover the dividend payment. I'll illustrate this in Example 2.9.

Example 2.9

A company has traded profitably for its first four years and has reinvested £24,000 in its business:

Retained profits

	£
Year 1	10,000
Year 2	5,000
Year 3	7,000
Year 4	2,000
Total	24,000

The £24,000 accumulated profits are known in law as *distributable reserves*, and I'll tell you more about them in the next chapter. Dividends can be paid until the distributable reserves reach zero. If the company makes a loss of £8,000 in the fifth year, but still wants to pay a dividend of £10,000, it would be able to do so. The retained loss for the year would be £18,000, which can be absorbed by the accumulated retained profits of £24,000. In fact the company could pay up to £16,000 in dividends (the accumulated retained profits of £24,000 less the £8,000 loss for the year).

The Companies Act places another restriction on the payment of dividends for UK public companies. They may only pay dividends when the value of their net assets (total assets less all liabilities including provisions for liabilities and charges) is not less than the total of their share capital and undistributable reserves. (Undistributable reserves are all the other reserves I'll talk about in the next chapter: the revaluation reserve, the share premium account, the capital redemption reserve, and any other reserve where the distribution is prohibited by the company's articles.) This means that whilst private companies can pay dividends if they have sufficient realised profits available, public companies may only do so after they have provided for any unrealised losses.

Shareholders don't have to approve all dividend payments. As long as it is legal, directors can pay interim dividends without the shareholders' approval. However, the shareholders at the Annual General Meeting must approve the final dividend, and the directors will devote a lot of time in determining how much should be paid.

Only private companies like paying dividends, although they are likely to have taken money out of the business well before they reach dividends! Private company directors are generally paying dividends to themselves, as in most private companies there are few shareholders who aren't also directors.

Public companies are different – the directors are proposing to pay dividends to strangers. The more the company pays as dividends, the less it can keep within the business for the next years' development and growth. Public companies use the same underlying principle for dividends as the one used to decide the level of salary increase for employees – they pay the least they can get away with! In fact the same things influence dividend decisions as influence salary decisions. It is a balance; they can't afford to disappoint the shareholders (they will vote with their feet and sell their shares). But neither can they afford to create unsustainable expectations (shareholders look for dividend growth, the dividend you pay this year creates an expectation about the size of the dividend that you will pay next year). To improve cash flow some companies offer a *scrip dividend*. A scrip dividend is where the shareholder receives extra shares instead of cash. This is often an attractive option for smaller shareholders as they can increase their stake in the company without paying dealing fees.

Most companies follow the Articles (the rules that govern the operation of the company) laid out in the Companies Act. If these Articles are followed, the only way the shareholders can change the dividend is to reduce it (probably about as likely as you asking your boss to reduce the size of your next salary increase)!

Following is IMI's note on dividends.

Dividends

After the balance sheet date the following dividends were proposed by the directors. The dividends have not been provided for and there are no income tax consequences.

	2008	2007
	£m	£m
12.7p per qualifying share (2007: 12.7p)	40.4	40.8

The following dividends were declared and paid by the Group during the year:

	2008	2007
	£m	£m
12.7p per qualifying ordinary share (2007: 11.7p)	40.7	39.2
8.0p per qualifying ordinary share (2007: 7.5p)	25.5	24.7
	66.2	63.9

The accounting judgements – defining the costs that relate to the sales

By now you know what the income statement looks like, and that operating profit is the most important element. Now I'd like to spend some time showing you how operating profit is calculated, as it's as much a matter of judgement as measurement, and you'll find that managers are involved in making many of the judgements that determine operating profit.

All companies make five major accounting adjustments to ensure that the costs charged to the income statement are those that relate to the sales made in the period:

Charges are made to the income statement to include:

▨ provisions for likely costs;

▨ accrued expenses;

▨ depreciation and amortisation.

> I've deliberately used the word 'charges' as they're nothing to do with cash.

And adjustments are made to exclude:

■ stock;

■ prepayments.

Companies involved in trading overseas have to make another adjustment, as they have to find a way to deal with exchange rates. I now want to show you how these adjustments affect both the income statement and the balance sheet.

Provisions

Companies have to make provisions to cover the likely costs that will arise in the future from the sales they have made in this period. These include provisions made for:

■ bad and doubtful debts;

■ obsolete stock (this may not be obsolete in the literal sense, but stock must be shown on the balance sheet at the lower of its cost or net realisable value);

■ warranty claims;

■ litigation;

■ rationalisation.

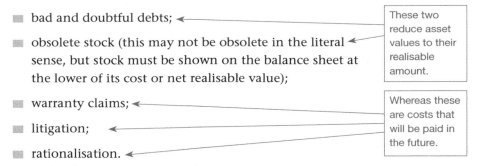

These two reduce asset values to their realisable amount.

Whereas these are costs that will be paid in the future.

You can see that I've categorised the provisions into two different types:

■ Those that are made to reduce an asset's value to the amount that the company expects to realise. (The general rule is that asset values should not be overstated, and that receivables and inventories should be shown at the lower of their cost or market value.)

■ Those that are costs the business will incur in the future as a result of the sales (warranty), or decisions (rationalisation), that have been made in the period.

I've made this distinction because the accounting treatment is different for the two different types of provision.

I'll start by looking at the first category, illustrating this by considering doubtful debt provisions. These provisions can be:

▦ specific, where each debtor is considered individually;

▦ general, where the same level of provision is applied to all receivables;

or

▦ a combination of the two, where perhaps large customers would be considered on an individual basis and smaller customers on a general basis.

The total provision is disclosed in the notes on the receivables (or inventories if the provision was for a stock writedown), where it may be referred to as an *impairment*.

Provisions can have an effect on reported profitability, and I'll illustrate this with a general provision for doubtful debts in Example 2.10.

Example 2.10

A company has decided to make a general provision of 4% to cover doubtful debts in the first year and, to keep the example simple, believed that this was also an appropriate percentage for the second year. I'll show you how this policy would affect the accounts over the two-year period. You'll see it has a significant effect on the company's reported operating profit.

	Year 1 £	Year 2 £	Profit growth
Outstanding invoices	100,000	110,000	
Less 4% provision	(4,000)	(4,400)	
Receivables on the balance sheet	96,000	105,600	
Profit before provisions	110,000	115,500	5%

Two things affect the company's reported profit in the second year – its provisioning policy, and the cash it receives from its first year's debtors. I'll show you two possibilities:

1 The company collects £98,000 from its first year's receivables.
2 The company only collects £94,000.

In the first option it collects more than expected, and so had '*over provided*' £2,000 in the first year. This means that it only needs to charge £2,400 into the second period's income statement to bring the provision to £4,400 (4% of £110,000). In the second option it had *under provided* and has to increase the

2.10 *continued*

charge to the income statement, to bring the provision to the 4% required. This means that its reported profit after provisions would be:

	Year 1	Year 2	Profit growth
	£	£	
Option 1	106,000	113,100	6.7%
Option 2	106,000	109,100	2.9%

Any reversal of a provision is shown in the in the income statement in the line where it was charged.

Now I'll consider those provisions made to cover future costs. These are shown on the balance sheet as provisions or, in accounts prepared using the UK's rules, *Provisions for liabilities and charges*. You know that provisions are only the managers' best guesses and are unlikely to be a totally accurate reflection of what happens. They are approximations and can be used by companies to move profit from one year to the next, as an over provision in one year could be written back later to boost profits when the cash is not needed.

Provisions are covered by IAS 37 (*Provisions, contingent liabilities and contingent assets*) and in the UK by FRS 12 (*Provisions, contingent liabilities and contingent assets*). The two standards are broadly similar, as they were developed at the same time. Provisions are only required when something has happened before the balance sheet date that gives rise to a measurable and clear obligation. The important words are:

- *Before the balance sheet date* – so you can't account for something that happens after that date.

- *Measurable and clear obligation* – so a board decision to restructure the business doesn't justify the creation of a provision, as it's only a decision not an obligation. The provision can only be made when the company has a detailed plan for the restructuring and there is an expectation that the plan will be implemented.

Provisions can only be made where there's a liability arising from a past event, and its probable future cash outflow can be measured. There are situations where the criteria for provisions won't be met. Perhaps there's only a possible obligation, or cash outflow that perhaps can't be measured. The accounting rules refer to these as *contingent liabilities* and they have to be disclosed in the notes to the accounts. Court cases are often disclosed as contingent liabilities, or could even be disclosed as a *contingent asset* in the notes to the accounts of the prosecuting company if it was probably going to win the case. I'll tell you more about these in Chapter 6.

Accrued expenses

These are outstanding invoices that relate to costs for items used in the period. You already know about accruals, even though you've probably never used the term. A lot of your personal costs could be accrued: gas, electricity, telephone. If they're not paid by direct debit they're paid quarterly in arrears. If you were trying to prepare an income statement for the month of December you would have to identify the costs that relate to the period. This means that you would have to try to work out what proportion of your next gas bill, etc. related to this period's sales. Companies do this to identify their accrued expenses – the costs of items they have used, but where they haven't received the invoice from their suppliers. Consequently, at the end of the financial year your accountants will send an email to all cost centre managers asking for a list of their accrued expenses.

I'll show you how accruals affect the accounts in Example 2.11.

Example 2.11

In the past two years a company has used and paid for electricity as follows:

	Year 1 £	Year 2 £
Electricity used	80,000	84,000
Electricity invoiced and paid for	65,000	83,000
Charge to the income statement	80,000	84,000
Accrued expenses	15,000	16,000
(*These are included in payables on the balance sheet*)		

The income statement is always charged with the costs *used*, not what has been paid for, as the cash flow is irrelevant. The accrued expenses in the second year are £16,000. £15,000 of the £83,000 paid during the second year related to the first year, so only £68,000 of this year's electricity has been paid for. Consequently the outstanding invoices, relating to costs used in sales and charged to the income statement, were £84,000 – £68,000 = £16,000.

The balance sheet shows what the company owes at its year end and its payables are analysed into those where the company has received an invoice (the trade payables), and those where it hasn't (the accrued expenses).

Depreciation, amortisation and impairment

Depreciation

Depreciation is something you know about. You buy something today, and it's not worth the same tomorrow. Some things depreciate more than others. Cars and computers generally depreciate faster than your other assets. Depreciation is a hidden business cost. The Companies Act requires companies to make a charge for depreciation to cover the cost of using their assets in the period. Once again, it's a *charge*, rather than a cash cost. Depreciation is the accountant's way of charging the costs of property, plant and equipment into the income statement over their life.

IAS16 (*Property, plant and equipment*) covers depreciation of most property, plant, and equipment. The charge to the income statement should be based on an asset's:

- cost;
- life;
- net residual value – this is its scrap value at the end of its life less any disposal costs.

It also requires that:

- Some large assets have to be subdivided into smaller assets if different parts of the asset have different lives (for example a furnace lining is unlikely to last as long as the furnace itself).
- Land and buildings are treated as separate assets, and land has an unlimited life and its depreciation is usually immaterial.
- Asset lives have to be reviewed annually, with the effects of any revision being spread over the asset's remaining life.
- The net residual value has to be reviewed annually, so that it's based on prices that are current at the balance sheet date.
- The method used to depreciate the assets is also reviewed annually to ensure that it is still the most appropriate method.

There are different methods that can be used to calculate the depreciation charge, and the resulting asset value shown on the balance sheet. I talked about some of them when I discussed deferred tax earlier. IAS 16 allows management to select the most appropriate method that allocates depreciation on a systematic basis over the asset's useful life. I'll just run through the main methods, assuming the residual value remains unchanged, and their effect on the accounts in Example 2.13.

Example 2.12

A company buys a machine for £10,490, believes it will last for five years and will have a scrap value of £490 in five years' time.

Now I'll calculate the depreciation charge and the asset values over the life of the asset. I'll start with the straight line method, as it's the one that most UK companies use.

The straight line method
The company has £10,000 to depreciate over five years, and makes an annual depreciation charge to the income statement of £2,000. It's called the straight line method of depreciation because both the depreciation charge and the asset value move in a straight line.

	Depreciation charge	Asset value
1st year	£2,000	£8,490
2nd year	£2,000	£6,490
3rd year	£2,000	£4,490
4th year	£2,000	£2,490
5th year	£2,000	£490

This is the commonest method of calculation depreciation, the next most popular approach is the reducing balance method.

Reducing balance
This is sometimes also called the double declining balance method. It uses a fixed percentage each year and applies this to the reducing value of the asset to arrive at the net realisable value. The percentage is calculated using the following formula, which gives the chosen residual value at the end of the life.

$$1 - \sqrt[n]{\frac{\text{residual value}}{\text{cost}}}$$

(*n* is the expected asset life)

In my example, this formula gives an annual percentage of 45.8%. But please don't let the formula fool you – it isn't any more accurate. All it does is calculate the percentage based on my assumptions about the asset's life and the net residual value. Using the reducing balance method gives the following depreciation charges and asset values:

		Depreciation charge	Asset values
1st year	£10,490 × 45.8%	£4,805	£5,685
2nd year	£5,685 × 45.8%	£2,604	£3,081
3rd year	£3,081 × 45.8%	£1,411	£1,670
4th year	£1,670 × 45.8%	£765	£905
5th year	£905 × 45.8%	£414	£491
			(there's a rounding error of 1)

Some companies prefer to use the reducing balance method, as they believe it gives a closer approximation to 'real' depreciation, which is usually higher in the earlier years.

Sum of the digits

This method is largely used by leasing companies in the UK, but it is widely used overseas, particularly in the United States. It gives a depreciation charge between the straight line method and the reducing balance method. The sum of the digits is simply the total of the number of years the asset is expected to last (1 + 2 + 3 + 4 + 5 = 15) and can be found quickly by using the formula:

$$\frac{n(n + 1)}{2}$$

Once again, n is the anticipated life.

Having found the sum of the digits, the next step is to find the depreciation factor for each year. In the first year depreciation is calculated at 5/15 of £10,000, in the second 4/15 of £10,000, and so on:

		Depreciation charge	Asset values
1st year	5/15 × £10,000	£3,333	£7,157
2nd year	4/15 × £10,000	£2,667	£4,490
3rd year	3/15 × £10,000	£2,000	£2,490
4th year	2/15 × £10,000	£1,333	£1,157
5th year	1/15 × £10,000	£667	£490

Some companies prefer this method because it gives higher charges in the early years, but is less extreme than the reducing balance method.

2.12 continued

Usage based methods

Some companies use depreciation methods that are based on the asset's use, expressing its life in production units, or hours, rather than years. This method of depreciation is often used for machinery and planes. Continuing the example, if the company believed that the machine would last for 20,000 hours, the annual depreciation charge would be based on the usage at £0.50 for each hour the machine is used (£10,000 ÷ 20,000).

	Hours used	Depreciation charge	Asset value
1st year	2,400	£1,200	£9,290
2nd year	3,600	£1,800	£7,490
3rd year	4,600	£2,300	£5,190
4th year	5,200	£2,600	£2,590
5th year	4,200	£2,100	£490

You can clearly see the effect that these different methods have on the depreciation charge, and therefore reported profitability and asset values, if you look at the chart below.

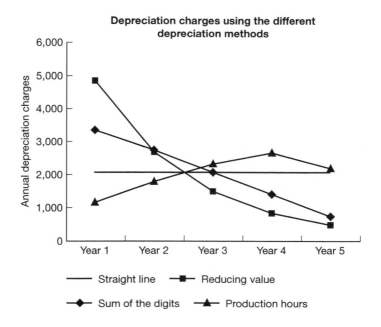

To summarise, when companies are calculating their depreciation charge they have four variables to consider:

- the cost;
- the asset's life;
- its net residual value;
- the depreciation method.

Any change in these will affect both profitability and asset values. Companies have to review asset lives, net residual value, and the appropriate depreciation method annually. This means that depreciation has to be based on the current market conditions.

 In essence FRS 15 (*Tangible fixed assets*) has similar requirements to IAS 16. However there are some differences that affect the depreciation charged to the profit and loss account:

- Residual values are based on the prices at the date when the asset was acquired, not current prices.
- Under certain circumstances renewals accounting is allowed for calculating the depreciation charge for infrastructure systems or networks.

Amortisation

If you look in a standard dictionary, you'll find that it suggests that amortisation is synonymous with depreciation. However, when accountants use the term amortisation they're referring to the depreciation of *intangible* assets. Essentially calculating amortisation is similar to calculating depreciation, as it's based on:

- either the asset's cost, or its fair value;
- the asset's life;
- its net residual value, which is normally zero;

▨ the depreciation method, which should reflect the way that company benefits from the intangible asset. If the benefit's pattern can't be reliably determined, the straight line method should be used. You'll find that most companies amortise their intangible assets using the straight line method.

Only intangible assets with finite lives, such as patents, are amortised. However, an asset with an indefinite life must have an annual impairment review to ensure that its value isn't overstated.

Acquisitive companies may have quite significant amortisation charges, as they have to capitalise intangible assets in acquisitions that wouldn't normally be shown on the balance sheet. (I'll discuss these in more detail in the next chapter.) Consequently, they often show an operating profit figure before and after the amortisation of acquired intangible assets.

Impairment

The underlying principle in valuing assets is that they shouldn't be shown on the balance sheet for more than can be recovered from their use in the business, or their sale. Consequently nearly all assets must be assessed at each reporting date to see if their value is impaired, and some assets must be assessed annually. (IAS 36 (*Impairment of assets*) does exclude some assets, such as inventories, construction contracts, deferred tax, as their accounting treatment is covered in other standards.) Both external factors (for example market or technology changes) and internal factors (for example changes in the way an asset is used) could indicate that the asset is impaired. An asset is impaired if its book value is higher than its 'recoverable amount', which is of a higher of its:

▨ net selling price (its market value less any cost to sell);

▨ value in use.

To calculate the value in use, companies have to estimate any future cash flows derived from the asset and then discount them using an appropriate discount rate.

Any impairment loss is recognised on the income statement and is disclosed separately if it's material, or in the notes if it's immaterial.

 FRS 11 (*Impairment of fixed assets and goodwill*) does not apply to current assets and there are some minor differences to IAS 36, which I will discuss in the next chapter.

Summarising depreciation, amortisation and impairment

Assets affect the income statement in two ways:

- Firstly, property, plant and equipment, and intangible assets have to be depreciated, or amortised, over their expected life.

- Secondly, if an asset's value falls, companies must make an impairment charge to the income statement so its value on the balance sheet reflects its commercial value.

Inventory or *stock*

As inventories haven't been shipped to the customer they aren't charged to the income statement, and any costs incurred for inventories are shown in the balance sheet. This means that stock valuation affects a business's cost of sales and reported profitability.

Inventories are shown on the balance sheet when a business controls them, expects them to generate future economic benefits (for example revenues or cash flows), and can reliably ascertain their value. They are analysed into their component parts, starting with raw materials and adding labour and overhead costs as the materials move through the production process. Inventories are shown on the balance sheet at the lower of their cost and net realisable value. (Net realisable value is the selling price less any further costs to completion and the estimated selling costs. This is designed to limit the costs that can be charged to stock.)

Companies have to determine the value the cost of goods used in sales, so they need to:

- measure the *volume* of units used in sales;

- calculate their *value*.

Measuring the volume of goods used in sales is theoretically very simple, as all companies use some form of stocktaking:

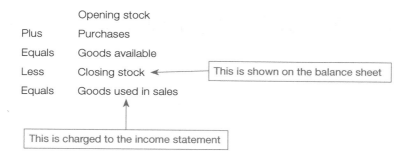

Whilst the process is simple it's not totally accurate, as anyone who has been involved in stocktaking knows!

Once the company has measured how many units it has in stock, they have to be valued. This is important, as small changes in stock values can have a disproportionate impact on reported profits in businesses where the materials cost is a large proportion of the total costs.

In practice valuing stock can be difficult and some guidance is given in the accounting rules. Companies have to cope with changing prices, and manufacturing businesses have to find a basis for valuing work in progress and finished goods.

To illustrate the difficulties I'll consider two different types of company:

■ **A retailer** – holding goods for resale.

■ **A manufacturer** – with materials stock, work in progress and finished goods stock.

Retailers

It's easier for retailers to value their stock, as they only have one type of stock – the goods they're intending to sell. A number of retailers find it useful to show stock at resale value in their internal management accounts. When they publish their accounts they adjust this figure to arrive at 'cost' by deducting their expected gross margin. This is called the retail method. This means that if they had a dress that they would sell for £100.00, with a gross margin of 50%, the stock value of the dress would be £50.00. The accounting rules allow companies to use the retail method, as long as it is a reasonable approximation of the actual cost.

The company's accounting policy for stock is always disclosed – for example, in its 2008 accounts Marks and Spencer discloses:

Inventories

Inventories are valued at the lower of cost and net realisable value using the retail method, which is computed on the basis of selling price less the appropriate trading margin. All inventories are finished goods.

Manufacturing businesses

Manufacturing businesses have more problems valuing their stock, as they have to cope with:

- **Different prices in the year** Manufacturers usually hold their stock for longer than retailers, and so they're more likely to have goods in stock that they have bought at different prices.

- **Complex valuation** They have different types of stock – materials, work in progress and finished goods stock. Labour and overhead costs have to be added to the value of the materials as they move through the production process, and are allocated to stock based on the business's normal activity levels.

To cope with these difficulties, accountants have developed a number of different approaches to valuing stock. The commonest methods are:

- first in first out (FIFO);

- weighted average cost;

- last in first out (LIFO).

I'll use Example 2.13 to show you the effect of using the three different methods:

Example 2.13

		Units	Unit cost £	Total cost £
1 January	Opening stock	1,500	1.00	1,500
28 February	Purchases	2,000	1.05	2,100
1 April	Purchases	1,500	1.06	1,590
30 June	Purchases	2,000	1.08	2,160
31 August	Purchases	2,200	1.10	2,420
30 November	Purchases	1,500	1.13	1,695
		10,700		11,465
31 December	Closing stock	1,000		

The company has bought units at different prices through the year, and has to determine the cost that will be charged to the income statement. It does this by establishing the value of the closing stock.

First in first out

This applies the principle of stock rotation to stock valuation. The first goods into the warehouse are assumed to be the first sent to the customer, so the latest deliveries will be in stock.

The inventory value on the balance sheet using FIFO will be £1,130 (1,000 units times the latest price of £1.13) and the cost of sales charged to the income statement will be £10,335 (11,465 − 1,130).

Weighted average cost

You have to use a weighted average, as a simple average isn't accurate enough. A simple average cost per unit would be:

$$\frac{£1.00 + £1.05 + £1.06 + £1.08 + £1.10 + £1.13}{6} = £1.07 \text{ per unit}$$

This means that £10,379 would be charged to the income statement and the stocks would be £1,070. Unfortunately this doesn't cover the total cost of purchases, £11,465. The inventories and the cost of sales total £11,449, so you'd lose £6 in the calculation. This isn't a large number, but it could be, and to be exactly right you have to use a weighted average.

The weighted average cost per unit is:

$$\frac{\begin{array}{l}(1,500 \times £1.00) + (2,000 \times £1.05) + (1,500 \times £1.06) \\ + (2,000 \times £1.08) + (2,200 \times £1.10) + (1,500 \times £1.13)\end{array}}{10,700} = £1.0714953$$

2.13 *continued*

Those extra decimal places guarantee the accuracy! The cost of sales will be £10,393.504 and the inventories £1,071.4953.

Last in first out

Last in first out charges the most recent deliveries into the profit and loss account. This means that the inventories on the balance sheet will be £1,000 and the cost of sales in the income statement will be £10,465.

Think about this for a minute – does this make sense? In the real world, would you send the newest stock to the customers before the oldest? The accounting standards agree with you, it isn't allowed by the international rule, IAS 2 (*Inventories*), and the UK's rule, SSAP 9 (*Stocks and long term contracts*), only allows companies to use it if it's the only way that the accounts show a true and fair view. (This is one of the major perceived obstacles to US companies using IFRS, as LIFO is widely used in the US where it is allowed for tax purposes.) The other point worth making is that my example is far too simple; to operate LIFO properly, companies have to calculate the last in each time they make a sale. This means that they would need a sophisticated accounting system to cope with the demands of operating LIFO.

You've seen that the three methods of valuing stock give different profits and different inventory values on the balance sheet:

	Cost of sales £	Inventories £
First in first out	10,335.00	1,130.00
Weighted average	10,393.50	1,071.50
Last in first out	10,465.00	1,000.00

Whilst these methods provide the basis for calculating the costs of goods used in sales, they don't cope with the problem of incorporating labour and production overhead costs into the value of work in progress and finished goods stock. Most companies' accounting procedures allow them to build in the cost of labour and production overheads as the materials move through the production process. But problems arise when production falls or rises dramatically, as the procedures assume 'normal' production levels. When production levels are abnormally low, any unallocated overheads are charged to the income statement. When they're high the allocated overheads are reduced, so that any stock isn't shown above its actual cost.

The international rule, IAS2 (*Inventories*), requires that if any item isn't interchangeable, or has been segregated for a specific contract, it is individually valued. Other stock items should be valued either on a first in first out basis or a weighted average cost. Different valuation methods can be used for different types of stock, but all similar stock must be valued using the same method.

The international rules require more disclosure than the UK's rules, including details of the value of inventories charged to the income statement, any material stock write downs and the value of inventories that have been written down below their cost. (This is referred to as the 'value of inventories carried at fair value less costs to sell'.)

Prepayments

This is an unusual accounting term as it actually means what it says! It's a payment made for goods that the business hasn't yet used. You're familiar with prepayments if you pay insurance and have a car. Insurance and road tax are both prepayments, you have to pay for them before you get any benefits.

As prepayments are payments in advance, they're not charged to the profit and loss account, as they do not relate to the sales made in the current period. I've illustrated this in Example 2.14.

Example 2.14

I'll assume that a company has a 31 March year end, but pays insurance premiums on 1 January.

On 1 January 2007 it paid £2,000 as an insurance premium. On 1 January 2008 the premium had risen to £2,800. The charge for insurance in the accounts for the year ending 31 March 2008 would be £2,200 (three-quarters of the payment made in 2007 – £1,500, and a quarter of the payment made in 2008 – £700). The balance of the 2008 payment (£2,100) would be charged to the 2009 profit and loss account. It would show on the 2008 balance sheet as a prepayment and is included with trade and other receivables (although in some countries you'll find that prepayments are shown separately on the balance sheet).

Currency adjustments

Any company exporting or importing goods, or that has a subsidiary or associate overseas, has to find a way of incorporating different currencies into its accounts. This can have a significant effect on a company's reported results, consequently I'll show you how they deal with the exchange rates. You'll find that the accounting treatment is different in individual companies and groups.

Exchange rate accounting problems

Exchange rates pose two problems:

- Which rate do you use?

- How do you account for any exchange differences?

The problems facing companies aren't that different from the ones you face when you're on holiday abroad and buy souvenirs. When you're thinking about the cost, do you use the rate in the resort or the rate you're likely to get on your credit card? You've had personal experience of 'exchange differences' if you've found that the rate that you thought you would get is different from the rate that appears on your credit card bill. Just like companies, sometimes you win and sometimes you lose!

Exchange rates can have a significant effect on companies' reported profits, particularly in those businesses where the costs are incurred in one currency and revenues are earned in another. This is quite common in industries such as shipping and oil, where revenues are earned in dollars, but a UK based company could incur most of its costs in sterling.

I'll illustrate this by looking at the profitability of the following dollar contract in Example 2.15.

Example 2.15

A company reports in sterling and has a contract that earns cash revenues of US$1,000 and has costs of £500. The reported sterling profit would vary widely according to the sterling : dollar exchange rate – I've used three rates ranging from parity to £1.00 = $2.00.

	£1.00 = US$2.00	£1.00 = US$1.50	£1.00 = US$1.00
Sales	500	667	1,000
Operating costs	(500)	(500)	(500)
Operating profit	0	167	500

You've seen that the reported profit ranges from zero to £500, a 50% operating margin! Now I'm sure you realise that this example is far too simple, there are many more problems than this. What if the cash received from the sale came in at a different rate than the exchange rate on the day of the sale? What exchange rate should you use? Should you take the sale at the rate on the day the sale was made, or the rate actually received? (If you think about it, this is a fairly common problem, as most companies give credit.)

There are five possible exchange rates that could be used:

■ **The closing rate** – the rate at the end of the financial year.

■ **The average rate** – the weighted average exchange rate during the year.

■ **The historical rate** – the rate on the date of the transaction.

■ **The spot exchange rate** – the current exchange rate.

■ **The forward/contracted rate** – the rate that the company actually gets.

IAS 21 (*The effects of changes in foreign exchange rates*) is based on two concepts:

■ The *functional currency* – this is the currency the company uses to measure items in its financial statements. The functional currency is the currency that is used in the business's main economic environment, consequently the bulk of the business's cash flows are in this currency.

- The *presentation currency* – this is currency that is used in the published financial statements. IAS 21 allows compares to present the accounts in any currency, and UK company law doesn't require UK companies to present their accounts in sterling.

These two currencies can be different, and the functional currency is often different from the presentation currency. Increasing globalisation means that most large groups don't have a single functional currency. Instead they have a number of functional currencies that are used to monitor and control the group. In some countries, businesses are required to report in the local currency, regardless of the functional currency. This is very common in groups where subsidiary companies will use their functional currency to determine their results, which may then have to be translated into the parent's presentation currency.

Companies can be affected by foreign currencies because they:

- have transactions in a foreign currency;

or

- have subsidiaries, associates or joint ventures whose accounting records are kept in a different currency.

I'd like to show you how they account for the effect of exchange rates; firstly within an individual company and then in a group.

Handling exchange rates in individual companies

The income statement

Items shown in the income statement are translated at either the rate of exchange at the date of the transaction or, if there have been no significant fluctuations, average exchange rates. Exchange differences may arise from the movement in exchange rates between the invoicing date and the payment date. These are charged to the income statement and affect the reported profit. I've illustrated this in Example 2.16.

Example 2.16

A company sells $450,000 of goods to an American client on 12 February when £1.00 = $1.50, giving a revenue of £300,000. (The sales will be recorded using US$1.50, as this is the exchange rate at the date of the transaction.) The cost of the goods was £275,000, giving an apparent profit of £25,000 on the deal. However, the company was paid on 28 March when the exchange rate was £1.00 = US$1.55.

The income statement will show revenue of £300,000 (450,000 ÷ 1.5), whereas the subsequent cash inflow will be only £290,323 (450,000 ÷ 1.55). The exchange loss of £9,677 will then be charged to the income statement:

	£
Revenue	300,000
Cost of sales	(275,000)
Exchange loss	(9,677)
Profit	15,323

A 3.33% change in exchange rates has reduced profit by 39%!

When sterling is strengthening, exporters lose both profit and cash, on the other hand importers win!

The balance sheet

I'll cover this now, although this balance sheet is covered in the next chapter, as exchange rate differences affect both documents.

The accounting treatment for exchange differences depends on the type of asset or liability. IAS 21 (*The effects of changes in foreign exchange rates*) classifies assets and liabilities as:

- ■ **Monetary assets and liabilities** These include both money that is held by the company (e.g. deposits and loans) and amounts that will be received and paid in money (e.g. receivables and payables). These are translated at the closing rate and any exchange differences are charged, or credited, to the income statement, unless other accounting rules require them to be shown as other comprehensive income (for example revaluation gains).

■ **Non monetary assets** These are divided into those that are shown at historical cost such as most plant and machinery, and those that are shown at fair value such as some investments. Assets shown at historical cost use the exchange rate when they were acquired, this means that their value is usually unaffected by exchange rate movements. (However, when the company conducts an impairment review it may have to consider exchange rates. For example stock is shown at the lower of its cost or net realisable value. The net realisable value would be translated at the exchange rate prevailing when the valuation was conducted. Consequently exchange rates could affect the calculation of an impairment loss.) Whereas those assets shown at fair value use the exchange rate when their fair value was determined.

Once the individual companies have accounted for the effect of exchange rates, a group has to consolidate them to reflect the group's position.

Handling exchange rates in groups

I have shown you how to account for transactions in foreign currencies in an individual company. I'll now move on to look at the other area where exchange rates affect the accounts – consolidating the results, assets and liabilities of a group's overseas subsidiaries.

The group financial statements should mirror the results, and the relationships, that are measured in the local currency before any consolidation. This means that usually:

■ Income and expenses are translated at the exchange rates at the date of the transaction, or average rates if this is a reasonable approximation.

■ Assets and liabilities on the balance sheet are translated at the closing rate on the balance sheet date.

■ All resulting exchange differences are shown as other comprehensive income and recognised in a separate component of equity – the *translation of foreign operations* (called the translation reserve in accounts prepared in accounting years starting before 2009).

■ Any business operating in a currency experiencing hyperinflation, such as Zimbabwe in 2008, must adjust both its current and comparative years' numbers to the current value before consolidation. Any gain or loss on its net monetary position is separately disclosed in its income statement.

The major exception to this is in the consolidated financial statements where the net assets in an overseas operation are hedged in some way. (A hedge is designed to minimise, or eliminate, a risk by moving in the opposite direction to the investment's value.) In this case they fall under the hedge accounting rules, which I'll discuss in more detail in the next chapter. Firstly, hedge accounting can only be used where the hedging relationship has been pre-designated and meets hedge effectiveness tests that must be met both at the outset and continuously. An effective hedge is where the change in value of the hedging instrument is the same as the change in value of the hedged item. This doesn't always happen, and these tests recognise that hedges aren't perfect and a hedge is split into its effective and ineffective parts. (The definition of an effective hedge is that the value of the hedged item is offset by the hedge within a range of 80–125%.) Any gain, or loss, on the effective portion is classified as other comprehensive income and taken to equity. Whereas the gains or losses on any ineffective part of the hedge are charged to the income statement.

 Unfortunately accounting for the effect of exchange rates is not straightforward in the UK, as there are currently two accounting rules and different companies use different rules:

- FRS 23, which is virtually identical to IAS 21 and is used by the few companies that have adopted FRS 26 (*Financial instruments: recognition and measurement*). SSAP 20 (*Foreign currency translation*) that is used by most UK companies.

There is a number of differences between SSAP 20 and IAS 21, and the main ones are:

- Companies can use the contracted forward rate for profit and loss account items.
- If a monetary item will be settled at a contracted rate, this rate should be used.
- If a subsidiary's trade is seen as a direct extension of the parent company's, it is treated as though it were part of the parent, with historical or average rates being used. This is called the temporal method.

Income statement summary

I've covered a lot of technical material, and I'd now like to summarise the key points that you need to remember in the table shown on the following pages.

Revenue	This is the cash sales in the period plus either the invoices raised, or the goods shipped during the period, depending on the company's accounting policy for recognising its revenue.
	Accounting for long-term contracts is different from normal accounting practice, as the revenue is recorded as the contract progresses and profit is recorded as it arises.
	Any payments in advance for sales in future periods will not be shown. They will be included in trade and other payables and shown as *deferred income*.
Operating costs	This is the cost of goods used in the sales in the period. The numbers are adjusted to:
	Include charges for:
	▪ *Accrued expenses*. These outstanding invoices are included in trade and other payables.
	▪ *Depreciation and amortisation*. The company gets the benefit of using its non current assets over a number of years. As the income statement must match costs to revenues, the depreciation and amortisation charges represent this year's use of these assets. There are different depreciation methods, giving different charges to the income statement and different asset values on the balance sheet.
	▪ *Provisions*. For likely future costs relating to either sales, or decisions that have been made during the period (for example, restructuring). The provisions may reduce asset values (bad debts, stock write downs) or relate to future costs. Unspent provisions relating to future costs are shown as provisions on the balance sheet. Provisions can only be made where there's a liability arising from a past event that has a measurable probable future cash outflow.
	And exclude:
	▪ *Prepayments*. These advance payments to suppliers are included in trade and other receivables, and are separately disclosed in the notes to the accounts.
	▪ *Inventories*. These are shown on the balance sheet. There are different methods of valuing stock, giving different charges to the income statement and different stock values on the balance sheet.
Exchange rates	In the income statement companies should use the actual exchange rate, but can use an average exchange rate as long as there hasn't been a significant change in rates during the period. However, exchange differences can arise from the movement in exchange rates between the invoicing date and the payment date, and these affect a company's reported profitability as they are shown in the income statement.

Sales, operating costs, and profit can be analysed between continuing and discontinued operations, but most companies using IFRS combine the after tax profit with the profit/loss arising from the sale of discontinued operations as a single figure 'Profit/loss from discontinued operation'. The analysis will then be shown in the notes.

Companies preparing their accounts using UK GAAP must show the discontinued operation's revenues and costs separately.

Continuing operations	These are operations that are expected to continue next year. If the business has made any acquisitions in the period, it must disclose, usually in the notes, the revenue and profit generated by acquisitions. If the acquisitions are material, there will also be pro forma information showing the revenue and profit for the financial year. *Profit and loss accounts prepared under UK GAAP show the acquisition's contribution to all line items from revenue to profit before interest.*
Discontinued operations	These are those operations that were closed, discontinued, sold during the year or have been classified as 'held for sale'.
Exceptional costs	An exceptional cost relates to normal business trading but is disclosed because it is either very large or 'material'. Most exceptional costs are no longer shown on the income statement, but are disclosed in the notes. *UK GAAP requires the following exceptional costs to be disclosed separately after operating profit if they are significant*: ▧ *profit, or losses, on disposal of fixed assets*; ▧ *profit, or losses, on disposal of businesses*; ▧ *restructuring costs*. Most UK companies using IFRS continue this practice showing operating profit before and after material restructuring and profits and losses from disposal of assets.
Profit, or losses, on sale of property, plant and equipment or businesses	All assets have a 'book value'. If their sale proceeds are different from their book value, the difference shows on the income statement as a profit or a loss. Profits, or losses, on sale of businesses are calculated in a similar way.
Financial income	This comprises: ▧ interest receivable and similar income; ▧ any 'fair value' (market value gains) arising from derivatives (things such as swaps, options and futures). A notional interest, representing the expected return on final salary pension scheme's assets, may be shown as 'Expected return on defined benefit pension plan assets'.
Financial expenses	This comprises: ▧ interest payable (the notes will attribute it to specific types of loan). ▧ preference dividends paid; ▧ any losses arising from derivatives when shown at 'fair value'. A notional interest charge on final salary pension schemes, representing the period's increase in the present value of the obligation now the benefits are one year closer to settlement, may be shown as the financing cost for pension scheme's liabilities.

Share of associate's profits or losses	An investment is classed as an associate when the investment is sizeable (usually 20–50% of the shares) and the company has the opportunity to be involved in, but doesn't control, the investment's decision making (*participating interest*).
	The company brings into its income statement operating profits in proportion to its investment in the company (i.e. if the company holds 30% of the shares, it incorporates 30% of the associate's profits). This is called *the equity method* of accounting. Companies preparing their accounts using IFRS show their share of the associate's after tax profits, *whilst those using UK GAAP show their share of operating profit* (*with any subsequent income and expense included on the relevant lines*).
Joint ventures	The accounting treatment for joint ventures is proposed to be the same as associates in the future. However, currently the accounting rules allow proportional consolidation, with the business's share of revenues and costs included in the line items on the income statement. *Companies preparing accounts using UK GAAP use the equity method, and also have to disclose the joint venture's turnover.*
Taxation	This can't be calculated directly from the published income statement, as profit for tax purposes is very different.
	It also includes an accrual, or prepayment, for tax called *deferred taxation*. Companies preparing their accounts using IFRS show deferred tax assets and liabilities on their balance sheet, *whereas those using UK GAAP include it in provisions for liabilities and charges*.
Minority or non-controlling interests	You'll find these when a company doesn't own all the shares in its subsidiaries.
	They represent the proportion of a subsidiary's profits that do not belong to the group. For example – if a subsidiary makes £100 after tax profits, and the group owns 60% of its shares. The group's income statement will show a deduction of £40 for minority interests, or non-controlling interests, to reflect the proportion of the after tax profits belonging to shareholders outside of the group.
	(If a company controls another, the other company is classed as a subsidiary. All of its sales, costs, assets and liabilities are included in the accounts, and the other shareholders' share is shown as a single line adjustment.)

IMI's income statement

IMI's income statement is shown on page 86. When you read it you'll find:

- Its operating profit starts with its segmental profit (the profit arising from their various businesses), and I'll be discussing this in detail in Chapter 6.

- It has included some gains and losses from hedges in operating profits, rather than other financial income and expenses. This is because they have been realised in the year.

▨ It has exceptional items arising from an investigation and associated fine and restructuring. So let me tell you a little about the investigation and the restructuring:

– The investigation arose when IMI discovered that payments were being made to commissioning agents in their Severe Service business in the US that were subsequently found to be illegal and were in breach of the company's policies and practice. (IMI had established policies and controls in place to guard against such activities, but these were circumvented through the collusion of a group of employees.) They contacted the US Department of Justice and the UK's Serious Organised Crime Agency and contracted forensic accountants at Ernst and Young to conduct an independent investigation. It is close to resolving the case with the US authorities, but may still have problems in other countries.

– In 2008 IMI completed its three-year restructuring programme to increase the percentage of manufacturing conducted in low cost economies from 25% to 35%. The restructuring charge is primarily for redundancies but it also includes plant transfer, installation and set up costs.

▨ It is disclosing the intangible amortisation and impairment relating to acquisitions separately. This is fairly standard, as most analysts use profit before one off impairment charges and amortisation of acquired intangible assets, as it helps them look at a company's underlying profitability and improves the comparability of accounts. (I'll be discussing acquired intangibles, and their amortisation, in the next chapter.)

▨ It has restated its 2007 numbers to reflect the changed presentation.

▨ Its revenues and operating profit have increased significantly, and you'll find out why in Chapter 6.

▨ It is a global business, as most of its tax is paid overseas.

▨ The operating costs are not shown on the income statement itself. That information is shown in the notes, and I have shown it on the page after the income statement. When you see the detailed information you'll find that the hedges affected both the revenue (which increased by £3.8 million) and the operating costs (which increased by £1.2 million).

CONSOLIDATED INCOME STATEMENT

FOR THE YEAR ENDED 31 DECEMBER 2008

	Notes	2008	2007
	2		restated
		£m	£m
Revenue	3,4,5	1,901	1,599
Segmental operating profit	3	266.3	207.8
Restructuring costs		(19.6)	(22.0)
Severe service investigation costs and fines		(26.3)	(4.9)
Acquired intangible amortisation and impairment		(13.2)	(10.9)
Other income	5	–	1.7
Economic hedge contract gain and losses		2.6	–
Operating profit	3,4,5	209.8	171.7
Financial income	7	85.6	81.1
Financial expense	7	(119.4)	(81.8)
Net financial expense	7	(33.8)	(0.7)
Profit before tax	8		
Before restructuring, investigation costs and fines, acquired intangible amortisation and impairment, other income and financial instruments excluding economic hedge contract gains and losses		254.7	205.5
Restructuring costs		(19.6)	(22.0)
Severe service investigation costs and fines		(26.3)	(4.9)
Acquired intangible amortisation and impairment		(13.2)	(10.9)
Other income		–	1.7
Financial instruments excluding economic hedge contract gains and losses		(19.6)	1.6
Total		176.0	171.0
Taxation	9		
UK taxation		(12.9)	(10.5)
Overseas taxation		(47.1)	(42.5)
Total		(60.0)	(53.0)
Profit of continuing operations after tax		116.0	118.0
Gain from discontinued operations (net of tax)	6	–	1.9
Total profit for the year		116.0	119.9
Attributable to:			

Equity shareholders of the company	112.9	117.0
Minority interest	3.1	2.9
Total profit for the year	116.0	119.9
Earnings per share	8	
Basic earnings per share	35.4p	35.4p
Diluted earnings per share	35.1p	35.3p
Basic earnings per share (continuing operations)	35.4p	35.4p
Diluted earnings per share (continuing operations)	35.1p	34.7p

5 Operating profit	2008 £m	2007 £m
Revenue (i)	1,900.6	1,599.2
Cost of sales (ii)	(1,144.1)	(964.4)
Gross profit	756.5	634.8
Selling and distribution costs (iii)	(228.0)	(201.1)
Administrative expenses (iv)	(318.7)	(263.7)
Other income (v)	–	1.7
Operating profit	209.8	171.7

i) Includes £3.8m economic hedge contracts net gain (2007: £nil).
ii) Includes £3.6m restructuring costs (2007: £5.2m) and £1.2m economic hedge contracts net loss (2007: £nil).
iii) Includes £2.2m restructuring costs (2007: £3.7m).
iv) Includes £13.8m restructuring costs (2007: £13.1m), £26.3m a Severe Service investigation costs and fines (2007: £4.9m) and £13.2m of acquired intangible amortisation and impairment (2007: £10.9m).
v) In 2007 the company sold its interest in Imagine, a Hong Kong based merchandising business, realising a profit of £1.7m.

3

The balance sheet and statement of financial position

Introduction

In this chapter I'll look at the balance sheet in detail, and when you've finished reading it you'll understand:

- *The things you'll find on a balance sheet.* I'll summarise these below and then discuss each one of them in detail later, so that you'll understand both the balance sheet and the wealth of information found in the notes to the balance sheet.

- *How the items on a balance sheet items are valued.*

- *The different ways that the balance sheet is presented in the accounts.*

The balance sheet is probably the only document that everyone regularly prepares, and yet it is the one that managers often find the hardest to understand! You've undoubtedly prepared a balance sheet, even though you didn't realise it.

Have you ever compared your lifestyle with someone else's? Perhaps you've looked at a friend and wondered how she can afford an expensive car, or an exotic holiday? You wondered whether she has won the lottery, or maybe it's all on credit cards? If you have, then you have prepared a balance sheet; in fact you've probably created a balance sheet that's pretty similar to a typical UK company's balance sheet. You look at what your friends have, deduct what you think they might owe, to find out what they are worth. That's a balance sheet!

Most people are much the same. I wonder if you have a group of friends that you think are intellectually similar, and work about as hard as you do. If they seem to be doing 'better' than you, you may well become dissatisfied and think about looking for another job. Most people mentally prepare their own balance sheets and compare their balance sheets with their friends' balance sheets. Your parents can tell you how well off you are, but you don't believe them if all your friends have better standards of living and aren't up to their ears in debt. Some of your friends can have better houses and cars, but they probably have bigger mortgages and credit card bills. Everyone has a different level of debt that they feel comfortable with (that's why you end up having rows with your partner about money – their debt comfort level is different from yours). Companies are exactly the same.

A balance sheet shows you what the company has (its assets) and what it owes (its liabilities) on a certain day. It is a snapshot of the business and is a useful tool for looking at a company's financial health. If you know what the company has and what it owes, you can see whether it is likely to be able to pay its debts when they fall due. Company balance sheets do appear to be more complicated than the ones we prepare for ourselves, and sometimes these detailed differences can obscure the more obvious similarities.

There are three main differences between personal balance sheets and those prepared by companies:

- The layout is more complicated, often having sub totals that are only useful once you understand what the balance sheet tells you.

- The jargon is unfamiliar, even though what it describes isn't.

- Companies have different types of loans, and company treasurers are becoming increasingly innovative, often constructing debt to attract a specific type of lender or investor.

Then to add to the complications – you'll usually find two balance sheets in the accounts. Most listed companies are not individual companies, but a *group* of companies. If you're looking at group accounts you'll find two balance sheets: a *consolidated balance sheet* for the whole group, and the *parent company's balance sheet* (sometimes the parent may be called the 'holding company', or just the 'company'). You have to imagine the group accounts like a family tree, but with a single parent at the top. Large businesses usually organise themselves into different divisions, and within these divisions there can be a number of operating companies. They then have a group structure like the one below.

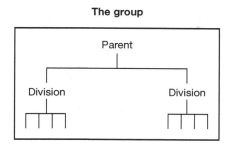

The Companies Act 2006 requires the parent company to prepare consolidated group accounts, and the consolidated balance sheet is the combined balance sheets of all the companies in the group including the parent. In the consolidation process some transactions cancel each other out (for example, a loan from one group company to another won't show on the consolidated balance sheet), so that the consolidated balance sheet reflects the group's position. (This is why the parent company often has more investments than the group. They're the shares they hold in the group companies and are cancelled out on consolidation with the subsidiary companies' share capital.) All of the companies in the group have to prepare their own accounts. However the law allows the parent company to present most of its financial statements in the group's accounts. (Section 408 exempts parent companies from presenting their income statement and related notes, as long as it discloses its profit for the financial year in the notes to the accounts. It still shows its own balance sheet, statement of total recognised income and expense, and statement of cash flows and their related notes. Most UK companies take advantage of this exemption.)

In financial analysis you're interested in the *consolidated group* balance sheet, as most of the other financial statements are consolidated group statements.

What will I find in a balance sheet?

A balance sheet is a photo of the company on a certain day identifying its assets, liabilities and shareholders' equity. Both the assets and liabilities are sorted into short term (less than a year) and longer term (more than a year). This classification is used in most companies, although the definition is slightly different in UK GAAP, but once again the terminology is different. Companies using IFRS call their long-term assets *Non current assets* (they're called *Fixed assets* in UK GAAP) and all companies refer to their short-term assets as *current assets*. IFRS calls a company's long-term liabilities *Non current liabilities*, whereas UK GAAP refers to them as *Creditors: amounts falling due in more than a year*. The short-term liabilities are called *Current liabilities* under IFRS and *Creditors: amounts falling due within a year* under UK GAAP. In the UK, a typical company balance sheet deducts its liabilities from its assets in order to show what the company is worth to its owners – adopting a 'net assets' presentation. This isn't the only way a balance sheet can be presented, and I'll tell you about the others later.

IFRS requires companies to classify their assets and liabilities as either current or non current, unless presenting their balance sheet on a liquidity basis makes the balance sheet more relevant. (Banks and other financial institutions do this, starting with their most liquid asset (cash) and liabilitiy, as the current and non current classification isn't a meaningful classification for their business.) Current assets and liabilities must be realisable within a year, and all other assets and liabilities are classified as non current. I've mentioned that there's a slight difference between the way that IFRS and UK GAAP classifies assets (the classification for liabilities is the same). IFRS defines the current assets and all other assets are non current. Whereas UK GAAP defines fixed assets, and all other assets are current. The Companies Act defines fixed assets as those assets the company intends to use on an ongoing basis, and all other assets are current assets. This creates differences in where some assets are shown on the balance sheet.

I'm going to discuss all balance sheet items in detail, but I'll start by summarising the balance sheet headings you'll find on most balance sheets.

Non current assets or *fixed assets*

These are either the assets:

■ The company doesn't intend to realise within the next 12 months – IFRS.

or

■ *The company intends to use on an ongoing basis – UK GAAP.*

You'll usually find at least three different types of non current assets on balance sheets:

- ▓ **Intangible assets** This term covers items such as brands or patents that have an obvious value to the company, but it's more difficult to determine their value objectively. The difference between the price paid to buy a company and its net asset value (called *goodwill)* can also be included in intangible assets, but if the value is material it is shown separately.

- ▓ **Property, plant and equipment, or** *tangible assets* The IFRS term 'Property plant and equipment' is self-explanatory, companies using UK GAAP refer to these as tangible assets.

- ▓ **Investments or financial assets** These are the long-term investments that the company intends to keep for more than a year. You'll find that IFRS and UK GAAP require that these investments are analysed into various types.

 Fixed assets are not the same as non current assets, as they are defined differently A fixed asset is something that is intended to be used on a continuing basis in the company's activities. This means that some items that would be shown as non current assets under IFRS, for example UK GAAP shows debtors falling due in more than a year as current assets.

Current assets

IAS 1 (*The presentation of financial statements*) defines current assets as an asset satisfying any of the following criteria:

- ▓ The business expects to realise it within its normal operating cycle, or within 12 months;

- ▓ The business intends to use or sell it within its normal operating cycle;

- ▓ The business is holding it primarily for trading purposes;

- ▓ It is cash, or a cash equivalent, that has no restrictions on its use;

Most companies' current assets include:

- Inventories or *stock*.

- Trade and other receivables or *debtors*.

- Investments or financial assets.

- Cash and cash equivalents or *cash*.

 Current assets are all the assets that are not fixed assets, and include cash and any assets held for resale. They are not necessarily all short term, as there is no legal requirement under UK GAAP to split assets on the balance sheet between those falling due within a year and more than a year. However, this information is given in the notes.

Current liabilities or *creditors*: *amounts falling due within a year*

This heading includes anything that might represent cash, or services, expected to go out of the business in the next 12 months. IAS 1 defines current liabilities as ones that satisfy any of the following criteria:

- The business expects to settle it within its normal operating cycle, or within 12 months.

- The business is holding the liability primarily for trading purposes.

- The business doesn't have the right to defer the settlement for at least 12 months. (This affects loans where the company has breached its banking covenants. Once the company breaches its banking covenants the loan is usually repayable on demand or within a few months. As the company has no right to defer the repayment for 12 months, the loan would be shown as a current liability regardless of its original repayment date.)

Companies using the international rules must show the details of their current liabilities on the balance sheet. Whereas most companies using UK GAAP show a total figure on the balance sheet, detailing the individual items in the notes to the accounts.

Non current liabilities, or *creditors*: *amounts falling due in more than a year*

These liabilities are largely debt, but would also include other cash, or services, expected to leave the business after a year. Again, companies using IFRS show all of these liabilities on the balance sheet itself, whereas companies using UK GAAP usually just show a total figure on the balance sheet with the details in the notes.

Shareholders' equity, or *capital and reserves*

This represents the owners' stake in the business. It includes the cash received from the shareholders, the profits reinvested in the business, any asset revaluations and some balancing items.

How is this information presented?

These headings form the building blocks of a balance sheet, but you know that you can take a picture from different perspectives. This means that balance sheets can be presented in different ways. Whilst the presentations may be different, the content of the balance sheet is the same – only the perspective has changed. You may find that although the degree of detail and the basis for valuations varies in other countries the information on the balance sheet remains broadly the same.

Most UK companies prepare the balance sheet from the shareholders' point of view, but this is a British perspective. Most other countries total their assets and liabilities, looking at the business from the point of view of everyone who has put money into the business, whether directly or indirectly. The UK's Companies Act refers to these presentations as Format One, the net assets presentation, and Format Two, the assets and liabilities presentation.

I've used the same numbers to show you four different balance sheet presentations:

▓ a typical UK balance sheet using IFRS

▓ the balance sheet presentation you're likely to find in the US and Asia

▓ a typical European presentation

▓ a balance sheet prepared using UK GAAP.

So let's look at a typical UK balance sheet prepared using IFRS.

Example 3.1

The net assets presentation

	£m
Non current assets	
Intangible assets	50
Property, plant and equipment	200
Investments	75
	325
Current assets	
Inventories	80
Trade and other receivables	270
Investments	40
Cash and cash equivalents	10
	400
Total assets	725
Current liabilities	
Interest bearing loans and borrowings	(130)
Trade and other payables	(120)
Current tax	(40)
Provisions	(10)
	(300)
Non current liabilities	
Interest bearing loans and borrowings	(100)
Provisions	(15)
	(115)
Total liabilities	(415)
Net assets	310
Equity	
Share capital	50
Share premium account	20
Revaluation reserve	40
Retained earnings	175
Total equity attributable to equity shareholders of the company	285
Minority interests	25
Total equity	310

Now let's look at the same information presented in the most popular global presentation of the balance sheet, an assets and liabilities presentation.

You'll find that some of the headings can be presented in a different order, for example in the US and Asia it's common to start with cash and present the assets and liabilities in order of liquidity.

The assets and liabilities presentation in order of liquidity

	£m
ASSETS	
Current assets	
Cash and cash equivalents	10
Investments	40
Trade and other receivables	270
Inventories	80
	400
Non current assets	
Investments	75
Property, plant and equipment	200
Intangible assets	50
	325
TOTAL ASSETS	725
LIABILITIES AND SHAREHOLDERS' EQUITY	
Current liabilities	
Interest bearing loans and borrowings	130
Trade and other payables	120
Current tax	40
Provisions	10
	300
Non current liabilities	
Interest bearing loans and borrowings	100
Provisions	15
	115
Total liabilities	415
Equity	
Share capital	50
Share premium account	20
Revaluation reserve	40
Retained earnings	175
Total equity attributable to equity shareholders of the company	285
Minority interests	25
Total equity	310
TOTAL LIABILITIES AND SHAREHOLDERS' EQUITY	725

In Europe the same information is usually presented horizontally, in reverse order of liquidity.

Example 3.3

A 'two sided' assets and liabilities presentation

	£m		£m
ASSETS		LIABILITIES AND SHAREHOLDERS' EQUITY	
Non current assets		Equity	
Intangible assets	50	Share capital	50
Property, plant and equipment	200	Share premium account	20
Investments	75	Revaluation reserve	40
	325	Retained earnings	175
		Total equity attributable to equity shareholders of the company	285
Current assets		Minority interests	25
Inventories	80	Total equity	310
Trade and other receivables	270	Current liabilities	
Investments	40	Interest bearing loans and borrowings	130
Cash and cash equivalents	10	Trade and other payables	20
	400	Current tax	40
TOTAL ASSETS	725	Provisions	10
			300
		Non current liabilities	
		Interest bearing loans and borrowings	100
		Provisions	15
			115
		Total liabilities	415
		TOTAL LIABILITIES AND SHAREHOLDERS' EQUITY	725

Companies using UK GAAP follow a slightly different presentation. They tend to use the net assets presentation and show two subtotals. The first is 'Net current assets', which deducts the short term liabilities from the current assets. The second is the 'Total assets less current liabilities', which adds the fixed assets to the net current assets. There's less information on the balance sheet about the liabilities, although you'll find it in the notes, and provisions are combined and shown under the heading 'Provisions for liabilities and charges'. This presentation is the first format in the Companies Act.

Example 3.4

A typical balance sheet prepared using UK GAAP

	£m
Fixed assets	
Intangible assets	50
Tangible assets	200
Investments	75
	325
Current assets	
Stocks	80
Debtors	270
Investments	40
Cash	10
	400
Creditors: amounts falling due within one year	(300)
Net current assets	100
Total assets less current liabilities	425
Creditors: amounts falling due after more than one year	(100)
Provisions for liabilities and charges	(15)
Minority interests[1]	(25)
	285
Capital and reserves	
Share capital	50
Share premium account	20
Revaluation reserve	40
Profit and loss account	175
	285

[1] Minority interests can be shown on either side of the balance sheet. I have shown them as a negative in the 'net assets side'. The alternative would be to report net assets of £310 million that would balance with the capital and reserves of £285 million plus the minority interests of £25 million giving £310 million.

Now you know what the balance sheet looks like, let's look at each item you'll find in more detail and find out how a company's assts are valued.

The balance sheet in detail

I'll now take you through each line of the balance sheet explaining how its value is determined.

Non current assets

I'll start by looking at the three types of non current assets shown on the balance sheet and how they're valued.

Intangible assets

Many businesses' ability to generate and develop future profits is not linked to assets that were traditionally shown on a balance sheet. For example, drug companies' future profits are linked to their patents which reflect their drug pipeline and ability to maintain margins. The revenue and subsequent profits of drinks and confectionery companies is affected by the strength of their brands. Customer relationships can be important to businesses that are selling 'business to business'. These can all be regarded as intangible assets, and in certain circumstances they're shown on the balance sheet.

The Companies Act identifies the following categories of intangible fixed assets:

- development costs;
- concessions, patents, licences, trademarks and similar rights and assets;
- goodwill;
- payments on account.

The international accounting standard, IAS 38 (*Intangible fixed assets*), introduces more intangible assets and defines and details the accounting treatment for them. So I'd like to tell you what can be shown as an intangible asset under the accounting rules, and then how its value is determined.

An intangible asset is an identifiable non-monetary asset that doesn't have a physical substance and is controlled by an entity and will generate future economic benefits (for example it could increase revenue or reduce costs). It:

■ can be sold, or transferred, or licensed separate from the business as a whole;

or

■ arises from contractual or other form of legal rights regardless of whether these rights are separable from either the business, or from other rights and obligations.

It can then only be shown on the balance sheet if it:

■ is probable that the company will receive future economic benefits from the intangible asset;

and

■ the asset's costs can be reliably measured.

A business can either acquire intangible assets or develop them itself. The accounting standard effectively precludes most internally generated intangible assets from being recognised on the balance sheet. The only internally developed assets allowed are development costs meeting specific criteria. Consequently, in practice, most intangible assets developed by the company itself can't be capitalised and their development costs are expensed as they're incurred. IAS 38 also specifically prohibits the capitalisation of internally generated goodwill, brands, mastheads, customer lists and publishing titles.

This means most intangible assets have been purchased, but not always on their own. What do I mean? A lot of intangible assets are purchased as part of an acquisition. When one company acquires another, its intangible assets *must* be capitalised if they can be reliably measured even when they weren't previously shown in the acquired company's financial statements. After an acquisition you'll find companies showing customer and supplier relationships as intangible assets, and many companies have a separate heading for 'acquired intangible assets' in the notes to their accounts.

Now you know what an intangible asset is, let's look at how you account for it.

If the intangible asset has been purchased it must initially be shown at its cost. Most intangible assets have a finite life, and these are usually amortised on a straight line basis over their life. Their value on the balance sheet can never exceed their fair value to the business. If there is any indication that their value has fallen the company must conduct an *impairment review*. The impairment review compares the asset's book value with its recoverable value (this is the higher of an asset's value for use in the business and its fair value less any costs that would be incurred to sell it). If this results in a reduction in the asset's value the company must make an impairment charge in the income statement. (A few intangible assets with a finite life are valued at their market value, using something called 'the revaluation model'. This can only be used where there's an active market for the intangible asset, and consequently it's rarely used.)

Intangible assets with an indefinite life do not have to be amortised, but have to have an impairment review if there's any indication that their value has fallen. (Indefinite doesn't mean infinite, just that the company expects the asset to generate cash inflows for the foreseeable future.)

Any impairment is disclosed separately on the income statement if it is material, or in the notes if it's an immaterial amount. This means that intangible assets affect the income statement in two ways:

- Firstly, they have to be amortised over their expected life. Acquisitive companies may have quite significant amortisation charges, as they have to capitalise intangible assets that wouldn't normally be shown on the balance sheet. Consequently, they often show an operating profit figure before, and after, amortisation of acquired intangible assets.

- Secondly, if their value falls, companies must make an impairment charge to bring the balance sheet value into line with the commercial value of the intangible asset.

 The definition of an intangible asset is largely the same, but the asset must be able to be sold separately from the business as a whole. This is an important difference, which particularly affects the recognition of legal and contractual rights, such as licences and acquired intangible assets.

I'd now like to discuss acquired intangible assets, development costs, goodwill and brands.

Acquired intangible assets

When a company acquires another company all its intangible assets must be recognised and measured. IFRS 3 (*Business combinations*) has an extensive list of acquired intangible assets. It includes many types of assets under the following headings:

- *Marketing related intangible assets* – including trademarks, internet domain names and newspaper mastheads.

- *Customer related intangible assets* – including customer lists, order backlogs, customer contracts and non contractual customer relationships.

- *Artistic related intangible assets* – including copyrights for books, plays and musical works.

- *Contract based intangible assets* – including licencing agreements, management contracts and broadcasting rights.

- *Technology based intangible assets* – including patented technology, databases and trade secrets.

 Under IFRS, when a company makes an acquisition, any rights arising from contractual or other legal rights and customer related intangible assets are shown as intangible assets. They are unlikely to be shown as intangible assets under UK GAAP, as FRS 10 (*Goodwill and intangible assets*) only allows intangible assets to be recognised if they can be sold separately from the business as a whole.

Research and development

Research and development is a problem for accountants. It's an investment in the long-term future of the business, but isn't always commercially successful. Just think about Blue Ray and HD, both great products but only one was commercially successful. Historically some countries capitalised all their research and development as an intangible asset, whereas others expensed it all through the income statement, and others expensed research but capitalised development costs.

IAS 38 requires companies to divide research and development into a research phase and a development phase. If it's impossible to distinguish these phases all expenditure must be treated as research. All research expenditure should be expensed to the income statement as it is incurred. Most development costs are also expensed, however some development expenditure *must* be capitalised if it meets certain conditions. This is development expenditure on new, or substantially improved, products or processes, where **all** of the following conditions are met:

■ The company intends to complete and subsequently use or sell the product.

■ The company has the ability to use or sell the product.

■ The product is technically feasible and commercially viable.

■ The related expenditure can be reliably measured.

■ The company has to demonstrate how the asset will bring it future economic benefits.

■ The company has all of the resources necessary to complete the project.

Any capitalised development costs are amortised over the periods that are expected to benefit from their use.

 SSAP 13 (*Accounting for research and development*) allows development expenditure to be capitalised if similar criteria are met, or it has a readily ascertainable market value. It can be capitalised if:

• there is a clearly defined project;
• the related expenditure is separately identifiable;
• it is reasonably certain that the project is both technically feasible and commercially viable;
• the project is expected to be profitable, having considered all current and future costs;
• the company has the resources to complete the project.

SSAP 13 is less stringent than IAS 38, as the company doesn't have to demonstrate the future benefits arising from the asset; it just has to have a reasonable expectation of future benefits.

Goodwill

I mentioned goodwill in the last chapter, but now I'd like to explain it in more detail. Goodwill arises as companies usually pay more to acquire another company than its business is worth on its balance sheet. What would you pay for a company that has net assets worth 50 million, but is generating 10 million profit a year? I know you'd pay more than 50 million, as you're not just buying the assets, you would also have another 10 million profit every year and some extra cash. The difference between the purchase price and the value of the business shown in the accounts is called goodwill. It is simply the difference between the purchase price of a company and the value of the net assets acquired – effectively a premium paid to acquire the company's future profits and cash flows.

I'll illustrate the accounting treatment for goodwill by using a simple example in Example 3.5.

Example 3.5

Firstly I need to tell you about my business – its net assets are currently £200 million, and I have agreed to buy the company I discussed earlier for £70 million in cash. My summarised balance sheet, before the acquisition, was as follows:

	£ million
Property, plant and equipment	200
Cash and cash equivalents	120
Other current assets	130
Current liabilities	(150)
Non current loans	(100)
	200

Shareholders' equity:	
Share capital	50
Retained earnings	150
	200

I now have to consolidate my newly acquired subsidiary into my accounts. Following the acquisition my cash reduces by the £70 million I paid to acquire the business. In exchange I'll receive its £50 million net assets. Now look what happens when I try to add up the two balance sheets to prepare my new balance sheet.

3.5 continued

	My business	Acquisition cost	Acquisition	Consolidated balance sheet
	£m		£m	£m
Property, plant and equipment	200		30	230
Cash and cash equivalents	120	(70)	0	50
Other current assets	130		50	180
Current liabilities	(150)		(20)	(170)
Long-term loans	(100)		(10)	(110)
	200		50	180
Shareholders' equity:				
Share capital	50			50
Retained earnings	150			150
	200			200

> These two numbers should be the same!

Now there's one thing you probably already know about balance sheets – they're supposed to balance! There are supposed to be two numbers at the bottom of the balance sheet that are the same. The consolidated balance sheet's net assets of £180 million should be the same as the shareholders' equity of £200 million! The balance sheet doesn't balance as I have paid more for a business than it was worth on its balance sheet – and that difference of £20 million is goodwill.

I can make the balance sheet balance in one of two ways:

- Reduce the shareholders' equity, by reducing the retained earnings by the amount of goodwill. Before December 1998 UK companies did this, and sizeable amounts of goodwill have been written off through retained earnings. Any goodwill previously written off through reserves remains there even when the companies they acquired are sold terminated (when it is deducted to arrive at the profit, or loss, on disposal). (For example, IMI discloses in its 2008 balance sheet that 'the aggregate amount of goodwill arising from relevant historical acquisitions prior to 1 January 2004 which had been deducted from the profit and loss account reserves and incorporated into the IFRS transitional balance sheet as at 1 January 2004 amounted to £364 million'.

■ Increase the net assets, by creating an intangible asset. All UK companies
have had to do this since for any acquisitions acquired since December 1998.

You will see that the balance sheet now balances:

	£m
Property, plant and equipment	230
Goodwill	20
Cash	50
Other current assets	180
Current liabilities	(170)
Long-term loans	(110)
	200
Shareholders' equity:	
Share capital	50
Retained earnings	150
	200

Unfortunately my example is quite simple, as the value of the acquisition's assets didn't change when they were consolidated and the cost was simply the cash I paid to acquire the business. It's rarely that simple, as the Companies Acts and the accounting standards require companies to consolidate the acquisition's assets and liabilities 'at their fair values as at the date of acquisition' and using the purchaser's accounting policies.

Consequently companies make two adjustments when consolidating acquisitions into the group accounts:

■ Aligning the acquisition's accounting policies with the group's.

■ Restating the values of the acquisition's assets and liabilities to fair values.

Goodwill can subsequently be revised, as it may take some time in a complex acquisition to identify all the assets, liabilities and contingent liabilities existing at the acquisition date and then perform a full, reliable fair value exercise. A company has 12 months from the acquisition's date to finalise the accounting and goodwill for an acquisition.

Goodwill is subject to an annual impairment review, although it must be reviewed more frequently if there is an indication that the goodwill has been impaired. Like all assets, goodwill cannot be shown on the balance sheet above its recoverable amount. The impairment review compares the value of the acquisition with the present value of its future cash flows and ensures that if there has been an overpayment any loss is recognised immediately.

IMI didn't make any acquisitions in 2008, but it acquired two companies in 2007. Here's its note on the acquisitions:

4 Acquisitions

There were no acquisitions during the year. The 2007 acquisitions of Pneumatex AG (Pneumatex) and Kloehn Company Limited (Kloehn) contributed £37m of additional revenue and £4.1m of additional operating profit in the year (2007: £15m and £1.8m respectively).

In 2007 the business of Kloehn, a leading US provider of specialist pumping and fluid handling systems for the life science sector, was acquired on 29 June 2007 which is reported within Fluid Power, and a 70% share in Pneumatex, a specialist provider of water conditioning equipment for building heating, cooling and related systems was acquired on 28 September 2007, reported within Indoor Climate.

2007 net assets acquired:

	Total 2007		
	Carrying values at acquisition	Fair value adjustments	Fair value of net assets acquired
	£m	£m	£m
Customer relationships		6.6	6.6
Order books		1.0	1.0
Property, plant and equipment	3.6	0.3	3.9
Inventories	8.3	(0.7)	7.6
Trade & other receivables	13.5	–	13.5
Trade & other payables	(10.0)	(3.9)	(13.9)
Tax	(1.5)	(0.5)	(2.0)
Net identifiable assets and liabilities	13.9	2.8	16.7
Minority share			(2.9)
			13.8
Other minority interests acquired			2.0
Total net assets acquired			15.8
Purchase consideration			53.3
Goodwill			37.5

Cash impact of acquisitions

	2007
	£m
Purchase consideration net of cash acquired	52.2
Deferred consideration to pay	1.1
Total	53.3

The methodology for arriving at fair value, intangible asset values and residual goodwill is described in the Accounting Policies in note 1(g) to these financial statements. The goodwill recognised on the acquisition principally relates to skills present within the assembled workforce, customer service capability and the geographical and sector presence of these businesses.

The fair value adjustments principally relate to harmonisation with Group IFRSs compliant accounting policies, recognition of intangible assets (which principally comprise the value of non-contractual customer relationships and the order book at acquisition) and the reflection of adjustments to move the carrying value of the identifiable net assets from cost to fair value.

You can see that the notes give you a lot of information about an acquisition:

▨ The fair value adjustments bring the asset values to their realisable value, align the accounting policies and recognise assets and liabilities that weren't previously shown in the accounts.

▨ Goodwill is the balancing item, the difference between the fair value of the assets and the consideration paid.

▨ You can also see how the acquisition has contributed to other aspects of the group's performance since its acquisition.

I've talked about companies paying more than the acquisition's net asset value. Sometimes it is possible to buy a company for less than its net asset value. In May 2000 BMW sold most of Rover Cars to the Phoenix Corporation for £10 – well below its asset value. In this case the company has made a 'bargain purchase', although it may not be a bargain purchase as you and I would understand the term. (The reason Rover was sold for £10 is that it was making huge losses.) The first thing the company has to do in this situation is to assess whether it has correctly identified all the assets acquired and the liabilities assumed. If this reassessment still results in a bargain purchase gain, the gain is shown in the income statement. It doesn't have to be shown on a separate line, however the company must disclose the amount of any gain that it has recognised and the line where it has been shown.

The rules are changing

IAS 3 has been revised as part of the convergence process, and will change the way companies account for acquisitions. Companies will have to apply this in their accounting years starting after July 2009. The major changes are:

- The scope of the standard has been widened to include mutual businesses and business combinations achieved solely through a contract.

- Transaction costs are expensed, reducing both the goodwill arising on the acquisition and the post acquisition profit.

- Minority interests are now called *non controlling interests*. Companies now have two choices for measuring the non controlling interests. They can either measure them:

    - At the value of their proportion of the acquisition's assets and liabilities (referred to as *partial goodwill*). This is the method prescribed in both the current IFRS 3 and UK GAAP.

  or

    - At their fair value (*full goodwill*). The second approach records goodwill on the non controlling interests as well as the acquired controlling interest. This means that goodwill will be higher, as both the goodwill attributable to the non controlling interest and controlling interest are shown. This is the method used in US GAAP.

- The definition of consideration has changed and now includes:

    - The fair value of any interest the company previously had in the acquired business. If these interests were not shown at fair value (for example the acquired business could have been an associate or joint venture) they are re-measured to their fair value, with any gain, or loss, shown in the income statement. This would include any gains that had previously been taken to equity.

      If the acquisition was previously listed on a stock exchange, fair value is the investment's market value. If the acquisition was unlisted, an alternative valuation model would have to be used.

    - Any contingent consideration (called *deferred consideration* or an *earn out*). It is very common for some of the payment for an acquisition to depend on future events, which could be post acquisition profits, the success of a major project, or a new product. The company has to include the fair value of the deferred consideration at the date of the acquisition, even if it is not probable at that time that it will be paid. (The current IFRS 3 only requires probable payments to be included as part of the consideration. This meant that deferred consideration subsequently increased the goodwill arising from the acquisition, if performance targets were met and payment of the deferred consideration became probable.) This requirement could be problematic if the deferred consideration relates to a research and development project. This could generate substantial profits over a number of years and the increased amounts due would probably be recognised as an expense in the income statement before the project generates any revenue.

The deferred consideration could be paid in cash or in shares. If it is payable in cash it is classed as a financial liability, and is re-measured to its fair value at every balance sheet date with any changes being shown in the income statement. If the deferred consideration is payable in ordinary shares it may not have to be re-measured through the income statement. This depends on the features of the deferred consideration and how the number of shares to be issued is determined.

▪ The disclosure requirements are increased, and an acquisitive business could easily add three pages to its financial statements for each acquisition made during the period. The additional disclosure requirements include:

- The amount of the acquisition related costs that have been expensed in the income statement, and the line on the income statement where these expenses have been reported.

- The method chosen for measuring the non controlling interests, and the amounts recognised for the non controlling interests.

- If the non controlling interest is measured at fair value, the company must disclose the valuation techniques and the key assumptions used.

- If the company had a prior investment in the acquisition, they have to disclose the fair value of the previously held equity interest and the amount of any gain or loss that has been recognised in the income statement.

- Details about the acquisition's receivables.

These changes will make a company's profit harder to predict and are likely to increase the volatility of reported profits. Whilst it is impossible to second guess how companies will cope with this, UK companies will probably show an operating profit before and after the effect of acquisitions to enable readers of the accounts to understand their underlying profitability.

The method chosen to measure the non controlling interest's share of the acquisition's net assets can have a significant effect on the goodwill arising on the acquisition, as I'll show you in Example 3.6.

Example 3.6

A predator acquires 80% of the shares in a company for 900. The fair value of 100% of the company's assets is 700. The predator believes that the fair value of the non controlling interest's investment in the company is 200. (You'll notice that this is less than the price paid by the predator. The predator paid 900 for 80% of a company, valuing the company at 1,125. 20% of 1,125 equals 225. However the predator's offer included a premium to acquire control of the company, consequently the non controlling interests are worth less.)

	Accounting policy	
	Share of nets assets	Fair value
Value of non controlling interests	140 (20% × 700)	200
Goodwill arising on consolidation	340 (900 paid + 140 non controlling interests − 700 fair value of the company's net assets)	400 (900 paid + 200 non controlling interests − 700 fair value of the company's net assets)

 FRS 10 (*Goodwill and intangible assets*) is concerned with accounting for goodwill. There is a number of differences between IFRS and UK GAAP:

- Goodwill should be amortised on a systematic basis over its useful life, usually a maximum of 20 years. If goodwill is regarded as having an indefinite life it isn't amortised, and is subject to an annual impairment review.
- A bargain purchase is called *negative goodwill*. Negative goodwill is shown separately from positive goodwill on the face of the balance sheet. It is subsequently written back into the profit and loss account over the periods expected to benefit.

- Any adjustments to the fair values, and goodwill, must be made in the financial statements for the first full financial year following the acquisition.

As from 2009/10, when the revised IFRS 3 came into use, there are additional differences between IFRS and UK GAAP:

- Transaction costs are included in the cost of the acquisition.
- If the company already has an investment in the acquisition, it is not restated to fair values.
- Minority interests can not be restated to fair values and, consequently, no goodwill is recognised for minority interests.
- The deferred consideration is only included in the goodwill calculation when it is probable that it will be paid.

Brand names

These can be quite substantial in acquisitive businesses in certain sectors. At 30 June 2008 Pernod Ricard had €7,068 million of brands they had acquired, largely through their acquisition of Allied Domecq and Seagram, shown as intangible assets on its balance sheet. To put this into context, its total assets were €19,472 million. As they've developed many of their brands themselves, or acquired them before the rules changed, only a relatively small proportion of their brand value is shown on the balance sheet.

The accounting profession has yet to resolve the problem of brand accounting, although most companies have their brands valued independently by companies such as the Interbrand Group. The valuation is derived from applying a multiple (based on the brand's strength in certain areas) to the brand's earnings. Both components of the formula (the multiple and the future earnings) are subjective. The other alternative valuation method is to discount the present value of the future cash flows arising from the brand, using the company's after tax weighted average cost of capital as the discount rate. The obvious problem with this method is the prediction of the future cash flows. But, whatever method the company uses to value their brands, the assumptions used will make the valuation subjective, and open to debate.

In its 2008 financial statements Pernod Ricard discloses:

Brands recognised in the context of business combinations – the fair value of identifiable acquired brands is determined using an actuarial calculation of estimated future profits or using the royalty method and correspond to the fair value of the brands at the date of acquisition. As the group's brands are intangible assets with indefinite useful lives, they are not amortised but are rather subject to an impairment test at least once a year and as soon as there is an indication that their value may have been impaired. Brands acquired as part of acquisitions of foreign entities are denominated in the functional currency of the acquired entity.

The note on intangible assets

The intangible assets are usually shown as a total on the balance sheet, although some companies analyse them between goodwill and others. If you want to see the components of intangible assets you have to look in the notes, where all the details are shown. IMI, in its note to the group, discloses both its assets and details of a goodwill impairment charge.

12 Intangible assets

	Goodwill	Capitalised development cost			Other acquired intangibles			Total
	Carrying amount £m	Cost £m	Amort-isation £m	Carrying amount £m	Cost £m	Amort-isation £m	Carrying amount £m	Carrying amount £m
At 1 January 2007	230.8	22.3	10.0	12.3	65.0	21.3	43.7	286.8
Exchange adjustments	(7.0)	0.5	0.2	0.3	1.3	1.3	–	(6.7)
Acquisitions	37.5	–	–	–	7.8	–	7.8	45.3
Additions	–	3.2	–	3.2	–	–	–	3.2
Amortisation for year			3.0	(3.0)		10.9	(10.9)	(13.9)
At 31 December 2007	261.3	26.0	13.2	12.8	74.1	33.5	40.6	314.7
Exchange adjustments	88.0	7.8	4.2	3.6	15.1	10.3	4.8	96.4
Transfers	(0.5)			–	0.5		0.5	–
Additions	–	5.1		5.1	–		–	5.1
Impairment	(6.0)		–	–		–	–	(6.0)
Amortisation for year			3.2	(3.2)		7.2	(7.2)	(10.4)
At 31 December 2008	342.8	38.9	20.6	18.3	89.7	51.0	38.7	399.8

Cumulative impairment recognised in good relation to goodwill is £6 m (2007: £nil). Management believe that the key assumptions on which the carrying value of goodwill is based are appropriate and any reasonable change in these assumptions will not lead to a materially different conclusion. Forecast year 3 cash flows were extrapolated in perpetuity at a 2.25% growth rate which is considered to be consistent with the long-term average growth rate in the industry. Pre-tax discount rates of between 10 and 15% are applied in determining the recoverable amounts of cash generating units. The discount rates are estimated based on the Group's cost of capital, which is calculated after consideration of market information, and risk adjusted for individual units' circumstances. No single cash generating unit represents a significant proportion of the total goodwill.

During the year, trading performance and order intake levels at Commtech (part of the Indoor Climate business) caused the Group to assess the recoverable amount of that business. The recoverable amount, being its value in use, was estimated by discounting the business forecast cash flows at 15%. Based upon this assessment the carrying value of the business was determined to be £6m higher than its recoverable amounts and an impairment loss against the acquired goodwill of that business was recognised. There were no impairments recognised in 2007.

The Group's estimates of impairments are most sensitive to increases in the discount rate used and the value of the third year's forecast cash flows which are extrapolated into perpetuity. Neither a 1% increase in the discount rate nor a 50 basis point decrease in the forecast cash flows would indicate any further impairment.

Now we've looked at intangible assets, let's move on to consider property, plant and equipment.

Property, plant and equipment

These assets are held by the business to use in generating sales, and aren't held for resale. (When the company decides to sell them they are shown separately after current assets, as 'non current assets held for resale'.)

When you are preparing personal balance sheets, you have a fair idea of what these assets are worth. Unfortunately the *book value* of a company's assets may not reflect its market value. You need to remember two things when you're looking at the property, plant and equipment on a balance sheet:

▓ *The company may not own these assets.*

▓ *Their values are affected by the company's depreciation and revaluation policies.*

Ownership of assets

In the introductory chapter I discussed the accounting principle of 'substance over form'. This says that if the company has the benefits, and risks, normally associated with owning an asset, the asset should be shown in the accounts, regardless of the legal position. This means that assets purchased under hire purchase agreements are included in tangible assets, even though the company doesn't own the asset until it has met certain conditions (normally when it has paid an agreed number of instalments).

A leasing agreement can also result in the company including assets in its property, plant and equipment that it doesn't own. (A lease gives one party, called the lessee, the rights to use an asset for an agreed period of time in return for a payment to the lessor.) Some leases also give companies most of the risks and rewards of ownership (*finance leases*), and these assets also appear as part of the property, plant and equipment. Other leases don't have these risks and rewards (*operating leases*), and the lease costs are expensed through the income statement. The accounting standard IAS 17 (*Lease accounting*) defines these two types of leases and details the appropriate accounting treatment for them:

- **Finance leases** The basic principle is that both the asset and the underlying liability should be shown on the balance sheet at the lower of the market value of the leased asset or the present value of the minimum leasing payments. Assets leased under finance leases are capitalised and usually depreciated over the shorter of the lease term and the anticipated useful life. However, if it is reasonably certain that the lessee will obtain ownership of the asset in the future, it can be depreciated over its economic life. The capital amount owed to the leasing company is included in the loans, split between the current and non-current parts. The subsequent lease rentals are then analysed into the capital element and the interest element. The capital repayment will reduce the amount owed to the leasing company, shown as debt, and the interest element of the lease rental is included in the interest charge on the income statement.

  The allocation between capital and interest payments is not straightforward, as the standard requires companies to use present value techniques to determine the split.

▨ **Operating leases** These are treated in the same way as any other short-term hire agreement. The assets don't show on the balance sheet and the lease rental is charged to the income statement as an operating cost. The notes to the income statement disclose the amount charged during the period, analysed between the hire of plant and machinery and other assets.

IAS 17 requires that land and buildings leases should be split, at inception, into two separate leases: a land lease and a buildings lease. Unless the legal ownership of the land is expected to pass to the lessee at the end of the lease term, leases of land are normally treated as operating leases. The buildings element will be classified as an operating or finance lease as appropriate.

As leasing agreements represent a contingent liability, the note on commitments also discloses the minimum amounts payable for non cancellable operating leases and finance leases for each of the following periods:

▨ within one year

▨ from one to five years

▨ after five years.

IMI's note on the group's operating leases discloses:

25 Operating leases

Non cancellable operating lease rentals are payable as follows:

	2008		2007	
	Land and buildings	Others	Land and buildings	Others
	£m	£m	£m	£m
Within one year	11.9	5.9	8.4	5.2
In the second to fifth year	36.1	12.6	25.3	10.5
After five years	18.9	0.1	19.2	0.1
	66.9	18.6	52.9	15.8

Operating lease payments represent rentals payable by the Group primarily for certain of its office properties.

Summarising leases

Whether a lease is a finance lease or an operating lease is important, as it affects where it shows in the accounts. However, as we're talking about the transfer of risks and rewards it's hard to have a definitive definition. However, I've summarised the major differences below:

	Finance leases	Operating leases
Risks and rewards associated with ownership	Yes	No
Lease transfers ownership to the lessee at the end of the term	Yes	No
The lessee has the option to purchase the asset at such a low price that it's reasonably certain that the option will be exercised	Yes	No
Lease term is ...	For the major part of the asset's life	Shorter than the asset's life
Lease rental equivalent to ...	Substantially all of the asset's fair value when discounted to its present value. (*UK rules are more specific defining it as the present value is at least 90% of asset's fair value*)	The interest on, and the repayment of, the asset's depreciation

Determining the cost

Property, plant and equipment is initially stated at its cost. This is not just the cost of acquiring the assets; it also includes any other costs the business incurs to make the property, plant and equipment operational. This includes the cost of any site preparation, delivery installation costs and relevant professional fees. It could also include the cost of dismantling and removing the asset and restoring the site. (This can only be included to the extent that such a cost is subsequently recognised as a provision.) A change to the international accounting rules (IAS 23 *Borrowing costs*) means that, for accounting periods that started in 2009, some borrowing costs must be included in the cost of the asset. These are the costs directly attributable to the acquisition, construction or production of property, plant and equipment that takes a substantial period of time to get ready for use, or sale. ('Substantial' is not defined, but an asset that takes more than a year to be ready for use would normally be eligible. The standard also allows the capitalisation of borrowing costs for inventories that have a long production period, such as wine and cheese.)

The capitalisation of borrowing costs starts when a company:

▦ starts the planning and construction process;

and

▦ is incurring expenses for the assets construction;

and

▦ is incurring borrowing costs that it wouldn't have incurred if it hadn't built the asset.

The capitalisation is suspended if the development is interrupted for an extended period and stops as soon as the asset is largely ready for use.

Depreciation of assets

Property, plant and equipment is usually shown on the balance sheet at cost less depreciation, with the main exception being land, where depreciation is usually immaterial so it's not depreciated. Some large assets are subdivided into smaller assets if different parts of the asset have different lives. In calculating the charge for depreciation companies have four variables to consider:

▦ the asset's cost;

▦ the asset's life, which must be reviewed at the financial year end to ensure it's still appropriate;

▦ its net residual value, which must be reviewed at the financial year end to reflect current residual values;

▦ the depreciation method, which must be reviewed at the financial year end to ensure that it's still the most appropriate method.

The notes to the accounts disclose the policies and methods used and here's IMI's accounting policy for property, plant and equipment:

h) Property, plant and equipment

Freehold land and assets in the course of construction are not depreciated.

Items of property, plant and equipment are stated at cost less accumulated depreciation (see below) and impairment losses (see accounting policy 'Impairment').

Where an item of property, plant and equipment comprises major components having different useful lives, they are accounted for as separate items of property, plant and equipment.

- Freehold buildings   25 to 50 years
- Plant and machinery   3 to 20 years

i) Leased assets

Leases where the group assumes substantially all the risks and rewards of ownership are classified as finance leases.

Plant and equipment acquired by way of a finance lease is stated at an amount equal to the lower of its fair value and the present value of the minimum lease payments at the inception of the lease, less accumulated depreciation (see above) and impairment losses (see accounting policy 'Impairment').

Payments made under operating leases are recognised in the income statement on a straight line basis over the term of the lease.

Lease incentives received are recognised in the income statement as an integral part of the total lease expense. The majority of leasing transactions entered into by the Group are operating leases.

Asset impairment

Most assets have to have an impairment review when circumstances suggest their values may have fallen. Impairment is measured by comparing an asset's book value to its 'recoverable amount'. The recoverable amount is the higher of its value:

- to the business by keeping and using it within the business;

- on the open market.

Most impairment losses are charged to the income statement as soon as a loss is recognised. The only exception is previously revalued assets, when the loss is less than the previous revaluations. In this case the impairment loss is shown as in the statement of recognised income and expense, or other comprehensive income, and reduces the value of the revaluation reserve (I'll illustrate this in the next section on revaluing assets).

Companies preparing their accounts using the UK's rules have to identify *why* the asset's value has fallen, as this determines where the loss is shown in the accounts. The asset's value could have fallen because there has been a general fall in market prices – then the loss would be shown on the statement of total recognised gains and losses and the revaluation reserve. On the other hand, if an asset's value has fallen because it has been damaged it would be charged to the profit and loss account.

Revaluation of assets

If you think about your own assets for a moment, they don't all depreciate. Property values increased remarkably until 2007, when they started to fall. When you and I think about our properties, we always think about their current market value, not the amount we paid for them. IAS 16 allows companies to revalue an *entire class of assets* to fair values. (This means that they can't just revalue one building; they have to revalue all buildings.) Fair value is the market value of land and buildings, and is usually the market value of plant and equipment. However, specialised assets are revalued using different methods. The valuations are normally conducted by professional valuer, and the valuations must be kept up to date, ensuring that an asset's book value isn't materially different from its market value.

You can always see if a company has chosen to revalue its assets, as it will have a 'revaluation reserve' in the shareholders' equity. I'll show you how this works in Example 3.7.

Example 3.7

A company has property, plant and equipment of £1,000,000 and share capital of £1,000,000. The share capital has been used to buy the property, plant and equipment, including a property costing £600,000. Property prices have been rising steeply and the company has had the property valued at £800,000 and decides to incorporate this value into its balance sheet. The revised balance sheet will be:

	£	
Property, plant and equipment	1,200,000	
Share capital	1,000,000	
Revaluation reserve	200,000	← The revaluation reserve reflects the £200,000 increase in the property's value.
	1,200,000	

There are three things I'd like to point out:

- Revaluation doesn't directly affect the income statement; it is shown in the statement of recognised income and expense, or comprehensive income. However, revaluation could affect the income statement indirectly through depreciation, as the depreciation charge would now be based on the buildings element in the £800,000, not the original cost of £600,000.

- The revaluation reserve is not a distributable reserve, which means it can't be used to pay dividends.

- The company's net worth has increased by £200,000. This will probably improve the company's borrowing powers and affects some of the ratios you'll use to analyse the company's performance. (I'll discuss these in detail in Chapter 10).

If the property subsequently falls in value (as commercial property did in 2008) it should be recognised in the accounts. In my example, the company could absorb a fall of £200,000 on the balance sheet. So if a fall in property prices reduces the property's value to £650,000, the revaluation reserve would fall by £150,000 to £50,000 and the reduction in value, the *impairment*, would be shown in the statement of recognised income and expense, or comprehensive income. However, if the value of the property fell to £500,000 the income statement would show an impairment charge of £100,000.

Companies choosing to revalue assets must disclose the following information in the notes to the balance sheet:

- The method and any significant assumptions used in estimating fair value.

- The date of the revaluation.

- Whether an independent valuer was used.

- The depreciated cost of each class of revalued assets.

- The revaluation surplus, detailing the change in the period and any restrictions on the distribution of the balance to shareholders.

Companies preparing their accounts using the UK's rules that choose to revalue must conduct a full valuation at least every five years with an interim valuation in the third year, and any other years where there is a material change in value. A qualified external valuer should be involved in the five-yearly full valuation of properties.

If a company has revalued its assets, and this affects its reported profitability (for example the revaluation has increased the depreciation charge), the profit and loss account must be followed by a *Note of historical cost profits and losses*. This tells you what the profit would have been had there been no asset revaluations, eliminating the distortions arising from different revaluation policies. It is only concerned with revaluation, and ignores the effect of different depreciation policies. It shows you what the profit before tax and the retained profit would have been if the company hadn't revalued.

The note of historical cost profits and losses

Now I'd like to give you a little test … You and I buy identical plots of land for £100,000, but I decide to revalue my land to £120,000 at the end of the first year. The following year, we both sell our land for £150,000. *What is our reported profit on the deal?* We both have £50,000 more cash in our pockets than we started with, but our reported profit is very different. You'll report £50,000, whereas I'll only show £30,000 profit, as I revalued my land and the profit is the difference between the book value and the cash received. You'll appear more profitable than I am, but our cash profit is exactly the same. The note on historical cost profits and losses resolves this problem, as it brings my profit into line with yours – £50,000.

You know that revaluation is optional. You also know that revaluation can affect profit in two ways:

- Firstly, it affects the profit, or loss, on disposal of the asset.
- Secondly, it could increase the depreciation charge if the revalued asset is depreciable.

The note on historical cost profits and losses was introduced in the UK to improve the comparability of reported profits. You'll see how this works if you read through my next example (Example 3.8), which is based on a depreciated asset to show you how the additional depreciation charge affects the balance sheet, and how it is shown in the note.

Example 3.8

Two companies, A and B, each buy a fixed asset for £1,000 at the start of the first year, and sell them for £750 on the last day of the third year. I'll keep it really simple by making cash their only other asset. Both companies have identical profits throughout the three years of £4,000 before depreciation. They both depreciate the asset on a straight line basis over five years (20% a year). Company B revalues its asset to £1,200 at the start of the second year, whereas Company A doesn't. The asset's life remains five years.

You know that the revaluation affects both the profit and loss accounts and the balance sheet.

Firstly I'll look at Company A's profit and loss accounts for the three years. Its profit after depreciation will be £3,800 each year (£4,000 less £200 depreciation). Its depreciation charge is £200 a year, so by the end of the third year its fixed asset has a book value of £400 (£1,000 – (3 × £200)). When it's sold for £750, it reports a profit on sale of fixed assets of £350. When you look at its balance sheet, you'll see that the asset's value reduces by £200 each year and cash increases by the profit before depreciation, plus the cash received from the asset's sale in the third year. (Remember depreciation is only a paper charge, not a real cash cost.)

Company A – Profit and loss accounts

	Year 1 £	Year 2 £	Year 3 £
Turnover	10,000	10,000	10,000
Profit before depreciation	4,000	4,000	4,000
Depreciation	(200)	(200)	(200)
Operating profit	3,800	3,800	3,800
Profit on sale of fixed assets	0	0	350
Profit for the year	3,800	3,800	4,150

Company A – Balance sheets

	Year 1 £	Year 2 £	Year 3 £
Fixed asset	800	600	0
Cash	4,000	8,000	12,750
	4,800	8,600	12,750
Share capital	1,000	1,000	1,000
Profit and loss account (retained earnings)	3,800	7,600	11,750
	4,800	8,600	12,750

Now Company B revalued its asset, and this complicates its accounts. Firstly its depreciation charge isn't so straightforward. It will be £200 in the first year, but at the start of the second year the asset's value increases to £1,200. This creates a revaluation reserve of £400 on its balance sheet (£1,200 less the book value of £800). The £1,200 then has to be written off over the remaining four years of the asset's life, increasing the annual depreciation charge to £300. When the asset is sold at the end of the third year its book value will be £600 (Its value, £1,200, at the start of the second year less two year's depreciation of £300), and the profit on sale of the asset will be £150.

Company B – Profit and loss accounts

	Year 1 £	Year 2 £	Year 3 £
Turnover	10,000	10,000	10,000
Profit before depreciation	4,000	4,000	4,000
Depreciation	(200)	(300)	(300)
Operating profit	3,800	3,700	3,700
Profit on sale of fixed assets	0	0	150
Profit for the year	3,800	3,700	3,850

Now I'll look at Company B's balance sheet. But before I do, I'll ask you a question. You learnt in the second chapter that companies can pay dividends when they're loss making as long as they have sufficient distributable reserves. These comprise the realised profits found in retained earnings, the profit and loss account reserve in UK GAAP. Now the question – *Should Company B's distributable reserves be lower than Company A's just because it's revalued its asset?* (You can see that its profit for the year is lower than Company A's for the last two years.) The UK's accounting rules say no – the distributable reserves should remain the same. To do this, the additional depreciation each year is transferred from the revaluation reserve to the profit and loss account reserve.

Company B – Balance sheets

	Year 1 £	Year 2 £	Year 3 £
Fixed asset	800	900	0
Cash	4,000	8,000	12,750
	4,800	8,900	12,750
Share capital	1,000	1,000	1,000
Revaluation reserve		300	0
Profit and loss account	3,800	7,600	11,750
	4,800	8,900	12,750

The revaluation reserve falls to £300, as the £100 additional depreciation is transferred to the profit and loss account to maintain the distributable reserve.

The balance on the revaluation reserve is transferred to the profit and loss account once the revaluation is realised.

In the third year the net worth of the two companies is the same for the first time since the assets were revalued, as the asset has been sold and the revaluation realised.

You need the note on historical cost profit and losses, as if you just looked at the profit and loss account Company A is more profitable than Company B. This is reflected in the common performance measures I've calculated below for the third year:

	Company A	Company B
Operating margin	$\frac{3,800}{10,000}$ = 38%	$\frac{3,700}{10,000}$ = 37.0%
Return on capital	$\frac{4,150}{12,750}$ = 32.6%	$\frac{3,850}{12,750}$ = 30.2%

It appears that Company A outperforms Company B, but you know that both businesses are, in reality, identical! Company B would follow its profit and loss account with a note of historical cost profits and losses that makes this obvious. Company B's profits are now the same as Company A's:

Note of historical cost profits and losses Company B – Year 3

	Year 3 £	Year 2 £
Reported profit	3,850	3,700
Realisation of revaluation gains of previous years	200	
Difference between the historical cost depreciation charge and the actual depreciation charge of the year calculated on the revalued amount	100	100
Historical cost profit	4,150	3,800

Once again, I've used a simple example. My reported profit is the profit for the financial year, however a published note of historical cost profits and losses starts with the profit before tax (in my example it's the same as the profit for the financial year). It then shows you the historical cost profit before taxation and the historical cost profit for the year. This note is useful if you are comparing the profits of two companies using UK GAAP in the same sector, but with different revaluation policies.

Now let's leave UK accounting and move back to IFRS.

IMI's note on property, plant and equipment

Once again, all the details are in the notes. The notes disclose their original cost, the accumulated depreciation to the balance sheet date, the asset's book value on the balance sheet date, and the amount of property, plant and equipment held on finance leases. You can see this in IMI's note.

13 Property, plant and equipment

	Land & buildings			Plant & machinery			Assets in course of construction	Total
	Gross book value	Depre-ciation	Net book value	Gross book value	Depre-ciation	Net book value	Net book value	Net book value
	£m	£m	£m	£m	£m	£m	£m	£m
At 1 January 2007	149.8	68.6	81.2	521.3	421.7	99.6	9.5	190.3
Exchange adjustments	7.2	3.5	3.7	18.0	14.1	3.9	0.4	8.0
Acquisitions	0.5	0.2	0.3	11.1	7.6	3.5	0.1	3.9
Additions	4.7	–	4.7	28.0	–	28.0	17.2	49.9
Disposals	(7.8)	(1.8)	(6.0)	(28.1)	(25.9)	(2.2)	–	(8.2)
Disposal of business	–	–	–	(0.3)	(0.2)	(0.1)	–	(0.1)
Transfers	0.4		0.4	10.8		10.8	(11.2)	–
Depreciation for year		1.5	(1.5)		34.4	(34.4)		(35.9)
At 31 December 2007	154.8	72.0	82.8	560.8	451.7	109.1	16.0	207.9
Exchange adjustments	47.2	22.4	24.8	143.6	115.5	28.1	2.7	55.6
Additions	3.5		3.5	31.1		31.1	14.3	48.9
Disposals	(6.8)	(5.8)	(1.0)	(42.7)	(40.8)	(1.9)	–	(2.9)
Transfers	0.7		0.7	17.5		17.5	(18.2)	–
Depreciation for year		3.9	(3.9)		39.2	(39.2)	–	(43.1)
At 31 December 2008	199.4	92.5	106.9	710.3	565.6	144.7	14.8	266.4

Included in the total net book value of plant and machinery is £1.1m (2007: £0.9m) in respect of assets acquired under finance leases. Depreciation for the year on these assets was £0.3m (2007: £0.3m).

Looking at this note you can see that IMI owns most of its assets, and that its plant and equipment are largely depreciated.

Investment properties

IAS 40 (*Investment property*) defines an investment property as a property that is held either to earn rental income and/or for capital appreciation. Investment properties must be shown separately and cannot be included as part of property, plant and equipment.

Initially they are shown at the purchase price plus any directly attributable costs. Companies then have the option of either revaluing them to their market value, or showing them at cost less depreciation. Once they have selected their accounting policy it must be used for all of their investment properties.

■ If they choose to show their investment properties at their market value any change in their value is recognised in the income statement in the period in which they arise.

■ If the company decides not to revalue they must depreciate them, and conduct impairment reviews, in the normal way. The investment properties' market value is disclosed in the notes.

 There are significant differences between IAS 40 and SSAP 19 (*Accounting for investment properties*) and the two major ones are:

• Investment properties must be shown at their open market value and cannot be shown at depreciated historical cost.
• Unless it's a permanent deficit, or its reversal, revaluation gains or losses are recognised in the statement of total recognised gains and losses not the income statement.

Investments

Investments are found in two places on the balance sheet, they can be non current assets or current assets. Their classification is determined by *why* the company is holding the investment, rather than the nature of the investment. An investment should be classed as a non current asset if the company does not intend to, is not able to, or will not be required to, sell it in the next year, otherwise it is classed as a current asset investment. IAS 1 requires investments to be classified into financial assets and investments accounted for using the equity method.

Like all assets, investments must be shown at cost less any necessary provisions. So if the net realisable value falls below the cost, or valuation, an impairment charge is made.

You'll often find three different types of long-term investments:

▦ Investments in subsidiaries.

▦ Investment in associated undertakings, joint ventures and other participating interests.

▦ Other investments, often called *available for sale investments* by companies using IFRS, or *trade investments* by companies using UK GAAP.

Investments are classified according to the degree of control or influence:

Classification	Degree of control/influence	Likely shareholding
Subsidiary	Sole control	More than 50%
Joint venture	Controlled jointly with other investors	If there's 3 investors 33% ... 4 investors 25% ...
Associate	Has the ability to exercise significant influence	20% or more
Other investments/available for sale investment	Has little/no influence	Significantly less than 20%

Let's have a look at these different investments and how companies account for them.

Subsidiaries

A subsidiary is a business that is controlled by another, called the parent or holding company. The parent consolidates the assets, liabilities, results and cash flows of its subsidiaries in the group accounts. This means that subsidiaries only show as a non current asset investment in the parent company's balance sheet (usually published alongside the group balance sheet). They don't show as investments in the group's accounts as all their assets and liabilities have been consolidated onto each line of the group's balance sheet.

Associates

An associate is a business which the investor doesn't control, but has the power to participate in the financial, operating and policy decisions of the business. The accounting rule (*IAS 28 Associates*) refers to this as a *significant influence*, and presumes it exists when the investor holds at least 20% of the company's voting rights. It is also presumed not to exist when the investor has less than 20% of the company's voting rights. However both of these presumptions can be rebutted if there is clear contradictory evidence.

Investments in associates are separately disclosed on the balance sheet. Unless they are held for sale, associates are accounted for using the 'equity method'. This is effectively a one line consolidation. Rather than detailing all of the associate's assets and liabilities, the group determines its share of the associate's net assets (including any goodwill arising from its acquisition). Initially this value is the cost of acquiring the investment in the associate. This is then increased, or decreased, to reflect the investor's share of the associate's retained profit or loss, since it acquired them. If the associate is loss making the investment may have no value on the balance sheet, as once the investor's share of the associate's losses is greater than the book value of its investment the value of the investment in the associate is reduced to zero. The company then only recognises any further losses if it has either the obligation to fund the associate, or has guaranteed to it. However, the value of an associate is not just affected by its profitability. Like other assets, investments in associates must be reviewed to see if their value has been impaired and any impairment is charged to the income statement.

It sounds complicated, so I'll show you how the equity method values an associate in Example 3.9.

Example 3.9

Firstly, let's keep it simple. An investor buys 30% of another company for £200,000 and has significant influence. The other company's total net assets at the date of acquisition were £500,000, and their fair value was £600,000. The associate made £100,000 after tax profit after its acquisition and paid a dividend of £10,000.

3.9 *continued*

When the investor makes the investment in the associate it will have a book value of £200,000, the cash paid to acquire the investment. (This includes goodwill of £20,000, as 30% of the fair value of £600,000 is £180,000.) At the end of the year the associate's value will have increased to £227,000.

Cost	200,000	
Plus investor's share of after tax profits	30,000	*(30% of 100,000)*
Less dividends received from the associate	(3,000)	*(30% of 10,000)*
Associate's book value	227,000	

Another way of establishing the associate's book value is to look at the investor's share of the associate's net assets. The associate's net assets at the end of the year were £590,000 (the original net assets of £500,000 plus the after tax profits of £100,000 less the dividends paid of £10,000).

The value of the associate comprises:

The investor's share of the associate's net assets	177,000	*(30% of 590,000)*
Plus goodwill	20,000	
Plus investor's share of after tax profits	30,000	*(30% of 100,000)*
Associate's book value	227,000	

Unfortunately, retained earnings aren't the only thing affecting equity and therefore net assets. And some items, such as property revaluation and foreign exchange translation differences, change the value of equity but aren't reflected in the company's after tax profits. This complicates the valuation. If the associate has recognised something directly in equity, the associate's value has to be adjusted to reflect the investor's share in the associate's net assets. I'll illustrate this by continuing my earlier example assuming that the associate also recognised £12,000 translation losses directly in equity. The associate's value falls to £223,400:

Cost	200,000	
Plus investor's share of after tax profits	30,000	*(30% of 100,000)*
Less dividends received	(3,000)	*(30% of 10,000)*
Less investor's share of exchange loss	(3,600)	*(30% of 12,000)*
Associate's book value	223,400	

You saw, in the last chapter, that the investor has to include its 30% share of the associate's after tax profits (£30,000) in its consolidated income statement.

Joint ventures

A joint venture is a long-term investment where two or more parties have a contractual arrangement to undertake an economic activity where there is a contractually agreed sharing of the control of this activity. IAS 31 (*Interests in joint ventures*) identifies three different types of joint ventures: jointly controlled 'entities', jointly controlled operations and jointly controlled assets. The accounting for jointly controlled entities is different from that for jointly controlled operations and jointly controlled assets, so let's have a look at how companies account for these joint ventures.

- **Jointly controlled entities** What is an entity? It's a business that trades. It could be in any legal form, so it could be a company or a partnership. Currently there are two ways that companies can account for these. They can either use the equity method I discussed earlier, or they can use *proportional consolidation*. (Proportional consolidation is just what you think it is. Imagine I control 30% of a joint venture, I consolidate into each line of my accounts 30% of its assets, 30% of its liabilities, 30% of its revenue and 30% of its costs.) However, proportional consolidation may not be allowed in the future, as in September 2007 the IAS issued a discussion document which proposes to remove this option. This would remove the main difference between IAS 31 and US GAAP.

- **Jointly controlled operations and jointly controlled assets** These don't involve the creation of a separate business. In a joint operation, each party uses its own resources and carries out its own part in a joint operation separately from the activities of the other parties in the joint venture. They own and control their own resources that are then used in the joint operation. Consequently each party accounts for its share of the assets, liabilities and cash flows under their contractual arrangement.

Jointly controlled assets are jointly owned, and each party accounts for its share of the assets, liabilities and cash flows under their contractual arrangement.

There is a number of differences between UK GAAP and IFRS. The main ones are:

- Proportional consolidation of joint ventures is not allowed, and the equity method must be used for both associates and joint ventures.
- Joint ventures use the 'gross equity method', showing the investors' share of the joint venture's assets and liabilities on the balance sheet.
- UK GAAP requires additional disclosures when associates, or joint ventures, exceed 15% of the investing group's:
  - gross assets;
  - gross liabilities;
  - turnover;
  - operating result (based on a three-year average).

If these thresholds are exceeded the investing company gives more information about the gross assets and liabilities, disclosing:

- fixed assets;
- current assets;
- liabilities due within a year;
- liabilities due in more than a year;
- any other information that is necessary to understand the total amounts disclosed, for example the size of the debt and its maturity.

If an individual associate or joint venture exceeds 25% of the thresholds shown above, the same information is disclosed for the individual investment.

Other investments

Accounting for non current investments is usually more complex in IFRS than UK GAAP. Other investments are regarded as financial assets by IAS 39 (*Financial instruments: recognition and measurement*). There are four categories of financial assets:

▨ financial assets at fair value through profit or loss;

▨ loans and receivables;

▨ held to maturity investments;

▨ available for sale financial assets.

This classification is important, as it determines the investment's valuation. So let's look at each type and see how the classification affects an investment's value.

Financial assets at fair value through profit or loss

These are subdivided into two types of assets: those that are held for trading, and those that the company has chosen to be in this category.

They are shown on the balance sheet at their fair value and any subsequent changes to their fair value are shown as a gain, or a loss, in the income statement.

Loans and receivables

These are non-derivative financial assets that aren't quoted in an active market and have fixed, or determinable, repayments. They usually arise when a business provides money, goods and services directly to a debtor and has no intention of trading the receivable.

These are shown at their amortised cost, using the effective interest rate method. (I'll explain this later.) The interest shown on the income statement is based on the effective interest rate.

Held to maturity investments

These are always classified as debt (loans and redeemable preference shares), as only debt has a finite life. The company must intend, and be able to, hold them to maturity. Both the intention and the ability to hold them to maturity must be assessed when the assets are acquired and then at each subsequent balance sheet date.

These are shown at their amortised cost, using the effective interest rate method. The interest shown on the income statement is based on the effective interest rate.

Available for sale financial assets

These are other investments, not falling into the previous two categories.

These are shown at their fair value, including transaction costs, and any gains or losses are recognised in the statement of recognised income and expense (comprehensive income) and equity. This means that their value doesn't affect the reported profit for the period. It is only recognised in the income statement when the gain, or loss, is realised.

The only exception to these rules is when you can't reliably measure the fair value of an unquoted equity investment. Then it is shown at cost. However, this rarely happens as most investments can be valued using discounted cash flow techniques.

Now I'd like to explain the effective interest method and amortised cost.

Effective interest method and amortised cost

Firstly, I need to identify the effective interest rate. This is the rate that exactly discounts the cash flows, excluding any credit losses, arising from the receipt/payments over the asset's life. You may already know this as the internal rate of return. Here's an example that will show you how the effective interest rate is calculated, and then how the interest shown on the income statement is calculated and the investment is valued on the balance sheet (Example 3.10).

Example 3.10

A company buys a bond for £934.70, including transaction cost of £34.70. The bond will pay £50 interest each year for the next five years, when it is redeemed for £1,200. I've used discounted cash flow, assigning the cost to a notional year 0, to calculate the effective interest rate of 10% (actually it's 9.99858% hence the rounding error of 5 pence):

	Cash flow	Discount factor @ 10%	Present value
Year 0	(934.70)	1.000	(934.70)
Year 1	50.00	0.909	45.45
Year 2	50.00	0.826	41.30
Year 3	50.00	0.751	37.55
Year 4	50.00	0.682	34.10
Year 5	1,250.00	0.621	776.25
			(0.05)

Now that you know the effective interest rate, I can show you the interest receivable that is shown in the income statement and the bond's value (its amortised cost) that's shown on the balance sheet:

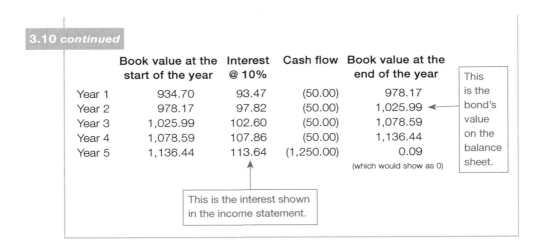

3.10 continued

	Book value at the start of the year	Interest @ 10%	Cash flow	Book value at the end of the year
Year 1	934.70	93.47	(50.00)	978.17
Year 2	978.17	97.82	(50.00)	1,025.99
Year 3	1,025.99	102.60	(50.00)	1,078.59
Year 4	1,078.59	107.86	(50.00)	1,136.44
Year 5	1,136.44	113.64	(1,250.00)	0.09

(which would show as 0)

This is the bond's value on the balance sheet.

This is the interest shown in the income statement.

My example is simple, as the bond wasn't impaired. Like most assets, investments have to be tested for impairment.

 Whilst the UK has rules that are very similar to IFRS they only apply to companies that are either listed or have adopted fair value accounting, which means that they are rarely used. Consequently most UK companies show their investments at cost less any impairment. Fixed asset investments can be shown at market value, or directors' valuation, with valuation gains and losses going through the revaluation reserve in the normal way. They can also be shown at a value that the directors believe is appropriate. This allows the investments to be valued using the rarely used 'marked to market', and then the resulting gain or loss would be shown in the income statement.

Fixed asset investments are classified as:

- shares in group undertakings;
- loans to group undertakings;
- participating interests;
- loans to undertakings in which the company has a participating interest;
- other investments other than loans;
- other loans;
- own shares.

Employee benefit net assets

This isn't the value of the employee benefit fund's net assets. It represents the amount that the employer can benefit from a surplus. The accounting standard imposes an 'asset ceiling', ensuring that any asset shown on the balance sheet doesn't exceed the future economic benefits it represents to the business.

 Companies preparing their accounts using UK GAAP would not show employee benefit net assets as a fixed asset. The after tax surplus, or deficit, in final salary pension funds is shown on the balance sheet, but is not included in the statutory headings. It is shown separately after net assets. (UK companies show a net asset figure before the pension scheme's asset or liability, and then after the pension scheme's asset or liability.)

Derivative financial instruments

You'll find these shown as assets and liabilities, and they can be both non current and current but I'll tell you about them here.

You may have come across the term 'hedging', as most companies hedge their exposure to movements in exchange rates and interest rates. Hedges are designed to minimise, or eliminate, a risk by moving in the opposite direction to an asset's, or liability's, value. Companies are exposed to a range of risks including commodity price changes, interest rate movements and movements in exchange rates. Hedging can be as simple as borrowing in dollars to hedge revenues earned in dollars. Or it can be more complicated, as a number of hedging products has been developed to help protect companies against these risks, and you'll find these referred to in accounts. You'll often find references to:

▪ *Forward rate agreements* These are usually used to hedge exchange and interest rate movements. They lock the company into a fixed rate and it receives this rate regardless of what happens in the market. Forward rate agreements provide certainty.

▪ *Options* This gives the right, but not an obligation, to buy or sell something at a fixed price for a fixed period of time. If the company can get a better rate it doesn't have to exercise the option. This gives flexibility, but the company has to pay for this flexibility and options are more expensive than forward rate agreements.

■ *Swaps* A swap is exactly what you think it is, it's an agreement between two parties to exchange cash flows over a period of time. The commonest swap is an interest rate swap, where companies exchange fixed rates for floating rates. Exchange rate swaps are usually used to finance overseas subsidiaries and associates. Loans are normally raised in the currency of the parent and then this loan is swapped into the preferred currency.

Now hedging is just like insurance – you can protect yourself against most things for a price! Hedging just passes the risk to someone else, so the cost increases with probability. If something's likely to happen, it's probably too expensive to cover yourself.

These hedging products are called *derivatives* – as their value is derived from something else. For example, the value of an exchange rate option depends primarily on the movements of exchange rates. So the option's value is derived from exchange rate movements. IAS 39 (*Financial instruments: recognition and measurement*) requires that all derivatives are shown at their fair value at the balance sheet date, and any subsequent gains or losses are recognised in the income statement, unless they qualify as hedging instruments in cash flow or net investment hedges (see below).

As companies have to reflect the changes in the fair values of most derivatives in their income statement, many companies opt to use *hedge accounting*. This changes the timing of the recognition of the gains and losses, so that both the hedged item and the hedge affects the income statement in the same period. This neutralises the effect of a fully effective hedge and reduces the volatility of companies' profits. IAS 39 allows companies to use hedge accounting if the business:

■ at the start of the hedge formally designates, and documents, the hedging relationship;

and

■ both at the start, and on an ongoing basis, can demonstrate that the relationship between the hedged item and the hedging instrument will be highly effective on an ongoing basis. This means that companies must test the hedge's effectiveness each period end to ensure that the hedge remains highly effective. (The accounting standard classifies a hedge as highly effective when the hedging instrument has changed within 80–125% of the hedged item. Outside of this range the hedge is regarded as ineffective, and hedge accounting can't be used.)

IAS 39 identifies three different hedges, which have slightly different accounting treatments. Firstly, I'll tell you how hedges are classified, and then I'll discuss their accounting treatment.

- *A fair value hedge* – this hedges the exposure of changes in the fair value of an asset, a liability, or a firm commitment that would affect the reported profit shown in the income statement.

- *A cash flow hedge* – this hedges the volatility in cash flows arising from an asset, a liability, a firm commitment, or a highly probable forecast transaction that would affect the profit shown in the income statement. Many cash flow hedges could also be classified as fair value hedges, but in a cash flow hedge the business must have a probable exposure to variability in the cash flows being hedged.

- *A net investment hedge* – this hedges the foreign currency risk on a net investment in a foreign operation.

Accounting for hedges

Where derivatives qualify for hedge accounting, the recognition of any resultant gain or loss depends on the nature of the hedge relationship and the item being hedged.

Fair value hedges

In a fair value hedge the value of the hedged item is shown at its fair value and adjusted for the gain, or loss, relating to the hedged risk. The hedging instrument, usually a derivative, is shown at its fair value and the resulting gain, or loss, is shown in the income statement.

This should mean that if the hedge is effective the gain, or loss, in the value of the asset, or liability, is offset by the gain or loss on the hedging instrument. So if a company enters into a swap agreement at the start of the year to switch a £100 million bond from fixed interest of 7.5% to a variable rate (LIBOR – **L**ondon **I**nter**b**ank **O**ffer **R**ate). This hedges against the movement in the fair value of the bond as interest rates change. On the same date it enters into an interest-rate swap to pay LIBOR and receive interest at 7.5%. The swap's terms are identical the bond's and this means the business will effectively be paying LIBOR rather than 7.5% interest. In the first year LIBOR is 6.0%, and the interest expense in the income statement is £6 million. The company receives £7.5 million from the swap's counterparty to pay the

interest on the bond and pays interest of £6 million to the counterparty. The company has made £1.5 million on its bet! This means that the swap has a positive value, the company has to show it at its fair value, which can be a quote from a dealer or derived using a valuation model. (A swap's fair value is the present value of the contractual cash flows. This means that changes in interest rates coupled with predicted changes in interest rates have a significant effect on its fair value.) I'll assume the swap's fair value is £2.5 million. It was worth nothing at the start of the year, now it's worth £2.5 million, and this will be recognised as a gain in the income statement. If the bond wasn't hedged, it would be shown at its amortised cost and any fair value changes wouldn't affect the income statement. But, because it's hedged and the hedge is fully effective, the bond's book value is adjusted by the fair value of the swap to reflect that its value has changed because interest rates have changed. The bond's value is increased on the balance sheet to £102.5 million. The income statement will include a gain on the swap agreement of £2.5 million, which is cancelled out by the loss of £2.5 million recorded for the bond (the liability has increased by this amount). The balance sheet shows the swap as an asset, which is cancelled out by the increase in the bond's value.

Now it's actually not quite this simple. I've talked about the hedge being effective – now what do I mean? A hedge is effective when the change in the value of the swap is **exactly** the same as the change in the bond's value. Unfortunately, hedging's like life – it's rarely this perfect! If there's a difference between the change in the value of the bond and value of the swap the hedge isn't fully effective. As the changes in the fair value of the swap are shown in the income statement, to offset the changes in the bond's value arising from interest rate changes, the ineffective part of the hedge is automatically shown in the income statement. So if the loan's fair value was £102.8 million and the swap's value was £2.5 million the reported profit would fall by £0.3 million, the ineffective part of the hedge. The hedge is still regarded as effective, as the hedging instrument (the swap) has changed by £2.5 million and the hedged item (the bond) has changed by £2.8 million. The swap's value is 89.29% of the change in the bond's value (2.5 ÷ 2.8), within the 80–125% range for a highly effective hedge.

Cash flow hedges

This follows the same basic principle that any ineffective part of the hedge must be charged through the income statement, but the effective part is initially shown as comprehensive income and in equity on the balance sheet. They are then reclassified to the income statement, when any gain, or loss, is realised. So if the swap agreement I used as an example earlier had been classified as a cash flow hedge, the £2.5 million gain on the swap would be shown in other comprehensive income, so once again has no effect on the company's reported profitability. The debt remains at £100 million, and the balance sheet is balanced by showing the £2.5 million in equity, as a *hedging reserve.*

Net investment hedges

The accounting treatment for these hedges is the same as cash flow hedges. This means that the exchange differences arising on consolidation remain in equity until the overseas operation is sold or closed.

 Unfortunately accounting for derivatives and hedges is not straightforward in the UK, as there are currently two sets of accounting rules and different companies use different rules. From 2005 all businesses had to apply the Companies Act disclosure requirements and FRS 25's presentation requirements. They will then apply either:

- FRS 25 (*Financial instruments: disclosure and presentation*) and in full combined with FRS 26 (*Financial instruments: recognition and measurement*). FRS 26 is identical to IFRS and must be adopted as part of a package, including other accounting rules, concerned with fair value accounting. Few UK companies have chosen to use these rules.
- FRS 4 (*Capital instruments*) and FRS 13 (*Derivatives and other financial instruments: disclosures*). Most companies have chosen to use these rules.

Most companies using UK GAAP use historical cost accounting, where derivatives are included in the balance sheet at a nil amount as their historical cost is effectively zero. Consequently, derivative financial instruments are rarely shown on their balance sheets. However they are disclosed in the notes, where companies must disclose their accounting policies and the fair values of their financial assets, financial liabilities, and any hedges.

Deferred tax assets

You may remember that I discussed deferred tax in Chapter 2, where I pointed out that there's usually a temporary difference between an asset's book value, which is shown at cost or valuation less depreciation to date, and its tax value. Sometimes this generates a deferred tax liability (a future tax payment) and at others a deductible difference. This deductible difference is a deferred tax asset (a future tax repayment or future credit note). Deferred tax assets represent the amounts the company expects to recover from the tax authorities in the future.

IMI is a good example; in 2008 it had £54.7 million deferred tax assets on its balance sheet. In the notes to the accounts it disclosed:

Unrecognised deferred tax assets and liabilities

Deferred tax assets of £26.1m (2007: 25.8m) have not been recognised in respect of tax losses. The majority of the tax losses have no expiry date, and the assets have not been recognised due to uncertainty over their recoverability.

 Deferred tax assets are included in debtors under UK GAAP.

Current assets

Current assets are a company's short-term assets that can be realised within a year.

Inventories or stock

IAS2 (*Inventories*) defines inventories as assets that are either:

- held for sale in the normal course of business;
- in the production process prior to a sale;
- materials or supplies that will be consumed in the production process (these are often referred to as consumable stores).

Companies usually show the total inventory figure on the balance sheet, disclosing the detail in the notes. The accounting rules allow companies to classify their stock in the most appropriate manner for their business.

When looking at stock you should understand:

▪ Not everything shown as inventories will be sold. Consumable stores are used within the business.

▪ A company may have inventories that are subject to reservation of title clauses, or hold consignment stock. The accounting principle of substance over form means that whoever bears the substantial risks and rewards normally associated with ownership shows the inventories in their accounts. This will involve identifying:

  – who has the right of return;

  – the customer's right to use the stock;

  – the stock's transfer price and deposits.

The note on inventories

The notes will disclose the various categories of inventory, stock write-downs and reversals, and the amount of stock that has been written down to net realisable value. You can clearly see this in IMI's note below:

---

15 Inventories

	2008 £m	2007 £m
Raw materials and consumables	115.0	89.5
Work in progress	105.8	85.6
Finished goods	112.7	76.9
	333.5	252.0

In 2008 the cost of inventories recognised as an expense within cost of sales amounted to £1,134.3m (2007: £954.3m). In 2008 the write-down of inventories to net realisable value and amounted to £7.1m (2007: £5.7m). The reversal of write-downs amounted to £0.9m (2007: £0.8m). The write-down and reversal are included in cost of sales. Write-downs and reversals in both years relate to ongoing assessments of inventory obsolescence, excess inventory holdings and inventory resale values across all the Group's businesses. The carrying value of inventories carried at net realisable value was £5.3m (2007: £3.9m).

Companies using UK GAAP include contract work in progress as part of stock. The Companies Act 2006 is stricter than the accounting rules, requiring stocks to be analysed under the following sub headings, but it allows directors to modify these if it is more appropriate for their business:

- raw materials and consumables;
- work in progress;
- finished goods and goods for resale;
- payments on account (these are payments made for items yet to be received).

Trade and other receivables

Trade and other receivables largely represent money owed to the business and are usually shown as a total on the balance sheet, with the analysis shown in the notes. The international rules are not prescriptive about the classification, but you would usually expect to see:

- **Trade receivables** – this is the amount owed for the company's reported sales in the period.

- **Other receivables** – these represent amounts owed to the company for its non trading activities. They may include amounts due from the sale of property, plant and equipment, businesses, and tax refunds.

- **Prepayments and accrued income** – accrued income is income that is earned by the balance sheet date, and has been included in the income statement, but the company is not entitled to bill or receive it yet. Typical examples are interest receivable and rental income, which may be due for payment on a different date.

- **Amounts owed by joint ventures and associates**.

- **Amounts owed by subsidiaries** – these are found in the notes to the parent company's balance sheet.

Companies with long-term contracts also disclose separately the amounts due from customers for contract work. You may remember from Chapter 2 that receivables are shown on the balance sheet net of any bad debt provisions, which have to be disclosed in the notes to the accounts.

Now, let's look at IMI's note on its trade and other receivables.

16 Trade and other receivables

	2008 £m	2007 £m
Falling due for payment within one year		
Trade receivables	347.3	286.7
Other receivables	21.9	16.1
Prepayments and accrued income	17.1	14.4
Other financial assets	12.2	8.3
	398.5	325.5
Falling due for payment after more than one year		
Other receivables	5.7	4.6
Other financial assets	4.3	2.5
	10.0	7.1
Total trade and other receivables	408.5	332.6
Receivables are stated after:		
Allowance for impairment	12.9	8.4

The group's exposure to credit market risks related to trade and other receivables are disclosed in note 19.

Note 19, nearly eight pages long, explains IMI's management of financial risk. It's in this note that IMI analyses its receivables and the impairment loss, which some companies report in the trade receivables note. Here's the relevant extract from IMI's note:

Impairment losses

The ageing of trading receivables at the reporting date was:

| | 2008 | | 2007 | |
| | Gross | Impairment | Gross | Impairment |
	£m	£m	£m	£m
Not past due	267.3	**(2.0)**	227.1	(1.5)
Past due 1–30 days	51.9	**(0.1)**	37.4	(0.4)
Past due 1–90 days	22.1	**(1.3)**	16.7	(0.9)
Past due 91 days to less than one year	18.9	**(9.5)**	13.9	(5.6)
Total	360.2	**(12.9)**	295.1	(8.4)

The movement in the allowance for impairment in respect of trade receivables during the year was as follows:

| | 2008 | 2007 |
	£m	£m
Balance at 1 January	8.4	7.0
Impairment loss/(gain) recognised	1.7	1.4
Exchange	2.8	–
Balance at 31 December	12.9	8.4

The impairment loss recognised of £1.7m relates to the movement in the group's assessment of the risk of non-recovery from a range of customers across all of its businesses.

 There are different classifications of debtors in UK GAAP. The Companies Act requires some to be shown separately, whereas others are required by the accounting rules and determined by the company's business practice. You're likely to find the following debtors disclosed in the notes to the accounts:

- *Trade debtors*.
- *Amounts owed by group undertakings*.
- *Amounts owed by participating interests* – these are investments, such as associates, where the company is involved in the decision making.
- *Other debtors*.

- *Loans to finance the acquisition of own shares* – these are primarily loans to employees to enable them to buy shares, or to facilitate transactions in the company's shares between employees, former employees and their immediate family.
- *Unpaid called up share capital*.
- *Prepayments and accrued income* – some companies show this as a major heading, but this would be very unusual in the UK.
- *Amounts recoverable on contracts* – this is the money owed for work done on long-term contracts.

There will also be a note disclosing the debtors falling due in more than a year, as they are included in current assets.

Factoring and securitisation

Having cash tied up in receivables can be a major problem in some companies, as profitable businesses can fail if they don't receive the money owed by their customers. It's a particular problem for small companies whose customers are often large companies seeking extended credit terms. Companies want to release the cash that's tied up in receivables, and factoring is an option used by many smaller companies.

So what is factoring? The company sells its invoices to a factoring company (they're usually part of a bank or an international factoring organisation), which usually advances them up to 90% of the invoice value. The balance will be paid (less the factor's fees) when the company's customer pays the invoice.

There are different types of factoring agreements and they may be:

▦ *Disclosed* – the customer deals with the factor, who manages the sales ledger.

▦ *Undisclosed* – the customer deals with the company, who manages its sales ledger in the normal way. This is also called *invoice discounting*.

▦ *With recourse* – if the customer does not pay (either in full, or by a certain date) the company repays the factor's advance.

▦ *Non recourse* – the factor cannot force the company to repay the advance.

▦ *With partial recourse* – there are some non refundable proceeds received by the company.

The important issue in a factoring agreement is which party has the risks and rewards associated with ownership. You now know that the business having substantially all of the rewards and risks normally associated with ownership must show the asset in its accounts. The word 'substantially' means it can be a matter of judgement. If the company has a 'recourse agreement' with its factoring company it would continue to show its receivables as an asset, with the advance from the factor being shown as a liability. However, if the agreement is a 'non recourse' one the company doesn't show the factored receivables as an asset. In a partial recourse agreement the value of the factored receivables is the total factored receivables less any advances that don't have to be refunded to the factor.

Factoring is a form of *securitisation*. Large companies often use their receivables as security for a loan in a process called securitisation. (You'll often see this term used in the notes to large companies' accounts. It just refers to a loan that is backed by the collateral of future income streams arising from one of the business's assets. A range of assets has been used to collatarise loans including credit card receivables, mortgages, car loans, film royalties and receivables.)

Companies have to disclose any securitisation of their assets in the notes to the accounts. For example Tate and Lyle in their note on trade receivables in their 2008 accounts disclosed that they had £50 million securitised trade receivables (their net trade receivables were £474 million):

> ... Included in trade receivables amounts received of £50 million (2007 – £95 million) in respect of securitised receivables, which are also included in current borrowings.

In the note on its current borrowings the £50 million receivables securitisation was shown on a separate line.

 In essence the accounting requirements of the UK's rule, FRS 5 (*Reporting the substance of transactions*), are the same as IAS 39. The difference is largely in the disclosure that is required for factoring agreements with any refundable advances. If the factoring agreement gives any recourse back to the company, it has to disclose in the notes to the accounts:

- That they are factoring.
- The amount of factored receivables at the end of the year.
- The cost of factoring – this is split between any administration costs and interest charges, which show on the appropriate lines of the profit and loss account.

Investments

These are classified and accounted for in the same way as non current asset investments, although in practice current assets are likely to be 'available for sale' or 'held for trading' investments.

▧ Available for sale investments are shown at their fair value and any gains or losses are recognised in the statement of income and expense (comprehensive income) and equity.

▧ Investments held for trading are those the company bought with the intention of selling in the short term. They are shown on the balance sheet at their fair value and any subsequent changes to their fair value are shown as a gain, or a loss in the income statement.

 Most current asset investments will either be short-term deposits or short-term loans to institutions such as building societies or banks, as most companies using UK GAAP define cash as something that is realisable within 24 hours. This means that any deposits, or loans, with a longer maturity are shown as current asset investments. It also includes marketable shares or other securities, which are usually shown at the lower of cost and net realisable value. However, they may be shown at market value with any change in the value usually being shown in the revaluation reserve. If the investments are valued using the rarely used 'marked to market', any gain or loss would be shown in the income statement.

The notes to the accounts will categorise the investments with listed investments shown separately and their market value is disclosed.

Cash and cash equivalents

Cash equivalents aren't casino chips! A cash equivalent is a short-term deposit with a maturity of less than three months. Or more precisely they are' short-term, highly liquid investments that are readily convertible to known amounts of cash and which are subject to an insignificant risk of changes in value ... an investment normally qualifies as a cash equivalent only when it has a short maturity of, say three months or less from the date of acquisition' (IAS 7 *Statement of cash flows*).

 Cash

Most companies using UK GAAP define cash as something that is realisable within 24 hours, as this is the definition of cash they use in the cash flow statement. (The Companies Act doesn't define cash.)

Non current assets held for sale

These are assets that are available for immediate sale, and where their sale is highly probable. Highly probable is when:

- there is evidence of management commitment;
- there is an active programme to locate a buyer and complete the plan;
- the asset is actively marketed for sale at a reasonable price;
- the sale is expected to be completed within 12 months from the classification date.

This means that these assets' value will be recovered primarily through their sale rather than through their continuing use. Their accounting treatment is covered by IFRS 5 (*Non current assets held for sale and discontinued operations*), which is primarily concerned with property plant and equipment and discontinued operations, as it does not apply to:

- deferred tax assets;
- financial assets covered by IAS 39;
- employee benefit assets;
- investment properties shown at fair value;
- agricultural assets shown at fair value;
- insurance contract assets.

It also covers 'disposal groups', which are defined as a group of assets, and directly related liabilities, that will be disposed of in a single transaction. Consequently, they include companies and discontinued operations held for sale. A discontinued operation is part of a business that:

▓ represents a separate major line of business, or geographical area;

▓ can be distinguished financially and operationally;

▓ is classified as 'held for sale' or one that has already been sold by the company (in which case it wouldn't be shown as part of non current assets held for sale).

Assets and disposal groups classified as held for sale must be:

▓ initially measured in accordance with relevant accounting standards;

▓ then shown at the lower of their book value and their fair value less any cost to sell;

▓ subsequently neither depreciated nor amortised;

▓ presented separately on the face of the balance sheet adjacent to current assets and liabilities.

Where a disposal group has both assets and liabilities, assets and liabilities should not be netted off. The assets held for sale should be presented separately in the balance sheet adjacent to current assets, and the liabilities should be presented separately adjacent to current liabilities. IFRS 5 also requires that the major categories of assets and liabilities should be separately disclosed. This is usually shown in the notes to the accounts.

 There is no accounting standard in the UK concerned with the sale of non current assets or disposal groups, although there is guidance on the presentation of discontinued operations. If a sale or termination has a material effect on a major business segment, this fact should be disclosed and explained.

Subsidiaries acquired exclusively for resale and expected to be sold within a year if their acquisition should not be consolidated and should be shown as current assets at the lower of cost and net realisable value.

Current liabilities *or creditors: amounts falling due within a year*

On the balance sheet these are classified as:

- trade and other payables;

- interest-bearing loans and borrowings;

- derivative financial instruments (these are shown separately if they are material);

- current tax liabilities;

- provisions.

Apart from current tax liabilities, each of these is then analysed in the notes, and I'll start by looking at trade and other payables.

Trade and other payables

These are disclosed in the notes to the accounts and I'll use IMI's note to explain them, as it's fairly typical. However if they had any joint ventures or associates they will also have to disclose on separate lines in this note any amounts they owed them:

18 Trade and other payables

	2008 £m	2007 £m
Trade payables	223.6	185.2
Bills of exchange payable	3.5	2.8
Other taxation	14.7	10.6
Social security	6.8	5.0
Other payables	1.4	1.0
Accruals and deferred income	165.4	140.4
Derivative liabilities:		
At fair value through income statement	23.9	1.5
Designated hedges	8.9	3.5
	448.2	350.0

You can see that IMI is disclosing its derivatives in this note. Most of the other payables are fairly self explanatory, but you probably haven't come across *bills of exchange* before. Now I wonder if you've ever written a post-dated cheque? Companies' post-dated cheques are called *bills of exchange*. Unfortunately it's not quite as simple as that, as bills of exchange are different from post-dated cheques in two respects as they:

▨ Are written by the supplier, and signed by the customer in an acknowledgement of the debt.

▨ Can be sold. Bills of exchange are what lawyers call *negotiable instruments* – this just means that you can sell them!

Bills of exchange normally have a maturity of three months. If the supplier wants the cash today, rather than in three months' time, he sells the bill. These bills are bought by discount houses. (Discount houses are specialist banks that borrow short-term money from commercial banks, and use the cash to buy various forms of short-term IOUs such as bills of exchange.) If the buyer of the bill has to wait three months for his money, he won't pay £100 today for a bill that gives him £100 in three months' time. He'll be losing three months' interest. Bills of exchange are *discounted*, effectively the interest is paid in advance with the discount reflecting the three months' interest that has been lost by the purchaser. This type of bill is called a *trade bill*; there is another kind called a *bank acceptance*.

An acceptance is similar to a post-dated cheque, but now has the equivalent of a cheque card number on the back. A bank guarantees payment, and then the acceptance can be sold. Once a bank puts its name on the bill it's guaranteeing payment, even if the company defaults. An acceptance sells at the lowest interest rates because the payment of the bill is certain.

Bills of exchange have been around for centuries, and have always been normal trade practice in import and export businesses. However treasurers often use acceptances as part of their short-term financing programmes, and a significant increase in acceptances could indicate the company is short of cash.

Interest-bearing loans and borrowings

Most financial liabilities are shown on the balance sheet at their amortised cost. (Usually the only exception is when the loan has been designated as a hedged item, and the hedge is effective, when their value is adjusted for the changes in the value of the risk being hedged.) I explained amortised cost in detail earlier in the chapter in the section on non current investments, but I'll summarise it again. The loans are initially recorded at the net proceeds received, and subsequently shown at their amortised cost. The finance costs,[1] are accounted for using the effective interest rate method and are added to the loan's book value of the instrument to the extent that they are not settled in the period. (This means that if the effective interest charge in the period was £94 but the company had only paid interest of £50 in the period, the loan's value would increase by £44.)

The loans and borrowings are analysed in detail in the notes. IMI analyses them in two places, firstly it gives analysis of the split between the secured and unsecured loans and then in its notes on financial risk management it gives detailed analysis of each individual loan, its book value, effective interest rate (if it's fixed), the loan's currency, contractual cash flows, loan repayment schedule, and the split between loans with fixed and floating rates. (I shall talk more about financial risk management in Chapter 6.)

Company treasurers have become increasingly sophisticated and raise funds from the cheapest source matching their needs. They are innovative in their use of short-term debt instruments, often tailoring them to attract a specific investor. Companies' short-term borrowings fall into two broad categories:

- Overdrafts and short-term loans from banks and other financial institutions.
- Issues of promissory notes (IOUs) that can be held by anyone and are bought and sold.

Now, I think you're probably familiar with bank overdrafts and short-term loans, but may be less familiar with the second category of short-term debt. A common form of a promissory note is commercial paper.

Commercial paper

Commercial paper has been widely used overseas since its creation in America in the 19th century. The commercial paper market started in 1986 in the UK, and commercial paper is another form of short-term unsecured borrowing in

---

[1] The finance costs include any premiums payable on the loan's settlement, or redemption, and any direct issue costs.

the form of a negotiable instrument. It is only available to high quality borrowers and in some markets (for example the US) companies must have their commercial paper credit rated. Large companies have used commercial paper as an alternative to bank overdrafts, as they are very cheap to establish, and have been cheaper than bank overdrafts. Whilst commercial paper maturities can be as long as five years, most issues tend to be very short dated (it is not unusual for commercial paper to have a three week maturity). It is issued at a discount to the face value, and is often 'rolled over' – with one tranche being repaid by the issue of another. The commercial paper market is one of the many markets that have been hit by the 'credit crunch'.

Provisions

These are the provisions the company has made that relate to costs that will be incurred in the future and relate to the sales the company has already made. The notes to the accounts give more details about the provisions, as you can see in IMI's note on provisions:

22 Provisions for liabilities and charges

	Due inside one year			Due outside one year		
	Restructuring	Investigation costs & fines	Total	Trade warranties	Other	Total
	£m	£m	£m	£m	£m	£m
At 31 December 2007	6.9	–	6.9	20.8	13.2	34.0
Exchange adjustment	1.7		1.7	3.9		3.9
Utilised during the year	(20.3)	(4.8)	(25.1)	(7.2)	(0.2)	(7.4)
Income statement	19.6	26.3	45.9	8.0	(2.0)	6.0
At 31 December 2008	7.9	21.5	29.4	25.5	11.0	36.5

We expect to reach final agreement in the near future on a settlement with the US Department of Justice in respect of certain irregular payments by our US subsidiary Control Components Inc (CCI) that violated the US Foreign Corrupt Practices Act. An investigation has also been completed into possible incidental breaches of US trade law by CCI. Legal costs of £4.8m were incurred during the year and an additional provision of £21.5m has been made for the expected fines and certain related legal costs, bringing the total expense for the year for these matters to £26.3m. Whilst we believe the estimate of these fines and costs to be reliable, the final determination of the fines will be subject to the agreement of the relevant authorities. It is anticipated that the provided fines and costs will be paid within one year.

The restructuring provision is expected to be fully utilised within one year. The provision balance reflects residual amounts committed but not spent in relation to a number of specific projects to relocate or reorganise operations and facilities and upgrade talent.

Trade warranties are given in the normal course of business and cover a range of periods typically of 1–6 years.

Other provisions are mainly environmental provisions, recognising the Group's obligation to remediate contaminated land at a number of current and former sites. Because of the long-term nature of the liability, the timescales are uncertain and the provision represents management's best estimates of these costs.

I'd like to translate some of the terminology used in this note. The term 'utilised during the year' represents the money spent in the year. Everything shown on the income statement line without brackets represents charges that have been made to the income statement; the £2 million shown in brackets in the other column has been credited to the income statement.

You can see that IMI's provisions are for restructuring, the severe service investigation, warranties and land remediation. It has nearly finished its restructuring programme; there are just a few outstanding items.

 Companies preparing their accounts using UK GAAP usually just show one figure for 'Creditors amounts falling due within a year', disclosing the details in the notes.

The provisions are shown separately as 'Provisions for liabilities and charges', which are not analysed between those falling due within a year and more than a year. They may be simply shown as 'deferred tax' and 'other provisions'; the degree of detail is determined by the need for the accounts to show a true and fair view.

Non current liabilities or *creditors falling due in more than a year*

On the balance sheet these are classified as:

- trade and other payables – the payables shown as non current liabilities are usually other payables;
- interest-bearing loans and borrowings;
- derivative financial instruments (these are shown separately if they are material);

▦ deferred tax liabilities;

▦ provisions;

▦ employee benefit obligations.

Interest-bearing loans and borrowings

Companies' long-term loans fall into two broad categories, similar to their short-term debt:

▦ Loans from banks and other financial institutions.

▦ Issues of bonds and other forms of loan stock which are offered to investors, and therefore can be held by the general public. They are bought and sold in the same way as shares.

Loans are initially recorded at the net proceeds received, and subsequently shown at their amortised cost unless they're an effective designated hedged item.

I'd now like to tell you about:

▦ the type of security offered for loans;

▦ traditional long-term bank loans;

▦ debentures and bonds;

▦ Eurobonds;

▦ notes;

▦ debt equity hybrids;

▦ preference shares.

Security for loans

Loans can be secured in one of two ways:

▦ **A fixed charge** When you have a mortgage the lender has a fixed charge on your house. This gives them a legal right to your house if you don't pay your mortgage, and you can't sell your house without the lender's permission. Fixed charges on company's assets work in exactly the same way. The lender has the legal right to specified assets and the company can't dispose of them without the lender's permission. Fixed charges tend to be given on long-term assets such as land, properties and ships. If the company falls into arrears or defaults on the agreement the lender can either:

- Repossess and sell the assets, giving any surplus to the company. This is also called *foreclosure*.

- Appoint a receiver to receive any income from the asset (for example property rents).

- **A floating charge** This is a general charge on the company's assets. Floating charges are usually taken on short-term fixed assets (such as plant and machinery and vehicles) and current assets. Whilst the such as has the legal right to a group of assets, the company continues to manage those assets in the normal course of business. (After all, the company has to be able to sell its stock – otherwise it couldn't trade!)

Some loans may be secured, but rank after all the other borrowings in the event of a liquidation. These are called *subordinated loans*. It is also common for a lending bank to require a company to seek the bank's permission before giving security to anyone else – this is called a *negative pledge*.

Here's IMI's note analysing the split between its unsecured loans and their finance lease liabilities (they don't have any secured loans, if they did they'd be separately disclosed secured loans):

17 Interest-bearing loans and borrowings

This note provides information about the contractual terms of the Group interest-bearing loans and borrowings. For more information about the group's exposure to interest rate and foreign currency risk, see note 19.

	2008 £m	2007 £m
Current liabilities		
Unsecured bank loans	–	4.6
Unsecured loan notes and other loans	46.4	0.3
Current portion of finance lease liabilities	0.1	0.1
	46.5	5.0
Non current liabilities		
Unsecured bank loans	216.1	185.7
Unsecured loan notes and other loans	155.0	119.7
Finance lease liabilities	0.4	0.1
	371.5	305.5

Long-term bank loans

A traditional long-term loan is like an interest only mortgage. All the company has to do on a day-to-day basis is pay interest, the loan is repaid either in full at the end of the term, or in stages. It is also possible to take the loan in stages; if the company doesn't want all the money at once, it can draw it down in specified tranches. The loan could either be with one bank, or syndicated amongst a number of banks.

In some industries (such as shipping) companies repay some of the capital as well as interest. Most of the loan is repaid in a final payment at the end of the loan.

Bonds and debentures

There is no real difference between a debenture and a bond: both are formally recognised in a written instrument, sold to the general public and may be secured or unsecured.

There is no precise definition of a debenture, either in practice or in law. A debenture is a negotiable instrument that is usually, but not always, secured and is covered by either a debenture deed or a trust deed.

▦ A debenture deed places a fixed or floating charge on the company's assets.

▦ A trust deed contains all the details of the debenture and may include clauses (called covenants) that restrict the company's operations in some way. (If these are important they are disclosed in the notes to the accounts.)

Bonds are also negotiable instruments offered to the general public that may, or may not, be secured on the company's assets. They are covered by a trust deed. A bondholder is entitled to receive a stream of interest payments, and the repayment of the principal at maturity.

Before a company has a bond issue it will have the debt credit rated. There are two types of rating agencies looking at companies:

▦ Agencies who look at the company from a supplier's point of view (such as Dun and Bradstreet) and help to answer the question 'Will I be paid if I supply goods or services to this company?'

■ Agencies who look at the company from the investor's point of view (such as Standard and Poor, Moody) to help to answer the question 'Will I lose all my money if I invest in this company?'

The last ones rate corporate debt and the best quality corporate debt is rated triple A. The rating is very important as it affects both the ability to sell the bonds (as ratings affect who can buy the bonds) and the rate of interest that the company will have to pay to be able to sell the bond. The higher the rating, the lower the risk; the lower the risk, the lower the interest! Bond interest is called the 'coupon' and is expressed as a percentage of the face value of the bond. The face value of the bond is unlikely to be the same as the current bond price. Bond prices historically have been influenced by two factors:

■ Relative interest rates – if current interest rates are 6% and the bond is paying 10% investors will pay a premium to buy the bond.

■ The current credit rating of the company – if the credit rating has fallen the interest may not reflect the current level of risk so the bond price falls.

(I've used the term 'historically' as at the time I'm writing the interest rates are falling, and corporate bond prices are also falling even when the company's credit rating is unchanged. Hopefully by the time you're reading this, the financial markets will have stabilised!)

Bonds are a flexible form of finance and you'll find many different types of bonds in company accounts. Banks and companies have been very innovative, custom designing bonds to attract specific investors. Bonds are an ideal vehicle for financial innovation, as there are four variables that can be modified:

■ **The security given for the bond** For example, banks can issue bonds that have our mortgages and credit card balances as collateral. Companies may securitise their receivables.

■ **The coupon paid** For example, some bonds are issued that don't pay interest, and are called *Zeroes*. They are issued at a discount. For example, a £10 million five-year bond may be issued for £6.209 million. This has an implied interest rate of 10% and the value of the bond would increase by 10% a year. All other things being equal, at the end of the first year the bond would be worth £6.83 million, at the end of the second £7.513 million, and so on until the end of the fifth year when the investors would receive the £10 million.

Some bonds increase the interest over the life of the bond (*step up bonds*), whereas others reduce it (*step down bonds*).

▨ **The repayment of the principal amount borrowed**. For example, the repayment of the principal in some bond issues is index linked. In others, the bond may be issued in one currency and repaid in another *(dual currency bonds)*.

▨ **The bond's maturity.** For example, a bond can have two maturity options – it might have a maturity of 30 years, with an option to reduce this to 10 years (*a retractable bond*), or a maturity of ten years with an option to extend it to 30 years (*an extendible bond*).

Eurobonds

Large companies often issue Eurobonds. The first thing you need to know is what the term 'Euro' means in this context, because it's very confusing as we now spend the Euro in parts of Europe. In this context, a currency becomes 'Euro' when it is traded outside of the country of origin and its banking regulations. Japanese yen on deposit in London are Euroyen, American dollars deposited in Tokyo are Eurodollars. Euro does not mean European, and isn't always the name of a currency.

A Eurobond is simply a bond issued outside the country of its currency that has few restrictions on its issue and trading. Companies don't keep a register of Eurobond holders (whereas they may for a domestic or foreign bond). The bond is sold in 'bearer' form (this means that whoever holds the bond claims the interest and repayment of the principal). As Eurobond interest is paid gross, they are very attractive to investors who wish to keep their affairs secret from the tax authorities!

Eurobonds are available to large, internationally known, high quality borrowers.

Notes

Notes are unsecured IOUs. They are negotiable instruments and usually have a short maturity, often less than a year. Some can be repayable at the option of the holders. (IMI has a lot of US dollar loan notes, but these are all long-term debt.)

Debt equity hybrids

There is an increasing number of instruments that are neither debt nor equity, but have the features of both. I'll discuss three that are commonly found in company accounts.

Convertible bonds

Holders of convertible bonds have the option of having a cash repayment, or converting the bond into a fixed number of ordinary shares. Convertibles have two advantages for the issuing company:

- The interest rate is lower, as the conversion option has a value.
- The company may not have to repay the loan, just issue additional shares (they will need shareholder permission to do this in the UK).

A convertible bond has two elements:

- A financial liability to repay the bondholder.
- a conversion option for a fixed number of shares.

The bond will have to be split between these two elements. The financial liability will be shown as debt, with its value being the present value of the bond discounted by the interest rate of a similar bond without a conversion option. The conversion option will be shown as part of the equity, with its value being the difference between the financial liability and the proceeds from the bond issue.

Mezzanine finance

The financial press often refers to something called 'mezzanine finance'. It is another example of a debt equity hybrid that tends to be used in young companies, or management buy outs and buy ins. Companies in these situations often find it difficult to raise finance.

Mezzanine finance is a subordinated loan (ranking behind the other loans) that has a higher rate of interest than the other debt (to reflect the increased risk) and is convertible into shares via:

- an option to convert all, or part, of the loan into equity;
- a warrant to subscribe for equity (a warrant gives the holder the right to subscribe at some future date for shares at a fixed price).

Mezzanine finance is treated in the same way as convertible bonds.

Preference shares

Although they're called 'shares', most preference shares are classed as debt not equity, as there is a contractual obligation to pay dividends, and often there is a redemption date. Preference shares have a fixed dividend that must be paid <u>before</u> other dividends can be paid. There is a number of different types of preference shares, and they can include one, or more, of the features outlined below:

■ **Cumulative** – If a company doesn't pay a dividend to a cumulative preference shareholder this year, the dividend is carried over into the following year and accumulates. This means that it's only postponing the payment. The preference dividend is referred to as 'in arrears' (which must be noted in the accounts) and no other dividend can be paid until all the preference dividend arrears have been paid.

■ **Redeemable** – These shares are redeemed (repaid) at a fixed date. This makes them fundamentally the same as debt, but with the dividend being paid out of after tax profits. They are common in two situations; management buy outs and bank rescues (the bank undertakes a debt equity conversion, turning loans into redeemable preference shares).

■ **Participating** – Shareholders may receive two dividends: a fixed dividend, and a variable dividend (usually a proportion of the ordinary dividend.

■ **Convertible** – Preference shareholders have the right to convert into ordinary shares at a predetermined rate, at some future date. These are treated as a debt equity hybrid and the conversion option would show as part of equity.

Although most preference shares are no longer regarded as equity, all the legal rules regarding shares continue to apply to them.

Deferred tax liabilities

This represents the company's future tax liabilities arising from the temporary differences between the tax value of assets and liabilities and their book value. The notes disclose the assets and liabilities that have generated these temporary differences and the movement in the deferred tax assets and liabilities during the year. You can see this in the note from IMI's accounts below:

14 Deferred tax assets and liabilities

Recognised deferred tax assets and liabilities

	Assets		Liabilities		Net	
	2008	2007	2008	2007	2008	2007
	£m	£m	£m	£m	£m	£m
Non current assets	12.7	15.8	(36.4)	(33.3)	(23.7)	(17.5)
Inventories	9.3	8.0	(8.0)	(5.7)	1.3	2.3
Interest-bearing loans and borrowings	5.8	1.5	(1.2)	(0.9)	4.6	0.6
Employee benefits and provisions	53.1	38.2	(4.5)	(8.8)	48.6	29.4
Tax value of loss carry forward recognised	7.0	3.6	–	–	7.0	3.6
	87.9	67.1	(50.1)	(48.7)	37.8	18.4
Set off of tax	(33.2)	(29.9)	33.2	29.9	–	–
	54.7	37.2	(16.9)	(18.8)	37.8	18.4

Deferred tax assets totalling £14.5m (2007: £11.7m) have been recognised relating to territories where tax losses were incurred in the year. It is anticipated that, based on forecasts, future taxable profits will be available against which the losses can be utilised.

Employee benefit obligations

These are defined benefit obligations at the end of the financial year. The deficit on the employee benefit schemes is the employee benefit obligation less the employee benefit asset (shown in non current assets).

Equity or *capital and reserves*

Shareholders' equity

This represents the owners' stake in the business, and shows the business's share capital and its reserves. Reserves can come from a variety of sources:

- The premium paid, above the nominal value, for the shares issued by the company – this is called *the share premium*, or the *share premium account.*

- This is largely the cumulative retained profit, less any losses, since the business started – this reserve is called *retained earnings,* or in UK GAAP the *profit and loss account.* The cash cost of any share buy backs is charged against retained earnings, as was goodwill arising from acquisitions they made before 1998 in the UK.

▥ The revaluation of the businesses' assets – this is called *the revaluation reserve*.

▥ The reserve arising from the cancellation, or redemption, of shares – this reserve is called the *capital redemption reserve*. This is now very common, as companies rationalised their capital structure in the last 20 years through share buy backs.

▥ If a company has merged with another company, the accounting treatment is different from an acquisition. There is no goodwill and the companies are treated as though they have always been combined. This often means that the merged company will have a *merger reserve*. This not allowed under IFRS unless it involves a group reconstruction.

▥ A reserve arising from the effect of exchange rates on the value of overseas subsidiaries – this reserve is called the *translation reserve*, and for accounting years starting in 2009 *translation of foreign operations*.

▥ A reserve arising from the gains, and losses, from effective portion of cash flow hedges unsurprisingly called *cash flow hedges*.

You might also find other reserves on the balance sheet, especially in other countries where statutory reserves are common. These are undistributable reserves made for the protection of creditors. They are established by transferring a percentage of the dividends, or profit, each year to the reserve until it equals a predetermined percentage of the share capital.

I'll now take you through the main components of shareholders' equity.

Share capital

In this section I'll tell you about:

▥ authorised and issued share capital;

▥ treasury shares;

▥ share issues;

▥ the different types of shares found in company accounts.

Authorised and issued share capital

Companies usually show two share capital numbers in the notes to the accounts: the *authorised* share capital, and the *issued* share capital. The authorised share capital is the amount that the company can issue at the moment. If the directors of the company want to issue more shares they have to seek approval from their shareholders. This normally just requires the passing of a resolution by a majority of the shareholders. (From October 2008, the Companies Act 2006 no longer requires UK companies to have an authorised share capital.)

The issued share capital on the balance sheet is the total number of shares currently in issue at their original value (this is called the *nominal* or the *par* value). All UK shares must have a par value that is determined when the company is started. Shares have to be issued for at least this amount, as they can't be issued below their par value. (This is not always true overseas – for example, in some American states you'll find shares with no par value and shares can be issued for any price.) The notes to the accounts usually describe the issued shares as *allotted* (the company has decided who is going to hold the shares), *called up* (they have asked for the money) and *fully paid* (they've received it).

Treasury shares

Since December 2003 the Companies Act has allowed most listed companies buying back their own shares out of distributable profits the option of holding these shares 'in treasury'. This means that they don't have to be cancelled and can be held for sale for cash at a later date or transferred into an employee share save scheme. They can subsequently be cancelled. The shares held in treasury can't exceed 10% of the issued shares, and the company can't exercise the treasury shares' voting rights and doesn't receive any dividend. In a few pages you'll see that at the end of 2008 IMI had 20.6 million treasury shares.

Share issues

Two things have affected a company's ability to issue more shares:

- Their authorised share capital.

- The Companies Act 2006 – This prevents companies from issuing shares to new investors without the existing shareholders' prior consent. S571 effectively 'disapplies' the other relevant sections of the Act by allowing companies to offer some shares to anyone, as long as 75% of their shareholders have agreed they can do this. However most major new issues are in the form of a *rights issue*.

In a rights issue, a company offers its existing shareholders the opportunity to buy new shares, in proportion to its existing holding, at a discounted price. The shareholders then have three alternatives:

▦ They can exercise their right to buy the share.

▦ The can sell their rights to buy the share (in practice this option is only available to large shareholders in listed companies, the smaller shareholders' profit will be wiped out by dealing fees).

▦ They can do nothing. The company usually sells the warrants to buy the shares on their behalf and sends them the proceeds.

Most share issues are *underwritten*. Underwriting is a form of insurance, provided by banks and financial institutions, where the underwriters agree to buy the shares if no one else wants them. This ensures that the company receives some cash from the rights issue.

Not all share issues raise cash. Companies can have *scrip*, *bonus* or *capitalisation* issues – they all mean the same thing! In these issues the company converts some of its reserves into share capital. The share price falls after the issue, as the company's market value hasn't changed and it is now spread over an increased number of shares. Companies usually do this when they believe their share price is too high.

Another way of reducing the share price, without capitalising reserves, is to have a share split. This reduces the nominal value of each share in issue. For example on 27 June 2002 the French building products company, Saint Gobain, changing the nominal value its shares from €16 to €4. This reduced the closing price of its shares from €161.259 to €40.065.

Both bonus issues and share splits reduce share prices. In a bonus issue, shareholders receive additional shares. In a share split, shareholders receive new shares in place of the old share.

Classes of share

You'll find different types of shares in company accounts including:

▦ deferred shares;

▦ ordinary shares;

▦ American depository receipts.

Companies may also issue warrants to allow people to subscribe for shares at some future date.

Deferred shares

These are often the founders' shares and are rarely seen now in company accounts. They either:

- do not receive a dividend until some future date, usually several years after issue;
- only receive a dividend after ordinary shareholders' dividends have reached a pre-determined level.

The shipping company P&O had deferred shares rather than ordinary shares, these dated from the time it became a limited company following the granting of a royal charter in 1840.

More recently they have been used in capital reconstructions, where there is a need to make the shares virtually valueless. In this case they rank behind the ordinary shares if the business fails.

Ordinary shares

These are the commonest form of shares, but they're not necessarily all the same. Companies can have more than one type of ordinary shares with differences in:

- voting rights;
- entitlement to dividend;
- ranking if the company is liquidated.

American depository receipts

You may find reference in some accounts to American depository receipts (ADRs), and although they aren't another type of share I'm discussing them here. An ADR is a mechanism used in the USA to simplify the procedures for holding shares in foreign companies. The shares are bought, on behalf of the American investor, and deposited in a bank outside of the USA. An American bank then issues ADR certificates to the American shareholder. The custodian bank then processes the payment of dividends, rights issues, etc.

ADRs may be traded on American stock exchanges if the company is registered with the Securities Exchange Commission and complies with their requirements (they are then called *sponsored ADRs*).

Reserves

You'll find that there is a number of reserves in company accounts. They can be classified into those that are *distributable* (this means that they can be used to pay dividends), and those that are *undistributable*. The only distributable reserve is the *retained earnings*, and not all retained earnings may be distributable.

You'll usually find the following reserves on a balance sheet.

The retained earnings, or the *profit and loss account*

This is the accumulated profits and losses made since the company started adjusted by two factors: goodwill written off before 23 December 1998, and any cancelled, or redeemed, shares.

As it contains the retained profits it is the only distributable reserve. However, not all of the reserve is 'distributable', as not all of the profits have been *realised*. (To be realised, the company must have received it either in cash or other realisable assets. Realisable assets include receivables and other assets that can easily be converted into cash.) This means that not all of the retained earnings are realised. A good example is when a company has made a 'bargain purchase' and has acquired a company for less than its net asset value (negative goodwill). The accounting rules require this to be shown as a profit, but it isn't a realised profit.

The revaluation surplus, or reserve

This represents the accumulated revaluations of assets. When previously revalued assets are sold, and the revaluation is realised, the revaluation is transferred from the revaluation reserve to the profit and loss account.

Whilst the revaluation reserve is not a distributable reserve, it can be used for a bonus issue.

The share premium account

Shares are usually issued at a premium to their nominal value, and this premium is shown in the share premium account. The only exception to this rule applies to companies using UK GAAP where shares are issued for an acquisition. (The company may then qualify for statutory share premium relief under Section 131 of the Companies Act. This allows companies, meeting certain criteria, to write off any goodwill arising on consolidation through the share premium account, via a merger reserve.)

Once a share premium has been created it is legally treated as part of the company's share capital, and is not a distributable reserve. It may however be used for:

■ writing off any expenses, commissions or discounts relating to share or debenture issues;

■ writing off the company's preliminary expenses;

■ providing for any premium repayable on the redemption of debentures;

■ a bonus issue.

The capital redemption reserve

Shares can generally only be bought out of distributable profits, or from the proceeds of a new share issue. A company creates a capital redemption reserve if it buys back, or redeems, its shares. These shares are then cancelled, and the issued share capital reduced accordingly. The authorised share capital is unaffected by the buy back.

The accounting for share cancellations and redemptions is as follows:

■ **Share capital** This is reduced by the nominal value of the shares purchased, or redeemed, and the amount is then transferred to a *capital redemption reserve*. This is a non distributable reserve of the company, which is separately disclosed on the balance sheet. (The principle underlying the Companies Act's requirements is that the total of the share capital and the undistributable reserves should remain unchanged following the repayment of share capital. This is achieved by transferring the nominal value of the shares bought, or redeemed, from issued share capital to the capital redemption reserve.)

▓ **Retained earnings** When shares are purchased from distributable profits, rather than a share issue, this is reduced by the total cost of the purchase. If the shares are purchased through another share issue, the retained earnings are only reduced if the buy back cost more than the cash the company received when the shares were issued. The retained earnings are then reduced by the difference between the cash received when the shares were issued and the cash paid to buy the shares.

When shares are held in treasury the nominal value remains in share capital until they are sold for cash, or transferred into an employee share save scheme. If they are subsequently cancelled their nominal value will transfer to the capital redemption reserve.

You'll see this when you look at IMI's note on share capital and reserves.

The merger reserve

You'll only find this when companies have merged and it reflects any:

▓ differences between the nominal value of the shares that have been issued and the nominal value of the shares received;

▓ existing balances on the new 'subsidiary's' share premium account and capital redemption reserve.

Minority interests or non controlling interests

You have discovered that minority interests are found when the group doesn't own all the shares in its subsidiaries, and that the revised IFRS 3 *Business combinations* calls these non controlling interests. The accounting standard allows two options for the initial measurement of the non controlling interests, which I discussed earlier in the chapter. This is subsequently adjusted by the minority interest's share of the profit and other comprehensive income.

IMI's note on share capital and reserves

23 Share capital and reserves

	Share capital £m	Share premium account £m	Hedging reserve £m	Translation reserve £m	Capital redemption reserve £m	Retained earnings £m	Total parent equity £m	Minority interest £m	Total equity £m
At 1 January 2007	90.3	155.2	(0.3)	(1.7)	1.6	167.6	412.7	3.9	416.6
Total recognised income and expense			1.9	(1.0)		138.5	139.4	2.9	142.3
Issued in the year	0.6	8.1					8.7		8.7
Dividends paid						(63.9)	(63.9)	(2.4)	(66.3)
Minority interest acquired (net)								2.0	2.0
Share-based payments (net of tax)						2.9	2.9		2.9
Cancellation of treasury shares	(6.3)				6.3		–		–
Acquisition of treasury shares						(93.3)	(93.3)		(93.3)
At 31 December 2007	84.6	163.3	1.6	(2.7)	7.9	151.8	406.5	6.4	412.9
Total recognised income and expense			(3.8)	68.1		58.6	122.9	5.3	128.2
Issued in the year	0.1	1.8					1.9		1.9
Dividends paid						(66.2)	(66.2)	(2.4)	(68.6)
Share-based payments (net of tax)						4.0	4.0		4.0
Shares held in trust for employee share schemes						(1.9)	(1.9)		(1.9)
Acquisition of treasury shares						(14.8)	(14.8)		(14.8)
At 31 December 2008	84.7	165.1	(2.2)	65.4	7.9	131.5	452.4	9.3	461.7

The aggregate amount of goodwill arising from relevant historical acquisitions prior to 1 January 2004 which had been deducted from the profit and loss reserves and incorporated into the IFRS transitional balance sheet as at 1 January 2004 amounted to £364m.

Share capital

	The number of ordinary shares of two 25p each			
	2008	2007	2008	2007
	m	m	m	m
Authorised	480.0	480.0	120.0	120.0
Issued and fully paid:				
In issue at the start of the year	338.3	361.0	84.6	90.3
Issued to satisfy employee share schemes	0.6	2.6	0.1	0.6
Cancellation of treasury shares	–	(25.3)	–	(6.3)
In issue at the end of the year	338.9	338.3	84.7	84.6
Of which held within retained earnings	20.6	17.2		

During the year 0.6m shares were issued under employee share schemes realising £1.9m.

The Company made purchases of a total of 3.7m (2007: 17.2m) of its own shares with an aggregate market value of £16.7m (2007: £93.3m) and the nominal value of £0.9m (2007: £4.3m), including dealing costs of £0.1m (2007: £0.5m). Of the 20.6m (2007: 17.2m) shares held within retained earnings, 1.5m (2007: 1.2m) shares with an aggregate value of £9.1m (2007: £7.2m) are held in trust to satisfy employee share scheme vesting.

IMI's note on share capital and reserves discloses:

■ They had a small share issue during the year (these were issued to employees).

■ They spent £16.7 million buying back shares, most of these were treasury shares but some were for employee share schemes. It is considerably less than the amount they spent, £93.3 million, in 2007.

■ They currently have 20.6 million shares in treasury.

■ Exchange rates increased IMI's net worth in 2008 by £68.1 million.

Summary

I've covered a lot of technical material, and I'd now like to summarise the key points that you need to remember.

The balance sheet is a snapshot of the company on a certain day, and like most snapshots it can be presented from different perspectives. Globally the most popular presentation groups assets and liabilities, whereas UK balance sheets usually look at the business from the shareholders' point of view.

You'll usually find two balance sheets in group accounts: one for the parent (sometimes called the *company*), and one for the group (sometimes referred to as the *consolidated* balance sheet). You are interested in the group's balance sheet, as this relates to the other financial statements. The parent's balance sheet is included in the group balance sheet, with its investment in the group companies cancelled out by the group companies' share capital.

I've summarised the important points about each balance sheet item in the table shown on the following pages. Some items may be shown as both current and non current, and I've explained them in the first place you could find them in a typical UK balance sheet. Key differences in UK GAAP are italicised.

Non current assets or fixed assets	These are assets that the company doesn't intend to realise within a year. *These differ from UK GAAP's fixed assets, which are the assets that the business intends to use on a continuing basis.*
Intangible assets	These assets are those that can either be sold, transferred or licenced separate from the business as a whole, or those arising from contractual or other form of legal rights. They are largely purchased intangible assets, apart from development costs meeting certain criteria. Acquisitive businesses have considerable intangible assets, as an acquired business's intangible assets *must* be capitalised (if they can be reliably measured) even if they weren't previously shown in the acquired company's balance sheet.
	Intangible assets can include internally generated software, brand names, patents and goodwill (see below). Acquired business's intangible assets also include customer and supplier relationships, and order books.
	Intangible assets with finite lives are *amortised* usually on a straight line basis. Their book value can not exceed their market value. If there is any indication that their value has fallen the company must conduct an impairment review and if necessary make an impairment charge to bring the asset's value to the higher of its value in use or its market value less any selling costs.
	UK GAAP only allows intangible assets to be recognised if they can be sold separately from the business as a whole, and have a market value that can be easily determined. This means that companies using UK GAAP are unlikely to recognise most acquired intangible assets.

Goodwill	This represents the difference between the cost of acquiring a company and the fair value of its assets. (The acquiring company will probably change the value of the assets. It modifies them to reflect the market values at the date of the acquisition and aligns the accounting policies to those of the group.)
	Only purchased goodwill, in other words that arising from an acquisition, can be shown on the balance sheet.
	IFRS requires companies to conduct an impairment review, at least annually, to ensure that its value is not overstated in the accounts. *UK GAAP requires companies to amortise goodwill on a systematic basis over its useful life.*
Property, plant and equipment or tangible assets	These are usually depreciated, ensuring that the cost of acquiring the asset is charged to the income statement over its useful life. (The only exceptions are land and investment properties shown at market value.) The deprecation methods and assumptions must be reviewed each year to ensure that they are still appropriate. If there is any indication that the asset's value has fallen the company must conduct an impairment review and if necessary make an impairment charge to bring the asset's value to the higher of its value in use or its market value less any selling costs.
	Companies have the option of revaluing assets to reflect current market values. If they choose to do this, the valuation is normally professional and has to be kept up to date. *UK rules are more prescriptive than IFRS, requiring a full independent professional valuation every five years, with an interim valuation in the third year, and any other year where there's a material change in value. If the company has revalued its assets, a revaluation reserve will be shown in the shareholders' equity.*
Investments	These are the company's long-term investments, and IFRS regards these as financial assets. It identifies four different types of financial assets and specifies their accounting treatment:

- Financial assets at fair value through profit or loss, which can either be those held for trading or designated as such. They are shown at their fair value and any subsequent changes to their fair value are shown as a gain, or a loss, in the income statement.
- Loans and receivables, which are shown at their amortised cost, using the effective interest rate method.
- Held to maturity investments, which is debt, and is shown at amortised cost, using the effective interest rate method.
- Available for sale financial assets, which are all other financial assets and are shown at their fair value and any gains, or losses, are shown in the statement of recognised income and expense, or comprehensive income. Most small investments are classified as available for sale.

If a company can't reliably measure the fair value of an unquoted equity investment, it is shown at cost.

Most companies using UK GAAP show their investments at cost less any impairment.

Investments in associates and joint ventures are shown separately on the balance sheet. Associates and joint ventures are usually valued using the equity method, showing the investor's share of the associate's net assets in a single line on the balance sheet. Jointly controlled businesses can be valued using proportional consolidation.

Companies using UK GAAP report their investments in joint ventures using the gross equity method, where the company's share of the joint venture's gross liabilities is deducted from its gross assets to arrive at its balance sheet value.

Employee benefit net assets	This represents the amount that the employer can benefit from a surplus. *Companies using UK GAAP would not show employee benefit net assets as a fixed asset. The surplus, or deficit, in final salary pension funds is shown separately on the balance sheet, after net assets.*
Derivative financial instruments and hedging	A derivative is a hedging product whose value is derived from something else. Swaps, options and futures contracts are classified as derivatives and can be both assets and liabilities. They are shown at their market value plus any transaction costs, and any subsequent gains and losses are shown as financial income or expense in the income statement unless they are designated as hedges.
	Hedge accounting changes the timing of the recognition of gains and losses, so that both the hedged item and the hedge affect the income statement in the same period. This means that profit is unaffected by an effective hedge, and is only affected by any ineffective part of the hedge.
	A hedge is fully effective when the change in value of the hedging instrument is the same as the hedged item. However it is still regarded as effective when the hedging instrument has changed within 80–125% of the hedged item. Hedges outside of this range are regarded as ineffective, and hedge accounting can't be used.
	IFRS classifies hedges as:
	▓ Fair value hedges, where the value of the hedged item and hedging instrument is shown at fair value and any gains or losses on revaluation are shown in the income statement.
	▓ Cash flow hedges, where the effective part is shown in reserves until the gain or loss is realised. Any ineffective part would be shown in the income statement.
	▓ Net investment hedges, which have the same accounting treatment as cash flow hedges.
	Most companies using UK GAAP use historical cost accounting, so derivatives are rarely included in the balance sheet as their historical cost is effectively zero. However they are disclosed in the notes, which disclose their accounting policies and the fair values of their financial assets, financial liabilities and any hedges.
Deferred tax assets	This is the amount that the company expects to recover from the tax authorities in the future. *Companies using UK GAAP include material deferred tax assets in debtors.*
Current assets	*If the company is using UK GAAP not all its current assets are short term, as they are simply those assets not satisfying the fixed asset definition. Debtors due in more than a year, which are often pension fund prepayments, are included as current assets.*
Inventories or stocks	Inventories must be shown at the lower of cost and market value. *Companies using UK GAAP include long-term contract work in progress in stocks.*
Trade and other receivables or debtors	Not all receivables represent a future cash inflow to the business, as they include prepayments.
	The notes to the group balance sheet will disclose trade receivables (the amount owed by customers), other receivables, prepayments and accrued income and amounts owed by joint ventures and associates.
	Companies using UK GAAP include debtors due in more than a year and also disclose in their note on debtors:
	▓ *loans financing the acquisition of own shares;*
	▓ *unpaid called up share capital;*
	▓ *deferred tax assets;*
	▓ *amounts recoverable on contracts.*

Investments	These are classified and accounted for in the same way as non current asset investments, and are likely to be 'available for sale' or 'held for trading' investments. They include all short-term investments that aren't classified as cash equivalents.
	As UK GAAP doesn't have cash equivalents, current asset investments include short-term deposits, loans to other organisations such as banks and building societies, marketable shares and other securities.
Cash and cash equivalents	This comprises cash and short-term deposits with a maturity of less than three months. A cash equivalent must have an insignificant risk of a change in its value.
Cash	*The Companies Act doesn't define cash, but most companies now use the same definition they use in the cash flow statement, which is a maturity of 24 hours or less.*
Non current assets held for sale	These are assets that are available for immediate sale, and where their sale is highly probable. Any assets are shown immediately after current assets, and liabilities immediately after current liabilities.
	UK GAAP doesn't require these to be shown separately, unless they're acquisitions bought exclusively for resale, when they're shown as current assets.
Current liabilities	
Interest bearing loans and borrowings	Companys' borrowings can be a mixture of loans from banks and investors. Loans from investors are usually negotiable instruments (can be bought and sold). All loans may be either secured on the company's assets or unsecured.
	These are shown on the balance sheet at their amortised cost, unless they have been designated as a hedged item, and the hedge is effective, when their value is adjusted for the changes in the value of the risk being hedged.
	Companies using UK GAAP usually don't recognise hedges, so loans are shown at amortised cost.
Trade and other payables	The notes to the accounts analyse these into trade payables, other tax, social security, other payables and accruals and deferred income, and amounts payable to joint ventures and associates.
Current tax	This is the amount payable to tax authorities in the next 12 months.
Provisions	These are the unspent provisions for likely future costs, which are shown as current and non current depending on when they will be realised.
Non current liabilities	
Deferred tax liabilities	This represents the company's future tax liabilities arising from the temporary differences between the tax value of assets and liabilities and their book value.
	Companies using UK GAAP include these in 'Provisions for liabilities and charges'.
Employee benefit obligations	This is the defined benefit obligation at the end of the year. The deficit/surplus on the employee benefit schemes is the employee benefit obligation less the employee benefit asset (shown in non current assets).
Shareholders' equity	
Share capital	These are the shares in issue at the end of the financial year, shown at their *nominal*, or *par*, value.

Share premium account	This represents the amount above the par value received by the company for its shares. For example – the par value of a share is £1 and the company receives £5. The share capital would increase by £1, and the share premium account by £4.
Hedging reserve	A reserve arising from the gains, and losses, from effective portion of cash flow hedges.
Translation reserve/ translation of foreign operations	A reserve arising from the effect of exchange rates on the value of overseas subsidiaries.
Merger reserve	A reserve arising from mergers and group reconstructions. (IFRS doesn't allow merger accounting, so these would arise from past mergers and group reconstructions.)
Revaluation reserve	This arises from the revaluation of assets.
Capital redemption reserve	This is created following a cancellation of shares after a share 'buy back'.
Retained earnings or profit and loss account	This represents the accumulated profits and losses reinvested in the business since it started. It may be adjusted by: ▦ The write off of goodwill arising from acquisitions made before 31 December 1998. ▦ Share buy backs. *Companies using UK GAAP will usually also include exchange adjustments in the profit and loss account.*
Minority interest/non controlling interests	This is the value of the net assets that aren't owned by the company's shareholders.

IMI's balance sheet

Now it's time to look at a 'real' balance sheet, and IMI's consolidated balance sheet is on the next page. You'll see that it follows the typical UK presentation you saw earlier and, having covered all the notes, you can now see the balance sheet itself. When you look at the balance sheet you need to remember that, as a global business, IMI was affected by the weakening of sterling during 2008. You'll find that there are considerable increases in intangible assets and property plant and equipment but, if you can remember the notes, this is partly explained by translation differences. (Exchange rates added £96.4 million to intangible assets and £55.6 million to property, plant and equipment.)

CONSILIDATED BALANCE SHEET

AT 31 DECEMBER 2008

	Notes	2008 £m	2007 £m
Assets			
Intangible assets	12	399.8	314.7
Property, plant and equipment	13	266.4	207.9
Employee benefit assets	20	2.4	1.3
Deferred tax assets	14	54.7	37.2
Total non current assets		723.3	561.1
Inventories	15	333.5	252.0
Trade and other receivables	16	408.5	332.6
Current tax		4.7	1.9
Investments	19	17.8	14.4
Cash and cash equivalents	19	123.9	106.5
Total current assets		888.4	707.4
Total assets		1,611.7	1,268.5
Liabilities			
Bank overdraft	19	(4.6)	(29.1)
Interest-bearing loans and borrowings	17, 19	(46.5)	(5.0)
Provisions	22	(29.4)	(6.9)
Current tax		(26.6)	(21.0)
Trade and other payables	18	(448.2)	(350.0)
Total current liabilities		(555.3)	(412.0)
Interest-bearing loans and borrowings	17, 19	(371.5)	(305.5)
Employee benefit obligations	20	(139.5)	(64.9)
Provisions	22	(36.5)	(34.0)
Deferred tax liabilities	14	(16.9)	(18.8)
Other payables		(30.3)	(20.4)
Total non current liabilities		(594.7)	(443.6)
Total liabilities		(1,150.0)	(855.6)
Net assets		461.7	412.9
Equity	23		
Share capital		84.7	84.6
Share premium		165.1	163.3
Other reserves		71.1	6.8
Retained earnings		131.5	151.8
Total equity attributable to shareholders of the Company		452.4	406.5
Minority interest		9.3	6.4
Total equity		461.7	412.9

Approved by the Board of Directors on 4 March 2009 and signed on its behalf by:

Norman B. M. Askew Chairman

4

The statements of recognised income and expense, comprehensive income and changes in equity

Introduction

The presentation of these financial statements is changing as part of the convergence process. Companies using the international rules in their financial years starting before January 2009 had two choices, either they could present:

- a statement of changes in equity (most overseas companies do this);

or

- a statement of recognised income and expense, often known by its acronym a SORIE, disclosing the information shown in a statement of changes in equity in the notes to its accounts. (Most UK companies do this, as it is similar to the UK's rules.)

For financial years starting after January 2009 companies have two choices, they can present a:

■ statement of changes in equity and a single statement of comprehensive income – combining the income statement and the income and expense recognised in equity (now called *comprehensive income*);

or

■ statement of changes in equity and two statements. One showing the components of profit and loss (an income statement), immediately followed by the other statement showing the components of other comprehensive income (a statement of comprehensive income).

This means that everyone will have to show the statement of changes in equity as a financial statement (so it can't be relegated to the notes), and they can merge the income statement and statement of recognised income and expense if they want to.

I'll start by looking at the current position under IFRS, then look at the requirements of UK GAAP, and finally the options for the future.

What's in a statement of recognised income and expense?

It shows all the movements in the shareholders' funds that the owners haven't either contributed to (such as a share issue), or benefited from (such as dividends or a buy back). You now know not all gains are shown in the income statement. Some gains are shown on the balance sheet until they are realised. So some transactions are shown immediately in the income statement, whereas others are shown in equity. This statement brings all these gains, or losses, together – showing any gain that the company has recognised during the year. As such, it bridges the income statement and the balance sheet, taking information from both statements showing you:

■ *the profit for the financial year;*

■ *any adjustments made during the year to asset valuations;*

■ *any differences in the net investments in overseas' businesses arising from changes in exchange rates;*

■ *any gains or losses shown in equity arising from cash flow and net investment hedges*;

■ *any actuarial gain or loss on post employment benefit assets and liabilities.* (This is just the difference between the amount the actuaries expected to receive and the amount they actually received. Most of these are shown in equity, as one year you could get more than expected and another year less. In the long run these differences should cancel out. I'll tell you more about this in Chapter 6);

■ *the effect that any changes in accounting policies or corrections of errors have had on each component of equity.*

It shows all the gains, and losses the company has recognised in the period that don't involve shareholders in their capacity as owners of the business. It won't show all the changes in the shareholders' equity, as some of them, such as changes in the share capital and dividends, are transactions with shareholders and are neither gains, nor losses, that have been recognised by the company. I'll show you how this works in the next example.

Example 4.1

During the year a company has:

- Revalued properties upward by £10 million.
- Sold a property for £5 million. This had been revalued from the cost of £3 million to £4 million. Consequently it reported a profit on sale of property of £1 million, which I've shown separately in the income statement so that you can follow the numbers.
- Written £2 million off an investment, reflecting a fall in its market value. The investment's value is still above its original cost.
- Issued shares with a nominal value of £5 million for £7 million.
- Written off through reserves an £11 million exchange loss on overseas net investments.
- Recognised a £2 million gain from the effective portion of its net investment hedges.

You'll see these transactions reflected in the income statement and balance sheet, where I've shaded the relevant entries.

4.1 *continued*

Extract from the income statement

	This year £ million
Revenue	1,000
Cost of sales	(650)
Gross profit	350
Administration expenses	(100)
Distribution costs	(150)
Profit on sale of property	1
Operating profit	101
Net financial expense	(11)
Profit before tax	90
Tax	(30)
Profit for the financial year	60

Balance sheets extracts

	This year £ million	Last year £ million
Non current assets		
Property, plant and equipment	520	500
Available for sale investments	8	10
	528	510
Current assets	536	450
Current liabilities	(350)	(300)
Non current liabilities	(270)	(260)
Net assets	444	400
Shareholders' equity		
Share capital	55	50
Share premium account	52	50
Retained earnings	280	250
Revaluation reserve	57	50
	444	400

4.1 continued

Note on share capital and reserves extracted from the notes to the balance sheet:

	Share capital £ million	Share premium account £ million	Revaluation reserve £ million	Translation reserve £ million	Hedging reserve £ million	Retained earnings £ million	Total £ million
At the beginning of the year	50	50	50	27	5	218	400
Total recognised income and expense				(11)	2	60	51
Issued in the year	5	2					7
Dividends paid						(20)	(20)
Transfer to retained earnings			(1)			1	0
Decrease in value of investment			(2)				(2)
Surplus on property revaluations			10				10
At the end of the year	55	52	57	16	7	259	446

I can now construct the company's statement of recognised income and expense.

Statement of recognised income and expense

	£ million
Gain on revaluation of properties	10
Loss on revaluation of available for sale investments	(2)
Effective portion of change in fair value of net investment hedge	2
Currency translation differences on foreign currency net investments	(11)
Income and expense net of tax recognised directly in equity	(1)
Profit for the year	60
Total recognised income and expense for the year	59

If the company had any minority interests, the recognised income and expense is analysed between that attributable to the company's shareholders and minority interests.

The statement clearly shows the relative importance to the company of profit, revaluations and currency adjustments. Now let's have a look at a real statement of recognised income and expense.

IMI's statement of recognised income and expense

Here you can clearly see the effect of weakening sterling and volatile markets. However, as they moved in opposite directions they had a limited effect on the IMI's equity:

	2008	2007 restated
	£m	£m
Foreign currency translation differences	73.4	(2.5)
Actuarial (losses)/gains of defined benefit plans	(77.4)	35.2
Change in fair value of other financial assets	–	4.2
Effective portion of change in fair value of net investment hedges	(5.3)	(3.3)
Income tax on income and expense recognised directly in equity	21.5	(11.2)
Income and expense net of tax recognised directly in equity	12.2	22.4
Profit for the year	116.0	119.9
Total recognised income and expense for the year	128.2	142.3
Attributable to:		
Equity shareholders of the Company	122.9	139.4
Minority interest	5.3	2.9
Total recognised income and expense for the year	128.2	142.3

The income statement and the statement of recognised income and expense are important measures of the company's financial performance during the year. However it is important that you understand why this may not reflect the changes in the shareholders' equity – the business's net worth. This information is found in the statement of changes in equity.

What's in a statement of changes in equity?

The statement of recognised income and expense showed you some of the changes in equity, but it ignored any changes arising from transactions with shareholders. (I told you about the share issue but it wasn't shown in the SORIE.) You saw in the note on share capital and reserves that the company had had a share issue and paid dividends. Both of these transactions changed the value of equity. The statement of changes in equity is this note! In addition to the recognised income and expense it discloses any transactions with shareholders including:

▨ share issues and redemptions;

▨ purchase and sale of treasury shares;

▨ dividends;

▨ the equity component of any debt equity hybrids like convertible bonds.

As most UK companies show a statement of recognised income and expense they currently disclose the information required in the statement of changes in equity in the notes to the accounts. Here's IMI's note:

23 Share capital and reserves

	Share capital	Share premium account	Hedging reserve	Translation reserve	Capital redemption reserve	Retained earnings	Total parent equity	Minority interest	Total equity
	£m	£m	£m	£m	£m	£m	£m	£m	£m
At 1 January 2007	90.3	155.2	(0.3)	(1.7)	1.6	167.6	412.7	3.9	416.6
Total recognised income and expense			1.9	(1.0)		138.5	139.4	2.9	142.3
Issued in the year	0.6	8.1					8.7		8.7
Dividends paid						(63.9)	(63.9)	(2.4)	(66.3)
Minority interest acquired (net)								2.0	2.0
Share-based payments (net of tax)						2.9	2.9		2.9
Cancellation of treasury shares	(6.3)				6.3		–		–
Acquisition of treasury shares						(93.3)	(93.3)		(93.3)
At 31 December 2007	84.6	163.3	1.6	(2.7)	7.9	151.8	406.5	6.4	412.9
Total recognised income and expense			(3.8)	68.1		58.6	122.9	5.3	128.2
Issued in the year	0.1	1.8					1.9		1.9
Dividends paid						(66.2)	(66.2)	(2.4)	(68.6)
Share-based payments (net of tax)						4.0	4.0		4.0
Shares held in trust for employee share schemes						(1.9)	(1.9)		(1.9)
Acquisition of treasury shares						(14.8)	(14.8)		(14.8)
At 31 December 2008	84.7	165.1	(2.2)	65.4	7.9	131.5	452.4	9.3	461.7

The aggregate amount of goodwill arising from acquisitions prior to 1 January 2004 which had been deducted from profit and loss reserves and incorporated into the IFRS transitional balance sheet as at 1 January 2004 amounted to £364m.

The statement of total recognised gains and losses

 Companies preparing their accounts using UK GAAP show a statement of total recognised gains and losses, which is similar to a SORIE. It follows a standard format, starting with the profit for the financial year, then you'll find asset revaluations, and finally currency adjustments. Some companies show a subtotal before currency adjustments, showing the recognised gains and losses before any changes in exchange rates.

I'll use a modification of my previous example to illustrate the STRGL in Example 4.2 (I assume that the company, like most companies using UK GAAP, has not recognised hedges).

Example 4.2

As before, during the year a company has:

- Revalued properties upward by £10 million.
- Sold some fixed assets for £5 million. These had been revalued from the cost of £3 million to £4 million. Consequently it reported a profit on sale of fixed assets of £1 million.
- Written £2 million off an investment, reflecting a fall in its market value after a valuation. The investment's value is still above its original cost.
- Issued shares with a nominal value of £5 million for £7 million.
- Written off through reserves an £11 million exchange loss on overseas net investments.

You'll see these transactions reflected in the profit and loss account and balance sheet, where I've shaded the relevant entries.

4.2 *continued*

Profit and loss account

	This year £ million
Turnover	1,000
Cost of sales	(650)
Gross profit	350
Administration expenses	(100)
Distribution costs	(150)
Operating profit	100
Profit on sale of fixed assets	1
Net interest payable	(11)
Profit before tax	90
Tax	(30)
Profit for the financial year	60
Dividends	(20)
Retained profits	40

Balance sheet extracts

	This year £ million	Last year £ million
Fixed assets		
Tangible assets	520	500
Investments	8	10
	528	510
Current assets	536	450
Creditors: Amounts falling due within a year	(350)	(300)
Creditors: Amounts falling due in more than a year	(200)	(200)
Provisions for liabilities and charges	(70)	(60)
	444	400
Capital and reserves		
Share capital	55	50
Share premium account	52	50
Profit and loss account	280	250
Revaluation reserve	57	50
	444	400

4.2 *continued*

The note on Reserves extracted from the notes to the balance sheet:

	Share premium account	Revaluation reserve	Profit and loss account	Total
	£ million	£ million	£ million	£ million
At the beginning of the year	50	50	250	350
Premium on issue of shares	2			2
Transfer from profit and loss account for the year			40	40
Transfer of realised profits		(1)	1	0
Decrease in value of investment		(2)		(2)
Currency translation differences on foreign currency net investments			(11)	(11)
Surplus on property revaluations		10		10
At the end of the year	52	57	280	389

Now I can show you the statement of total recognised gains and losses:

Statement of total recognised gains and losses

	£ million
Profit for the financial year	60
Unrealised surplus on revaluation of properties	10
Unrealised loss on investment	(2)
	68
Currency translation differences on foreign currency net investments	(11)
Total recognised gains and losses for the year	57

Companies preparing their accounts using the UK's rules don't have to show a statement of changes in equity (although the information is disclosed in the notes on share capital and reserves). But they do show a reconciliation to the movements in the shareholders' funds to complete the picture. It may be found either in the notes, or following the statement of total recognised gains and losses.

The reconciliation of movements in shareholders' funds
There are two ways that the recognised gains can be reconciled to the movement in the shareholders' funds. The first starts with the total recognised gains in the period.

4.2 continued

First reconciliation option

	£ million
Total recognised gains	57
Dividends	(20)
New share capital subscribed	7
Net addition to shareholders' funds	44
Opening shareholders' funds	395
Closing shareholders' funds	439

The other alternative starts with the profit for the financial year, rather than the recognised gains and losses:

Second reconciliation option

	£ million
Profit for the financial year	60
Dividends	(20)
Other recognised gains and losses relating to the year (net)	(3)
New share capital subscribed	7
Net addition to shareholders' funds	44
Opening shareholders funds	395
Closing shareholders' funds	439

This is the presentation illustrated in the accounting standard, but is less 'user friendly' than the first, as it is more difficult to identify the total recognised gains. To do this you have to add the profit for the financial year of £60 million to the other recognised gains and losses of −£3 million. This gives the £57 million gains recognised during the year.

The effects of the revisions to IAS 1 on the financial statements

The presentation of the income statement will change in financial years starting in 2009, when the revised IAS 1 (*Presentation of financial statements*) is applied. The main changes to the presentation of financial statements are:

■ Companies can combine their income statement and their SORIE into one financial statement – the statement of comprehensive income. Alternatively they can show two statements: an income statement and a statement of comprehensive income. (This means that the term 'statement of comprehensive income' may mean different things to different companies.) If companies choose to show two statements, the statement of comprehensive income immediately follows the income statement. (There appears to be no reason why this couldn't be on a separate page as long as it's on the next page.) This means that UK companies who have used a SORIE can effectively continue to have two separate financial statements, as long as the other comprehensive income is shown immediately after the income statement.

■ All companies must show their statement of changes in equity as a financial statement, which means it can't be relegated to the notes.

■ Most of the financial statement's names are changed in the revised standard, and there are also some other changes in terminology:

– Firstly you've already read about *comprehensive income*.

– The balance sheet is referred to as a *statement of financial position*.

– The cash flow statement is referred to as a *statement of cash flows*.

However, as companies don't have to use the new terminology, it's possible that the change in the names may only be of academic interest to trainee accountants who are expected to use them in their exams. As the standard isn't affecting the presentation of accounts yet, I have no idea how many companies will adopt the new names.

■ If the company applies a new accounting policy retrospectively, or makes any other retrospective changes (this could happen if it's corrected material errors) it has to show its balance sheet at the beginning of the earliest comparative period.

■ Companies have to disclose, either in the statement or the notes, the tax and any reclassification adjustments relating to comprehensive income.

The statement of comprehensive income

I'd like to show you what the combined statement of comprehensive income could look like, and tell you about some of the changes in the terminology. To do this I'll continue with my previous example, expanding the income statement to include all of the required entries.

Example 4.3

Income statement

	This year £ million
Revenue	1,000
Cost of sales	(650)
Gross profit	350
Distribution costs	(150)
Administration expenses	(100)
Profit on sale of property	1
Operating profit	101
Interest receivable	6
Other financial income	2
Interest payable	(16)
Other financial expense	(3)
Profit before tax	90
Tax	(30)
Profit for the financial year	60

And here's their statement of recognised income and expense:

Statement of recognised income and expense

	£ million
Gain on revaluation of properties	10
Loss on revaluation of available for sale investments	(2)
Effective portion of change in fair value of net investment hedge	2
Currency translation differences on foreign currency net investments	(11)
Income and expense net of tax recognised directly in equity	(1)
Profit for the year	60
Total recognised income and expense for the year	59

These are then combined in the statement of comprehensive income:

Statement of comprehensive income

	This year £ million
Revenue	1,000
Cost of sales	(650)
Gross profit	350
Distribution costs	(150)
Administration expenses	(100)
Profit on sale of property	1
Operating profit	101
Interest receivable	6
Other financial income	2
Interest payable	(16)
Other financial expense	(3)
Profit before tax	90
Tax	(30)
Profit for the year	60
Other comprehensive income:	
Gain on revaluation of properties	10
Loss on revaluation of available for sale investments	(2)
Effective portion of change in fair value of net investment hedge	2
Currency translation differences on foreign currency net investments	(11)
Other comprehensive income for the year, net of tax	(1)
Total comprehensive income for the year	59

Companies with minority interests subsequently analyse the profit and the comprehensive income into that attributable to the company's shareholders and the minority interests. (Minority interests will be called non controlling interests.)

5

The statement of cash flows

Introduction

The success and survival of every organisation depends on its ability to generate and acquire cash. We all understand the importance of cash flow. Companies survive when they have cash, and fail when they don't. This means that you have to understand a company's cash flow and you will be interested in a company's ability to generate cash for itself, and acquire it from other sources. You can clearly see this in the statement of cash flows, called the *cash flow statement* if the accounts relate to financial years starting before 2009, or are prepared using the UK's rules.

The statement of cash flows identifies the business's cash movement in the period. It shows where the cash came from and where it was spent. It is purely concerned with the movement of cash, so the accounting adjustments found in the other financial statements don't affect the cash flow statement. One thing that you'll notice is that the cash flows shown on the cash flow statement are often different from the charges shown in the income statement. This is because the income statement accrues income and expenses as they're earned, whereas the cash flow shows them when they are received and paid.

I think it's the most important financial statement, as cash is the one thing that can't be created – the company either has cash or it hasn't! By looking at the movement of cash, you have a much clearer idea of the company's financial stability and viability.

What is in a statement of cash flows?

IAS 7 (*Statement of cash flows*) requires all companies, including parent companies, preparing their accounts using IFRS to prepare a statement of cash flows, which summarises the company's cash flows during the period. It classifies cash flows into three headings: operating activities, investing activities and financing activities. However, companies are allowed to classify their cash flows within these headings in the most appropriate way for their business. Consequently there are some presentational differences between companies for some line items:

- *Operating activities* – these are the company's principal revenue generating activities together with any other activities that are neither investing activities nor financing activities. It usually starts with profit after tax (but it can start with any profit figure). It includes taxation and can include interest and dividends paid. However, both interest paid and dividends paid are normally shown as financing cash flows.

- *Investing activities* – this usually covers the cash returns from investments as well as investment within the business. Consequently it includes the cash flows arising from the purchase and sale of non current assets and acquisitions and disposals together with investment income.

- *Financing* – this usually includes the financing costs of interest and dividends as well as any financing cash flows arising from changes in share capital and loans. Bank overdrafts can be included in the financing cash flows, but in the UK are usually shown as part of cash and cash equivalents if they're repayable on demand and form an integral part of the company's cash management. (Companies are allowed to include bank overdrafts as a negative cash and cash equivalent when their cash position regularly fluctuates from positive to negative.)

The statement of cash flows then finishes with the changes in cash equivalents, which may, or may not, be shown net of any bank overdrafts.

You can see that companies have some flexibility in positioning interest and dividends in their statement of cash flows. The accounting standard allows companies to choose how they classify them as long as they are separately disclosed and the classification is consistently applied from one period to another. Some companies like to show interest and dividends paid as operating activities, as it enables readers to see if the company can pay its interest and dividends from its operating cash flows. (In my own analysis spreadsheets I always include interest paid as an operating cash flow as it enables me to quickly see whether a company has generated enough cash in the year to pay its interest. Somehow, I don't think it's prudent for companies to have to increase their borrowings to pay the interest on their existing loans!) Most companies, however, show interest and dividends received as investing activities, and interest paid as financing activities. Financial institutions always show interest as an operating cash flow, as it's their main source of revenue.

Foreign currencies are usually translated at the exchange rate on the date of the cash flow, although a weighted average rate can be used for immaterial transactions if it's a fair approximation to the actual rate. Exchange gains and losses are not shown on the statement of cash flows, as they are paper adjustments rather than cash flows. However, the effect of exchange rates on cash and cash equivalents is shown so that a reconciliation can be made between the cash and cash equivalents at the start of the period with those at the end of the period.

Companies also have to disclose:

▨ any material non cash transactions relating to an investing or financing transaction, even if it doesn't show on the statement of cash flows;

▨ the components of cash and cash equivalents and a reconciliation with the cash and cash equivalents shown on the balance sheet;

▨ any significant amounts of cash and cash equivalents that can't be used by the group.

The cash flow statement in detail

I'll now look at the items shown in the cash flow statement in more detail, and illustrate them with a simple cash flow statement. Firstly I'll show you the cash flows you will find under each heading, and then the cash flow statement as it appears in the accounts. I'll show interest paid as an operating item.

Cash flows from operating activities

There are two ways that companies can calculate their cash flow from their trading activities, which I'll call the cash 'generated from operations'. You will often find this subtotal shown on UK listed companies' statements of cash flows, as it equates to the operating cash flow shown under the UK accounting rules. The stock exchange encouraged companies to show this when companies changed from the UK rules to the international rules, as it facilitated comparisons with previous years.

I'm going to show you the simpler, but rarely used, option first. I'm sure that you'll find it easy to understand, as it shows the period's cash receipts and payments for operating items.

Cash flow generated from operations:

	£m
Cash received from customers	910
Cash paid to suppliers	(530)
Cash paid to, and on behalf of, employees	(200)
Other cash paid	(100)
Cash generated from operations	80

Whilst this approach is straightforward, much easier to follow, and its use is encouraged by the standard, very few companies use it. Most companies start with profit and then add back any paper charges (primarily depreciation and amortisation) that have been made in determining the profit, to show the cash that *will* be generated from this period's trading. This is then adjusted for any changes in the working capital, to arrive at the cash generated from operations during the year. Now let's have a look at the most popular presentation:

		£m
	Operating profit	80
	Depreciation and amortisation	40
Less	Increase in inventories	(20)
Less	Increase in receivables	(90)
Plus	Increase in payables	70
	Cash generated from operations	80

> The 120 million total of operating profit and depreciation and amortisation (EBITDA) is the cash the business *will* receive from the period's trading. But it's only received 80 million as an additional 40 million had to be invested in working capital.

You can see that both approaches give you the same answer: 80. However, the first approach tells you *what* the operating cash flow is; the second tells you *why* it's 80 million. That's why it's the most popular presentation! The company will receive 120 from its trading. This is called EBITDA (an acronym standing for *E*arnings, another word for profit, *B*efore *I*nterest, *T*ax, *D*epreciation and *A*mortisation. It is calculated by adding the depreciation and amortisation charge to the operating profit. You'll find it's an important comparative measure in financial analysis, which I'll discuss further in later chapters). However, the company has only generated 80 because it has had to increase its working capital.

You'll notice that I started from operating activities with the company's operating profit, as it made it easier to explain. In fact companies can start with any profit figure. However if you start with profit for the financial year you have to adjust for more items to arrive at the operating cash flow, as most items shown below operating profit aren't operating items. Even if they were, the amounts shown in the income statement are unlikely to be the same as the cash flow. I've added back depreciation and amortisation because they are accounting adjustments and not cash items. Provisions are another obvious non cash item, as a charge has been made to the income statement but no cash may have left the business. You also find other charges that are added back, for example share-based payments. You'd also have to adjust for financial income, financial expense and the company's share of associates and joint ventures' profits.

Now I need to deduct the interest and tax paid to arrive at the cash flow from operating activities:

	£m
Operating profit	80
Depreciation and amortisation	40
Increase in inventories	(20)
Increase in receivables	(90)
Increase in payables	70
Cash generated from operations	80
Interest paid	(85)
Tax paid	(10)
Net cash used in operating activities	(15)

> *Now you can see why I decided to show interest as an operating item rather than a financing one. The company isn't generating enough cash in the period to pay its interest and tax bills!*

Now let's look at the cash flows from investing activities.

Cash flows from investing activities

These are the cash flows from the purchase and sale of non current assets, current investments, acquisitions and disposals, and usually any interest and dividends received.

	£m
Purchase of property, plant and equipment	(130)
Purchase of investments	(20)
Investment in associate	(10)
Purchase of subsidiary X, net of cash acquired	(200)
Proceeds from sale of property, plant and equipment	25
Interest received	30
Dividends received	10
Net cash used in investing activities	(295)

So now you can see that, although the company hasn't generated enough cash to cover its interest and tax bills, it has spent significant amounts on new equipment, investments and an acquisition. Either it had a lot of cash or required a large injection of capital. So let's look at the financing cash flows.

Cash flows from financing activities

These are either receipts from, or repayments to, the external providers of finance. The receipts could arise from share issues and additional long-term borrowings. The payments could include purchases of own shares, the redemption of bonds and loan repayments (and interest payments in most companies' statements of cash flows). In my example below the company had the following financing cash flows:

	£m
Proceeds from share issue	250
Increase in borrowings	50
Repayment of borrowings	(20)
Repayment of obligations under finance leases	(40)
Dividends paid	(30)
Dividends paid to minority interests	(5)
Net cash from financing activities	205

So now you know that my company had a cash outflow of £15 million from operating activities, an outflow of £295 million from its investing activities and an inflow of £205 million from financing. This means that its cash and cash equivalents fell by £105 million. They started with cash and cash equivalents of £165 million, the movement in exchange rates reduced them by £5 million and the closing cash and cash equivalents was £55 million.

And here's their statement of cash flows:

	£m
Cash flows from operating activities	
Operating profit	80
Depreciation and amortisation	40
Increase in inventories	(20)
Increase in receivables	(90)
Increase in payables	70
Cash generated from operations	80
Interest paid	(85)
Tax paid	(10)
Net cash used in operating activities	(15)
Cash flows from investing activities	
Purchase of property, plant and equipment	(130)
Purchase of investments	(20)
Investment in associate	(10)
Purchase of subsidiary X, net of cash acquired	(200)
Proceeds from sale of property, plant and equipment	25
Interest received	30
Dividends received	10
Net cash used in investing activities	(295)
Cash flows from financing activities	
Proceeds from share issue	250
Increase in borrowings	50
Repayment of borrowings	(20)
Repayment of obligations under finance leases	(40)
Dividends paid	(30)
Dividends paid to minority interests	(5)
Net cash from financing activities	205
Net decrease in cash and cash equivalents	(105)
Cash and cash equivalents at the beginning of the period	165
Effect of exchange rate fluctuations on cash held	(5)
Cash and cash equivalents at the end of the period	55

There are considerable differences between IAS 7 and FRS 1 (*Cash flow statements*):

- Not all companies have to prepare cash flow statements and the following companies do not have to do prepare them:
  - Small private companies (I gave you the definition of a small private company in Chapter 1).
  - Subsidiary companies where more than 90% of the voting rights are controlled within the group, providing that the group's consolidated accounts are publicly available.
  - Mutual life assurance companies owned by their policyholders.
  - Pension schemes.
  - Open ended investment funds meeting certain conditions.
- All the cash flows exclude any recoverable VAT, and similar sales taxes. (IAS 7 does not specify whether the cash flows should be shown gross or net of VAT and similar sales taxes.)
- Foreign currencies are translated at the same rate used in the profit and loss account, unless the actual rate is used. (This means that companies can use the closing rate.) The actual rate can be used for cash flows within the group to ensure that these cancel out in the consolidated cash flow statement.
- The cash flows relate to movements in cash, rather than cash and cash equivalents. Cash is defined as cash in hand and investments repayable on demand, with less than 24 hours' maturity, less any bank overdrafts and other loans repayable on demand. This means that cash equivalents are shown under a separate heading of 'Management of liquid resources'.
- Exchange differences on cash are regarded as non-cash items and consequently are not reported on the face of the cash flow statement.
- FRS 1 is more prescriptive about where cash flows are shown and classifies the cash flows into nine headings:
  - *Trading* – these cash flows are shown under the heading 'Operating activities'. This is equivalent to the optional subtotal 'Cash generated from operations' shown by most UK companies reporting under IFRS.
  - *Dividends from joint ventures and associates.*
  - *Interest, dividends received and any dividends paid to preference shares and minority interests* – these are shown under the heading '*Returns on investment and servicing of finance*'.
  - *Tax* – these are shown under the heading 'Taxation'.
  - *Buying and selling fixed assets* – these are shown under the heading of '*Capital expenditure and financial investment*'. (This heading can be shortened to capital expenditure, if the company hasn't bought or sold any fixed asset investments during the period. The heading then reflects the actual cash flows.)

- *Buying and selling businesses* – these are shown under the heading '*Acquisitions and disposals*'.
- *Dividends paid to ordinary shareholders* – these are shown as '*Equity dividends paid*'.
- *Short-term investments shown as current asset investments* – these investments are used to manage a company's net debt, or net funds, position rather than for its investment potential. Any deposits maturing in more than 24 hours will be included under the heading '*Management of liquid resources*'.
- *Shares and loans* – these shown under the heading '*Financing*'.

The first seven headings must be presented in the order above, and companies can take subtotals at any point.

- The cash flow statement then finishes with the increase, or decrease, in cash. The definition of cash includes short-term deposits and other investments maturing in 24 hours less any borrowings repayable on demand.
- You'll also find reconciliations to:
  - Net debt – linking the cash flow statement to the balance sheet.
  - Operating profit – linking the cash flow statement to the profit and loss account.

These reconciliations may either follow the cash flow statement or be shown in the notes. Most companies show a reconciliation to net debt below the cash flow statement and use the reconciliation to operating profit to identify the operating cash flow.

This means that the cash flow statement prepared using UK GAAP looks very different from that prepared using IFRS. I've compared a cash flow statement prepared using UK GAAP with one prepared using IFRS in Chapter 7.

IMI's cash flow statement

IMI's cash flow statement is on the next page and you'll find that they have a strong and positive cash flow in both 2007 and 2008, with 2008 having a particularly strong operating cash flow.

CONSOLIDATED STATEMENT OF CASH FLOWS

FOR THE YEAR ENDED 31 DECEMBER 2008

	2008	2007
	£m	£m
Cash flows from operating activities		
Profit for the period	116.0	119.9
Adjustments for:		
Depreciation	43.1	35.9
Amortisation	16.4	13.9
(Profit)/losses from discontinued operations (net of tax)	–	(1.9)
Other income – disposal of business	–	(1.7)
Gain on sale of property, plant and equipment	(0.2)	(0.1)
Financial income	(85.6)	(81.1)
Financial expense	119.4	81.8
Equity-settled share-based payment expenses	3.9	3.1
Income tax expense	60.0	53.0
Decrease/(increase) in trade and other receivables	17.6	(12.6)
Decrease/Increase in inventories	(9.2)	(18.6)
(Decrease)/increase in trade and other payables	(7.2)	20.5
(Decrease)/increase in provisions and employee benefits	14.4	(6.6)
Cash generated from the operations	288.6	205.5
Income taxes paid	(54.4)	(37.1)
	234.2	168.4
Additional pension scheme funding	(16.8)	(15.6)
European commission fine	–	(32.8)
Net cash from operating activities	217.4	120.0

Cash flows from investing activities

Interest received	12.4	7.2
Proceeds from the sale of property plant and equipment (including £1m from discontinued operations in 2007)	3.1	8.3
Sale of investments	0.1	0.1
Purchase of investments	(0.8)	(1.2)
Income from investments	0.7	–
Acquisition of subsidiaries, net of cash required	–	(52.2)
Disposal of businesses (net of cash disposed)	–	2.0
Acquisition of property, plant and equipment	(47.6)	(49.9)
Capitalised development expenditure	(5.1)	(3.2)
Net cash from investing activities	(37.2)	(88.9)

Cash flows from financing activities

Interest paid	(29.0)	(19.9)
Purchase of own shares	(16.7)	(93.3)
Proceeds from the issue of share capital for employee share schemes	1.9	8.7
(Repayment)/drawdown of borrowings	(45.5)	110.7
Dividends paid to minority interest	(2.4)	(2.4)
Dividends paid	(66.2)	(63.9)
Net cash from financing activities	(157.9)	(60.1)
Net increase/(decrease) in cash and cash equivalents	22.3	(29.0)
Cash and cash equivalents at the start of the year	77.4	103.6
Effects of exchange rate fluctuations on cash held	19.6	2.8
Cash and cash equivalents at the end of the year*	119.3	77.4

* Net of bank overdrafts

Notes to the cash flow appear in note 24.

You can see that IMI starts with profit for the period, rather than operating profit, and consequently has to add back all the non operating items of income and expense together with any other non cash items such as the gain on sale of property, plant and equipment and equity-settled share-based payment expenses. (These must be charged to the income statement, as they're a component of salaries, but their cash flow is a financing cash flow that occurs when the shares are bought.) You'll also see that the income tax expense is added back and replaced with the tax that's paid during the year. (Remember the statement of cash flows will show the cash movement rather than the income earned and the costs relating to the income earned in the period that shows on the income statement.) If it started with operating profit, it would have the same operating cash flow but with fewer adjustments:

	2008	2007
	£m	£m
Cash flows from operating activities		
Operating profit	209.8	171.7
Adjustments for:		
Depreciation	43.1	35.9
Amortisation	16.4	13.9
Other income – disposal of business	–	(1.7)
Gain on sale of property, plant and equipment	(0.2)	(0.1)
Equity-settled share-based payment expenses	3.9	3.1
Decrease (increase) in trade and other receivables	17.6	(12.6)
Increase in inventories	(9.2)	(18.6)
(Decrease)/increase in trade and other payables	(7.2)	20.5
(Decrease)/increase in provisions and employee benefits	14.4	(6.6)
Cash generated from the operations	288.6	205.5
Income taxes paid	(54.4)	(37.1)
	234.2	168.4
Additional pension scheme funding	(16.8)	(15.6)
European commission fine	–	(32.8)
Net cash from operating activities	217.4	120.0

IMI's operating cash flow increased by 81% in 2008, and the cash generated from operations was improved largely by:

▓ increasing EBITDA by £47.8 million (see below)

▓ the turnaround in working capital, which generated another £11.9 million (see below)

▓ the turnaround in provisions and employee benefits of £21 million, which reduced profits with no corresponding cash flow.

The combination of these explains £80.7 million of the £83.1 million improvement in the cash flow from operations.

EBITDA

	2008	2007
	£m	£m
Operating profit	209.8	171.7
Depreciation	43.1	35.9
Amortisation	16.4	13.9
EBITDA	269.3	221.5

Change in working capital

	2008	2007
	£m	£m
(Decrease)/increase in trade and other receivables	17.6	(12.6)
Increase in inventories	(9.2)	(18.6)
(Decrease)/increase in trade and other payables	(7.2)	20.5
Change in working capital	1.2	(10.7)

There were no acquisitions in 2008, and this largely explains the reduction in the cash outflow from investing activities. In both years IMI had surplus cash before financing. In 2008 it was £180.2 million, and in 2007 it was £31.1 million.

In 2007 IMI was re-balancing its capital structure, buying back shares and drawing down loans. The net additional cash flow was insufficient to cover its dividend and interest payments, so in 2007 it decreased its cash and cash equivalents by £29 million. However, you know that it largely funded its acquisitions from the current year's cash flow.

In 2008, whilst it still bought back shares in the first half of the year, it repaid £45.5 million of its loans and after paying interest and dividends increased its cash and cash equivalents by £22.3 million.

6

Other information found in the accounts

Introduction

You'll find that there's other information in the accounts that provides you with some useful insights into a company's financial performance. Firstly you'll find information about a group's different businesses in the segmental analysis. You'll also find information about its:

- accounting for employee benefits, including pensions;
- contingent liabilities;
- commitments for future capital expenditure;
- events after the reporting period;
- transactions with related parties;
- financial risk management;
- the financial review;
- the operating review.

Reading, and understanding, this information improves your understanding of the company's financial performance, as it enables you to see:

- *how well the company has performed in specific areas;*

- *if it could face problems in the future;*

- *whether, and how, the company has changed between the date of the accounts and their publication.*

Segmental analysis

You know that most of the accounts you see are consolidated group accounts. Companies such as IMI have different businesses, and trade throughout the world. The group accounts show you the total picture, but how useful is it? When you're trying to understand a business's performance you want to know *where* the company is making its profits and *where* it's trading. Unless you know that, how can you make a realistic assessment of the risks facing the business and its long-term prospects? You have to have more detailed information about the company's activities and its performance in different markets. You'll find this information in the notes to the income statement. You'll probably find revenue, profits, assets and liabilities analysed between the different businesses and, if it's appropriate, geographically. This analysis is called *segmental reporting*.

The presentation and definition of operating segments are changing during 2009 as part of the convergence process. Companies whose accounting year starts before 1 January 2009 can continue to use IAS 14 (*Segment reporting*), whereas those with accounting years starting after this date will use IFRS 8 (*Operating segments*) which is similar to the US accounting standard. When companies adopt IFRS 8 their reported segments and the information disclosed may, or may not, change. It depends on how they applied IAS 14 in the past. IFRS 8 requires companies to identify their operating segments on the basis of the internal management reports reviewed by their 'chief operating decision maker' when allocating resources to the business and assessing its financial performance. So if their segments reflected their management accounts there will be little change, although segments can now include ones that are primarily involved in internal trading (IAS 14 limited segments to those that earned the majority of their revenue from *external* sales). There is a number of consequences in moving to this 'management approach':

▦ Different companies operating in the same sector will identify different segments and disclose different information. The reporting is driven by their management accounts, and the information may not be comparable. (On the other hand, it will give useful insights into the company's management information and controls.)

▦ IAS 14 determined segments on an audited view of economic risks and returns and then used a similar test to identify the segments shown in the accounts (these are called *reportable segments*).

▦ Segmental information may not be consistent over time, as the segmental information shown in the accounts changes as management reporting changes.

▦ Segmental disclosures are based on internal reporting, and consequently may not reflect IFRS. You've already seen this, as IMI shows its segmental operating profit assuming that all its currency and metals hedges were effective, as it believes that this gives the best measure of the business's underlying operating performance.

Determining reportable operating segments is a two stage process; firstly companies have to identify all of their operating segments, then they have to determine those that they have to show in the accounts. The operating segments are the parts of the business generating revenue and incurring expenses whose results are regularly reviewed by the company's chief operating decision maker and where there is separate financial information available reflecting their activities.

Companies have to disclose separately any segment whose:

▦ reported revenue is more than 10% of the total operating segments' revenue;

▦ reported profit, or loss, is 10% or more of the greater of:

  – the combined profit of all of the profitable operating segments;
  or
  – 10% or more of the greater of the combined loss of all of the loss making operating segments;

▦ assets are more than 10% of the combined assets of all of the operating segments.

The external segmental revenue shown in the accounts must be at least 75% of the company's revenue and this means that some of the segments could be below the 10% threshold. The standard doesn't prescribe the number of segments, although it acknowledges that there may be a practical limit. Consequently it allows homogenous operations to be combined, even if individually they exceed the thresholds. Combined segments must have similar economic characteristics (such as long-term average gross margins, competitive, operating and financial risks), and similar products, production processes, distribution channels and customers.

As the segments follow the management accounts, they could be based on businesses or countries and geographic areas. It all depends on the way that their chief operating decision maker reviews information.

Once the segments have been determined, companies disclose the following information for each of their operating segments:

- general information about each segment;
- revenue (analysed between external revenue and internal inter segment revenue);
- interest revenue and interest expense (this is relevant for financial institutions);
- any material item of revenue or expense;
- depreciation and amortisation and any other material non cash items
- profit or loss;
- the business's share of profits and the amount invested in investments accounted for using the equity method (associates and joint ventures);
- tax;
- capital expenditure (this is probably defined differently from the way it's defined in your organisation, as it comprises additions to non current operating assets – property, plant and equipment, and intangible assets);
- assets;
- liabilities.

Other detailed disclosures of performance and resources are required if the chief operating decision maker regularly reviews them. Companies also have to give some additional geographical information and information about their dependence on major customers:

▨ *Geographical information* – External revenues have to be analysed both by product and geographically. Companies also have to disclose any additions to their non current operating assets geographically.

▨ *Major customers* – If one of a company's customers represents 10%, or more, of its revenue it must disclose this together with the total revenue earned from each major customer together with their operating segment.

As the segmental information may only reflect 75% of the company's revenue, and is based on internal reporting, companies also have to reconcile the segmental information with information shown in the financial statements.

Business segments using IAS 14

Companies with financial years starting before January 2009 can continue to use the old accounting standard, IAS 14. This requires companies to identify two sets of segments (business and geographical) using a risks and rewards approach, with the business's internal reporting system providing the starting point for identifying the segments. One set of segments is regarded as 'primary', disclosing more information, and the other 'secondary'. If the business's risks and returns are primarily affected by differences in its products or services, its primary reporting format will be its business segments. If different countries, or geographical areas, predominantly affect the business's risks and returns, its primary reporting format will be geographical. The starting point for determining the predominant influence on the business's risks and returns is the business's management structure and reporting systems, so there may not be significant differences in the segments identified using the two accounting standards. (IFRS 8 requires the information shown in the accounts to be the measure reported to the management, whereas segmental information shown under IAS 14 follows IFRS rather than management accounting. You'll see this when you look at IMI's note on segmental reporting. It has adopted the new accounting rule in its 2008 accounts, and include economic hedge contract gains and losses in its segmental operating profit, as this is the way it's reported in their management accounts.)

There are different levels of disclosure required for primary and secondary segments. The disclosures required for the primary segments disclose the same information required by IFRS 8 and are shown in the bulleted list above. The disclosures for the secondary reporting segments include the segment's revenue, assets and capital expenditure. Companies don't have to disclose the profits for their secondary segments.

 Most companies have to disclose segmental information in the notes to their accounts. The Companies Act requires that all companies disclose their turnover and profit, or loss, before tax for each class of business and each geographical market that differs substantially from one another. All public and large private companies are required to give more information by SSAP 25 (*Segmental reporting*). However, the Companies Act exempts companies from giving segmental information if their directors believe its disclosure would be 'seriously prejudicial'.

Companies have to disclose both product based segments and geographical segments where the turnover (*external sales*), or the profit and loss, or the net assets are 10%, or more, of the total. (This analysis only has to be given for associated undertakings, when their profit and loss or their net assets are 20%, or more, of the total.) They disclose their turnover, profits (or losses) before tax, and operating assets (this is net operating assets: the operating assets less the operating liabilities) by class of business and geographical segment.

Whilst segmental information is very useful you can't always rely on being able to use this information in your analysis, as even using UK GAAP companies can change their reporting to reflect changes in their business.

IMI's note on segmental analysis

IMI used IFRS 8 in its 2008 accounts, a year earlier than required, so its segmental analysis has changed to reflect the presentation shown in its management accounts. It now gives information about segmental restructuring costs and amortisation of acquired intangible assets.

3 Business and geographical segments

The Group has adopted IFRS 8 'Operating segments' in these accounts. Segmental information is presented in the consolidated financial statements for each of the Group's continuing primary operating segments. The operating segment reporting format reflects the Group's management and internal reporting structures. Inter-segment revenue is insignificant. Comparative segmental information is presented on a consistent basis with the exception that information on economic hedge contract costs is not available for 2007 and the cost to develop it would be excessive. Due to the relative stability of currencies in 2007 any impact is not considered to be material.

The Group includes the following five operating segments and activities:

Fluid Controls

Severe Service

Design, manufacture, supply and service of high performance critical control valves and associated equipment for power generation plants, oil & gas producers and other process industries.

Fluid Power

Design, manufacture and supply of motion and fluid control systems, principally pneumatic devices, for original equipment manufacturers in commercial vehicle, life science, print, packaging and other industries.

Indoor Climate

Design, manufacture and supply of indoor climate control systems, principally balancing valves for large commercial buildings and thermostatic radiator valves for residential buildings.

Retail Dispense

Beverage Dispense

Design, manufacture and supply of steel and carbonated beverage dispense systems and associated merchandising equipment for brand owners and retailers.

Merchandising

Design, manufacture and supply of point of purchase display systems for brand owners and retailers.

Information regarding the operations of each reporting segment is included below. Performance is measured based on segmental operating profit before restructuring, Severe Service investigation costs and fines, acquired intangible amortisation and impairment and other income. Segmental operating profit is also reported as if economic currency and metals hedges were effective for financial reporting purposes. This measure gives a more meaningful indication of the underlying performance of the segments because either the quantum, the one-off nature, or volatility of these items would otherwise distort underlying trading performance. Business segments enter into forward currency and metal contracts to provide economic hedges against the impact on profitability of swings in rates and values in accordance with the Group's policy to minimise the risk of volatility in revenues, costs and margins. Business segmental operating profits are therefore charged/credited with the impact of these settled contracts. In accordance with IAS 39, these contracts do not meet the technical provisions required for hedge accounting and gains and losses are recorded in net financial income and expense.

	Segmental revenue		Segmental operating profit	
	2008	2007	2008	2007 restated
	£m	£m	£m	£m
Fluid Controls	1,390	1,140	217.8	163.8
Severe Service	443	362	81.3	55.9
Fluid Power	666	571	91.3	75.4
Indoor Climate	281	207	45.2	32.5
Retail Dispense	507	459	48.5	44.0
Beverage Dispense	305	285	27.6	24.8
Merchandising	202	174	20.9	19.2
Segmental result	1,897	1,599	266.3	207.8

Reconciliation of reported segmental revenue and operating profit

	Revenue		Profit	
	2008	2007	2008	2007
	£m	£m	£m	£m
Segmental result	1,897	1,599	266.3	207.8
Restructuring costs			(19.6)	(22.0)
Severe Service investigation costs and fines			(26.3)	(4.9)
Acquired intangible amortisation and impairment			(13.2)	(10.9)
Other income			–	1.7
Economic hedge contract gains and losses	4	–	2.6	–
Total revenue/operating profit reported	1,901	1,599	209.8	171.7
Net financial expense			–	(0.7)
Profit before tax			176.0	171.0

Balance sheet

	Segment assets		Segment liabilities	
	2008	2007	2008	2007
	£m	£m	£m	£m
Fluid Controls	**1,067.6**	834.0	**324.6**	249.4
Severe Service	378.9	284.6	140.0	96.7
Fluid Power	529.2	413.1	121.7	103.4
Indoor Climate	159.5	136.3	62.9	49.3
Retail Dispense	**319.0**	258.8	**89.3**	72.8
Beverage Dispense	175.4	130.3	56.0	41.5
Merchandising	143.6	128.5	33.3	31.3
Total	**1,386.6**	1,092.8	**413.9**	322.2

Reconciliation of segment assets and liabilities to Group balance sheet

	Assets		Liabilities	
	2008	2007	2008	2007
	£m	£m	£m	£m
Segment assets and liabilities	1,386.6	1,092.8	413.9	322.2
Corporate items	21.6	14.4	104.4	71.9
Employee benefits	2.4	1.3	139.5	64.9
Investments	17.8	14.4	–	–
Net borrowings	123.9	106.5	422.6	339.6
Net taxation and others	59.4	39.1	69.6	57.0
Per group balance sheet	**1,611.7**	1,268.5	**1,150.0**	855.6

Other information

	Restructuring costs		Capital expenditure		Depreciation and amortisation	
	2008	*2007*	*2008*	*2007*	*2008*	*2007*
	£m	*£m*	*£m*	*£m*	*£m*	*£m*
Fluid Controls	12.3	14.5	44.5	41.1	39.9	39.6
Severe Service	0.9	0.1	10.6	9.0	9.8	11.6
Fluid Power	10.0	14.1	25.1	26.0	22.9	21.7
Indoor Climate	1.4	0.3	8.8	6.1	7.2	6.3
Retail Dispense	7.3	7.5	9.2	11.4	12.9	9.5
Beverage Dispense	4.4	7.1	6.5	7.6	6.8	4.4
Merchandising	2.9	0.4	2.7	3.8	6.1	5.1
Total continuing operations	19.6	22.0	53.7	52.5	52.8	49.1
Corporate	–	–	0.3	0.6	0.7	0.7
Total operations	19.6	22.0	54.0	53.1	53.5	49.8

Revenue by geographical destination

	2008	2007
	£m	*£m*
UK	183	188
Germany	266	209
Rest of Europe	533	423
USA	517	460
Asia/Pacific	249	202
Rest of world	149	117
Total continuing operations	1,897	1, 599
Economic hedge contract gains and losses	4	–
Total	1,901	1,599

Segmental analysis of non current assets by geographical origin

	Carrying amount of non current assets	
	2008	2007
	£m	£m
UK	123.3	123.7
Germany	88.9	64.9
Rest of Europe	184.8	138.5
USA	220.8	163.6
Asia/Pacific	40.4	26.1
Rest of world	8.0	5.8
Total continuing operations	666.2	522.6

The results in respect of discontinued operations are set out in note 6.

You can use this information to understand where IMI's revenues and profits are generated, and where they're restructuring and investing. The segmental information tells you some interesting things, some of which I've summarised below:

▦ *Revenue* – Most of its revenue (73% in 2008) comes from the Fluid Controls business, and fluid power alone is 35% of the IMI's 2008 revenue. IMI may be based in the UK, but it's a global business. Europe is IMI's biggest market, representing almost 52% of 2008's revenue, with Germany alone contributing 14%. America is its next biggest market, generating over 27% of revenue in 2008, followed by Asia Pacific, which generated over 13% of its revenue.

▦ *Profit* – Fluid Controls makes the most profit (82% of the 2008 profit), with Fluid Power representing 34% of IMI's 2008 profit.

▦ *Profit margin* (operating profit/revenue) – The best operating margin is in Severe Service, which had an operating margin of 18.4% in 2008. Beverage dispense has the lowest margin in 2008 of 9.0%.

■ *Return on capital invested* – You'll see when I analyse IMI's four-year performance that I've looked at the return on capital for each of the segments (although the numbers aren't perfectly comparable because of the change in reporting). To calculate this I've deducted the liabilities from the assets to arrive at each business's net assets. The best return on capital is in Indoor Climate, which had a return of nearly 47%, and the worst was Merchandising with a return of just under 19%.

Employee benefits

The accounting standard IAS 19 (*Employee benefits*) identifies four types of employee benefits:

■ **Short-term employee benefits** – These include wages, salaries, holiday entitlement, sick leave, profit-sharing and bonuses and non-monetary benefits such as private healthcare, company cars, subsidised goods or services. These are charged to the income statement as the employee earns the benefits.

■ **Termination benefits** – These can only be recognised when the company has a detailed formal plan, with no realistic possibility of withdrawing, from either:

– making employees redundant

or

– offering a package in order to encourage voluntary redundancy.

Any benefits that are due after 12 months have to be discounted to their present value.

■ **Post-employment benefits** – Such as pensions, other retirement benefits, post-employment life insurance and post-employment medical care, which I'll discuss fully below.

■ **Other long-term employee benefits** – These include sabbatical leave, long-term disability benefits. The accounting treatment of long-term employee benefits is similar to post-employment benefits (see below), with actuarial gains and losses and past service cost recognised immediately in the income statement.

I'd like to consider accounting for pensions in more detail, where I'll be focusing on accounting for final salary pension schemes.

Accounting for post-employment benefits

The main post-employment benefits companies offer to employees are pensions, and whilst pensions accounting appears esoteric, the way companies account for pensions has a significant effect on their reported financial performance. Consequently you need to understand some of the more important principles of pension accounting if you want to interpret a set of accounts.

Different types of company pension scheme

Pension schemes can be classified in two ways:

▓ Firstly, whether they're funded, or not. In a funded scheme companies make payments to a separate pension fund holding the fund's assets. However, many overseas pension schemes are 'unfunded'. This means that the company has a large pension provision in its accounts, as it doesn't make any payments to a separate fund.

▓ Secondly, by the type of pension offered to employees. Pension schemes can be classified as:

– A *money purchase,* or *defined contributions,* scheme. The contributions are invested and the employee's pension is determined by the scheme's investment performance. If the investment performance is poor, the employee's pension is poor.

– A *final salary,* or *defined benefits,* scheme. The employee is entitled to receive a proportion of his salary on retirement that is totally unrelated to the scheme's investment performance. If the scheme under performs, the company has to make additional contributions to honour its obligations to the employee. The recent poor performance in the stock market, coupled with past 'pension holidays', has led to many companies either closing these schemes to new employees, or converting them into money purchase schemes. The risk in a final salary scheme lies with the employer.

Now just think about money purchase schemes and defined benefit schemes for a moment. Pension costs are staff costs and have to be charged to the income statement as the employee earns the benefits. Now, accounting for money purchase schemes is simple – the employer's contributions in the period are charged to the income statement.

But it's difficult to work out the employer's cost in final salary schemes, as there are so many variables that interrelate with one another, including:

- the employees' final, or average, salary – this determines the size of the pension they'll receive in the future;

- their remaining lifetime as a pensioner – this determines how long the pension will be paid;

- the returns that will be made on the fund's investments – this determines the balance between the payments to the fund and the fund's eventual value.

If you think about it, the pension costs in a final salary scheme can only be accurately determined when the scheme is wound up. But that's not an acceptable accounting option – companies have to make a charge to the income statement for the cost of providing pensions as they're benefiting from the employee's services. So companies have to find a way to predict both the pension benefits and the investment returns. This is calculated by an actuarial valuation, which must be kept up to date and is usually done every three years. The actuarial valuation:

- determines the size of the fund needed to meet its obligations;

- assesses whether the fund is in surplus or deficit;

- accounts for the surplus, or the deficit, in calculating the pension cost for the period;

- determines the scheme's contribution rate.

I'll take you through these in more detail later. Now, once actuaries have found a way to spread the cost of providing the pension over the working lives of the employees, the pension cost can be charged to the income statement. But what should you do if the fund is in deficit? In a final salary scheme, the employer guarantees a pension regardless of the fund's investment performance. If the fund can't meet its obligations the employer has to make up the shortfall. This means that the employer is ultimately responsible for the employee's pension. This means that a pension fund deficit shows on an employer's balance sheet as a liability.

The first thing the actuaries have to do is to determine the size of the fund that's needed to meet the fund's obligations.

The size of the fund

It's actually quite complicated to determine this, as you have to start by making some assumptions based on the answers to the following questions:

▦ How many staff will stay with the scheme until they retire?

▦ When will they retire?

▦ What will they be earning when they retire?

▦ How will the fund perform until they retire?

▦ How long will the employees live after they've retired?

▦ Will the fund's return be large enough to cover its liabilities?

Actuaries then carry out valuations to determine the size of the fund needed to meet the pension liabilities. The fund is then discounted to its present value, and IAS 19 requires companies to use the yield on high quality corporate bonds (whilst this isn't defined it's understood to be those that are rated at least AA) as the discount rate. (It effectively assumes that the pension funds are invested entirely in corporate bonds and ties the value of the fund to current bond yields. While some schemes are heavily invested in corporate bonds, most schemes have a mix of assets and tend to rely heavily on stock market investments.) If you've ever done any present value calculations you all know that it's precise (lots of decimal places), but not necessarily accurate. It's very vulnerable to the underlying assumptions, which is why they have to be disclosed in the notes to the accounts. But it's also affected by the discount rate: the bigger the discount rate the lower the present value. Now I'm writing this in 2009, when we're right in the middle of the 'credit crunch'. Investors have become more risk averse and are demanding higher interest rates on corporate bonds, particularly those in the financial services sector. This has increased the yield on corporate bonds. If the pension fund was fully invested in corporate bonds, as some are, it wouldn't be a problem. However most funds invest in shares, commercial property and bonds. All of these have gone down in value,

but the fund's valuation is only linked to the bond yield. This means that pension liabilities are appearing to shrink at the same time as world financial markets are in a state of turmoil and investment returns are falling! A recent study reveals that the pension liabilities of the UK's 350 biggest companies are understated by about £160 billion because of the discount rates used.

If you read the accounts, the notes on employee benefits will disclose firstly the mix of assets held in the fund, and then secondly the sensitivity to changes in assumptions. Here's IMI's in 2008:

e) Market value by category of assets at 31 December

	2008				2007			
	UK	Overseas post employment	Overseas non-post employment	Total	UK	Overseas post employment	Overseas non-post employment	Total
	£m	£m	£m	£m	£m	£m	£m	£m
Equities	413.1	36.6	–	449.7	583.1	28.1	–	611.2
Bonds	352.1	61.6	–	413.7	339.0	47.9	–	386.9
Property	49.6	2.6	–	52.2	32.3	5.1	–	37.4
Other	23.0	19.6	–	42.6	76.8	11.7	–	88.5
Total	837.8	120.4	–	958.2	1,031.2	92.8	–	1,124.0

j) Sensitivities

The balance sheet liability is sensitive to changes in the assumptions used to place a value on the defined benefit obligation, in particular to the discount rate and the implied life expectancy, and to changes in the market value of the fund's assets, in particular to equity market movements. As set out in 20 (a) above the IMI Pension Fund constitutes around 80% of the total liabilities and 87% of the total assets of the Group's long-term employee benefit arrangements as at 31 December 2008. It is therefore appropriate to consider the sensitivities to changes in key assumptions in respect of the fund and these are illustrated below.

Increase in defined benefit liability as at 31 December 2008

	£m
Discount rate 0.1% pa lower*	14
Increase of one year in life expectancy from age 65*	25
10% fall in equity markets*	40

*in each case all other assumptions are unchanged

You can see that in 2008 IMI's funds represent a balanced portfolio, with only 43% of their funds invested in bonds, 47% in equities, with the balance invested in property and other investments. The valuation of its funds was sensitive to changes in the discount rate, life expectancy assumptions and equity markets. The most important sensitivity factor is the discount rate, as a 1% change in the discount rate increases the pension deficit by £140 million.

The notes disclose the actuarial assumptions, which historically have been seen as very conservative (tending to overestimate salary increases and underestimate the fund's performance). These are long-term assumptions, which actually look quite optimistic in the light of the current market turmoil so it's not surprising that IMI's actual return in 2008 was less than the expected return.

You can see this in the extract from IMI's disclosures on its pension schemes:

	Weighted averages					
	31 Dec 2008		31 Dec 2007		31 Dec 2006	
	UK	Overseas	UK	Overseas	UK	Overseas
	% pa	% pa	% pa	% pa	% pa	% pa
Inflation rate	2.8	2.2	3.3	2.2	3.0	1.7
Discount rate	6.5	4.9	5.9	4.9	5.1	4.2
Expected rate of salary increases [1]	4.0	2.8	5.0	2.9	4.7	2.8
Rate of pension increases [2]	2.8	0.5	3.3	0.5	3.0	0.6
Rate of increase for deferred pensions[2]	2.8	0.5	3.3	0.5	3.0	0.6
Medical cost trend rate [3]	n/a	5.0	n/a	5.0	n/a	5.0
Expected return on equities	7.9	7.0	7.8	6.9	7.8	6.2
Expected return on bonds	5.8	3.9	4.9	4.0	4.7	3.5
Expected return on property	7.0	4.9	6.6	4.9	n/a	4.0
Expected return on other assets	3.8	2.5	4.5	3.3	4.2	2.5
Overall expected return on assets[4]	6.9	4.7	6.6	4.8	6.8	4.5

[1] includes a 0.2%pa as the average effect of the age by age promotional scale for UK.
[2] in excess of any Guaranteed Minimum Pension (GMP) for UK.
[3] initial rate of 8.5%pa (9.0%pa in 2007, 9.5%pa in 2006) reducing by 0.5%pa each year to 5%pa. Assumed healthcare cost trend rates do not have a significant effect on the amount of recognised in the income statement or the obligations.
[4] based on the distribution of assets set out below.

The charge to the income statement

As you know, the income statement uses the accruals principle and consequently is charged with the cost of providing pensions over the period that the company benefits from the employees' services. This means that the accounting charge for pensions can be very different from the cash cost of funding the pension schemes. For example, in 2008 IMI paid £16.8 million additional contributions into the defined benefits pension scheme to help to reduce the deficit. Whereas, the charge to the income statement disclosed in the notes was:

b) Components of the pension expense recognised in the income statement for the year ended 31 December

	2008				2007			
	UK	Overseas post employment	Overseas non-post employment	Total	UK	Overseas post employment	Overseas non-post employment	Total
	£m	£m	£m	£m	£m	£m	£m	£m
From defined benefit schemes								
Current service cost	7.8	4.9	1.4	14.1	12.2	4.4	0.9	17.5
Interest cost (in financial expense)	59.9	7.1	0.8	67.8	53.2	5.3	0.6	59.1
Expected return on assets (in financial income)	(66.6)	(5.0)	–	(71.6)	(66.5)	(3.1)	–	(69.6)
Past service costs	–	0.3	0.5	0.8	–	–	0.5	0.5
Recognition of gains	–	–	(1.0)	(1.0)	–	–	(0.1)	(0.1)
Settlement/curtailment	–	(0.1)	(1.9)	(2.0)	–	(0.3)	–	(0.3)
Total defined benefit pension expense	1.1	7.2	(0.2)	8.1	(1.1)	6.3	1.9	7.1
Pension expense from defined contribution schemes	0.8	4.8	–	5.6	0.6	5.9	–	6.5
Total pension expense	1.9	12.0	(0.2)	13.7	(0.5)	12.2	1.9	13.6

Pension expenses have been recognised within operating costs except where shown.

Let me explain each of these and some of the other things that may be charged to the income statement:

▨ *The current service cost* – This is the charge based on the actuarial assumptions.

▨ *Past service costs* – These arise if the company improves the benefits it offers to employees.

▨ *Interest cost* – This represents the increase in the period of the present value of the obligation because the benefits are now one year closer to settlement. It is simply calculated by multiplying the chosen discount rate by the present value of the obligation in the period. This may be shown in other financial expense or as part of operating costs.

▨ *Expected return on the pension fund's assets* – This is the fund's expected return using the actuarial assumptions. This may be shown in other financial income or in the operating costs. Unless the pension fund is invested in corporate bonds this is likely to be much larger than the interest cost, as the bond rate is likely to be lower than the planned return on the fund's assets. (Shares have a higher risk and should theoretically offer a better return.) You can see this when you look at IMI's 2008 accounts; its financial cost arising from its defined benefit liabilities was £67.8 million, whereas the expected return on its pension plan assets was £71.6 million. A net return of £3.8 million.

▨ *Actuarial gains and losses* – This is the difference between the fund's actual performance and its expected performance (called *experience gains*) and the effect of any changes in the actuarial assumptions (for example companies have had to amend their assumptions to reflect that we will live longer in retirement than previous pensioners). If you deduct the experience gains from the expected return, you have the fund's actual return.

Not all of these have to be recognised, as IAS 16 allows companies to only take *some* of these into the income statement. I need to explain what I mean by 'some'. The international standard takes the view that, in the long-term, actuarial gains and losses could offset one another. Consequently it currently allows three policies that companies can use:

– *The corridor approach* – As long as the actuarial gains and losses remain within 10% they don't have to show them in the income statement. However, when they are above 10% they are shown in the income statement – but only to the extent that they are greater than 10%. (Now you know it's unlikely to be that simple – the question to ask is '10% of what?' It's currently the greater of the present value of the fund's obligation at the start of the year and the fair value of the fund's assets. (There's a proposal to change this, so that all changes are recognised in the period they occur. However in the discussion paper the IASB is seeking views about where the gains and losses should be recognised.) This means that in practice the gains and losses, or to be more precise a *percentage* of the gains and losses, are recognised in the following year, as they're based on the fund's valuation at the start of the year not the end. This is usually spread over the average remaining working lives of both current and former employees to determine the charge to the current period's income statement. Companies using this approach defer the recognition of gains and losses within the 10% corridor. (This is important, as if they're unrecognised they're not shown in the accounts although they are disclosed in the notes.) The standard allows the corridor approach as the IASB recognises that the interrelationship of the underlying assumptions makes it difficult to measure the company's obligation precisely and the valuation represents an estimate which really represents a range around the best estimate. The size of the deficit, or surplus, can change rapidly from one year to next affecting companies' retained earnings, distributable profits and dividend policies. However, the corridor approach may disappear as part of the convergence process, and the IASB has already issued a discussion paper suggesting full and immediate recognition of actuarial gains and losses.

- *Faster recognition* – Companies can charge more than the current year's proportion of all of the actuarial gains, as IAS 19 allows any systematic method that results in faster recognition of actuarial gains and losses as long as it is applied to gains and losses, and consistently applied from one period to another. If they use a faster method, the actuarial gains and losses are shown in the income statement.
- *Full recognition* – The final option is to recognise all of the actuarial gains and losses attributable to the current period. In this case, companies can show the actuarial gains and losses either in profit or loss or in the statement of recognised income and expense (comprehensive income). Most UK companies recognise them as other comprehensive income, as this reflects the UK's accounting requirement. If companies choose to recognise actuarial gains and losses in other comprehensive income, this policy must be applied to all defined benefit plans and all actuarial gains and losses.

This approach makes the disclosures in the notes to the accounts easier to follow, stabilises the pension costs charged to the income statement, and reported earnings per share, but also volatises the value of the equity reported on the balance sheet.

The choice of approach has been influenced by historical practice and whether the company prefers a stable profit figure (full recognition) or balance sheet (the corridor approach or faster recognition).

▧ *Settlements and curtailments* – Settlements could arise from buying out the employees' rights and curtailments arise when the company has a redundancy programme.

The effect on the balance sheet

Most companies show both retirement benefit net assets and liabilities on their balance sheets. IMI shows an asset of £2.4 million and a liability of £139.5 million, which equates to the deficit of £137.1 million.

The surpluses and deficits shown on the balance sheet include any actuarial gains and losses that haven't been recognised in the income statement, as it shows the value of the fund's assets and liabilities at the end of the year. The £2.4 million is clearly not the value of the post-retirement fund's assets; it represents the amount that the employer benefits from a surplus plus any unrecognised actuarial losses and past service costs. (The employer benefits from surpluses in the form of reduced future contributions, or a refund from the scheme, or a combination of the two. These have to be discounted to their present value.) The accounting standard imposes an 'asset ceiling', to ensure that any asset shown doesn't exceed the future economic benefits it represents to the business. So the £2.4 million is the present value of the future benefits that IMI will be able to realise from its post-retirement surpluses.

The notes also tell you more information about the surplus or deficit. A surplus arises when the fund's value is greater than the amount it needs to satisfy its liabilities. Given the conservatism of the actuarial assumptions, in the past when investment returns outpaced wage inflation it was relatively easy for a pension fund to be in surplus. Unfortunately, this trend has now reversed and most companies' pension funds are in deficit, as recent poor investment returns are shrinking fund values at a time when many staff are electing to take early retirement options in restructuring programmes.

Here's an extract from the notes to IMI's 2008 accounts that shows you how its deficit was calculated (I've highlighted the numbers shown on the balance sheet):

Reconciliation to the balance sheet as at 31 December

	2008				2007			
	UK	Overseas post employment	Overseas non-post employment	Total	UK	Overseas post employment	Overseas non-post employment	Total
Funded schemes in surplus:	£m	£m	£m	£m	£m	£m	£m	£m
Fair value of assets	–	21.4	–	21.4	–	61.2	–	61.2
Present value of defined benefit obligation	–	(17.4)	–	(17.4)	–	(56.4)	–	(56.4)
	–	4.0	–	4.0	–	4.8	–	4.8
Restriction due to asset ceiling	–	(1.6)	–	(1.6)	–	(3.5)	–	(3.5)
Recognised asset for defined benefit funded schemes	–	2.4	–	2.4	–	1.3	–	1.3
Funded schemes in deficit:								
Fair value of assets	837.8	99.0	–	936.8	1,031.2	31.6	–	1,062.8
Present value of defined benefit obligation	(881.4)	(124.4)	–	(1,005.8)	(1,034.6)	(38.1)	–	(1,072.7)
Present value of obligation for unfunded schemes	–	(55.2)	(15.3)	(70.5)	–	(42.4)	(12.6)	(55.0)
Recognised liabilities for defined benefit obligations	(43.6)	(80.6)	(15.3)	(139.5)	(3.4)	(48.9)	(12.6)	(64.9)
Recognised net liability for defined benefit obligations	(43.6)	(78.2)	(15.3)	(137.1)	(3.4)	(47.6)	(12.6)	(63.6)
Total fair value of assets	837.8	120.4	–	958.2	1,031.2	92.8	–	1,124.0
Total present value of defined benefit obligation	(881.4)	(197.0)	(15.3)	(1,093.7)	(1,034.6)	(136.9)	(12.6)	(1,184.1)
Asset ceiling		(1.6)		(1.6)		(3.5)		(3.5)
Restriction due to asset ceiling				-				-
Recognised net liability for defined benefit obligations	(43.6)	(78.2)	(15.3)	(137.1)	(3.4)	(47.6)	(12.6)	(63.6)

You will also find in the notes an analysis of the change in the present value of the defined benefit obligation and the fair value of the assets detailing the following information.

The present value of the defined benefit obligation:

- The opening present value
- The current service cost
- The past service cost
- Interest cost
- Employee contributions
- Actuarial gains and losses, analysed between those arising from experience, and those arising from changes in assumptions
- Benefit payments
- Settlements or curtailments
- Purchase/sales of businesses
- Currency movements
- The closing present value

The fair value of the assets:

- The opening asset value
- Expected return on assets
- Actuarial gains and losses
- The company's contributions, analysed between normal contributions and any additional contributions
- Employee's contributions
- Benefit payments
- Settlements or curtailments
- Purchase/sales of businesses
- Currency movements
- The closing asset value

The effect on the statement of recognised income and expense (other comprehensive income)

Companies recognising all actuarial gains and losses immediately have the option to take the actuarial gains and losses through the statement of recognised income and expense (other comprehensive income). Most UK companies do this.

 FRS 17 (*Retirement benefits*) has a narrower scope than IAS 19, as it is only concerned with retirement benefits. However, it is broadly similar to IAS 19, with some additional disclosure requirements, but there are some differences and the main ones are:

- Full actuarial valuations, conducted by a professionally qualified actuary, must be made at least every three years. In the intervening period the most recent valuation should be updated at the balance sheet date.
- The pension obligations should be discounted by the AA corporate bond rate that has the same currency and term.

- Actuarial gains and losses must be taken to the statement of total recognised gains and losses in the period in which they arise. FRS 17 does not allow the spreading of actuarial gains and losses.
- The asset, or the liability, shown on the balance sheet is solely the surplus/deficit in the defined benefit pension scheme.

Pension accounting and financial analysis

Pension accounting can have a significant effect on comparative financial analysis as:

■ Firstly, it affects reported operating profit and profit before tax, as companies can decide where they show some of their pension costs:

- Some companies include interest cost and the expected return on the scheme's assets in operating costs, whereas others show them as other financial income and expenses. Normally the expected return should be greater than the interest cost, so this affects the comparability of operating margins. However, it may be relatively small. If IMI had included the interest cost and the expected return in operating costs its operating margin would have increased from 14% to 14.2%.

- Most UK companies recognise all actuarial gains and losses immediately and take them through the statement of recognised income and expense. This means that they don't affect a company's reported profitability, but do affect its equity. Whereas overseas companies often use the 'corridor approach', where some of their actuarial gains and losses are taken through the income statement affecting reported profitability. If they're within the 10% corridor, no actuarial gains and losses affect the income statement, and their equity is also unaffected by the unrecognised gains and losses. However, to the extent that their gains and losses exceed the 10% corridor they are taken directly to the income statement. This may make their profits more volatile if there are significant market movements, changes in bond yields or actuarial assumptions.

■ The pension fund will affect the company's net assets, and its distributable reserves (thus affecting possible dividend payments). Some ratios may have to be adjusted to take account of this.

Contingent liabilities

I briefly mentioned contingencies when I talked about provisions in the earlier chapters covering the income statement and the balance sheet. A contingency is a possible gain or liability that hasn't happened by the balance sheet's date.

IAS 37 (*Provisions, contingent liabilities and contingent assets*) covers the accounting treatment for contingent assets and contingent liabilities. Whilst all provisions are effectively contingent, a contingency differs as it:

■ requires one, or more, events that aren't totally within the business's control to occur to confirm the existence of the contingency;

■ is unable to be classified as a provision within the rules, as it either isn't probable that it will happen, or its cash outflow can't be reliably measured.

Whilst companies don't provide for contingent liabilities, so there's neither a charge to the income statement or a liability on the balance sheet, they have to disclose contingent liabilities in the notes to the accounts unless there's only a remote possibility that the liability will ever be realised. Contingent assets can never be recognised in the financial statements, and can only be disclosed in the notes when it's probable that the company will receive some economic benefits, such as cash, in the future.

You'll find that companies regularly disclose some contingencies (such as bank guarantees, discounted bills, performance bonds), whereas they're reluctant to disclose others. A good example is contingent liabilities arising from court cases. Most companies don't like disclosing them, as they feel that it might jeopardise their position – implying that they believe they'll lose the case. Companies are also unwilling to show the financial effect of a breach of the law, although the disclosure would probably result in it not being seen as a contingency but as a liability. When you read IMI's note on contingencies you'll find that its contingencies are largely related to court cases and guarantees.

 IAS 37 and FRS 12 (*Provisions, contingent liabilities and contingent assets*) were developed at the same time, so there are no significant differences between the two rules.

IMI's note on contingencies

---

27 Contingencies

Following completion of the European Commission investigations into allegations of anti-competitive behaviour in the EU among certain manufacturers of copper tube and copper fittings, the Company has paid fines of £31.3m in February 2005 and £32.8m in January 2007. Both of these fines are the subject of ongoing appeals. In preparing the financial statements, the directors have not anticipated the outcome of either appeal due to the inherent uncertainty of such processes. The copper tube appeal was heard in 2008 and a judgement is expected in the first half of 2009, the copper fittings appeal has yet to be heard.

We expect to reach final agreement in the near future on a settlement with the US Department of Justice in respect of certain irregular payments by our US subsidiary Control Components Inc (CCI) that violated the US Foreign Corrupt Practices Act. An investigation has also been completed into possible incidental breaches of US trade law by CCI. At 31 December 2008 there is a provision for these expected fines and certain related legal costs of £21.5m.

The Korean authorities have recently announced an investigation into the improper payments made to Korean entities. Subject to the foregoing paragraph, at this date, it is not possible to assess the level of any fines, defence or other costs arising from these or any other actions which may be taken in connection with the Severe Service investigation or the timing of any such actions and accordingly no provision has been made for them in these financial statements.

Group contingent liabilities relating to guarantees in the normal course of business and other items amounted to £80m (2007: £56m).

Commitments for future capital expenditure

You'll find a note on capital commitments disclosing the contracted capital expenditure for the following year. This is often a useful note to refer to, as it gives some indication of the company's investment plans and future cash flows.

IMI's note on commitments

You can see that IMI's contracted capital expenditure is unchanged at £9.2 million:

---

26 Commitments

Group contracts in respect of future capital expenditure which had been placed at the balance sheet date amounted to £9.2m (2007: £9.2m).

Events after the reporting period

The accounts tell you about the company on its balance sheet date, but a lot could have happened in the company during the months between taking the snapshot and authorising the accounts for publication. These are called events after the reporting period and are covered by IAS 10 (*Events after the reporting period*).

▨ *Adjusting events* – These give you extra information about conditions that were known about on the balance sheet date. The extra information allows the company to adjust its figures to show a more accurate view. For example, perhaps the company has made a bad debt provision for a customer's account. If the customer goes into administration a month after the date of the balance sheet, the company's view is confirmed. The total amount outstanding would be written off, but it would only be disclosed if it was so large that its disclosure was necessary for the accounts to reflect a true and fair view.

▨ *Non adjusting events* – These occurred after the balance sheet date. They could include acquisitions, disposals, announcing (or starting) a major restructuring programme and share issues. They have to be separately disclosed in the notes to the accounts and the company gives an estimation of their financial effect, where it's possible.

IMI's note on events after the reporting period

---

29 Post balance sheet events

On 1 January 2009 the 19.1% minority interest in Display Technologies LLC, part of the Merchandising group, was acquired by the Group under the terms of the original purchase agreement. Based on the contracted pricing mechanism the cash consideration is expected to be around £20m.

Related party transactions

Relationships between related parties are a normal part of business life. However, dealings between related parties can have a material effect on a company's performance and its financial position. There could be an asset sale, or trading between companies that is controlled by the same group. When these have been made at arm's length and at fair value there's no cause for concern. Unfortunately this isn't always the case. If there is any possibility that transactions have not been fairly conducted, the shareholders have a right to know. The financial statements have to contain sufficient disclosures to make readers aware of the possibility that the company's reported financial position, and its profitability, might have been affected by transactions with related parties.

IAS 24 (*Related party disclosures*) defines related parties, and they include:

- subsidiaries;
- fellow subsidiaries;
- associates;
- joint ventures;
- the businesses and its parent's key management personnel (including close members of their families);
- parties who have control/joint control or significant influence over the business (this can include close family members);
- post-employment benefit plans.

A related party transaction involves the transfer of resources, services or obligations between related parties regardless of whether anything is charged.

IAS 24 requires that all companies should disclose the name of the parent (if it isn't disclosed elsewhere in the accounts), the name of the ultimate controlling party if it's different from the parent, together with the name of the next most senior parent that produces financial statements available for public use, if neither their parent nor the ultimate controlling party does so. These have to be disclosed whether or not any transactions have taken place.

If there had been any related party transactions the company must disclose:

▦ the nature of the related party relationship;

▦ the amount of the transaction;

▦ the amount of any outstanding balances, including:

  – their terms and conditions

  – whether they are secured

  – the nature of the consideration to be provided

  – details of any guarantees;

▦ provisions for bad and doubtful debts and any charge made during the period;

▦ any other information that is necessary to ensure an understanding of the potential effect of the relationship on the financial statements.

 FRS 8 (*Related party disclosures*) is broadly similar to IAS 24. There are however some differences including:

- The related parties include:
  – anyone who actively cooperates with others to exercise either control or influence over the business (these are referred to as 'concert party members');
  – any business that manages, or is managed by, the company under a management contract.
- The related parties names must be disclosed.
- Pension contributions, and disclosures, representing a breach of a legal duty of confidentiality are exempt from disclosures.

IMI's note on related party transactions

---

28 Related party transactions

Transactions between the company and its subsidiaries, which are related parties, have been eliminated on consolidation and are not disclosed in this note.

Certain short term quasi loan arrangements arose from time to time during the year in connection with transactions involving Martin Lamb, the aggregate amount of which did not at any time exceed £1,250, being less than the relevant statutory limits for small transactions of this nature as provided in Section 332 (1) of the Companies Act 1985 and, from 1 October 2007, Section 207 (1) of the Companies Act 2006.

Detailed information concerning directors' emoluments, shareholding, options and retirement benefits are shown in the Remuneration Report on pages 46 to 60.

Directors are considered to be the key management personnel.

Financial risk management disclosures

In Chapter 3 you learnt how companies use hedging to minimise, or eliminate, risks by using hedging instruments such as swaps that move in the opposite direction from an asset's or liability's value. When you're analysing a company, you're interested in the risks it's facing and how it manages them. You'll find a range of disclosures in the accounts explaining some of the risks the company is facing in a long note to the accounts. Whilst this is a long note it's well worth reading, as you'll find information about a company's exposure to risks and what it has put in place to minimise its exposure to these risks. I'll list the information companies have to disclose in this note and select some of IMI's disclosures to show you how useful it can be in financial analysis. In this note companies disclose information about:

- Overview – This tells you who's responsible for managing the business's financial risks and identifies the main risks they are exposed to. Like most companies, IMI's main risks are credit risk, liquidity risk and market risk.

- The company's exposure to each individual risk and a review of how the company manages these risks. IMI's credit risk arises from receivables and cash balances at banks. The note details the company's exposure and quantifies the risks. From this note you learn that:

- Around 4% of its revenue comes from its largest single customer. So if its largest customer failed, IMI wouldn't!

- Surplus cash is deposited with highly rated banks, and the maximum exposure to any one bank was £20 million. So if a bank collapsed, IMI would continue to trade.

- At the end of the year it had undrawn committed borrowing facilities (these are agreed, unused and therefore available for the company to use) of £154 million (up from £60 million in 2007), of which £115 million expires in a year, £3 million in one to two years and £36 million expiring after two years. So it has funds in place if it needs them.

- Its metal purchases in the year were £30 million, so its exposure to movements in commodity prices was relatively low.

- The company's banking covenants are based on net debt to EBITDA and net interest to EBITDA, and they complied with them 'comfortably'.

▦ The main currencies of their assets excluding cash, cash, debt, exchange contracts and net assets. IMI's main currencies are sterling, US dollars and euros.

▦ Interest rate risk profile of financial assets and liabilities, analysed between fixed and variable rates in the companys' main currencies. This analyses their debt and exchange contracts and their assets and exchange contracts, showing the currencies and disclosing whether they're floating or fixed rate. The weighted average fixed interest rate and the weighted average period that it is fixed are also shown in this table.

▦ A term and debt repayment schedule. Their cash and debt is analysed disclosing each individual loan showing:

- the fixed effective interest rate;

- their value shown in the accounts their 'carrying value';

- the total contractual cash flows (these are capital and interest payments);

- an analysis of these cash flows showing how much must be repaid next year, in one to two years time, two to three years, three to four years, four to five years, and in more than five years.

- A table detailing all the financial assets and liabilities and analysing them between those shown at:
  - designated fair value;
  - other derivatives at fair value;
  - available for sale assets;
  - amortised cost;
  - total carrying value;
  - fair value.
- Details of their exposure to credit risk. This:
  - details their financial assets;
  - analyses the trade receivables geographically and by business segment;
  - tells you the percentage of the trade receivables owed by their largest customer. In 2008 it's a food and beverage company that represented 1.2% of IMI's receivables;
  - the impairment loss table I showed you in Chapter 3.
- Details of their exposure to market risk. IMI's key market risks are changes in interest rates, exchange rates and metal costs. It then analyses its sensitivity to any changes in interest rates, sterling and base metal costs, in the table shown below, where you can see that changes in the value of sterling have the largest effect on its reported financial performance.

Sensitivity analysis table

	1% decrease in interest rates	1% increase in interest rates	10% weakening in Sterling	10% strengthening in Sterling	10% increase in base metal costs	10% decrease in base metal costs
	£m	£m	£m	£m	£m	£m
At 31 December 2008						
Impact on income statement gain/(loss)	1.2	(1.2)	16.6	(16.6)	(1.4)	1.4
Impact on equity gain/(loss)	–	–	19.7	(19.7)	–	–
At 31 December 2007						
Impact on income statement gain/(loss)	1.3	(1.3)	17.5	(14.3)	(2.6)	2.6
Impact on equity gain/(loss)	–	–	13.6	(11.1)	–	–

 There are fewer disclosures in accounts prepared under UK GAAP. However, larger companies disclose:

- the company's objectives, policies and strategies for managing risk;
- interest rate risk profile of financial assets and liabilities, analysed between fixed and variable rates in the company's main currencies;
- currency exposures;
- fair values of financial assets and liabilities;
- gains and losses on hedging agreements.

The operating and financial reviews

All companies in the UK, with the exception of small companies, are required by the Companies Act 2006 to publish a business review as part of their directors' report. (This also applies to companies overseas, as the requirement arose from the EU Accounts Modernisation Directive.) The business review should identify the financial and non-financial key performance indicators and comprise:

- a fair review of the company's business;

- a description of the principal risks and uncertainties facing the company;

- a balanced and comprehensive analysis, reflecting the size and complexity of the business, of:

  - the development and performance of the company's business during the financial year;

  - the position of the company's business at the end of the financial year.

Quoted companies have to provide additional information. For example they have to include:

- the main trends and factors that are likely to affect the future development, performance and position of the company's business;

- information about environmental matters, the company's employees, and social and community issues.

Most large companies publish a voluntary operating and financial review containing the same information, which has to be cross-referenced in the directors' report to avoid unnecessary duplication. IMI's cross-referencing in its directors' report is fairly typical:

Business review

Section 417 of the Companies Act 2006 requires the Company to present a business review in this report. The information that fulfils the business review requirements can be found in this report and the following sections of this report. All of the information detailed in these sections is incorporated by reference into this report and is deemed to form part of this report:

- Our goals and how we are achieving them on pages 4 and 5;

- Measuring our business performance on pages 6 and 7;

- Group operating review (including Statement from the Chairman and Chief Executive on pages 8 to 21);

- Financial review on pages 22 to 27; and

- Responsible business on pages 28 to 33.

If you want to understand the company you should always read the operating review, as it identifies:

▨ the main factors influencing both the company as a whole and its various businesses;

▨ the way that these have varied in the past, and are expected to vary in the future.

And also gives you:

▨ a full discussion of the operating results and the business' s dynamics, including the main risks and uncertainties facing the business.

The financial review is also very useful if you prefer words to numbers, as it discusses the financial statements and the company's financial performance. There's a lot of information in IMI's financial review, and this is where you'll discover *why* its revenues and profits increased. You also see how they monitor the business's performance and what financial key performance indicators it uses. I think it's always important to read the financial review if you want to understand the business's financial performance, so you can now read IMI's financial review.

IMI's financial review

The Group has elected to adopt IFR S8 'Operating segments' early and presents the segmental financials in accordance with this new standard. As referred to in note 2 to the financial statements amortisation of internal development costs is now included in segmental operating profit. Economic hedge contract gains and losses are also included in segmental revenues and segmental operating profit. Other accounting policies are consistent with those applied for the year ended 31 December 2007.

In 2008 revenue, segmental operating profit margin and adjusted earnings per share again all showed significant progress over the prior year. Organic revenues were up 5%, excluding the impact of exchange rates and acquisitions.

In Fluid Controls, the Severe Service business continued to trade well with project activity in the oil and gas and power markets remaining firm. Fluid Power performed well overall. However performance in the second half was impacted by a sharp decline in volumes in certain markets including general pneumatics, in-plant automotive and European commercial vehicles resulting from the global economic downturn. The Indoor Climate business continued to deliver good organic growth and also benefited from a strong performance by Pneumatex which was acquired last year. The thermostatic radiator valve business also benefited from increased refurbishment activity in Germany, helped by recent legislation in respect of energy efficiency.

In Retail Dispense, the Beverage Dispense business experienced a sharp reduction in demand in the second half from the major soft drinks bottlers in both North America and Europe. The UK beer market continued to be challenging. Merchandising performed well with a good second half benefiting from strong shipments to a major US supermarket chain.

The Group has continued to make further progress towards its long-term operating margin target of 15%, with the segmental operating profit margin at 14.0% (2007: 13.0%).

Total revenue for the year from continuing operations increased to £1,901m (2007: £1,599m), up 19% or £302m, of which £37m (2%) came from acquisitions, £85m (5%) from organic growth and £179m from a gain on translation reflecting the impact of exchange rate movements.

Segmental operating profit at £266.3m (2007: 207.8m) increased by 28%. Acquisitions accounted for £4.1m of the increase and translational foreign exchange movements positively impacted by £27.0m. The Fluid Controls businesses, Severe Service, Fluid Power and Indoor Climate, accounted for £217.8m (2007: 163.8m) or 82% (2007: 79%) of these profits and the Retail Dispense businesses, Beverage Dispense and Merchandising accounted for £48.5m (2007: £44.0m) or 18% (2007: 21%) of the total.

Interest costs for the year on net borrowings at £16.1m (2007: £12.8m) were covered 17 times (2007: 17 times) by earnings before interest, tax, depreciation, amortisation and impairment and other income of £269.3m (2007: £219.8m).

The net credit from pension fund financing under IAS 19 was £3.8m (2007: £10.5m), income from investments of £0.7m (2007: nil) and a loss arose on the revaluation of financial instruments and derivatives under IAS39 of £22.2m (2007: gain of £1.6m) reflecting the significant volatility in exchange rates during the year. The majority of this adjustment is a non-cash accounting adjustment required under IAS 39 for financial instruments that the Group holds to provide stability of future trading cash flows and does not reflect the underlying trading performance of the Group.

Profit before tax, from continuing operations before restructuring, Severe Service investigation costs and fines, acquired intangible amortisation and impairment, other income and financial instruments excluding economic hedge contract gains and losses at £254.7m (2007: £205.5m) is 24% ahead of the prior year.

We have completed a three year programme to raise the level of the Group's manufacturing undertaken in low cost economies from 25% to about 35%, restructuring costs were £19.6m (2007: £22.0m). The majority of these were in the Fluid Power business, £10.0m (2007: £14.1m) and the Beverage Dispense business, £4.4m (2007: £7.1m). The majority of these costs are redundancy costs but they also include plant transfer, installation and set up costs.

Acquired intangible amortisation and impairment was £13.2m (2007: £10.9m). During the year, the trading performance and order intake levels at Commtech (part of the Indoor Climate business) caused the Group to assess the carrying amount of that business. This assessment resulted in an impairment of £6.0m being recognised in the second half. Profit before tax was £176.0m (2007: £171.0m), an increase of 3% over the prior year.

Additional months of the Kloehn and Pneumatex businesses, which were both acquired in 2007, together contributed revenue of £37m and operating profit of £4.1m.

A summary of the major changes in revenue and profit over each six month period compared to the prior period is as follows:

	Revenue	PBTRA*	PBT**
	£m	£m	£m
First half			
2007	781	93.8	76.8
Effects of currency translation	59	9.5	9.5
Acquisitions/disposals	23	1.9	1.9
Organic growth	48	15.1	15.1
Net interest cost		(2.7)	(2.7)
Other financing items		(3.4)	(3.4)
Financial instruments excluding economic hedge contract gains and losses			1.1
Restructuring costs			5.3
Investigation costs and fines			(2.7)
Acquired intangible amortisation and impairment			2.8
2008	911	114.2	103.7

	Revenue £m	PBTRA* £m	PBT** £m
Second half			
2007	818	111.7	94.2
Effects of currency translation	120	17.5	17.5
Acquisitions/disposals	11	2.2	2.2
Organic growth	37	12. 3	12.3
Net interest cost		(0.6)	(0.6)
Other financing items		(2.6)	(2.6)
Financial instruments excluding economic hedge contract gains and losses			(22.3)
Restructuring costs			(2.9)
Investigation costs and fines			(18.7)
Acquired intangible amortisation and impairment			(5.1)
Other income			(1.7)
Economic hedge contract gains and losses	4		
2008	990	140.5	72.3
Year	1,901	254.7	176.0

* Profit before tax from continuing operations before restructuring, investigation costs and fines, acquired intangible amortisation and impairment, other income and financial instruments excluding economic hedge contract gains and losses.
** Continuing operations profit before tax.

Half-year analysis

The comparison for the first and second halves of the year is as follows:

	Change %	2008 £m	2007 restated £m
Revenue			
First half	+17	911	781
Second half	+21	990	818
	+19	1,901	1,599
Segmental Operating profit			
First half	+28	120.6	94.1
Second half	+28	145.7	113.7
	+28	266.3	207.8
PBTRA*			
First half	+22	114.2	93.8
Second half	+26	140.5	111.7
	+24	254.7	205.5
Restructuring costs			
First half		(5.6)	(10.9)
Second half		(14.0)	(11.1)
		(19.6)	(22.0)
Other			
First half			
Severe Service investigation costs and fines		(2.7)	–
Second half			
Severe Service investigation costs and fines		(23.6)	(4.9)
Other income		–	1.7
		(26.3)	(3.2)
Acquired intangible amortisation and impairment			
First half		(3.5)	(6.3)
Second half		(9.7)	(4.6)
		(13.2)	(10.9)

Financial instruments excluding economic hedge contract gains and losses			
First half		1.3	0.2
Second half		(20.9)	1.4
		(19.6)	1.6
Profit before tax			
First half	+35	103.7	76.8
Second half	−23	72.3	94.2
	+3	176.0	171.0

* Profit before tax from continuing operations before restructuring, investigation costs and fines, acquired intangible amortisation and impairment, other income and financial instruments excluding economic hedge contract gains and losses.

Taxation

The effective tax rate for the year on profit before tax was maintained at 31% after adjusting for the Severe Service investigation costs and fines (2007: 31%). Before this adjustment the effective tax rate was 34%. The reductions in the UK and German corporate tax rates that became effective in 2008 have had a beneficial impact but this was offset by an increase in the effective tax rate for our Severe Service business. After taxation of £60.0m (2007: £53.0m) the profit on continuing operations was £116.0m (2007: £118.0), a decrease of 2%.

Earnings per share

Basic earnings per share (EPS) was maintained at 35.4p (2007: 35.4p). The Board considers that a more meaningful indication of the underlying performance of the Group is provided by adjusting the basic EPS on continuing operations to state earnings before the after tax cost of restructuring, Severe Service investigation costs and fines, acquired intangible amortisation and impairment, other income, and financial instruments excluding economic hedge contract gains and losses. Details of this calculation are given on pages 82 to 83. On this basis the adjusted EPS from continuing operations was 54.1p, an increase of 29% over last year's 41.9p.

Cash flow

The Group's cash flow statement is shown on page 64. The change in net debt is summarised in the table below. The cash flow from continuing operations was £238m (2007: £160m). This represents a conversion rate of segmental operating profit after restructuring costs into operating cash flow of 97%. Capital expenditure on property, plant and equipment amounted to £48m (2007: £50m) which was equivalent to 1.1 times depreciation (2007: 1.4 times). Expenditure on research and development in the year was £38m (2007: £31m), of this amount development costs capitalised in the year were £5m (2007: £3m).

After payment of interest and tax, the free cash flow generated from operations was £168m (2007: £110m) and, after paying the additional pension contribution, free cash flow before corporate activity was £151m (2007: 61m). The dividends paid during the year totalled £66m (2007: £64m), which were covered 2.3 times by this cash flow. The conversion of foreign currency borrowings at the year end resulted in an increase of £133m (2007: £13m) in reported net debt.

Net debt at the year end was £299m (2007: £233m). The year end net debt to EBITDA ratio was 1.1.

	2008 £m	2007 £m
EBITDA*	269.3	219.8
Working capital requirements	1.2	(10.7)
Capital expenditure	(47.6)	(49.9)
Capitalised development costs	(5.1)	(3.2)
Capital sales/other	20.5	3.6
Operating cash flow (continuing)	238.3	159.6
Tax paid	(54.4)	(37.1)
Interest paid (net)	(15.9)	(12.7)
	168.0	109.8
European Commission fine	-	(32.8)
Additional pension scheme funding	(16.8)	(15.6)
Free cash flow before corporate activity	151.2	61.4
Acquisitions and disposals net of cash acquired including acquired debt	-	(50.2)
Dividends paid to equity shareholders	(66.2)	(63.9)
Dividends paid to minorities/other	(2.4)	(2.4)
Purchase of shares (net)	(14.8)	(84.6)
Currency translation	(133.4)	(13.0)
Change in net debt	(65.6)	(152.7)
Opening net debt	(233.1)	(80.4)
Closing net debt	(298.7)	(233.1)

* Earnings before interest, tax, depreciation, amortisation and impairment, and other income.

At the end of 2008 the US loan notes totalled £201m, with a weighted average maturity of 6.7 years and unsecured bank loans totalled £221m. In early 2008 $100m of the US loan notes maturing in 2009 were refinanced out to 2018 with a further $50m added to this tranche. £50m of bilateral bank facilities were also extended to 2011. In addition £125m of new banking facilities were agreed during the year and a further £25m facility was agreed in January 2009.

Share buybacks

In the first half of 2008, the Company bought back to be held in treasury 3.1m (2007: 17.2m) of its shares at a cost of £14.8m (2007: £93.3m) and in the second half 0.6m shares were purchased at a cost of £1.9m to be held in employee benefit trust for management share based incentive plans.

No further shares were repurchased in the second half as the Board determined it was sensible to maintain a strong balance sheet in the context of the global economic downturn.

Dividend

The Board has recommended a final dividend of 12.7p, maintained at last year's level. This makes a total dividend for the year of 20.7p, an increase of 2%. The total cost of the final dividend is expected to be £40m, giving a total cost of £66m in respect of the year ended 31 December 2008. Dividend cover based on adjusted earnings is 2.6 times.

Pensions

The IMI Pension Fund remains the largest employee benefit obligation within the Group. Like many other UK companies, the Fund is very mature having significantly more pensioners and deferred pensioners than active participating members.

The Group completed the triennial actuarial valuation of the UK defined benefit pension plan as at 31 March 2008. This valuation resulted in a funding deficit of £118m. A recovery plan has been agreed with the pension fund Trustee that requires additional cash contributions from the company of £16.8m each year until July 2016. The first of these additional contributions was made in December 2008. The funding position will be reviewed again no later than March 2011 and should there no longer be a funding deficit, these additional contributions would cease.

The IAS 19 deficit at 31 December 2008 for the Group's employee defined benefit pension plans was £137m, up from £64m in the prior year. The increase was mainly due to changes in the market value in the underlying assets of the scheme.

Treasury policy

IMI's centralised Treasury function provides treasury services to Group companies including funding liquidity, credit, foreign exchange, interest rate and base metal commodity management. It ensures that the Group operates within Board approved guidelines in order to minimise the major financial risks and provide a stable financial base. The use of financial instruments and derivatives is permitted where the effect is to minimise risk to the Group. Compliance with approved policies is monitored through a control and reporting system.

There have been no changes in the year or since the year end to the major financial risks to the Group or the way in which they are managed.

Foreign exchange and interest rate risk

Further information on how the Group manages its exposure to these financial risks is shown in note 19 to the financial statements. The translation impact on the 2008 segmental operating profit was an improvement of £27.0m. The most important foreign currencies for the Group remain the Euro and the US Dollar. If current exchange rates of US $1.44 and €1.13 had been applied to our 2008 results, it is estimated that both revenue and segmental operating profit would have been 15% higher. The relevant rates of exchange for the year were:

	Average		At 31 December	
	2008	2007	2008	2007
Euro	1.26	1.46	1.03	1.36
US dollar	1.85	2.00	1.44	1.99

Return on capital employed

Return on capital employed, defined as operating profit before acquired intangible amortisation and impairment as a percentage of closing net assets, was 48% (2007: 44%). This equates to a post tax return of 33% (2007: 31%) at the underlying tax rate of 31% (2007: 31%).

Economic value added

Economic value added is defined as the net operating profit after tax (NOPAT) on continuing operations before restructuring costs less a capital charge. The capital charge is arrived at by applying the after tax weighted average cost of capital (WACC) to the average invested capital (net assets plus net debt, but net debt excludes the IAS 19 pension deficit). For 2008 the net operating profit before restructuring costs, but after charging £26.3m Severe Service investigation costs and fines, was £229.4m and after tax the NOPAT was £151.2m. The Group's invested capital at the beginning of 2008 was £646.0m, comprising £412.9m of net assets and £233.1m of net debt. The equivalent amounts at the end of 2008 were £760.4m, £461.7m of net assets and £298.7m of net debt. The average invested capital was £703.2m. Applying the 2008 WACC of 8% to the invested capital gives a charge of £56.3m. The economic value added in 2008 was £94.9m, representing an increase of 8% over the 2007 economic value added of £88.0m.

Going concern

The Group's business activities, together with the factors likely to affect its future development, performance and position are set out in the Group Operating Review on pages 8 to 21. The financial position of the Group, its cash flows, liquidity position and borrowing facilities are described in this Financial Review. In addition, note 19 to the financial statements includes the Group's objectives, policies and processes for managing its capital; its financial risk management objectives; details of its financial instruments and hedging activities; and its exposures to credit risk and liquidity risk.

The Group has considerable financial resources together with long-standing relationships with a number of customers, suppliers and funding providers across different geographic areas and industries. The Group's forecasts and projections, taking account of reasonably possible changes in trading performance, show that the Group is able to operate within the level of its current bank facilities without needing to renew facilities expiring in 2009. As a consequence, the directors believe that the Group is well placed to manage its business risks successfully despite the current uncertain economic outlook. Additionally, as part of the Group's normal ongoing funding review, the Group has received indicative offers, of additional funding facilities and confirmation of the lenders' intention to agree to the renewal of a number of existing facilities.

After making enquiries, the directors have a reasonable expectation that the Company and the Group have adequate resources to continue in operational existence for the foreseeable future. Accordingly, they continue to adopt the going concern basis in preparing the annual report and financial statements.

Share price and shareholder return

The share price at 31 December 2008 was 271.75p (2007: 393.75p), a decrease of 31% over the year. Based on the year end share price, the total dividend of 20.7p represents a yield of 7.6%.

Douglas M. Hurt

Finance Director

4 March 2009

A comparison of IFRS and UK GAAP

Introduction

You've learnt that the financial statements prepared using IFRS and UK GAAP are different, and I've discussed the major differences as we've progressed through the book. However I'd like to summarise them in this chapter, and show you how the same information would be shown in IFRS financial statements and those prepared using UK GAAP. I'll start by looking at the main differences and then you can see the financial statements.

The main differences between the international rules and UK GAAP

There are a number of differences between IFRS and UK GAAP that affect financial analysis. They include:

▪ IFRS tends to be more complex than UK GAAP and has a 'fair value focus', with more assets and liabilities shown on the balance sheet. Most of these are shown at fair values and most of the changes in fair value affect the income statement. This has had two effects on the financial statements:

- It has increased the volatility of reported profits and net asset values. (In the current volatile economic environment some senior European politicians are actively seeking a return to the historical cost accounting base previously used in most European countries.)

- Retained earnings are not necessarily the same as distributable profits. One of the principles of UK GAAP is that profits should only be shown when they are realised, whereas most of the fair value gains and losses reported using IFRS are unrealised.

- IFRS offers more flexibility in the presentation of the income statement, as it only specifies the *minimum* line items that should be presented, and operating profit doesn't have to be shown. However, companies can show additional line items and sub totals to help readers understand the company's financial performance. Profits and losses on sale of assets and restructuring costs have to be disclosed if they're material, but don't have to be shown on the income statement itself. This means that it's important to read the notes to the accounts, particularly if you're looking at overseas accounts where there hasn't been a history of separate disclosure on the income statement. Otherwise you may be unable to understand a company's underlying performance.

- If the business has decided to close, or sell, any of its operations during the year companies using IFRS usually show the discontinued operation's profit after tax for the period and the profit, or loss, on disposal plus any costs to sell as a single figure on the income statement, with the components of this figure detailed in the notes to the accounts. The discontinued operation's revenue, expenses and profit before tax have to be disclosed in the notes to the accounts, but they can be shown on the profit and loss account if they're clearly separated from those of the continuing operations. The previous year's income statement is comparative, as it is restated to show the business as discontinued. UK GAAP requires the full disclosure on the profit and loss account itself.

Under IFRS the discontinued operation's assets and liabilities are shown separately on the balance sheet as 'held for sale', whereas they are not separated under UK GAAP. The discontinued operation's cash flows are disclosed either on the cash flow statement or in the notes.

■ If a company makes an acquisition, it must disclose in the notes to the income statement the acquisition's revenue and profit both since the acquisition date and for the whole period. (Companies are required to show you what the revenue and profit would have been if the business had been acquired at the beginning of the period. If this is impracticable, the company must disclose this and explain why it is impracticable.) Companies using UK GAAP show the acquisition's profits separately, since the date of acquisition, in the profit and loss account, disclosing it as a separate component of continuing operations.

■ Financial instruments (a term embracing most investments traded in the stock markets and money markets such as bonds and shares) and derivatives (spin-offs derived from a basic instrument, such as options and futures) are widely used by companies to manage their exposure to risks. The international rules require that most of these are revalued to their market value at the end of the financial year, with any profit or loss shown in the income statement as part of other finance income or expense. (The accounting rules have a wider definition of financial instruments than the commonly used one that I've given above – they define them as 'a contract that gives rise to an asset in one entity and a financial liability or equity in another'. This means that it includes cash, receivables and payables. Receivables are shown net of bad debt provisions: a realisable value rather than a market value.)

Most UK companies do not recognise derivatives in their accounts, so they are 'off balance sheet', although they're disclosed in the notes to the accounts. There are UK rules similar to IFRS, but most companies don't use them. This can have a significant effect on reported profitability. (This is illustrated by Virgin Atlantic's profit in 2009. It is a private UK company using UK GAAP, and in May 2009 reported a net profit for the financial year, ending in February, of £45 million. Singapore Airlines have a 49% stake in Virgin Atlantic and account for it as an associate. Singapore Airlines use IFRS, and in its financial year ending March 31 reported S$400,000 (just under £929,000, as S$1 = £0.4307) profits for its 49% stake, indicating the profit for its financial year using IFRS would have been around £1.895 million not £45 million! The IFRS requirement to recognise derivative losses accounted for most of the difference. Virgin Atlantic did not provide the notes to the accounts, although they will be available from Companies House by the end of the year.)

- Companies using IFRS show the group's share of associates and joint venture's *after* tax profits, shown before tax, whereas UK GAAP requires companies to show their share of operating profit and subsequent line items. This means that the group's reported profitability is affected by the associate's and joint venture's exceptional items, interest and tax charges when the accounts are prepared using UK GAAP.

- IFRS requires more disclosure of segmental information in the accounts, and is moving to a 'management focus' in accounting years starting after January 2009. (This means that the presentation and measures will reflect the management accounts, rather than the statutory accounts prepared using IFRS.) At least 75% of the business's revenue has to be analysed into the business segments that reflect the management of the business.

  Whilst most companies using UK GAAP provide segmental information, the Companies Act allows them to not disclose any segmental information if their directors believe its disclosure would be 'seriously prejudicial'.

- There are some differences in accounting for final salary pension schemes. UK GAAP separates pension costs for final salary schemes into operating costs and financing costs, whereas the international standard only specifies the components of the cost, not where they are shown in the income statement. Most companies using IFRS include all of the costs as staff costs in the relevant operating cost line, however many UK companies still show the expected return and the financing costs as part of finance income and expense. UK GAAP requires all actuarial gains and losses to be shown in the statement of total recognised gains and losses, whereas IFRS permits three approaches to recognising actuarial gains and losses:

  - Only recognising, in the income statement, those differences that fall outside a 10% 'corridor'. Most companies overseas use this option.

  - Recognising, in the income statement, more actuarial gains and losses using any systematic method that is applied consistently.

  - Immediately recognising all the actuarial gains and losses either in the income statement or the statement of recognised income and expense (comprehensive income). Most UK companies use this option, as it is the same as UK GAAP.

  IFRS requires companies to accrue for short-term employee benefits, such as holiday pay, whereas there is no equivalent requirement in UK GAAP, as the rules only cover post-retirement benefits.

▨ Companies using UK GAAP systematically amortise goodwill; whereas companies using IFRS don't amortise it, instead they review it annually in an impairment review.

▨ Companies using IFRS are likely to have more other intangible assets, and associated amortisation charges, than those using UK GAAP. Acquired intangible assets and certain development costs must be shown as intangible assets.

▨ IFRS classifies assets and liabilities as 'current' (effectively realisable within a year) and non current (realisable in more than a year). This means that companies using IFRS show material receivables due in more than a year as non current assets, whereas companies using UK GAAP show them as current assets.

▨ Deferred tax is prominent in the financial statements of companies using IFRS, with deferred tax assets and liabilities shown on the balance sheet. UK GAAP includes them in provisions for liabilities and charges, disclosing the detail in the notes. Companies using IFRS have additional deferred tax assets arising from goodwill and any pension deficits.

▨ The international rules don't allow tax assets and liabilities to be offset.

The presentation of the financial statements

Financial statements prepared under international rules look very different from those prepared by users of UK GAAP. Whilst they're essentially the same, the language and headings are different.

Firstly, let's see the information that must be shown in the financial statements using the different rules.

IFRS		UK GAAP
For financial years starting before 1/1/2009	For financial years starting after 1/1/2009	

IFRS		UK GAAP
The balance sheet IAS 1 requires that assets and liabilities are analysed between current and non current and, as a minimum, include the following: ■ Property, plant and equipment ■ Investment property ■ Intangible assets ■ Financial assets ■ Investments that are accounted for using the equity method ■ Biological assets ■ Trade and other receivables ■ Assets held for sale ■ Trade and other payables ■ Provisions ■ Financial liabilities ■ Current tax assets and liabilities ■ Deferred tax assets and liabilities ■ Liabilities held for sale ■ Minority interests ■ The parent's issued capital and reserves	**The statement of financial position** IAS 1 requires that assets and liabilities are analysed between current and non current and, as a minimum, include the following: ■ Property, plant and equipment ■ Investment property ■ Intangible assets ■ Financial assets ■ Investments that are accounted for using the equity method ■ Biological assets ■ Trade and other receivables ■ Assets held for sale ■ Trade and other payables ■ Provisions ■ Financial liabilities ■ Current tax assets and liabilities ■ Deferred tax assets and liabilities ■ Liabilities held for sale ■ Non controlling interests ■ The parent's issued capital and reserves	**The balance sheet** The balance sheet's presentation is prescribed in The Companies Act, which allows two presentations. The first presentation, used by most UK companies, arranges the balance sheet vertically with assets shown above liabilities. Two subtotals are shown: ■ 'Net current assets/ (liabilities)', which deducts the creditors' falling due in a year from the current assets ■ 'Total assets less current liabilities', which adds fixed assets to the net current assets The second presentation is a 'two sided' presentation with assets on the one side and liabilities and capital and reserves on the other A balance sheet usually shows: Fixed assets ■ Intangible assets ■ Tangible assets ■ Investments ■ Associates and joint ventures Current assets ■ Stocks ■ Debtors ■ Investments ■ Cash

		Creditors: amounts falling due within a year[1]
		Creditors: amounts falling due in more than a year[1]
		Provisions for liabilities and charges
		Pension fund asset/liability
		Minority interests
		Capital and reserves[2]

[1] Liabilities are usually shown as a total on the balance sheet, with the details in the notes
[2] Most reserves are shown separately on the balance sheet

An income statement

As a minimum an income statement discloses:

- Revenue
- Finance costs
- Share of profits, or losses, of associates and joint ventures accounted for using the equity method
- A single amount comprising the total of the after tax profit of discontinued operations plus the after tax profit, or loss, on disposal
- Tax expense
- Profit, or loss, for the period

A statement of comprehensive income

This can presented in two ways:

- A single statement, showing all items of income and expense recognised in the period

or

- Two statements – The first comprising a separate income statement, showing the components of profit or loss. The second statement beginning with profit, or loss, showing the components of other comprehensive income (Statement of comprehensive income). This should be shown immediately after the income statement

As a minimum the single statement comprises:

- Revenue
- Finance costs
- Share of profits, or losses, of associates and joint ventures accounted for using the equity method

A profit and loss account

This is more detailed than income statements prepared using IFRS

- Turnover, operating costs and operating profit must be analysed between continuing operations (split between acquisitions and existing business) and discontinued operations.
- The share of joint ventures turnover must be disclosed
- The group's share of associate's and joint venture's operating profit must be shown immediately after operating profit and their share of all line items to profit after tax must be disclosed
- Profits/losses on the sale of assets, businesses and restructuring costs must be separately disclosed after operating profit
- Interest is usually netted off and shown as net interest payable/receivable

■ A single amount comprising the total of the after tax profit of discontinued operations plus the after tax profit, or loss, on disposal

■ Tax expense

■ Profit, or loss, for the period

■ Each component of other comprehensive income.

■ The share of comprehensive income in associates and joint ventures accounted for using the equity method

In the two-stage approach, this is split between the income statement and a statement of other comprehensive income

A note of historical cost profits and losses

This is a memorandum, rather than a financial statement, and is only shown if the company has revalued its assets and the revaluation has affected the reported profit. It shows you what the company's profit would have been if they hadn't revalued

A statement of changes in equity or a statement of recognised income and expense	A statement of changes in equity	A statement of total recognised gains and losses
This can show either:	This shows all the changes in equity and reconciles the opening and closing balances of each component of equity disclosing the changes arising from:	This shows:
■ All the changes in equity (a statement of changes in equity)		■ The profit, or loss, before the deduction of dividends
or		■ Any adjustment to asset valuations and any other unrealised gains
■ The changes in equity excluding any transactions with the owners – The statement of recognised income and expense	■ Profit or loss ■ Each item of other comprehensive income ■ Transactions with shareholders, acting as shareholders	■ Any translation differences ■ Prior period adjustments
If a business has opted to account for the full actuarial gains and losses outside the income statement it must use a SORIE	Both profit and total comprehensive income are analysed between the amounts attributable to non controlling interests and the owners	The information shown in a statement of changes in equity is found in the note on reserves

The SORIE shows:

■ The profit, or loss, before the deduction of dividends
■ Any adjustment to asset valuations required to be shown on the SORIE
■ Any translation differences

A cash flow statement

Cash flows are shown under three headings:

■ *Operating activities* – This includes tax and can include interest and dividends paid. However these are usually shown as part of financing activities
■ *Investing activities* – This includes the cash flows arising from the purchase and sale of non current assets, acquisitions and disposals and investment income (interest and dividends received)
■ *Financing activities* – This covers the cash flows arising from shares and loans and may include bank overdrafts. However, they would be shown as part of cash if they're repayable on demand and form an integral part of the company's cash management

It finishes with the change in cash and cash equivalents and reconciles the opening cash to the closing cash

A statement of cash flows

Cash flows are shown under three headings:

■ *Operating activities* – This includes tax and can include interest and dividends paid. However these are usually shown as part of financing activities
■ *Investing activities* – This includes the cash flows arising from the purchase and sale of non current assets, acquisitions and disposals and investment income (interest and dividends received)
■ *Financing activities* – This covers the cash flows arising from shares and loans and may include bank overdrafts. However, they would be shown as part of cash and cash equivalents if they're repayable on demand and form an integral part of the company's cash management

It finishes with the change in cash and cash equivalents and reconciles the opening cash to the closing cash

A cash flow statement

Cash flows are categorised under nine headings:

■ *Operating activities* – These are just the cash flows from the company's trading.
■ *Dividends received from associated undertakings and joint ventures*
■ *Returns on investment and servicing of finance* – This is interest and most of dividends received and paid. Dividends paid to ordinary shareholders are excluded.
■ *Taxation*
■ *Capital expenditure and financial investment* – These are the cash flows from buying and selling fixed assets
■ *Acquisitions and disposals*
■ *Equity dividends paid* – These are the dividends paid to ordinary shareholders
■ *Management of liquid resources* – These are short-term investments that are readily disposable
■ *Financing* – These are the receipts from, or payments to, the external providers of finance

It finishes with the changes in cash and bank overdrafts and a note that reconciles the movement in cash to the change in net debt. Anything shown as cash is usually realisable within 24 hours

Now let's see the different presentations using IFRS and UK GAAP. I've simplified the example to make it easier to follow, so there are no additional deferred tax assets and no financial instruments.

The income statement/profit and loss account

You'll find a profit and loss account prepared using UK GAAP rules below. I've followed the commonest presentation, where the costs are shown functionally.

Profit and loss account for the year ending 31 December 2xxx (UK rules)

	£m	£m	£m
	Continuing operations	Discontinued operations	Total
Turnover	700	300	1,000
Cost of sales	(420)	(180)	(600)
Gross profit	280	120	400
Distribution costs	(60)	(70)	(130)
Administrative expenses	(40)	(30)	(70)
Other operating income	10		10
Operating profit	190	20	210
Share of associate's operating profits	20		20
Restructuring costs	(20)		(20)
Provision for loss on disposal of discontinued operations		(15)	(15)
Profit on sale of fixed assets	10		10
Profit before interest	200	5	205
Interest receivable – Group			10
Interest payable:			
Group			(55)
Associates			(5)
Net interest payable			(50)
Net return on retirement assets and liabilities			1
Profit on ordinary activities before taxation			156
Taxation on profit on ordinary activities *			(46)
Profit on ordinary activities after taxation			110
Minority interests			(10)
Profit for the financial year			100

* The notes would disclose that tax relates to the following:	Group	(44)
	Associates	(2)

If the company had revalued its assets and this had affected its profits, this would be followed by a Note of historical cost profits and losses, showing you what the profit would have been if the company hadn't revalued its assets.

Now let me show you how this *might* look using the international presentation assuming the group discloses all operating costs in the income statement (rather than the notes) and shows an operating profit line. (As there is no prescribed format, only *minimum* line headings, it's impossible to be definitive.) I have tried to keep it simple and comparable, so I have assumed that there are no development costs that have to be capitalised, no derivatives (so there's no revaluation gains or losses to be recognised), and there's no impairment losses. This means that the sale of the discontinued operation has been agreed and fixed so the company can make a provision; otherwise the asset's value would be reduced after an impairment review.

Income statement for the year ending 31 December 2xxx (International rules)

	£m	
	Total	
Revenue	700	*It is now called revenue, and only the continuing business's revenue and operating costs have to be shown. (Companies can disclose discontinued operations revenue, expenses, and profit before tax separately on the income statement. If they don't it's found in the notes.)*
Cost of sales	(420)	*The financing costs/return of defined benefits pension schemes may be included in operating profit. I've shown it as other financial income. Immaterial profits/losses on sale of assets are also included in operating profit, and don't have to be separately disclosed. Administrative expenses are £2m less, as goodwill is not amortised.*
Gross profit	280	
Distribution costs	(60)	
Administrative expenses	(38)	
Other income	10	
Operating profit before exceptional items	192	*Most UK companies show operating profit before and after restructuring costs, although they don't have to.*

Restructuring costs	(20)	*Restructuring costs are charged to operating*
Profit on sale of property	10	*profit, and companies overseas would charge*
Operating profit after exceptional items	182	*them to the appropriate line heading, with material amounts disclosed in the notes. I've shown the profit on sale of assets as an exceptional item, as it is 'material' and would have to be separately disclosed. (UK companies usually show these on their income statements.)*
Interest payable and similar charges	(55)	*Interest can't be shown net. I've shown the net return of £1m as other financial income,*
Other financial income	1	*but many companies don't net it off and show*
Interest receivable	10	*both income and expense. (Other finance income and expense also includes gains and losses on financial instruments which I have ignored.)*
Share of associate's after tax profits	13	
Profit on ordinary activities before tax	151	
Taxation	(38)	*The tax charge has been reduced by the associate's and discontinued operation's tax charges.*
Profit for the year from continuing operations	113	
Loss for the year from discontinued operation	(1)	*This is the discontinued operation's after tax profit of £14m less the provision of £15m for the loss on its disposal. These are detailed in the notes to the accounts, along with its revenue, expenses and profit before tax.*
Total profit for the year	112	
Attributable to:		
Equity shareholders	102	
Minority interests	10	

You can see that the reported profit is £2 million higher, as goodwill hasn't been impaired and IFRS doesn't require it to be systematically amortised.

Now let's see how the balance sheet looks when presented using the different rules. You'll find that there's more information on the balance sheet itself. Firstly I'll show you a typical UK GAAP balance sheet, using the net assets presentation, and then re-present it using IFRS. (Both rules also allow the assets and liabilities presentation.)

The balance sheet

Balance sheet as at 31 December 2xxx (UK rules)

	£m
FIXED ASSETS:	
Intangible assets	45
Tangible assets	222
Investment in associated undertaking	38
Investments	12
	317
CURRENT ASSETS:	
Stocks	70
Debtors	200
Investments	50
Cash	71
	391
CREDITORS: AMOUNTS FALLING DUE WITHIN ONE YEAR	(160)
Net current assets	231
Total assets less current liabilities	548
CREDITORS: AMOUNTS FALLING DUE AFTER MORE THAN ONE YEAR	(150)
PROVISIONS FOR LIABILITIES AND CHARGES	(39)
NET ASSETS EXCLUDING RETIREMENT BENEFITS ASSETS AND LIABILITIES	359
Retirement benefits net assets	41
Retirement benefits net liabilities	(46)
NET ASSETS INCLUDING RETIREMENT BENEFITS ASSETS AND LIABILITIES	354

CAPITAL AND RESERVES:

Called up share capital	50
Share premium account	40
Revaluation reserve	13
Capital redemption reserve	10
Shares held in employee share ownership trusts	(10)
Profit and loss account	223
Shareholders' funds	326
MINORITY INTERESTS	28
	354

Balance sheet as at 31 December 2xxx (International rules)

£m

Assets	
Goodwill	50
Intangible assets	2
Property, plant and equipment	170
Investment in associate	38
Available for sale financial assets	13
Employee benefit net asset	41
Trade and other receivables	10
Deferred tax assets	1
Total non current assets	225
Inventories	50
Trade and other receivables	140
Other financial assets (investments)	10
Cash and cash equivalents	101
Total current assets	301
Non current assets held for sale	132
Total assets	758

> Goodwill is usually shown separately and isn't amortised. There are more intangible assets including some development costs and all acquired intangible assets.

> UK rules include long-term debtors in current assets where they're disclosed in the notes. Long-term receivables, usually other receivables, are discounted so their value is unlikely to be the same. There are more deferred tax assets arising from goodwill and pension deficits.

> The assets and liabilities of the discontinued operations are shown as non current assets and liabilities held for sale. I've assumed the assets and liabilities comprise:
>
> | | |
> |---|---:|
> | Property, plant and equipment | 52 |
> | Inventories | 20 |
> | Receivables | 50 |
> | Cash | 10 |
> | Payables | (15) |
> | Current tax | (5) |
> | Deferred tax | (4) |
> | Borrowings | (40) |

Liabilities

Bank overdraft	(10)
Borrowings and finance leases	(40)
Current tax	(25)
Trade and other payables	(65)
Provisions	(16)
Total current liabilities	**(156)**

Financial liabilities, current tax, and trade and other payables are separately disclosed on the balance sheet.

Provisions are analysed into short and long term.

Liabilities directly associated with non current assets held for sale	(64)

Borrowings and finance leases	(100)
Employee benefit obligations	(46)
Trade and other payables	(10)
Provisions	(10)
Deferred tax liabilities	(10)
Total non current liabilities	**(176)**

The employee benefit obligation less the employee benefit net asset equals the pension deficit of £5m.

Deferred tax was included in provisions for liabilities and charges.

Total liabilities	**(396)**

Net assets	**362**

Equity

Issued capital	50
Share premium	40
Reserves	18
Retained earnings	226
Total equity attributable to equity holders of the parent	**334**

Only the retained earnings have to be shown on the balance sheet itself.

Minority interest	28
Total equity	**362**

If the company has any derivatives, they are recognised on the balance sheet at their fair value. They can be both assets and liabilities, and be both current and non current.

The statements of total recognised gains and losses and the recognised income and expense

Whilst this would normally follow the income statement, I'll show you the two statements here, as they use information from both the income statement and the balance sheet.

Firstly let's look at the statement of total recognised gains and losses prepared using UK GAAP.

Statement of total recognised gains and losses (UK rules)

	£m
Profit for the financial year	100
Unrealised surplus on revaluation of properties	3
Currency translation differences	4
Actuarial gains and (losses) on defined benefit pension scheme	(1)
Total recognised gains and losses for the year	106

> These are charged to the profit and loss account reserve.

This is followed by a note reconciling the recognised gains and losses with the changes in the shareholders' funds:

Reconciliation to movements in Group shareholders' funds

	£m
Profit for the financial year	100
Dividends	(40)
Other recognised gains and losses relating to the financial year	6
New ordinary share capital issued	5
Net increase in shareholders' funds for the year	71
Shareholders' funds at the start of the year	255
Shareholders' funds at the end of the year	326

Now let's see how this would be presented using IFRS before the changes in 2009:

Statement of recognised income and expense (IFRS)

	£m
Unrealised surplus on revaluation of properties	3
Revaluation of available for sale securities	1
Currency translation differences	4
Actuarial gains and (losses) on defined benefit pension scheme	(1)
Net income net of tax recognised directly in equity	7
Profit for the financial year	112
Total recognised gains and losses for the year	119
Attributable to:	
Equity shareholders	108
Minority interests	11
	119

Companies using the international rules, which aren't presenting the single statement of comprehensive income, in their financial years starting after January 2009 must start their *statement of comprehensive income* with the period's profit.

The cash flow statement and statement of cash flows

Now let's look at the last financial statement, the cash flow statement. I'll start with the presentation used in UK GAAP and which has more classifications than one prepared using the international rules.

Cash flow statement for the year ended 31 December 2xxx (UK rules)

	£m
Operating activities	
Operating profit	210
Depreciation and amortisation	15
Increase in stocks	(10)
(Increase) in debtors	(20)
Increase in creditors	10
Cash inflow from operating activities before restructuring costs	205
Restructuring costs	(20)
Cash inflow from operating activities after restructuring costs	185
Returns on investment and servicing of finance	
Interest received	10
Dividends paid to minority interests	(2)
Interest paid	(55)
Net cash outflow from returns on investment and servicing of finance	(47)
Taxation	
Tax paid	(35)
Tax refund	5
Net cash outflow from taxation	(30)
Capital expenditure and financial investment	
Purchase of tangible fixed assets	(30)
Purchase of fixed asset investments	(2)
Sale of tangible fixed assets	15
Net cash outflow from capital expenditure and financial investment	(17)
Acquisitions and disposals	
Investment in associated undertaking	(5)
Net cash outflow from acquisitions and disposals	(5)
Equity dividends paid	(40)
Net cash flow before management of liquid resources and financing	46
Management of liquid resources	
Cash withdrawn from 7 day deposit	30
Cash placed on 14 day deposit	(20)
Net cash flow from management of liquid resources	10
Financing	
Proceeds of share issue	5
Additional loans	30
Repayment of loans	(40)
Net cash inflow from financing	(5)
Increase in cash for the period	51

The cash flow statement is followed by a note that reconciles the increase in cash with the movement in net debt:

Reconciliation of net cash flow to movement in net debt:

	£m
Increase in cash for the period	51
Cash outflow from decrease in debt	10
Cash inflow from decrease in liquid resources	(10)
Change in net debt resulting from cash flows	51
Net debt at the start of the year	(130)
Net debt at the end of the year	(79)

Cash flow statements prepared using the international rules contain the same information, but are presented slightly differently. There are fewer headings and different definitions of operating activities, financing and cash.

As you now know companies using IFRS have some flexibility in the classification of some of their cash flows. For example, interest and dividends paid can be shown as an operating, or a financing cash flow. The statement of cash flows finishes with the changes in cash equivalents, which may, or may not, be shown net of any bank overdrafts.

To help you follow the example, I'll show you the cash flow statement starting operating activities with operating profit. (Companies can start with any profit figure. Operating profit is more comparable with UK GAAP and there are fewer adjustments to make.) I've shown interest and dividends paid as financing cash flows, as this is the most common presentation and it's different from the presentation I used earlier.

So let's have a look at the same cash flow statement prepared using IFRS:

Statement of cash flows for the year ended 31 December 2xxx (IFRS)

	£m
Operating activities	
Operating profit	192
Depreciation and amortisation	10
Changes in working capital:	
(Increase) in inventories	(10)
(Increase) in receivables	(10)

Increase in payables	10
Cash generated from continuing operations before restructuring costs	192
Restructuring costs	(20)
Cash generated from continuing operations after restructuring costs	172
Cash from discontinued operations	13
Cash generated from operations	185
Tax paid	(30)
Cash from operating activities	155

This optional sub-total is the same as the operating cash flow under UK rules.

Investing activities

Purchase of property, plant and equipment	(30)
Investment in associate	(5)
Purchase of available for sale investment	(2)
Sale of property, plant and equipment	15
Interest received	10
	(12)

Financing

Proceeds of share issue	5
Additional loans	30
Loan repayment	(40)
Dividends paid to minority interests	(2)
Dividends paid	(40)
Interest paid	(55)
	(102)

Change in cash and cash equivalents	41
Less cash in business held for sale	(10)
Cash and cash equivalents at the start of the year	70
Cash and cash equivalents at the end of the year in continuing business	101

Companies also disclose the effect of exchange rates on the value of their cash and cash equivalents.

How do I analyse the accounts?

8

How do I analyse the accounts?

Introduction

Welcome to the world of the amateur detective! You're now entering the part in the book where you start to understand what the accounts do (and don't) tell you about a company's financial performance. Like any good detective, you'll probably have as many questions as answers, but you should be able to make sense of what is going on. Interpretation starts with understanding – it's only after you've understood the wealth of information you'll find in the accounts, that you can start to analyse and interpret it.

I'm now going to show you how to do this in a structured way. You've already looked at the accounts, and reading through them is the starting point for financial analysis. You'll now move on to:

- identify the components of a business's financial performance;
- complete a financial analysis;
- interpret your analysis.

You'll discover the main elements of a business's performance, how they're measured, and develop a structured approach for analysing any company's accounts. The subsequent interpretation involves taking this analysis of isolated factors and bringing it together into a coherent whole. All the factors interact with one another to reveal the company's financial performance.

Starting your analysis

Analysis doesn't start with ratios – it starts with *understanding*. You have to think before you calculate! The first thing that you need to do is read the company accounts, and to start to understand what's been happening in the company in the period. Once you've done this, look at the financial statements, starting with the revenue shown in the income statement. I then move line by line through the income statement and the balance sheet, trying to think about *why* things might have changed. You may already have discovered some of the important factors influencing the company's financial performance in the operating and financial review, or the business review in the directors' report of smaller companies.

Why start with revenue? Well if you think about it, sales drive some of the costs and some of the assets on the balance sheet and revenue is a combination of volume and price.

The income statement

Sales, costs and profit

I'll start with costs. Some costs move in line with sales – the more you sell the bigger the cost. Materials' cost is the best example of this. The more valves IMI makes, the bigger the metal cost charged to the income statement. Rent on the other hand is a different type of cost. The company has to pay its rent regardless of the level of production, whereas most material costs are only incurred when another unit is produced. Some costs move with sales and others don't, and consequently costs can be described as being variable or fixed. Fixed costs are those that don't increase proportionally with volume, whereas variable costs do – the more you make, and sell, the bigger the cost. This doesn't mean that fixed costs are constant. They increase over time, and will also increase when the business's volumes increase. Sometimes, if the company has an additional order, it needs to run another shift, or move to a larger factory. Fixed costs increase in 'steps', and are only fixed within certain levels of volume and certain periods of time. I've illustrated this in the graph below, where the fixed costs are £1m until sales reach 800 units, when they increase to £1.3 million.

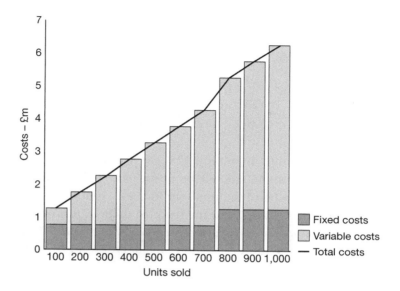

Fixed costs aren't necessarily constant, but they don't increase *proportionately*. Now I'll show you how this affects a company's profitability by adding sales to the graph, but I'll keep the units sold below 800 to keep the graph simple.

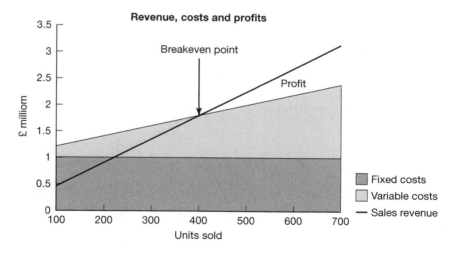

You can see that the company has to sell 400 units before it covers all of its costs, and breaks even. It only starts to make a profit when it sells 401 units, and the more it sells the bigger the profit. But the profit growth percentage isn't constant – just look at the following table.

Units sold	400	450	500	550	600	650	700
	£ million	£ million	£ million	£ million	£ million	£ million	£ million
Sales revenue	1.800	2.025	2.250	2.475	2.700	2.925	3.150
Variable costs	(0.800)	(0.900)	(1.000)	(1.100)	(1.200)	(1.300)	(1.400)
Fixed costs	(1.000)	(1.000)	(1.000)	(1.000)	(1.000)	(1.000)	(1.000)
Operating profit	0.000	0.125	0.250	0.375	0.500	0.625	0.750

Every 50 units sold add £125,000 to the operating profit. When the units increase from 450 to 500, profit increases by £125,000 – an increase of 100%. However, when the units sold increase from 650 to 700, profit increases by the same £125,000, but the reported increase is now only 20%. *Profit volatility increases as a company approaches its breakeven point.* If a company is close to its breakeven point it can report large increases in its profit with small increases in volume, but it's actually a riskier company. (It works both ways – small falls in its volumes generate large falls in its profits. Think about how the recession is hitting companies' profits, and some industries may become unviable if the current reductions in volume continue for any length of time.)

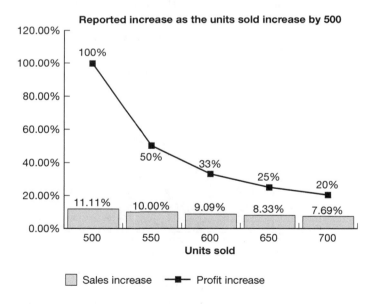

Now look at the effect that the relatively smaller increase in sales has on the company's reported profit margin:

Units sold	400	450	500	550	600	650	700
Operating profit margin	0.00%	6.17%	11.11%	15.15%	18.52%	21.37%	23.81%

Unfortunately, in their published accounts, companies don't analyse their costs into fixed and variable costs, so you can't work out their breakeven point. But I hope that you now understand:

■ Some costs move with sales.

■ Profit moves disproportionaly, as not all costs are variable.

■ The percentage change in a company's profits, and its profit margins, increase the closer the company gets to its breakeven point.

Sales and assets

If a company doubles its sales, what do you think would happen to its working capital – its inventories, trade receivables, and trade payables? Assuming that the company is operating at optimum efficiency, you wouldn't be surprised if these doubled too. Working capital tends to move in line with volumes. Property, plant and equipment, on the other hand, tend to behave in the same way as fixed costs. They have a capacity constraint; once this 'trigger point' is reached the company has to invest more in property, plant and equipment. The additional property, plant and equipment are used to support higher levels of sales. This means that you expect:

■ working capital to move in line with sales volume;

■ property, plant and equipment to move in 'steps', increasing when the company hits a capacity ceiling.

Now you understand this, I'd like to run through the key items in the income statement, and think about why they might have changed. You'll see that it's common sense, not rocket science, but approaching the analysis in this way is useful as it:

■ helps you understand the company's performance and interpret the data;

■ identifies the appropriate ratios to use.

Revenue

The revenue is the number of units sold times the selling price. Now just think about *why* the company's revenue could change.

It could change because of changes in:

- prices;
- volume;
- mix;
- exchange rate movements could affect exporting and global companies;
- a combination of a number of these factors.

Now in the operating and financial review, you'll find information about which of these could have affected the revenue. (For example in 2008 exchange rate movements increased IMI's reported revenue by £179 million, an 11% increase, and its segmental operating profits by £27.0 million, an increase of more than 10%. To find the effects of prices, volumes and mix you need to look at the operating review: IMI's is in Chapter 13.)

Material costs

These aren't disclosed in every company's accounts, but some companies disclose them. Materials' cost, as a percentage of revenue, could have changed if:

- The company has had to pay more for its materials.
- The company is using more materials. This could have arisen from:
  - the company's selling different products, or a different mix of products;
  - manufacturing difficulties are leading to increased scrap levels.
- Adverse exchange rates have increased the material costs.
- There could be a combination of a number of these factors.

Staff costs

These are always disclosed in the notes to the accounts and could change if:

- The company is paying higher salaries.
- The company has changed the type of staff it employs, and is employing more expensive staff.

- ▦ The company is employing more staff.

- ▦ There could be a combination of a number of these factors.

> The common theme in all the explanations for changes in revenue, materials, and staff costs is changes in the volume, price, mix or a combination of these. However, there's another possibility that would explain some of the changes, linked to mix. The company's acquisitions, or disposals could have changed the business's revenue and profitability. You can see this if you look at the disclosures in the notes to the accounts about acquisitions and disposals.

Other costs

The other costs could change if:

- ▦ the company's volume caused the fixed costs to move up, or down, a 'step';

- ▦ the company is paying more, or less, for some of its costs.

Interest

There are two things you should remember about interest:

- ▦ Interest received relates to average cash balances and interest paid relates to average borrowings.

- ▦ If the company both receives and pays interest, the business may be seasonal.

The financial review will give you additional information about peak, and average, borrowings if the business is seasonal.

The balance sheet

Again I recommend that you adopt a line by line approach in understanding the balance sheet. I'm always interested to see where the company has spent its money, and at this stage in the analysis I focus on the business's assets.

Intangible assets

Intangible assets will have changed if:

- They've fallen because the company has amortised them. This will be disclosed in the income statement and the notes.

- The company has:

  - bought, or sold, intangible assets – this will be shown on the cash flow statement;

  - acquired, or sold, another company resulting in changes in goodwill and intangible assets – this will be disclosed in the notes. (You may recall that IMI's 2007 acquisitions increased goodwill by £37.5 million and other intangible assets by £7.6 million.)

- The company has developed intangible assets. This capitalisation of costs will be disclosed in the notes to the accounts.

Property, plant and equipment

There is a number of reasons why property, plant and equipment values could have changed:

- Firstly, you should expect property, plant and equipment values to fall, as most of them have to be depreciated. The depreciation charge is disclosed in the notes to the accounts.

- The company has capitalised some costs – charged them to property, plant and equipment. In the UK this is usually disclosed in the notes to the accounts on staff costs. WorldCom did disclose that it was capitalising costs on page 89 of its 2001 accounts:

> We construct certain of our own transmission systems and related facilities. Internal costs directly related to the construction of such facilities, including interest and salaries of certain employees, are capitalized. Such internal costs were $625 million ($339 million in interest), $842 million ($495 million in interest) and $858 million ($498 million in interest) in 1999, 2000 and 2001, respectively.

This meant that it had disclosed that it had charged $286 million staff costs to transmission systems in 2001, $347 million in 2000, and $360 million in 1999: a total of $993 million – a long way short of the over $7 billion subsequently revealed!

▩ The company has bought, or sold, some property, plant and equipment – this will be shown in the cash flow statement and the notes to the accounts.

▩ The company has revalued its assets. Go to the statement of recognised income and expense, or the statement of comprehensive income to discover this. (There will be a corresponding movement in the revaluation reserve in the balance sheet, but you'll have to check this in the notes as an upward revaluation could be eliminated on the balance sheet if they'd sold some previously revalued assets.)

A common theme is emerging … all property, plant and equipment can change if the company has bought some, sold some, or is recognising a different value. In a multinational business, such as IMI, its values will also change if the year end exchange rate used to consolidate them into the group accounts differs from the rate used the previous year. This will be disclosed in the statement of total recognised gains and losses and the notes to the reserves.

If the company has bought or sold property, plant and equipment, you need to think about why it's doing so. They could be replacing existing assets, upgrading technology, or manufacturing new products requiring different machinery. Or it may simply be that the property, plant and equipment were bought, or sold, when they bought or sold a business. (This will be disclosed in the notes about acquisitions and disposals.)

Now I'll consider working capital, and you would expect this to move in line with sales. Consequently, I'm looking at changes in working capital in relation to changes in revenue. However, the change could arise from the variables affecting the company's revenue, and have nothing at all to do with its control of working capital. So you should also bear in mind the possible reasons for revenue changes I summarised earlier.

Inventories change by a different percentage to the revenue

Inventories need to be analysed into their component parts, as different things can cause their changes. Price, mix and volume could all cause stock differences. I'll start by looking at raw materials, which could have changed for a number of reasons, including:

■ a change in the price paid for materials;

■ a change in the volume of stock held;

■ a change in the mix of stock held;

■ a combination of the above.

Work in progress is partly manufactured orders and changes in the value of work in progress could also be caused by two factors in addition to those shown above:

■ an increase, or decrease, in orders;

■ a manufacturing problem;

■ a change in the price paid for materials and/or labour;

■ a change in the mix of stock held;

■ a combination of the above.

And changes in the finished goods stock could be caused by another two new factors:

■ A fall, or increase, in orders towards the end of the year. (This may also be reflected by changes in raw materials' stock.)

■ The company has developed a new product, and initially is building up its inventories prior to the product launch. The following year inventories will fall, as the new product is launched.

Trade receivables change by a different percentage to the revenue

You must use trade receivables, not the total receivables shown on the balance sheet, as only trade receivables relate to revenue. Changes in trade receivables could have arisen for a number of reasons, including:

■ A change in the quality of the company's credit control procedures.

■ An increase, or decrease, in the sales towards the end of the year.

■ A change in the company's payment terms.

■ A change in the type, or location, of the company's customers. (Different industries, and countries, have different standard payment terms.)

■ There could be a change in the number of queries on the company's invoices – increasing queries is a common indication of administration problems and new computer systems.

■ If receivables are rising, it could indicate that one of the company's major customers has a cash flow problem, or it's managing its own cash flow.

■ If receivables are rising it could indicate that customers are unwilling to pay because of poor product quality, or late deliveries.

Trade payables change by a different percentage to the revenue

■ There could have been an increase, or a fall, in the purchases towards the end of the year. This should be reflected by a corresponding change in stock.

■ A change in the suppliers' payment terms.

■ A change in the type, or location, of the company's suppliers. (For example moving to low cost manufacturing locations can reduce trade payables and increase inventories. It's common practice for payment terms for items manufactured in China to be fob (freight on board). This means the customer has to pay as soon as the goods are loaded onto the ship. The legal ownership, usually referred to as 'title', often also changes at this point meaning that the goods are shown as stocks in the customer's accounts as soon as it's loaded onto the boat. Even if you're making the products in your own factories, stock usually increases, as the products can spend a month on a ship before it reaches your warehouse.)

■ A change in the mix of the company's purchases.

■ If the supplier has administration problems, the company may be querying the accuracy of the invoice. Its payables will rise, until the company has an accurate invoice. When the problem is resolved, the payables will fall, as the company will be prepared to pay once the invoice is correct.

■ If payables are rising it could indicate that the company is unwilling to pay because of poor product quality, or late deliveries. This could have a 'knock on' effect on the company's own business.

■ The company has a cash flow problem.

I've given you some possible reasons for year on year changes, and they could reflect good news (inventories are increasing because the company is about to launch a new product), or bad news (inventories are increasing because customers don't want to buy the company's products). You'll find some answers when you read through the accounts. Other factors may combine to offer you a plausible scenario, but don't be surprised if you still have as many questions as answers.

And now, a few words about ratios

In this part of the book I'll introduce you to the ways that a company's financial performance is measured, and you'll find that this means I'll use lots of ratios. However, you already know that the most important tool in financial analysis isn't in this book. It's one you already have – your common sense! Your common sense will help you identify creative accounting, and assess the company's financial performance. Financial performance is only *measured* by using financial ratios. And you'll find that most ratios only quantify what you can already see. They measure it to six decimal places, and give you a feeling of comfort as they tell you that you were right in the first place! Ratios are reassuring, but they're not the only way to understand a business's performance. In interpretation workshops I've been known to divide the group into two: one with calculators who are allowed to calculate ratios, the other group having no calculators and asked not to calculate any ratios. (I tend to rely on the fact that most of us couldn't calculate ratios without a calculator.) The quality of the interpretation is never the same, and the 'ratio free' group always have a better understanding of the company's performance! Whilst I'm going to introduce you to lots of ratios, I'm not actually a great ratio fan. There's a tendency for people, who are just starting financial analysis, to become overly obsessed with them. They are only a means to an end, and it's so easy to lose sight of what the ratios actually tell you. There is no need to calculate every ratio I've illustrated in this book, I don't. You'll use the ratios that help you understand the company's performance in specific areas. The ratios you choose to use should be determined by the things you spotted when you read through the accounts, and why you wanted to look at the company's financial performance in the first place.

When you start your analysis you will find that ratios are not as easy to calculate as you first thought. Most people want to see nice standard formulas that they can program into a spreadsheet, input the accounts, press the return key and get the ratios. Sadly it isn't quite that simple. (If it was, you wouldn't need financial analysts in the city, computers would do the job for considerably less money!) You have to think about which numbers should be included in the ratios.

Take the return on capital employed (sometimes called the return on assets or return on investment) – this is a ratio that most managers have heard about. It tells you the return the company is making on the capital it uses. It's an important measure, as it allows you to rank companies' financial performance, and identifies whether their return is good enough to compensate for the investment risk. It's often calculated by using the following formula (I'll explain why in Chapter 10):

$$\frac{\text{Profit before tax and interest}}{\text{Capital employed}}$$

But is that the best profit figure to use? The profit before tax includes operating profit, profit (or losses) on sale of property, plant and equipment, and exceptional items. Should these be included? Or will they distort the ratio?

And what about the capital employed? Traditionally, this is the long-term capital tied up in the business – the shareholders' equity plus any non current liabilities. But company treasurers often fund the business using short-term debt – should this be included? Should you include provisions, as no cash has left the business? It would certainly make calculating the ratios easier. In accounts prepared using UK GAAP you could just lift the number off the balance sheet from the total assets less current liabilities line. Should you take account of the different policies that different companies have in accounting for goodwill and revaluation of assets? You'll need to read Chapter 10 to find the resolution to this debate!

You have to decide what should be included in the ratios, and different people have different views. If you read analysts' reports, you'll find that different analysts often report different returns on capital for the same company. Why? Their definitions are slightly different, some making considerable adjustments to improve the comparability of the company's numbers, and others just using the numbers from the published accounts. Different views about how to calculate the ratios could give you different views about the company's financial performance. So the ratios aren't always what they appear to be. Most managers like ratios because they think they are an objective measure of the company's performance. Unfortunately, they aren't. Reporting ratios to six decimal places is confusing precision with accuracy. You have to decide how to calculate them, and you must always remember that they are based on numbers that represent the 'best' picture that the company could present. Ratios give you a feel for what is going on in the company. In isolation they are meaningless, and you always need to look at trends. Ideally you would need to look at the company's performance over a number of years, and within the context of its sector.

And remember you need to have a consistent approach when you're analysing different companies, otherwise you introduce another variable – yourself!

And I've a final comment to make about ratios and financial analysis. Remember that, when you're analysing accounts, the accounts you're using are historical; you're largely looking at what has happened which may not be a good predictor of what *will* happen. Things change, and in 2009 they're changing fast. You've seen that IMI reported revenue increases of 19% and profit increases of 28%. In its announcement of preliminary results it stated that:

Since late November trading conditions have deteriorated across many of our end markets. The sectors such as automotive and commercial vehicles have suffered a sharp contraction, as has investment in factory automation as businesses seek to rein back capital expenditure in the face of balance sheet concerns and poor forward visibility. Construction markets, particularly within the once fast-growing regions of Eastern Europe and Dubai, have also contracted sharply, as access to credit has evaporated.

Whilst pockets of resilience do exist, with energy markets remaining buoyant for our Severe Service business; increased Government investment in infrastructure providing new opportunities throughout Fluid Power and Indoor Climate businesses; and the consumer focus on value and comfort purchases presenting new product opportunities for both the Beverage Dispense and Merchandising businesses; the prevailing picture is one of significant retrenchment. For the three months to the end of February, like-for-like revenues for the group of around 15% lower than the equivalent period last year, reflecting sharply lower activity in the Fluid Power business, down nearly 30% on last year, partly offset by continued growth in severe service.

We took significant and decisive management action early to respond to these challenges, and this has been and continues to be focused in four key areas: …

The four key areas are: resource allocation, capacity alignment, product margins, and cash optimisation. For example in the three months since December it's already 'released' 10% of the global workforce, and have implemented short time working arrangements where they can. This view, and the actions they're taking to minimise the effect on their business was reiterated in page 10 of the annual report. If you want to read more about this you'll find it in Chapter 13, where you will find IMI's taken rapid steps to try to minimise the effects of the recession on its business.

What's in this part of the book?

In this section of the book I'll cover analysing a business's:

▓ *Solvency – Can the business pay its debts when they fall due?*

This is obviously the crucial question – it's insolvent businesses that go bust, not unprofitable ones. You have to be able to identify whether the company is likely to have any problems with its bank, or its suppliers. If they do have problems, are they likely to be able to resolve them? This chapter will help you identify if the company has any current, or potential, solvency problems.

▓ *Profitability – Is the business profitable?*

This chapter helps you identify if the profitability of the company has changed, why it's changed, and whether any improvement is likely to be sustainable. The profitability of the company needs to be considered in detail to find out:

– if the company is more or less profitable than it used to be;

– if it's more, or less profitable, than its competitors;

– why?

▓ *Cash – Is the business managing its cash in the most effective way?*

The cash flow statement is your starting point for looking at the way the company manages its cash. You need to know where the company is getting its money from, and what it's spending its money on. Is it tapping the right sources of funds, considering the type of expenditure? Is it living within its means? What is the company's approach to managing its cash resources? Is it conservative or innovative? There are different risks and opportunities associated with different strategies.

■ *Investment performance – Are they satisfying their shareholders?*

In most financial analysis you look at the business from the investor's point of view. It gives you information about the company's ability to have a rights issue, or to make an acquisition. You will be able to tell whether it is under performing the market and is a possible take over target. Understanding the stock market perspective is an important management skill. Sometimes the market undervalues companies – why? Does it matter?

■ *Interpreting the data – What does it all mean?*

Analysing the information is only the first step in conducting the analysis. We must tie all the information together to understand what is really going on in the company. This chapter will integrate the analysis to form a view of IMI's financial performance over the last four years.

In each chapter I'll identify the key issues, the principal ratios, and what they tell you. I'll also calculate each ratio twice: firstly using the simple accounts on the following pages, and then using IMI's 2008 accounts. So, by the time you've read this section of the book, you will be able to analyse and interpret a set of company accounts.

You'll find it useful to look at the simple accounts I'll be using to illustrate the ratios, shown on the following pages, before moving on to the next chapter.

Income statement

Revenue	100,000
Cost of sales	(60,000)
Gross profit	40,000
Distribution costs	(10,000)
Administration expenses	(20,000)
Operating profit	10,000
Interest	(6,000)
Profit before tax	4,000
Tax	(2,000)
Profit for the year	2,000

The notes to the accounts disclose that the interest receivable is 1,000, the interest payable is 7,000 and the company is proposing to pay 1,000 dividends to its shareholders.

Balance sheet

Non current assets:	
Property, plant and equipment	100,000
Current assets:	
Inventories	10,000
Trade receivables	25,000
Cash and cash equivalents	5,000
	40,000
Total assets	140,000
Current liabilities:	
Bank overdraft	(10,000)
Trade payables	(15,000)
Other payables	(3,000)
Current tax	(1,000)
Provisions	(1,000)
	(30,000)
Non current liabilities:	
Loan (at 10% interest)	(60,000)
Total liabilities	(90,000)
Net assets	50,000
Shareholders' equity:	
Share capital (nominal value 1.00 each)	20,000
Retained earnings	30,000
	50,000

Cash flow statement

Cash flows from operating activities

Operating profit	10,000
Depreciation	1,000
Increase in inventories	(2,000)
Increase in receivables	(5,000)
Increase in payables	3,000
Cash generated from operations	7,000
Tax paid	(1,500)
Net cash from operating activities	5,500

Cash flows from investing activities

Purchase of property, plant and equipment	(15,000)
Disposal of property, plant and equipment	2,000
Interest received	1,000
Net cash from investing activities	(12,000)

Cash flows from financing activities

Issue of ordinary share capital	5,000
Additional loan	5,000
Interest paid	(7,000)
Dividends paid	(1,000)
Net cash from financing activities	2,000

Decrease in cash and cash equivalents	**(4,500)**
Cash and cash equivalents at the start of the year	**9,500**
Cash and cash equivalents at the end of the year	**5,000**

9

Solvency

Introduction

When you're analysing a company, your first concern has to be whether the company is still going to be trading next year. What are the chances of it going into administration? If it looks likely, then doing any further analysis seems a waste of time! So you start financial analysis by looking at a company's solvency, as this gives you an indication of whether or not it has a long-term future.

A business is solvent when:

- its assets exceed its total liabilities (this means that it has a positive net worth);
- it can pay its debts when they fall due.

I'll look at solvency on three timescales:

- 'Could the company pay all of its short-term liabilities immediately?'
- 'Will the company be able to meet its short-term obligations?'
- 'Is the company likely to be able to meet its medium- and long-term obligations?'

When you're looking at a company's solvency you'll find that most of the information is on the balance sheet, as it is this snapshot that shows you the business's assets and liabilities.

Immediate solvency/liquidity

Immediate solvency is the same as *liquidity*, as liquidity is the term used to describe the company's ability to pay its short-term liabilities on time. The question this analysis answers is 'Could the company pay all its short-term creditors if they all wanted to be paid today?' It is the most pessimistic view of solvency, as you are imagining that all of the company's creditors falling due in a year are demanding immediate payment. To answer the question you have to identify the assets that the business could turn into cash within a day. You know these assets are going to be found in the current asset section of the balance sheet, as it would take more than a day to sell its long-term assets. So let's look at the current assets in my example, and try to identify the ones that you think could be realised in a day.

Current assets:
Inventories	10,000
Trade receivables	25,000
Cash and cash equivalents	5,000
	40,000

Not as easy as it sounds, is it? It does depend on the type of company that you're analysing. Most manufacturers would be unable to sell their inventories in a day, particularly as part of it would be in work in progress and no one would want unfinished goods. However, some retailers could sell their stock that quickly. You have to understand the company you're analysing if you want to determine its 'liquid assets' – those that can be sold quickly to generate cash. Retailers would normally be able to realise all of their current assets; most manufacturers would only be able to realise their receivables (you may remember that they can 'factor' them), and their cash and cash equivalents. This is the standard definition of liquid assets used in accounting textbooks, as it's right for most companies. If I use this definition, the liquid assets are 30,000 – the total current assets of 40,000 less the inventories of 10,000. These are then compared with the current liabilities of 30,000.

$$\frac{\text{Liquid assets}}{\text{Current liabilities}} = \frac{30,000}{30,000} = \textbf{1.00}$$

This means that the company has £1.00 in liquid assets for every £1.00 it owes. So it's unlikely to have an immediate liquidity problem. As long as a large customer doesn't collapse, they shouldn't have any difficulties. This ratio of liquid assets to short-term liabilities has three names – it can be called the:

▨ quick ratio;

▨ liquid ratio;

▨ acid test.

Now, you know that this is a pessimistic measure, but is it appropriate? That largely depends on whether you think that everyone is likely to ask for their money back immediately. To find this out, you need to discover whether the company is likely to be having difficulties with its suppliers or the bank. How long is it taking to pay its suppliers? Well there's two ways to find this out. UK companies have to disclose their policy for paying their suppliers and should disclose their payable days in their directors' report. However you've already seen that many companies don't disclose them and just tell you something such as 'the group pays its suppliers on a timely basis', and so you may well have to work out the payment period for yourself. This company has trade payables of 15,000 at the end of the year, and if you knew its purchases in the period you could calculate how long the company is taking to pay its suppliers.

Unfortunately, you'll only find materials' purchases disclosed on the least popular income statement presentation, so you're unlikely to be able to calculate an accurate figure. Some analysts use cost of sales as an approximation to purchases, but this can mean different things to different companies. Consequently, if you want to compare companies using different presentations of their income statement, or definitions of their cost of sales, you have to find a different approach. Most analysts look at the trade payables in relationship to revenue and, although it's wrong, it's consistently wrong and enables you to compare one company with another! (You should remember that you are only trying to identify whether the company may have a problem, not quantify it to six decimal places. You're unlikely to be able to quantify it exactly anyway, as the balance sheet only shows you the year end 'best view'.) You do not need to have a Mensa-sized intellect to know that if revenue is at £3 million, and trade payables are at £1.5 million – the company has a problem.

Whichever way you choose to calculate it you should still get the same trend (unless the profit margins have fluctuated wildly during the period), although not the same answer! So let me show you how to work out roughly how long a company takes to pay its suppliers. Firstly I need some information from the income statement.

Revenue	100,000
Cost of sales	(60,000)
Gross profit	40,000
Distribution costs	(10,000)
Administration expenses	(20,000)
Operating profit	10,000

And then I need to know the trade payables. I've shown them separately on the balance sheet, as I've made it nice and simple, however, the actual heading you'll normally find is trade and other payables, and you're only interested in the trade payables, so you have to read the notes to find the number you're looking for. Why am I only interested in the *trade* payables? They're the ones that relate to the expenses charged to the income statement. I can now calculate the *payable days*, also known as the *creditor days*, or the *payment period*.

Firstly, I'll base the calculation on revenue:

$$\frac{\text{Trade payables}}{\text{Revenue}} \times 365 = \frac{15,000}{100,000} \times 365 = \textbf{54.75 days}$$

Now when I base the calculation on the cost of sales the payment period increases to over 91 days:

$$\frac{\text{Trade payables}}{\text{Cost of sales}} \times 365 = \frac{15,000}{60,000} \times 365 = \textbf{91.25 days}$$

(I'm multiplying by 365 in both calculations, as the trade payables represent the money owed on a given day and both the revenue and the cost of sales are for the whole year.)

You can see that using revenue as the denominator has the effect of understating payable days. Even assuming the worst view, the company is taking three months to pay its suppliers. Whilst this is a long time, its suppliers are probably unlikely to be threatening liquidation – yet!

When you're looking at liquidity, you're taking a pessimistic view. You are assuming that all the current liabilities have to be repaid today. This is only likely to happen if someone is going to force the company into administration. The payment period is a good indicator of whether the company is experiencing difficulties paying its suppliers.

Short-term solvency

Now I'd like to extend the time period and look at short-term solvency. Here you're trying to see if the company can meet all its short-term liabilities. You do this by looking at the relationship between the current assets and the current liabilities. So I'm now assuming that the company has sufficient time to sell its Inventories. Here's the relevant information from the balance sheet in my example:

Current assets:	
Inventories	10,000
Trade and other receivables	25,000
Cash and cash equivalents	5,000
	40,000
Current liabilities:	
Trade payables	(15,000)
Other payables	(5,000)
Bank overdraft	(10,000)
	(30,000)

> You can see that the company has more current assets than current liabilities, so it has more than a pound for every pound it owes. Companies using UK GAAP show a subtotal at this point called 'Net current assets/(liabilities)', which would be 10,000 in my example.

The company has 1.33 in its short-term assets, for every 1.00 in its short-term liabilities. This ratio called the *current ratio*:

$$\frac{\text{Current assets}}{\text{Current liabilties}} = \frac{40,000}{30,000} = \textbf{1.33}$$

Whether a current ratio of 1.33 is good, or bad, depends on a number of things that are largely determined by the company you're analysing. For example consider:

▒ **Grocers** – When you look at grocers' accounts you will find that they tend to have net current *liabilities*, as their short-term liabilities are greater than their short-term assets. If you look at Tesco's 2008 accounts you find that it has total current assets of £5,992 million and its current liabilities are £10,263 million, giving a current ratio of just over 0.58. The company has 58 pence for every pound it owes! Now does this mean that Tesco's is on the brink of insolvency? Of course not – just think about its business for a moment: it doesn't carry much stock, gives limited credit to customers who use credit cards, but has the usual credit terms with its suppliers. The very nature of its business allows it to have negative working capital. People shop there almost every day and so it's fairly safe in not having its short-term liabilities covered by its short-term assets. It's the grocers' business model. As long as it has access to sufficient cash to pay the suppliers it needs to pay today, the company is OK as its customers will give it more cash tomorrow.

■ **Manufacturing companies** – Manufacturers have more current assets than retailers. They have more inventories – there's raw materials, work in progress and finished goods. They're often carrying retailers' stock, giving retailers normal corporate credit terms and have the same terms with their suppliers. Consequently you can see that manufacturers should have higher current ratios than retailers. How large the current ratio needs to be depends on the type of manufacturing business. It really depends on how long it takes them to convert their materials back into cash. The longer it takes them the more they need, and should have, in current assets to cover their creditors. A heavy engineering company, which may have a nine-month production cycle, could need as much as 2.5; whereas for a confectioner a current ratio of 1.4 is acceptable.

This means that current ratios can't be viewed in isolation – they have to be considered in the light of the company's business, and over a period of time. The size of the current ratio is determined by the interrelationship of two factors:

■ How long does it take the company to convert its materials into cash – the shorter the period, the lower the ratio.

■ How frequently do people buy the product – the greater the frequency, the lower the ratio.

Long- and medium-term solvency

Now I'm taking a longer-term view and there is a number of different indicators of a business's longer-term solvency:

■ positive net worth;

■ gearing (also referred to as *leverage*);

■ interest cover;

■ its terms and debt repayment schedule;

■ any undrawn committed borrowing facilities.

When you're looking at a company's ability to meet its long-term obligations you need to discover whether:

▓ Its assets cover its liabilities.

▓ It has borrowed too much money:

 – Can it afford the loans it has?

 – Can it repay the loans when they're due?

I'll start by looking at whether the company's assets cover its liabilities.

Net worth

The first thing that you can check is that the company's total assets exceed its total liabilities, and by how much. The bottom line on a UK company's balance sheet shows you this instantly, as the net worth is the same as the net assets. If you look at the balance sheet extract below you'll see that the company in my example has a net worth of 50,000.

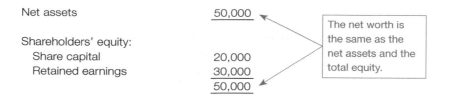

Net assets		50,000
Shareholders' equity:		
Share capital	20,000	
Retained earnings	30,000	
	50,000	

The net worth is the same as the net assets and the total equity.

Unfortunately it's not always that simple, as the net worth on the balance sheet can be influenced by a number of factors.

▓ **Revaluation of assets** – Revaluing assets increases a company's net worth. Now this may not be important unless you're comparing companies. Only a few companies revalue their assets, and in some countries revaluation is not allowed. So it is often difficult to make realistic comparisons of companies' net worth.

▓ **Exchange rate movements** – The value of overseas investments moves in line with exchange rates, and most of these adjustments are shown on the statement of recognised income and expense, or comprehensive income. The net worth of multinational companies with overseas subsidiaries is affected by exchange rate movements and their net worth can be more volatile. However, you can see the effect of exchange rate movements on the company's net worth and adjust for it if you need to.

- **Goodwill write offs** – You've already seen that UK companies can have sizeable amounts of goodwill written off through their reserves for acquisitions made before December 1998. This means that they have a lower net worth than an overseas company operating in a country where goodwill has always been shown as an intangible asset.

- **Provisions and deferred tax** – You've learnt that UK companies can make provisions when they have a measurable obligation, but in other countries provisions can be based on directors' decisions. Provisions are charged against profits and either reduce asset values or are shown as a liability. Either way they reduce a company's net worth. Deferred tax works in the same way.

Gearing

Now I'd like to move on to look at gearing, this measures the amount of debt a company has. But before I show you how to calculate it, I'll show you *why* it might be important. I'm now going to show you two balance sheets. I'm comparing the company in my example with another company in the same sector. They both have the same amount of capital invested in their business, and the same profits, but a different balance of debt to their shareholders' investment.

	My company	A competitor
Non current assets:		
Property, plant and equipment	100,000	100,000
Current assets:		
Inventories	10,000	10,000
Trade and other receivables	25,000	25,000
Cash and cash equivalents	5,000	5,000
	40,000	40,000
Total assets	140,000	140,000
Current liabilities:		
Trade payables	(15,000)	(15,000)
Other payables	(5,000)	(5,000)
Bank overdraft	(10,000)	(10,000)
	(30,000)	(30,000)

	My company	A competitor
Non current liabilities:		
Loan (at 10% interest)	(60,000)	0
Total liabilities	(90,000)	(30,000)
Net assets	50,000	110,000
Equity:		
Share capital	20,000	80,000
Retained earnings	30,000	30,000
	50,000	110,000

You can see that they both have the same amount of capital invested in the business, but all of the competitor's long-term capital has come from its shareholders. The competitor's business is safer in a recession. My company has to pay interest regardless of its profitability and at some time the loan has to be repaid. The competitor doesn't have a legal obligation to pay dividends, only interest; if times are bad it can reduce, or waive, its dividend. But in boom times my company would offer investors the best return. My identical profit could be shared amongst fewer shareholders, and I would have the opportunity to pay four times my competitors' dividend. Think back over the last ten years … Companies bought back their shares, increased their debt, and offered great returns to investors. (I'll tell you why they did this in Chapter 12.) But when the global recession took hold, suddenly all those companies with little, or no, debt start to look much more attractive!

It's obvious that my company has borrowed more than its competitor, but I have to find a way of measuring this – hence the gearing ratios. Gearing measures the proportion of borrowed money, either to the total capital (the traditional way of calculating gearing), or to the shareholders' stake in the business (the city's and bank's approach). There are a number of ways that companies can calculate their gearing, and I'll show you how to calculate all of them.

The gearing ratios

I'll calculate the gearing ratios using the example shown in 'my company', starting with the traditional approach.

Traditional gearing calculation

I've called this the 'traditional' way of calculating gearing, but as the other two ratios are called something else perhaps this is the gearing ratio! This method for calculating a company's gearing expresses the loans as a percentage of the total capital invested in the business. This capital invested, also called the *capital employed*, is all the loans (the lenders' investment) and the equity (the shareholders' investment). It shows how much of the total capital invested has been borrowed. In my example the loans and bank overdrafts are 70,000 and the equity is 50,000, so the total capital invested is 120,000.

$$\frac{\text{Loans}}{\text{Capital invested}} = \frac{10,000 + 60,000}{120,000} = \textbf{58.33\%}$$

If you calculate gearing in this way it will always be less than 100%, now look at what happens when I calculate it using the investors' approach.

Investors' gearing

This looks at the relationship between debt and the shareholders' stake in the business, often called the *equity*. This ratio is usually called the *debt to equity ratio* and there are three different ways that this can be calculated, each using a slightly different debt figure:

- long-term debt;
- all debt;
- net debt.

I'll show you how to calculate all three.

Long-term debt to equity ratio

$$\frac{\text{Long-term loans}}{\text{Equity}} = \frac{60,000}{50,000} = \textbf{120\%}$$

This tells you that the company's long-term loans are 20% greater than its equity. This ratio is rarely used today.

All debt to equity ratio

This is a measure that is often used by banks and credit rating agencies and it adds the overdraft, and any other short-term debt, to the long-term loan. It is also a more appropriate measure when looking at smaller private companies, which have limited access to long-term loans.

$$\frac{\text{Total debt}}{\text{Equity}} = \frac{70,000}{50,000} = \textbf{140\%}$$

The total debt is 40% greater than the equity. Companies in the US and Asia usually use this version of the debt to equity ratio.

Net debt to equity ratio

This is the commonest way of calculating gearing in Europe. It deducts the cash and cash equivalents from the total debt and looks at the business's net debt in relation to its equity. It tends to be a better measure when looking at multinational companies which may have both cash balances and bank overdrafts, with the cash balances in one country and bank overdrafts in another. This could arise if there are early redemption penalties attached to the debt (just like your mortgage). There are three other reasons why this could occur:

▨ The business could be seasonal, and the company only has this amount of cash at its year end.

▨ It is very difficult to take cash out of some countries, as they have *remittance restrictions*. Consequently companies may have an overall cash surplus, but are reluctant to use it to repay loans in a country with remittance restrictions.

▨ Multinational businesses often use debt, rather than equity, to finance their 'start up' activities in developing countries.

Whatever the reason for maintaining both cash balances and debt, a number of companies could pay off their loans and are described as having *negative gearing*. (Whilst it doesn't sound good, it just means that their cash and short-term deposits at the year end are greater than their loans.) This has made net gearing the most popular way of calculating gearing.

$$\frac{\text{All debt} - \text{Cash and cash equivalents}}{\text{Equity}} = \frac{65,000}{50,000} = \textbf{130\%}$$

Whilst this is the commonest way of calculating gearing in Europe, you should choose the definition of gearing that seems the most appropriate for the company you are analysing.

How you calculate gearing is largely irrelevant as long as you're consistent, although gearing based on only long-term debt is inappropriate if the company has changed the maturity of its debt during the period of analysis. (A move from long-term to short-term debt would reduce the apparent gearing using this measure, which is why it has fallen out of favour.) It is important that you calculate your own gearing figures, and don't rely on the ones chosen in the company accounts. If borrowing becomes a problem, finance directors will always pick the most flattering definition and sometimes it changes from one set of accounts to the next!

You've seen that there are different ways to calculate gearing, but does gearing matter? Does it really matter that a company has borrowed a lot of money? The answer is ... maybe, or may be not – it all depends! There are two factors I'd have to consider before answering the question:

- **Are the company's profits increasing or declining?** The company in my example has to pay at least 6,000 a year interest (10% of 60,000) regardless of its profitability. If its profits increase and debt remains the same interest becomes an increasingly smaller proportion of its profits, but if they fall interest could eliminate any profits the company makes.

- **Can the company afford to service and repay the debt?** To do this you have to look at the interest cover and the terms and debt repayment schedule.

A final word of warning about gearing ratios

All the methods use the equity, so the gearing ratios have the same problems I talked about when discussing a company's net worth. The revaluation of assets and goodwill write offs may have reduced the value of reserves. If you were making comparisons you should:

- **Exclude the revaluation reserve** – Revaluation of assets is not allowed in some countries, whilst in others it is done for tax reasons.

- **Add back any goodwill previously written off through reserves** – Companies usually disclose this in the notes to the reserves, if not you may have to refer to their transitional accounts when they first adopted IFRS.

▦ **Add back the provisions** – Companies using IFRS or UK GAAP make provisions once an obligation exists, whereas others may make provisions when either the management, or the tax authorities, feel they would be prudent.

However, for most purposes it is worth bearing in mind that revaluations and goodwill arising from past acquisitions may affect the ratios. Whether this is important, or not, depends on the amount involved and whether this has changed significantly during your analysis' period.

You now know that gearing defines how much a company has borrowed, now let's move on to answer the all important question – can they afford to borrow this much?

Interest cover

This is the measure of affordability. You know that it's often possible to borrow more money that you can afford. The terms 'sub prime' and 'toxic debt' are now part of everyday language. Companies were also lent more than they could afford, relying on their profits growing in the long-term to enable them to repay their loans. The interest cover ratio tells you if a company can afford its current level of debt by showing you how many times interest can be paid from the available profit. It is simply calculated by dividing the profit before interest by the net interest payable. I'm using the following extract from my example's income statement to calculate interest cover.

Operating profit	10,000	Interest is 60%
Interest	(6,000)	of the company's
Profit before tax	4,000	operating profit!

Now remember I said that ratios *quantify* what you can already see, and interest cover is no exception. However, it doesn't express interest as a percentage; it tells you how many times the company could pay the interest bill from its profits by dividing interest into the available profit.

$$\frac{\text{Profit before interest}}{\text{Net interest payable}} = \frac{10,000}{6,000} = \textbf{1.67 times}$$

It's obvious that the company could have a problem repaying its loans, unless it either has lots of cash or its profits rise. After all, interest is only a percentage of the money that it has borrowed. Does this business have any cash, and is it generating any cash? Well, if you remember its financial statements in the last chapter, it has 5,000 cash at its year end, and had a decrease in its cash and cash equivalents during the year of 4,500. It paid interest of 7,000 and dividends of 1,000, and increased its loans and share capital during the period. This means that it's reliant on profit growth to be able to repay its loans. The only comfort is that the long-term loan is at a fixed rate so the company is only exposed to increases in interest rates on its short-term borrowings.

Interest cover is an important ratio, as it's a common lending covenant. This means that if interest cover drops to a certain level, usually 2.5 times if it's based on profit (that means that interest is 40% of the company's profit), the loan has to be renegotiated or even repaid. (Since the move to IFRS most new interest cover covenants are based on EBITDA, which I'll discuss later in the chapter, as this is seen as a more appropriate measure.) If you read the *Financial Times* at the moment it's often referring to companies being in breach of their banking covenants, and having to sell off part of their business or have a rights issue to repay their loans. They're also paying their lenders significant amounts of money to renegotiate the covenants and defer their covenant testing dates. They borrowed money when the global economy was expanding, their profits have now fallen, they're in breach of covenant and need to renegotiate them.

Now I've calculated interest cover from profit, as this is the normal way it's calculated. However, interest is paid from cash and it can also be useful to look at the cash interest cover using the cash flow statement. I've extracted the relevant numbers from my example's cash flow statement, where the cash flows for interest are the same as the interest shown in the income statement:

Cash generated from operations	7,000
Tax paid	(1,500)
Net cash from operating activities	5,500
Interest paid	(7,000)
Interest received	1,000
Net interest paid	(6,000)

The cash flow that's usually used for this ratio is the pre tax cash flow, as this is the same basis as that used for a profit based interest cover. In my example this is the cash generated from operations of 7,000. This is even worse!

$$\frac{\text{Operational cash flow}}{\text{Net interest paid}} = \frac{7,000}{6,000} = \textbf{1.17 times}$$

Had the interest paid been shown as an operating cash flow, the net cash from operating activities would have been negative. You can see that if profits are falling this could pose serious problems for the company.

High levels of borrowing and poor interest cover are indications of possible future solvency problems. Interest cover is crucial, if you look at the large companies that went bust during the last recession and those currently having difficulties, they're highly geared companies with low interest cover. In fact you probably don't even need to be highly geared, your borrowings could be relatively low, but you could still have poor interest cover. The important question is – can the company afford its current level of debt? In my example, the answer is clearly 'no'.

A small complication – capitalising interest

I talked about capitalising interest in Chapter 2, and you saw that in its 2008 accounts Tesco's charged 29% of its interest charge to property, plant and equipment and all companies must adopt this accounting policy in the future. When you're calculating interest cover you need to remember that the interest shown on the income statement may only be a *fraction* of the interest cost incurred. I'll show you why this might be important by using a different example:

Operating profit	70,000
Interest income	15,000
Interest expense	(35,000)
Profit after interest	50,000

It looks like the net interest payable is 20,000, however there is a note in the accounts analysing the interest expense and this discloses:

Interest payable	60,000
Interest capitalised	(25,000)
Interest expense	35,000

What is the interest cover? A lot of analysts would say 3.5 times, but is it? How do you think its bankers would calculate this? You're calculating a ratio because it gives you useful information and you're using interest cover as an affordability measure. Whether interest is charged to fixed assets or the income statement is irrelevant. (That's why interest cover calculated from the cash flow statement is so useful, even though it is still unusual to find it included in any analysis.) Banking covenants are concerned with the *payment* of interest, not where it's charged. You might also be comparing companies having different accounting policies on capitalising interest. This means that you'd have to include the capitalised interest in the interest charge, preparing an adjusted interest cover.

$$\frac{\text{Profit before interest}}{\text{Adjusted net interest payable}} = \frac{70,000}{45,000} = \textbf{1.56 times}$$

Its interest cover doesn't look quite so good now!

The terms and debt repayment schedule

Now you've discovered that the company in my example is relying on future profit, and cash, growth to repay its loans. It certainly couldn't repay them now. So the next question you have to answer is – *when* do the loans have to be repaid? The answer lies in the terms and debt repayment schedule, which is disclosed in the notes to the balance sheet. The note for the company in my example is:

	Effective interest rate	Carrying value	Contractual cashflows	0 to <1 year	1 to <2 years	2 to <3 years	3 to <4 years	4 to <5 years	5 years and over
Cash and cash equivalents	Floating	5,000	5,000	5,000	–	–	–	–	–
Bank overdraft	Floating	(10,000)	(10,000)	(10,000)	–	–	–	–	–
Secured bank loans	10%	(60,000)	(67,500)	(6,000)	(61,500)	–	–	–	–
Total		(65,000)	(72,500)	(11,000)	(61,500)	0	0	0	0

Now you haven't seen one of these before, so I'd like to explain the heading 'contractual cash flows'. This is the cash flow arising from the repayment of debt and any committed interest cash flows. The bank overdraft is repayable on demand, so it shows as falling due in a year and there isn't any committed interest added to its value as the interest charge depends on the size of the overdraft. Early in the second year the whole of the loan has to be repaid, this means that, unless the company has significant undrawn committed borrowing facilities, its cash flow has to improve significantly in the next two years to enable it to repay the loan.

The notes to the accounts will also disclose the undrawn committed borrowing facilities, which are analysed into those expiring within a year, between one to two years, and more than two years.

It is difficult to reach any definite conclusions without knowing anything about the company, and only having one year's cash flow. (You'd really need to understand the trends in the company's cash flow.) But if the company's cash flows remain at this level it will experience difficulties in repaying the debt unless it can:

▨ *Repay existing loans with new loans.* To determine if this is possible you'd need to ask yourself whether lenders would view the business as a good risk taking into account things such as its relative performance, market conditions and interest cover?

▨ *Generate sufficient cash to repay the loans.* This doesn't have to come from its operations, it may be able to generate cash by reducing its working capital, or selling some of its assets.

▨ *Have a share issue.* A number of major companies have managed to obtain cash from a rights issue, just by highlighting the alternatives!

Summary of the solvency ratios and analysis

I've introduced you to a number of ratios, and some of the other things you need to consider to assess a company's solvency. I'd now like to summarise how these ratios are calculated, and why you use them.

▨ **The liquid ratio, the quick ratio or the acid test** – These are the three names for the ratio that measures a company's *liquidity*. It compares the assets that the company can quickly realise as cash (usually the current assets less inventories) with the company's current liabilities. This is a pessimistic view, as you are assuming that all the company's current liabilities have to be repaid today. This is only likely to happen if creditors have been waiting so long for payment that they decide to force the company into administration. The *payment period*, or *payable days*, is a good indicator of whether the company is having difficulties paying suppliers, as it gives an indication of how long the company takes to pay them. This is usually calculated by dividing the trade payables by the company's revenue and multiplying by 365. A more accurate, but less comparative, formula uses cost of sales, rather than revenue, as an approximation to purchases.

- **The current ratio** – This is concerned with short-term solvency, and looks at the relationship between the company's assets that can be realised within a year and the liabilities it has to repay in the next year. The size of the ratio is determined by the nature of the company's business and the interrelationship between the length of time the company takes to convert its materials into cash, and the frequency that its customers buy its products.

- **Net worth** – This tells you if, and by how much, the company's total assets exceed its total liabilities. It is the bottom line on the balance sheet, and is the same as the net assets and the total equity. In practice, however, you may have to make a number of adjustments to get a comparable number.

- **Gearing, or leverage** – This measures the relationship of the company's debt either to its equity, or capital employed. The most popular gearing ratio in Europe is the net debt to equity ratio, which expresses the company's net debt (all loans less cash and cash equivalents) as a percentage of its equity. You may have to adjust the company's reported equity to get a comparable measure. Gearing just quantifies how much has been borrowed, to find out if this level of debt is a problem you have to look at the company's interest cover, its terms and debt repayment schedule and its cash flow statement.

- **Interest cover** – This is an affordability measure that divides profit before interest by the net interest payable. It is an important ratio, as it's a common lending covenant. If interest cover falls to a certain level the loan has to be either renegotiated or repaid. A company that has a low interest cover is relying on future profit, and cash, growth to repay its loans. If you're comparing companies with different accounting policies, or are concerned about a possible breach of banking covenant, you'll need to adjust the net interest payable to exclude capitalised interest.

Interest cover can also be calculated from the cash flow statement, by dividing the operating cash flow by the net interest paid.

▦ **The terms and debt repayment schedule** – This is a note to the accounts that tells you the contracted cash flows arising from the company's debt and when the loans have to be repaid. It is very important if the company has a low interest cover. (If it's struggling to pay the interest, which is only a small percentage of the amount it's borrowed, you know it's going to have difficulties repaying the loans.) The loan repayment schedule tells you if it's going to have to repay any loans in the near future. It's also worth checking in this part of the notes whether the company has any committed, undrawn borrowing facilities.

▦ **Using cash and the cash flow statement** – The balance sheet identifies how much cash the business has at its year end, and the cash flow statement shows you how much it generated during the year. Looking at the two helps you understand whether the company is likely to have any difficulties repaying its loans on time.

IMI's solvency in 2008

You've seen how to calculate the ratios from a simple set of accounts. Now I'd like to show you how to calculate them from a real set of accounts. And, as you've probably guessed, it's going to become more complicated. I'll just be calculating the ratios for 2008 using IMI's accounts, and will show you the trend when I analyse their accounts in Chapter 13.

I'll follow the same procedure and show you how to measure IMI's:

▦ immediate solvency, or liquidity;

▦ short-term solvency;

▦ long- and medium-term solvency.

Immediate solvency – liquidity

This is measured by the ratio called the acid test (which is also called the liquid or the quick ratio), which looks at the relationship between the company's liquid assets and its current liabilities. I've extracted the relevant lines from IMI's 2008 consolidated balance sheet and ticked their liquid assets:

		Liquid asset?
Current assets		
Inventories	333.5	✗
Trade and other receivables	408.5	✓?
Current tax	4.7	✗
Investments	17.8	✓
Cash and cash equivalents	123.9	✓
	888.4	
Current liabilities		
Bank overdraft	(4.6)	
Interest bearing loans and borrowings	(46.5)	
Provisions	(29.4)	
Current tax	(26.6)	
Trade and other payables	(448.2)	
	(555.3)	

You'll notice that I've excluded all of its inventories and the current tax asset, as they can't be realised immediately. I've also put a question mark by trade and other receivables and that's because there's a slight complication in IMI's accounts as the notes disclose that they include £10 million receivables due in more than a year. This means that its liquid assets are receivables falling due in a year, investments and cash and cash equivalents totalling £540.2 million (398.5 + 17.8 + 123.9). It has total current liabilities of £555.3 million, so its acid test in 2008 is 0.97:

$$\frac{\text{Liquid assets}}{\text{Current liabilities}} = \frac{540.2}{555.3} = \textbf{0.97}$$

If all their creditors asked for immediate repayment, IMI would be able to pay them 97 pence for every pound they owe. Their liquid assets almost cover their current liabilities. This ratio is really only important if it is taking a long time to pay, although even then IMI has more than enough liquid assets to pay them. But I'd like to show you how to calculate the ratio, so let's see how long IMI are taking to pay suppliers.

To do this I need some numbers from its 2008 accounts – the revenue, cost of sales and trade payables. The revenue was £1,900.6 million, the cost of sales before exceptional items was £1,140.5 million, and the trade payables were £223.6 million at the end of the year.

I'll calculate the creditor days based on both revenue and the cost of sales:

$$\frac{\text{Trade payables}}{\text{Revenue}} \times 365 = \frac{223.6}{1,900.6} \times 365 = \textbf{42.9 days}$$

$$\frac{\text{Trade payables}}{\text{Cost of sales}} \times 365 = \frac{223.6}{1,140.5} \times 365 = \textbf{71.6 days}$$

As you're not using this ratio to compare IMI's performance with another company, the payable days based on cost of sales is more reliable. This suggests that suppliers are waiting 72 days to be paid. This is about the national average, so it's unlikely that suppliers will be forcing IMI into administration.

Now let's have a look at IMI's short-term solvency.

Short-term solvency

This is measured by the current ratio, which measures the relationship between the company's assets that can be realised within a year and its liabilities that will have to be realised within a year. It's 'within a year' and 'realised' that are important, and this means that you can't always use the total current assets. You now know that IMI has receivables falling due in more than a year of £10 million and these have to be excluded. Consequently the current asset figure that would be used in the current ratio is £878.4 million (£888.4 million total current assets – £10 million receivables falling due in more than a year).

$$\frac{\text{Current assets}}{\text{Current liabilities}} = \frac{878.4}{555.3} = \textbf{1.58}$$

IMI has £1.58 in realisable current assets for every £1.00 it owes. It doesn't look likely that it will have any short-term solvency problems, now let's see if it could have any problems in the long-term.

Long- and medium-term solvency

There's a number of things to consider when looking at IMI's longer-term solvency – its net worth, gearing, interest cover, terms and debt repayment schedule and committed borrowing facilities, and its cash balances and cash generation.

Net worth

You know that this should be very simple to identify, as it's the total equity found on the bottom line of most UK balance sheets. You're only glancing at this to make sure it's a positive number and that the company's total assets are greater than its total liabilities. Whilst you could do some adjustments to make the numbers internationally comparable it's probably not worth it, as this is just a rough check.

Firstly let's look at IMI's equity shown on its 2008 balance sheet.

Equity	
Share capital	84.7
Share premium	165.1
Other reserves	71.1
Retained earnings	131.5
Total equity attributable to equity shareholders of the Company	452.4
Minority interest	9.3
Total equity	461.7

IM's net worth is £461.7 million, with £452.4 million being funded by its shareholders and £9.3 million being funded by the minority shareholders in some of its subsidiaries. Now you know that a company's net worth can be influenced by a number of factors, so let's see how these have affected IMI's net worth.

▨ **Revaluation of assets** – IMI hasn't revalued its property, plant and equipment but, like all companies, does show its financial instruments at fair value. Some of these adjustments are shown in other financial income and expense, whereas others are charged directly to equity. You'll recall that in its financial review it reported a revaluation loss of £22.2 million on its financial instruments in 2008. This reduced profits and net worth. (In 2007 the situation was different, as it had a net financial income of £1.6 million.) Another £3.8 million was charged directly to the hedging reserve.

▨ **Exchange rate movements** – There were significant exchange-rate movements during 2008 as sterling weakened against all major currencies and IMI's translation reserve increased by £68.1 million.

▨ **Goodwill write offs** – You know that before 1998 IMI wrote off £364 million goodwill against its retained earnings. This is important – just compare that with the current level of retained earnings!

▨ **Provisions and deferred tax** – The net deferred tax asset increased by £3.6 million, largely as a result of the increased pension deficit. The provisions increased by £25.0 million, largely as a result of the Severe Service investigation. The net effect of these was to reduce the reported net worth by £21.4 million.

Although people talk about a company's net worth being important, and it does influence some of its credit ratings, I'm not sure how relevant it is. Its net worth has been significantly reduced because it was highly acquisitive before 1998, when the accounting rules required goodwill to be written off through reserves. 2008's market volatility had a dramatic effect on the value of IMI's financial instruments, and the value of its overseas investments. The Severe Service investigation has reduced the business's net worth, however this is a liability that will be a cash outflow next year, so I'm less concerned about that. I'll be returning to the usefulness of net worth, or net assets, in Chapter 12.

Gearing

Now, you know that there are a number of gearing ratios and usually you only calculate one of them. But I'm going to calculate all of them so you know how to calculate them from published accounts. I'll calculate:

- the traditional gearing ratio;

- long-term debt to equity;

- all debt to equity;

- net debt to equity.

Traditional gearing

This shows how much of the invested capital has been borrowed. It expresses the loans as a percentage of the company's capital employed, which is all the loans (the lenders' investment) and the equity (the shareholders' investment).

Firstly, I'll take the loans. IMI had, at the end of December 2008, £51.1 million in loans that are due to be repaid in a year (the bank overdraft of £4.6 million plus the interest bearing loans and borrowings of £46.5 million), and £371.5 million due to be repaid in more than a year. So its long-term debt is £371.5 million, and its total debt is £422.6 million.

Now, the equity is shown on the bottom line of the balance sheet but you've learnt that it's not necessarily that simple; if you want to make some international comparisons you may have to make some adjustments. You may decide that, for the purpose of your analysis, it's unnecessary. But I'll show you how to make the adjustments, just in case you feel you need to make them. So I'll calculate the gearing ratios using two equity figures – one based on the unadjusted accounts, and an adjusted one.

Its total shareholders' investment is £461.7 million, with £452.4 million coming from its shareholders and £9.3 million coming from minority interests. But the retained earnings have been affected by:

- £65.9 million unspent provisions. Provisions represent future cash outflows, and if the companies that you are comparing use IFRS then it probably isn't important. However different countries have different rules about provisions, and in some countries they're tax driven. This means that you may have to add back the provisions in order to make the numbers comparable.

- £364 million goodwill has been written off for businesses it acquired before December 1998. This is money that has been invested in the business, and in most countries goodwill has always been shown as an intangible asset. You can see that £364 million represents a significant reduction in the value of IMI's equity.

▨ The net deferred tax asset of £37.8 million, which is only a 'paper asset' not involving a current cash flow. It is logical that if a deferred tax liability, another provision, is added to the reported equity, a deferred tax asset should be deducted.

It hasn't revalued its properties, so its adjusted equity is £853.8 million (£461.7 million + £65.9 million + £364.0 million − £37.8 million). If the company you're analysing has revalued, you'll have to exclude the revaluation reserve if you're comparing it with companies that haven't revalued their assets.

Consequently its adjusted capital employed is £1,276.4 million (loans of £422.6 million + adjusted equity of £853.8 million) and its unadjusted capital employed is £884.3 million (loans of £422.6 million + unadjusted equity of £461.7 million).

Now I can calculate its traditional gearing ratios, firstly based on the unadjusted figures:

$$\frac{\text{Total loans}}{\text{Unadjusted capital employed}} = \frac{422.6}{884.3} = \textbf{47.8\%}$$

I'll now calculate the same ratio using the adjusted capital employed. The gearing falls by almost 15%:

$$\frac{\text{Total loans}}{\text{Adjusted capital employed}} = \frac{422.6}{1{,}276.4} = \textbf{33.1\%}$$

Long-term debt to equity

This is a different approach to the gearing calculation, this time expressing the long-term loans as a percentage of the shareholders' investment in the business. IMI has long-term loans of £371.5 million, unadjusted equity of £461.7 million, and adjusted equity of £853.8 million.

Using its unadjusted equity, its long-term debt to equity ratio is 80.5%.

$$\frac{\text{Long-term loans}}{\text{Unadjusted equity}} = \frac{371.5}{461.7} = \textbf{80.5\%}$$

Using the adjusted equity, its long-term debt to equity ratio falls to 43.5%:

$$\frac{\text{Long-term loans}}{\text{Adjusted equity}} = \frac{371.5}{853.8} = \textbf{43.5\%}$$

All debt to equity

This looks at the relationship of the company's total borrowings to the shareholders' investment. IMI's total debt is £422.6 million. Using its unadjusted equity, its all debt to equity ratio is 91.5%.

$$\frac{\text{Total loans}}{\text{Unadjusted equity}} = \frac{422.6}{461.7} = \textbf{91.5\%}$$

Using the adjusted equity, its all debt to equity ratio falls to 49.5%:

$$\frac{\text{Total loans}}{\text{Adjusted equity}} = \frac{422.6}{853.8} = \textbf{49.5\%}$$

Net debt to equity

This is the most widely used definition of gearing in Europe and looks at net borrowings as a percentage of the shareholders' investment. At the end of December 2008, IMI had cash and cash equivalents of £123.9 million, and this is deducted from the total debt to give net debt of £298.7 million (422.6 – 123.9).

Using its unadjusted equity, its net debt to equity ratio is 64.7%.

$$\frac{\text{Total loans} - \text{Cash \& cash equivalents}}{\text{Unadjusted equity}} = \frac{298.7}{461.7} = \textbf{64.7\%}$$

Using the adjusted equity, its net debt to equity ratio falls to 35%:

$$\frac{\text{Total loans} - \text{Cash \& cash equivalents}}{\text{Adjusted equity}} = \frac{298.7}{853.8} = \textbf{35.0\%}$$

You have seen that gearing can be calculated in many different ways. Goodwill, revaluations and provisions, and deferred tax change the equity and, whilst it doesn't matter when you're looking at one year in isolation, it can distort the trends shown by your analysis. Consequently, if they have changed significantly during the period you need to adjust the reported figures to have a comparative basis. Once you have a common base, you then select the most appropriate gearing calculation to use. This is largely determined by the company's capital structure – after all it would be pointless using a measure based on long-term debt if all the company's borrowings are short term! The net debt to equity ratio usually offers the best basis for comparison.

IMI is not highly geared, and now it's time to see whether it can afford the debt it has.

Interest cover

This looks at the company's ability to service its debt and you can calculate it from both the income statement and the cash flow statement. I'll start by calculating the interest cover from the income statement, as this is the usual way it's calculated. Here's the relevant extracts:

Extracts from the income statement and the notes		
	As published	Net of exceptional items
Operating profit	209.8	268.9
Interest expense	26.3	26.3
Interest income on bank deposits	(10.2)	(10.2)
Net interest payable	16.1	16.1

Now your first problem ... which profit are you going to use? Do you use the published operating profit, or the adjusted operating profit? To help you decide let's think for a moment about why you're interested in interest cover. It's an affordability measure, and you're trying to identify if the company is likely to have any difficulties with its banks. Normally you're trying to look at trends, to see if it's getting better or worse. If you're interested in trends you need to exclude the operating exceptional items, as they're 'one offs'. So, on balance, the most appropriate figure to use as a measure that shows you the underlying affordability trend is the group operating profit before exceptional items.

When you've decided on the best profit figure to use, calculating the interest cover is a matter of simple arithmetic. I'll show you both:

$$\frac{\text{Group operating profit before exceptionals}}{\text{Net interest payable}} = \frac{268.9}{16.1} = \textbf{167 times}$$

This is the underlying interest cover, and would be the best figure to use for comparisons. The published interest cover is lower at 13 times:

$$\frac{\text{Group operating profit}}{\text{Net interest payable}} = \frac{209.8}{16.1} = \textbf{13.0 times}$$

Either way you can see that IMI has no problem supporting its current level of borrowings, even if its halved it would still have an adequate interest cover.

I mentioned earlier in the chapter that most banking covenants, including IMI's, are now linked to EBITDA rather than profit. You also read in my summary of IMI's financial risk management note that it is comfortably within its banking covenants. So let's quantify 'comfortable'.

EBITDA is operating profit plus depreciation and amortisation. You'll find EBITDA in IMI's financial review and you can find the depreciation and amortisation and impairment charges in the notes to the accounts or on the statement of cash flows. You'll notice that I'm not adding back less amortisation to the profit before exceptional items, as the amortisation of acquired intangible assets is one of the exceptional items and hasn't been charged to profit so it doesn't need to be added back.

	As published	Net of exceptional items
Operating profit	209.8	268.9
Depreciation	43.1	43.1
Amortisation charged to profit	16.4	3.2
EBITDA	269.3	315.2

You can see I've calculated an adjusted EBITDA, as well as a published EBITDA. If you're looking at trends, and trying to make comparisons you'll need to use an adjusted EBITDA to see IMI's underlying performance, but I'll show you both calculations:

$$\frac{\text{Adjusted EBITDA}}{\text{Net interest payable}} = \frac{315.2}{16.1} = \textbf{19.6 times}$$

$$\frac{\text{EBITDA}}{\text{Net interest payable}} = \frac{269.3}{16.1} = \textbf{16.7 times}$$

Now let's look at the cash flow statement and see how its cash based interest cover looks.

Cash flow statement extracts

Firstly here's the operating cash flow.

Cash generated from the operations	288.6
Income taxes paid	(54.4)
	234.2
Additional pension scheme funding	(16.8)
European Commission fine	–
Net cash from operating activities	217.4

The cash based interest cover would use cash of £271.8 million (the cash generated from operations of £288.6 million less the additional pension contribution of £16.8 million). Now I need the interest received, shown as an investing cash flow, and the interest paid, shown as a financing cash flow.

Interest paid	29.0
Interest received	(12.4)
Net interest paid	16.6

You'll notice that the net interest *payable* on the income statement is slightly different from the interest *paid* shown on the cash flow statement. Interest is accrued on the income statement, whereas the cash flow statement is only concerned with the interest that is received and paid during the year.

You don't need to calculate the ratio to know there's no problem. But I still will calculate it to show you how it's done. Its interest cover rises to just over 16 times.

$$\frac{\text{Cash generated from operations}}{\text{Net interest payable}} = \frac{271.8}{16.6} = \textbf{16.4 times}$$

It's clear that IMI has no problem affording its current borrowings, and its interest cover indicates that its business could support much higher levels of borrowings.

Now let's see when it's loans have to be repaid.

The terms and debt repayment schedule

IMI's terms and debt repayment schedule is disclosed in the notes to the accounts, and here's the relevant part of the note for 2008:

19.4 Terms and debt repayment schedule

	Effective interest rate	Carrying value	Contractual cashflows	0 to <1 year	1 to <2 years	2 to <3 years	3 to <4 years	4 to <5 years	5 years and over
Cash and cash equivalents	Floating	123.9	124.0	124.0	–	–	–	–	–
US loan notes 2009–2022	6.83–7.17%	(59.0)	(75.2)	(38.6)	(1.7)	(1.7)	(15.5)	(0.7)	(17.0)
US loan notes 2009–2014	Floating	(37.3)	(42.2)	(12.0)	(0.8)	(0.8)	(0.8)	(0.8)	(27.0)
US loan notes 2018	5.98%	(104.2)	(161.0)	(6.2)	(6.2)	(6.2)	(6.2)	(6.2)	(130.0)
Finance leases	Various	(0.5)	(0.5)	(0.1)	(0.2)	(0.1)	(0.1)	–	–
Bank overdraft	Floating	(4.6)	(4.6)	(4.6)	–	–	–	–	–
Unsecured bank loans	Floating	(216.1)	(238.2)	(8.6)	(55.4)	(112.8)	(61.4)	–	–
Other unsecured loans	Floating	(0.9)	(0.9)	(0.9)	–	–	–	–	–
Total		(298.7)	(398.6)	53.0	(64.3)	(121.6)	(84.0)	(7.7)	(174.0)

You can clearly see that IMI has more than enough cash to pay the contractual cash flows on its debt for the next year, and would have enough left to pay over 80% of the next year's debt contractual cash flows.

IMI's cash and cash generation

IMI is good at generating cash. You've already seen that IMI has cash of £123.9 million at the end of December 2008, and had net debt of £298.7

million. If you look at its cash flow statement in 2008 there was an increase in its cash and cash equivalents of £22.3 million, which was increased by the effect of exchange rates on the cash and cash equivalents it held at the end of the year. And this was after £16.7 million spent buying back its own shares, and repaying loans of £45.5 million.

You may recall that in its financial review it rewrote the cash flow statement to identify a slightly different operating cash flow – free cash flow. It started with EBITDA and then adjusted this for any working capital requirements, net capital expenditure, and capitalised development costs. This gave it an operating cash flow of £238.3 million, which it compared with its profit after restructuring costs of £246.7 million. This gave it a conversion rate of 96.6%. (This ratio is affected by its profitability, capital expenditure and control of working capital.) Once it deducted the tax and net interest paid and the additional pension scheme funding that left it £151.2 million before any corporate activity. This cash could be used to acquire businesses, pay dividends, buy back shares or repay debt.

Not only can it generate cash it can also raise it, even during the credit crunch. You will remember in Chapter 6 that at the end of 2008 it had undrawn committed borrowing facilities of £154 million, and when you read its financial review you found that in January 2009 a further £25 million facility had been agreed.

What have we learned?

Well, IMI's so solvent it probably wasn't worth measuring it and calculating the ratios. The ratios are measuring what you can already see, and you don't have to calculate every ratio to understand a business's financial performance. In isolation the ratios tell you very little and, in IMI's case, the only reason you'd do them is to see if there's any trend in its solvency. Is it becoming more solvent, or less solvent?

10

Profitability

Introduction

Imagine that you have come into a lot of money … If you suddenly won five million pounds, how would you choose your investments? You'd naturally want a good return, but I wonder how you feel about risk. Would you be prepared to lose all of your money? I thought not, I didn't think you'd want to have to go back to work again! You'd probably compare any return you're offered with the rate that you could get from a building society. For most of us, this would be a 'risk free rate' (in as much as anything can be risk free). If you had a lot of money, you could probably find a better risk free rate, but building society interest rates are a reasonable benchmark.

If the risk increased you'd expect the investment to offer a better return. Comparing risk and return is an everyday activity; we do it when we look for jobs (are you in the best paid job available?), in just the same way as when we plan our investments. Most people are risk averse, a small increase in risk means that you'd want to see a substantial increase in the return. Other people aren't, and embark on lifestyles (and investments) that you would find too risky to even contemplate.

When you're looking at a company's financial performance you want to be able to make comparisons, particularly if you're an investor choosing your investments. You want to compare its profitability to a risk free rate, and to other businesses in the same sector. Any company you choose has to beat the risk free rate, as investing in a company is never risk free. The investment return you'd find acceptable is determined by two factors: your personal attitude to risk, combined with the risk inherent in the company. You would want to see a higher return from a car company than a grocer: we all have to eat every day but don't have to buy a car every year! The return on capital employed ratio, sometimes called the return on assets or the return on investment, enables you to have a basis for comparing the overall profitability of companies.

It's also important for another reason. During the 1990s some consultants in the US developed a concept called 'shareholder value'. They 'discovered' that companies add value for their shareholders when their return on capital is greater than their cost of raising the capital. If it costs 10% to finance the business, the return on capital must be greater than 10%! The greater the difference between the return on capital and the cost of capital the greater the valued added to the investment, or destroyed if the return is less than the cost. The consultants believe that this value added is the major determinant of share price movements, and this approach has become one of the main ways that shares are valued. So the return on capital is a useful measure for both comparing companies and explaining share price movements.

The return on capital is exactly what it says – it measures the return that's generated on the capital used by the company. It usually defines the capital as the total capital invested in the business, regardless of whether it is in the form of equity or debt. This allows you to compare companies with different capital structures, identifying which company is generating the best return overall. (If you were concerned purely with the return for the shareholders, you would calculate another ratio (the return on equity) which is discussed in detail in Chapter 12.)

You will discover that companies can improve their return on capital in a number of different ways, and it is important to understand why the return on capital has changed. Then you can understand whether any improvement is a 'one off', or whether it represents a sustainable increase.

In this chapter I will be looking at the return on capital ratio in detail and showing the ways that companies try to improve it.

What is the definition of the return on capital employed?

It has traditionally been defined as:

$$\frac{\text{Profit before interest and tax (PBIT or EBIT)}}{\text{Capital employed}}$$

However, both companies and analysts use slightly different definitions. Companies have a tendency to choose a definition that improves their reported return on capital trend, and analysts tend to use a definition that improves the company's comparability. So, although there appears to be a nice simple formula to programme into your spreadsheet, it may not be the best definition to use if you're comparing different companies' financial performance. I have another problem – I'm not sure that one definition of return on capital is enough. I like to do two: one looking at the business's return on total capital, and another looking at a return on capital based on the company's trading activities – a return on the company's operating capital.

I'll start by looking at a return on total capital employed, and then adapt it for the company's trading activities. I mentioned in the last chapter that calculating the capital employed is not as simple as it seems if you want to be able to compare a company's performance over time, and with its competitors. Companies change their accounting policies, they restructure, buy and sell businesses. When you're trying to make comparisons you have to find a way to eliminate, or at least minimise, these differences. This means that you can't necessarily use profit before interest and tax in the ratio, and may have to make some adjustments to arrive at a comparable capital employed. I'm going to show you how to do this in the next few pages.

PBIT – why has this profit been selected?

Firstly I'd like to explain why this profit figure has traditionally formed the basis for the return on capital calculation. You know the return on capital is a useful comparative tool that's used to compare a company's performance in two ways:

▪ **Over time** – You have to use a profit before tax, as the tax rules change from one year to the next. If you're looking at a company's performance over a period of time you have to ignore the factors outside its control.

▪ **With other companies in the same sector** – You want to be able to compare companies with different capital structures. Now if you think about the income statement for a moment, interest comes out of before tax profits. Whereas, dividends are shown after tax. Using profit before interest ensures that you are comparing apples with apples!

But PBIT isn't a perfect profit figure to choose if it includes 'one off' items of income and expense, such as restructuring costs or profits on the sale of property, plant and equipment. Most companies using IFRS include exceptional items in operating profit (although most UK companies usually show operating profit before and after exceptional items), whereas those using UK GAAP have to show some exceptional items after operating profit. You can also have inconsistencies arising from depreciation and amortisation charges. How could you compare a business using Japanese accounting rules, where depreciation is effectively determined by the tax authorities, with a company using IFRS. You're always trying to look at trends and this means that you have to identify the company's underlying profitability and attempt to eliminate international differences. So you start with operating profit and make some adjustments.

So let's see what you might have to adjust.

Gains, or losses, on sale of property, plant and equipment

As these are included in operating profit they are part of profit before interest and tax. Now in essence they reflect an under depreciation, or over depreciation, of assets. But they're not an ongoing source of profits and including them affects the return on capital, but rarely represents sustainable profits, or losses. Unless they're so small that they're immaterial I don't include them in the profit used in the return on capital employed calculation, as they can destroy the ratio's comparability. (In 2008 IMI's were £200,000, and as this is immaterial in the context of an underlying operating profit of £266.3 million I have ignored them.)

You can easily find the gains and losses on disposal of property, plant and equipment that have been included in the operating profit by looking at the operating cash flow on the cash flow statement. They will be listed as part of the adjustments that have to be made in order to arrive at the company's operating cash flow.

Eliminating the differences arising from depreciation and amortisation – EBITDA

I've mentioned EBITDA before. It's an important measure that's frequently referred to in the financial press. You know that it is an acronym standing for *E*arnings (another word for profit) *B*efore *I*nterest, *T*ax, *D*epreciation and *A*mortisation. It is calculated by adding the depreciation and amortisation charge to the operating profit. Why would anyone want to do that?

In a nutshell, you do this because you want to compare one company with another and different depreciation and amortisation policies affect the reported profit. Depreciation and amortisation are charged to operating profit, and operating profit is one of the business's key performance indicators. For example, how can you compare the operating profit of ...?

▪ Two shipping companies, one with an old fully depreciated fleet and the other having a new modern fleet. The shipping company with the old fleet whose ships are fully depreciated could report a much higher profit figure than the one with the new fleet.

▪ A UK business, where depreciation is a management judgement, with a Japanese one where the depreciation charge is determined by the tax rules.

▪ A business that has moved into different industries through its own efforts with a predatory one that's bought its way in and has had to recognise acquired intangible assets.

EBITDA allows you to make comparisons of businesses even in different countries, with different accounting policies and different strategies. It's also an important measure because it more closely aligns the profit with the cash flow, as it represents most of the cash that the business *will* receive from the current period's trading. (The other big 'paper' charges that don't affect cash are provisions and impairment, if you added these to EBITDA you have the total future cash flow from the period's trading.)

I was asked to compare five global companies in the same sector, and identify their relative strengths and weaknesses. Two used US accounting rules, one

IFRS, one Japanese rules and the other Korean rules. The only way to compare their profitability was to use EBITDA for their return on capital and operating margin. I also had to adjust their asset values back to cost, to eliminate the differences arising from different depreciation and amortisation charges.

Exceptional items

Most exceptional items are included within the appropriate cost heading, although some are disclosed separately. Exceptional items are by definition unusual, and not expected to occur on an ongoing basis. The return on capital employed is intended to be a comparable measure so these should be excluded, as long as you believe the item is truly exceptional. Most analysts regard restructuring costs and the amortisation arising from acquired intangible assets as exceptional items. I shall exclude both, when I'm analysing IMI, as I'm looking at the business over a four-year period and want the numbers to be comparable.

Associates and joint ventures

Associates and joint ventures are problematic, as their after-tax profits are shown as a single number before tax. You then have two choices, you either:

- Include the company's share of it profits or losses, even though these profits are not comparable with the other profits that you will use. If they're not significant this probably won't matter.

or

- Exclude them totally, excluding its profits and deducting them from the capital employed, and calculate a separate return on capital for the associates and joint ventures. On balance I think this is probably the best, and simplest, solution.

And what about the income from the company's other investments?

And finally there's the problem that the company's other investments have been funded from its invested capital, so shouldn't the income the company receives from them be included in the profit figure? If you're going to be consistent with the number used for capital employed you have to include any income from its investments and interest receivable.

A revised profit figure

As you're using return on capital as a comparability measure, you need to eliminate one offs. Consequently the most appropriate figure to use for the calculation of the business's return on total capital employed would be:

> Operating profit − Exceptional items including material gains or losses on the sale of property plant and equipment + Interest receivable and similar income

However if you were just looking at the return on the business's trading activities you would ignore the return from the business's investments and use:

> Operating profit − Exceptional items including material gains or losses on the sale of property plant and equipment

Now you've found a comparable profit figure, let's move on to look at the capital employed.

What is the capital employed?

The capital employed is the total investment in the business – the lenders' and the shareholders' investment. But you've probably guessed by now that deciding on the figure to use won't be as easy as it sounds! If you look on the internet, you'll find that the definition most websites give for capital employed is the total assets less the current liabilities. This is the traditional definition, which equals the total of the equity and the non current liabilities. Now in some situations this may be an acceptable measure to use, and you may choose to use this definition, as it's simple. But sadly it isn't always appropriate if you're comparing companies' performance, and I'd like to explain why.

Firstly I'll look at the shareholders' investment.

Adjusting the equity

Unfortunately the published reserves may not be a comparable measure for a UK company, as they are affected by the company's accounting policy on revaluation and any goodwill that was previously written off through reserves. You've already seen this in the last chapter, where I discussed the adjustments that you have to make. If you are comparing companies that have different revaluation policies you need to exclude the revaluation reserve to make the numbers comparable. You already know that IMI has a sizeable amount of goodwill, £364 million, written off through its retained earnings. If I compared IMI with another company overseas, which had always shown goodwill as an intangible asset, I have to add back the £364 million otherwise its capital employed isn't comparable with the other company.

A brief word about provisions and deferred tax

Some analysts include provisions and net deferred tax as part of the capital employed, arguing that they've already been charged to the income statement but haven't been spent, so the cash is still within the business. They feel that logically they should be considered as part of capital employed, as if they hadn't been charged to profit the equity, and therefore the capital employed, would be greater. The provisions and any deferred tax have reduced the equity, no cash has left the business and so, on balance, I think that they should be part of the capital employed, particularly if you're making international comparisons and the companies are using different rules.

And there's another possible adjustment you may like to think about

Cast your mind back to Chapter 6 and the discussion on pensions accounting ... the accounting rules require that final salary pension scheme's recoverable surpluses and deficits are shown on the balance sheet. Now you know that balance sheets have to balance. When companies adopted IFRS, or FRS 17 if they're using UK GAAP, their retained earnings were affected (they were reduced by any deficit and increased by any recoverable surplus). The size of the deficit is affected by company contributions and the fund's performance. The company's contributions can reduce any deficit, and most companies with deficits are making additional contributions. The fund's actual performance is split into two: its expected performance, which all companies charge to the income statement, and the actuarial gains and losses. This means that the value of a company's equity changes with the annual valuation of its final salary pension schemes. The problem is exacerbated if you're comparing a UK company with one overseas. Although they both may be using IFRS, the financial statements may not be directly comparable, as most overseas companies use the corridor approach that stabilises their balance sheets, although it can make earnings more volatile, by recognising only those actuarial gains and losses outside of the 10% corridor. Most

UK companies have traded stable earnings, as actuarial gains and losses don't affect their income statements, with unstable equity.

Research in 2008 by Fassshauer, Glam, and Street identified that the major European companies in its sample who used the corridor approach overstated their equity by an average of 3.43% and understated their net pension liability by 41.02%. So you can see that pension accounting affects the comparability of the financial statements and the ratios, but in practice the trade off in time and comparability means that it's probably not worth adjusting for it unless you're an analyst. (At the time I'm writing this a lot of analysts are actually revising pension liabilities upwards, as they think they're understated. Economists at Goldman Sachs think that if the duration of pension liabilities is 20 years and companies changed from an average discount rate of 6.1% to 4.8% (current gilt yields plus a 1% premium for an AA rated corporate bond) the FTSE 100 pension liabilities would rise by £93 billion.) But you're not an analyst and you're probably 'time poor', so you have to make a compromise. If you are trying to look at trends in the business's operating performance, and want to remove any 'one offs' from your calculation and feel that the value of the pension fund is having a significant effect on equity and capital employed, you may need to make an adjustment. (You can adjust the equity, and capital employed, by adding any deficit, and deducting any surplus to the reported equity.) On the other hand, you may feel it's more prudent to include pension fund surpluses, or deficits, and I'd be very surprised if you felt the need to adjust them!

Identifying the loans

If you think about the traditional definition of capital employed it only included the company's long-term debt, as the return on capital was seen as a measure of the return on the long-term investment in the business. However, company treasurers often switch from long-term to short-term debt if the rates are more attractive. This short-term debt is part of the capital invested in the business, and in these 'credit crunch' days banks often prefer to give companies short-term debt, particularly 'on demand' bank overdrafts, as they feel there's less risk involved. Even if you don't make any other adjustments, I think that you have to include all of the company's loans in the capital employed.

Some companies and analysts use a net debt figure, deducting cash from the total debt. Whilst it does simplify the profit figure (it eliminates the need to include interest received), it doesn't always provide a realistic measure of a company's capital employed. The balance sheet is a snapshot, showing the company's cash balance on a certain day. That day often reflects the company's best position, when its cash levels are at their highest. The company has raised loans because it feels that it needed the money to fund its business, and no one likes to pay interest if they don't have to. Companies usually have large cash balances for one of three reasons:

- It's a short-term situation, and the cash will be spent in the near future.
- The cash is locked up somewhere (maybe there are remittance restrictions).
- The company feels that it's prudent to have large cash balances.

Consequently, on balance I think that the cash should not be netted off from the debt in the return on total capital employed measure. I've included the interest received on cash balances as part of the profit measure, to be consistent in the treatment of investments. However, although all companies need cash to survive, cash isn't one of the company's trading assets and is not used in calculating a company's operating capital employed.

And businesses up for sale?

You've discovered that if a company is intending to sell a business, it is classed as a discontinued operation. This means that it shows the discontinued operation's after tax profits after the continuing operation's after tax profits and its assets and liabilities are shown separately on the balance sheet as 'held for sale'. This means that its profits are not included in the return on capital calculation, so logically its net assets should also be excluded.

And a final thought – is it appropriate to use the capital employed at the year end?

The profits are earned *during* the year, and the capital employed is a year end 'snapshot' figure. To be technically accurate you should use an average capital employed figure but if there's been no significant changes during the year, the year end figure will be good enough to show you the trend. However, the average capital employed is the most appropriate measure to use if the company had discontinued any of its operations during the period.

A revised total capital employed figure

Having thought through all the issues, the most appropriate figure to use for the calculation of the business's return on total capital employed would be:

Adjusted shareholders' equity + Minority interests + Total debt + Provisions + Net deferred tax – Associates and joint ventures – Net assets of business's held for sale

And now the basis for calculating the operating capital employed

And if you were only interested in the return on the business's operating activities you ignore the business's investments and some of the non operating assets and liabilities. You would also have to exclude cash and cash equivalents, as they include deposits with up to three months' notice. This doesn't strictly reflect the commercial reality, as some cash would have to be available to run the business's operations. (Some analysts try to work out the cash the business needs for its operations, and exclude the 'excess cash'. However, this is subjective and it's probably easier to exclude all cash and cash equivalents.)

Instead of basing the operating capital employed on the funding, I think it's easier to look at the operating assets and liabilities. To generate sales, a business invests in property, plant and equipment and working capital. In this analysis I define working capital as inventories, *trade* receivables and *trade* payables, so I don't include all the receivables and payables. You'll understand why I do this later on.

A business is also likely to have intangible assets. They are problematic. You know that intangible assets include goodwill, which represents the difference between the amount paid to acquire a company and the net assets acquired. Although it's a balancing item, the company paid to acquire it. Companies are prepared to pay more than a company's asset value because they're also acquiring future revenue, profit streams and cash flows. Intangible assets also include brands, patents, order books and capitalised development expenditure, which also represent future revenues, profit streams and cash flows. However, apart from brands and patents, they don't necessarily generate current revenue and they're not controlled by the company's operational management. Consequently I think that, in most situations, they aren't part of the operating assets, as the managers in the business can't control them. However, if you were analysing a drinks company, such as Pernod Ricard, or a pharmaceutical company, such as GlaxoSmithKline, you would include brands and patents, as they drive the business's sales.

This means that my usual definition of operating capital employed is:

Property, plant and equipment + Inventories + Trade receivables – Trade payables

The two comparable return on capital formulae are...

Return on total capital employed:

$$\frac{\text{Operating profit} - \text{Exceptional items} + \text{Interest receivable and similar income}}{\text{Adjusted shareholders' equity} + \text{Minority interests} + \text{Total debt} + \text{Provisions} + \text{Net deferred tax} - \text{Associates and joint ventures} - \text{Net assets of business's held for sale}}$$

Return on operating capital employed:

$$\frac{\text{Operating profit} - \text{Exceptional items}}{\text{Property, plant and equipment} + \text{inventories} + \text{Trade receivables} - \text{Trade payables}}$$

Now at last I can calculate the return on capital employed using my example. You'll find it's so simple that I don't have to make any of the adjustments I've discussed, but the situation will be very different when I calculate them for IMI!

Calculating the return on capital employed

I'm using the numbers from my example, and have extracted some information from the accounts so that I can show you the appropriate numbers to use in the calculation.

Income statement extract:

Revenue	100,000
Cost of sales	(60,000)
Gross profit	40,000
Distribution costs	(10,000)
Administration expenses	(20,000)
Operating profit	10,000
Interest receivable	1,000
Interest payable	(7,000)
Profit before tax	4,000

> 11,000 profit is used in the return on total capital employed ratio, and 10,000 in the return on operating capital employed.

Here's the balance sheet:

Non current assets:	
Property, plant and equipment	100,000
Current assets:	
Inventories	10,000
Trade receivables	25,000
Cash and cash equivalents	5,000
	40,000
Total assets	140,000
Current liabilities:	
Bank overdraft	(10,000)
Trade payables	(15,000)
Other payables	(3,000)
Current tax	(1,000)
Provisions	(1,000)
	(30,000)
Non current liabilities:	
Loan (at 10% interest)	(60,000)
Total liabilities	(90,000)
Net assets	50,000
Shareholders' equity:	
Share capital (nominal value 1.00 each)	20,000
Retained earnings	30,000
	50,000

Calculating a return on capital employed without any adjustments

If you decided that you didn't want to make any adjustments, calculating the return on capital employed is simple:

$$\frac{\text{Operating profit} + \text{Interest received}}{\text{Total equity} + \text{Total debt}} = \frac{11,000}{120,000} = \textbf{9.17\%}$$

I think that you have to use the total debt, as this is an integral part of the finance being used in the business.

If you want to compare your company with other companies in the sector you're probably going to have to make some adjustments, so let's see how to do this. They'll be fairly simple in my example and will be a little more complicated when I look at IMI.

Identifying the adjusted capital employed

Reported total equity	50,000
Total provisions	1,000
Net deferred tax	0
Goodwill written off against retained earnings	0
Adjusted equity	51,000
Bank overdraft (short-term debt)	10,000
Bank loan (long-term debt)	60,000
Total debt	70,000
Adjusted capital employed	121,000

This means that the company's return on its adjusted total capital employed is:

$$\frac{\text{Operating profit} + \text{Interest received}}{\text{Adjusted capital employed}} = \frac{11,000}{121,000} = \textbf{9.09\%}$$

(If you wanted to use the average capital employed; let's assume that the opening total capital employed was 109,000 and the average capital employed 115,000 ((109,000 + 121,000) ÷ 2), a return on average total capital employed of 9.57%. As the capital employed increased during the year, using an average improves the company's return on capital.) I shall calculate the other profitability ratios using the capital employed at the company's year end.

Identifying the adjusted operating capital employed

Property, plant and equipment	100,000
Inventories	10,000
Trade receivables	25,000
Trade payables	(15,000)
Working capital	20,000
Operating capital employed	120,000

(This is very close to the adjusted capital employed, as in my simple example I'm only excluding cash of 5,000 and other payables of 3,000 and current tax of 1,000. The 5,000 cash – 3,000 other payables – 1,000 current tax is the 1,000 difference between the two capital employed figures. You'll find much bigger differences in real companies' accounts.)

In my example the return on operating capital employed is:

$$\frac{\text{Operating profit}}{\text{Operating capital employed}} = \frac{10,000}{120,000} = \textbf{8.33\%}$$

You now know how to calculate the return on capital, and can see that this company has a return on total capital of 9.09% and a return on operating capital of 8.33%, but what does it tell you? It's a figure in isolation, and you have no idea if this figure is good or bad. To understand this you would need to know:

▨ What were their returns on capital in preceding years?

▨ What is the risk free rate (for example building society or money market rates)?

▨ What returns on capital do other companies in the sector get?

▨ What's their cost of capital?

All ratios need to be looked at in context, as they're meaningless in isolation. At the moment I'm just showing you how to calculate them. In Chapter 13 they'll start to mean something, when I review IMI's financial performance over four years.

You now understand that:

- Conceptually the return on capital is a simple ratio, it quantifies the return that the company is earning on the capital it uses. However, you've seen that deciding what should be included in the ratio is more problematic. The profit can be affected by a number of 'one off' transactions, and the company's accounting policies influence the capital employed shown on the balance sheet.

- The return on operating capital employed is the most important element of the return on total capital employed.

I'd now like to show you how companies can improve their return on operating capital employed.

Improving the return on operating capital employed

If a company wants to improve its return on operating capital employed it either improves its profitability, and/or improves its asset utilisation. This is reflected in the following two ratios:

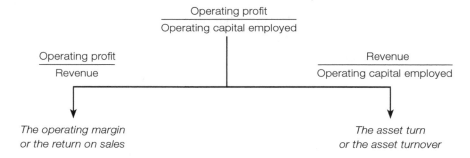

$$\frac{\text{Operating profit}}{\text{Operating capital employed}}$$

$$\frac{\text{Operating profit}}{\text{Revenue}}$$

$$\frac{\text{Revenue}}{\text{Operating capital employed}}$$

The operating margin or the return on sales

The asset turn or the asset turnover

If you can remember simple arithmetic, you'll see that the return on capital is a straight multiplication of the two subsidiary ratios I've shown above, as the revenue cancels out to give you the return on capital employed! This means that the return on capital is the multiplication of the operating margin and a ratio known as the asset turn, or the asset turnover. The asset turn tells you how many pounds' worth of sales (or in my example it's pence) are generated for every pound of operating capital invested in the business. It is a measure of how efficiently the company is utilising its capital. A fall in this ratio indicates the company is becoming less efficient, requiring more capital for each pound's sales. Whereas a rise in the asset turn indicates improved efficiency.

I'll now show you these ratios for the company in my example.

Operating margin: *Asset turn:*

$$\frac{10,000 \times 100}{100,000} = 10\% \qquad \frac{100,000}{120,000} = \mathbf{0.833}$$
(or 83p for every £ of capital invested)

And just to check that the arithmetic works … 10% × 0.833 = 0.0833, or 8.33%.

This company needs to improve its return on operating capital, and it can do this by:

▦ improving its operating margins;

 and, or

▦ using its the assets more effectively to either generate more sales from the same assets (and therefore capital employed), or the same sales using less capital.

I'll start by considering how it can improve its profit margins.

Improving the profit margins

The operating profit margin, or return on sales, can be analysed into its component parts:

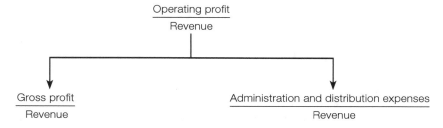

You can see that if the company wants to improve its operating profit margin it increases its gross margin or reduces its overhead cost ratio, as the operating margin is the gross margin minus the overhead cost ratio.

In my example these ratios are:

Gross margin:

$$\frac{40,000}{100,000} \times 100 = \mathbf{40\%}$$

Overhead cost ratio:

$$\frac{30,000}{100,000} \times 100 = \mathbf{30\%}$$

And just to check that the arithmetic works ... 40% – 30% = 10%.

You must remember that the gross margin isn't always a comparable measure, as different companies may define cost of sales in different ways.

Improving the gross margin

If a company wants to improve its gross margin, it must reduce costs or grow revenues. It can do this if it:

- increases its prices;

- reduces its cost of sales;

- changes its sales and product mix – If it can increase the proportion of its sales coming from higher margin activities, its gross profit will improve.

Improving the overhead cost ratio

If a company wants to improve its overhead cost ratio, it must reduce its administration and distribution costs or grow revenues. It can do this if it:

- increases its prices;

- increases its volumes;

- reduces its administration and distribution costs.

Improving the asset turn

The asset turn looks at sales in relation to the capital that is invested in the business. This capital is used to finance the business's assets; consequently to improve this ratio a company has to improve its asset utilisation. Now I'd like you to think for a moment about the balance sheet, and those assets that are used to generate the business's revenue. They're the business's property, plant and equipment and its working capital. (In some companies you might also include some of their intangible assets, as they're also used to generate revenue. However, not all companies capitalise brands and patents, so it might distort some comparisons.) You'll also have to adjust the working capital, as not all of the receivables and payables relate to the business's revenue. Some of the receivables and payables relate to asset purchases and sales. So if you're trying to assess a company's operating performance you have to just include the trade receivables and trade payables in the operating working capital figure.

You can then analyse the asset turn into its component operational parts:

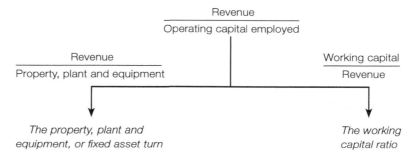

You can see that improving the asset turn is a combination of doing two things: using property, plant and equipment more effectively, and reducing the company's working capital requirements. You'll also notice that the arithmetical simplicity of the model has now collapsed. This has happened largely because of the way that the ratios are calculated; and partly because of the data that's excluded from the ratios. However the two ratios do cover the key drivers of a company's asset utilisation.

The property, plant and equipment turn identifies how many pounds of sales are generated by every pound invested in property, plant and equipment. If the company wants to improve its profitability, it's investing in property, plant and equipment either because it wants to increase its sales, or it wants to reduce its costs. Working capital is usually expressed as a percentage of sales showing how many pence (although sometimes it can be pounds) you would have to have tied up in the working capital to generate each pound of sales.

The company, in my example, has 100,000 invested in property, plant and equipment, 10,000 in inventories, 25,000 in trade receivables, and 15,000 in trade payables. Consequently these ratios are:

Property, plant and equipment turn	Working capital
$\dfrac{100,000}{100,000} = \mathbf{1.00}$	$\dfrac{20,000}{100,000} = \mathbf{20\%}$, or 20p for each £1 of sales

The 20,000 for the working capital comprises:

	Inventories	10,000
plus	Trade receivables	25,000
less	Trade payables	15,000
		20,000

Improving the property, plant and equipment turn

The property, plant and equipment can be broken down into its component parts:

- land and buildings;

- plant and machinery;

- motor vehicles.

If you felt that it was appropriate you could calculate ratios for these:

$$\frac{\text{Revenue}}{\text{Land and buildings}} = \text{Land and buildings turn}$$

$$\frac{\text{Revenue}}{\text{Plant and machinery}} = \text{Plant and machinery turn}$$

$$\frac{\text{Revenue}}{\text{Motor vehicles}} = \text{Motor vehicles turn}$$

I haven't analysed the property, plant and equipment turn in my example, so I can't calculate these ratios. Clearly it would be ridiculous to do all of these ratios, you'd just have a lot of facts and no information. You need to identify the type of asset that is helping to generate the sales. So if you were analysing Tesco's it may be appropriate to do the land and buildings turn, Corus the plant and machinery turn, Maersk the vehicles turn.

Improving the working capital ratio

The working capital ratio is important, as it is an indicator of management efficiency. An efficient management team would be trying to reduce inventories and receivables, whilst managing its payables ethically. You now know that the company needs to have twenty pence cash tied up in its working capital for every pound of sales. I can now analyse this in more detail, identifying how many days' stock the company is carrying, how many days' credit it's giving, and how many days' credit it's taking.

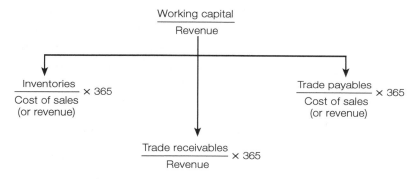

Now let's look at how the company is managing the individual components of working capital: its inventories, receivables and payables.

Inventories

There are two different ways of looking at stocks. Either you calculate how many times a year the company converts its stock into sales (its inventory turn), or you calculate how many days' stock the company is carrying (its inventory days). They're different ways of measuring the same thing, and you should use the measure you find easier to understand and are most familiar with.

Inventory turn

Companies often use this measure in their internal management accounts. In retailing, the stocks relate to the merchandise that has been sold in the period. A manufacturer's stocks relate to the materials, labour and production overheads used in sales. Now you may recall that these figures are not always shown in the published income statement, and you'll find that analysts usually calculate inventory turn (and inventory days) using slightly different figures.

Cost of sales is the closest approximation to the materials, labour, and production overheads used in sales. If you're analysing one company, cost of sales would be an appropriate basis for analysing inventories. Unfortunately if you were trying to compare a company with others it may not be comparable, as cost of sales means different things to different companies. Most analysts use revenue as the denominator. Even though it is wrong it is consistently wrong, and allows them to make comparisons between companies! However, it creates other problems if you are comparing companies with very different profit margins.

I've calculated inventory turn, using both revenue and cost of sales below:

Revenue based

$$\frac{\text{Revenue}}{\text{Inventories}}$$

$$\frac{100{,}000}{10{,}000} = \textbf{10 times}$$

Cost of sales based

$$\frac{\text{Cost of sales}}{\text{Inventories}}$$

$$\frac{60{,}000}{10{,}000} = \textbf{6 times}$$

Based on revenue, the company converts its inventory into sales ten times in a year. The higher the inventory turn, the more efficient the management.

Inventory days

This is the alternative way of looking at stock, and is calculated in a similar way to the way I calculated creditor days in Chapter 9.

Revenue based

$$\frac{\text{Inventories}}{\text{Revenue}} \times 365$$

$$\frac{10{,}000}{100{,}000} \times 365 = \textbf{36.5 days}$$

Cost of sales based

$$\frac{\text{Inventories}}{\text{Cost of sales}} \times 365$$

$$\frac{10{,}000}{60{,}000} \times 365 = \textbf{60.8 days}$$

(Remember that I'm multiplying by 365 to align the time period, as I'm using the sales for the year and the stock on one day.)

You can see how using revenue, rather than the cost of sales, understates inventory days and inventory turn. As the calculation of inventory days is inaccurate it is important that it's looked at in context. Is the control of inventories improving (the inventory days are falling), or does this company have lower inventory days than other companies in its sector?

Receivables

Calculating receivable days is very simple:

$$\frac{\text{Trade receivables}}{\text{Revenue}} \times 365$$

In my example the company is giving 91.3 days' credit to its customers:

$$\frac{25{,}000}{100{,}000} \times 365 = \textbf{91.3 days}$$

Receivable days are also called *the collection period*.

Payables

You may recall from Chapter 9 that payable days are calculated using one of the following formulas:

Sales based

$$\frac{\text{Trade payables}}{\text{Revenue}} \times 365$$

$$\frac{15{,}000}{100{,}000} \times 365 = \textbf{54.8 days}$$

Cost of sales based

$$\frac{\text{Trade payables}}{\text{Cost of sales}} \times 365$$

$$\frac{15{,}000}{60{,}000} \times 365 = \textbf{91.3 days}$$

Payable days may also be called *the payment period*.

The hierarchy of ratios

I have evolved a hierarchy of ratios, showing how the return on operating capital employed is determined by its subsidiary ratios. If the return on capital changes, you want to know *why* it has changed. Although I've portrayed it as having arithmetical simplicity, in fact it isn't as simple as it appears, as I've only included the receivables and payables relating to the company's revenue. The other receivables and payables will include prepayments and accrued expenses, which do relate to a company's operating activities but aren't used in standard calculations of receivable and payable days.

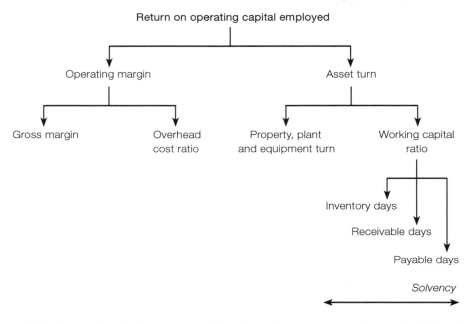

This hierarchy helps you to identify why a company's profitability has changed, and how effectively it is utilising its operating assets. This return on operating capital is the driver of a company's return on total capital employed. Small changes in the subsidiary ratios have a disproportionate effect on the return on capital, because of the multiplying relationship between the operating margin and the asset turn. You need to identify the changes in these ratios if you want to understand a company's underlying performance. Some changes will generate 'one off' improvements, whereas others will provide ongoing benefits. Companies improve their return on capital by improving the subsidiary ratios by focusing on improving profit margins, utilising their property, plant and equipments more effectively, and minimising their working capital.

The working capital ratios also affect the business's solvency, and you've seen that high payable days make the acid test a very relevant ratio to use. After all, if suppliers have been waiting six months for their money they may feel they've little to lose in forcing the company into administration! Companies can improve their return on capital by reducing the working capital, but this adversely affects the solvency ratios and both the current ratio and the acid test will fall.

Using EBITDA

I mentioned earlier in the chapter that EBITDA is a comparable profit measure that closely aligns profit with the cash flow. It's particularly useful when you're comparing companies using different accounting rules. You can use it to determine a comparable return on capital and operating margin, but you can't accurately calculate gross margins and the overhead cost ratio, as you don't know the depreciation that has been charged to these costs. (Companies usually classify amortisation as an administrative expense.)

To illustrate these ratios, I've calculated an EBITDA-based return on adjusted capital employed, and a return on operating capital employed for the company in my example. To calculate EBITDA you add the depreciation and amortisation charge (there's only depreciation in my example, as there aren't any intangible assets) to the operating profit. You can find the depreciation and amortisation charges in the notes to the accounts, or they're shown on the cash flow statement.

Operating profit	10,000
Depreciation	1,000
EBITDA	11,000

The return on total adjusted capital employed is 9.9%:

$$\frac{\text{EBITDA + Interest received}}{\text{Capital employed}} = \frac{12,000}{121,000} = \textbf{9.9\%}$$

The return on operating capital employed is 9.2%:

$$\frac{\text{EBITDA}}{\text{Operating capital employed}} = \frac{11,000}{120,000} = \textbf{9.2\%}$$

The EBITDA margin is:

$$\frac{\text{EBITDA}}{\text{Revenue}} = \frac{11,000}{100,000} = \textbf{11.0\%}$$

Summary of the profitability ratios

I've introduced you to a hierarchy of profitability ratios, and I'd now like to summarise how these ratios are calculated, and why they're important.

■ **The return on capital employed** – This is the most important measure of a company's profitability, but unfortunately it is easier to understand than to calculate. It measures the percentage profit the company is making on the capital that is invested in its business. This return should be greater than the cost of financing the business (its cost of capital), and a risk free rate. Unfortunately there is no standard definition, with the only consensus being that the profit used should be a profit before both interest and tax. Some analysts exclude all exceptional items, some use operating profit. Defining the capital employed is even more problematic. You can't rely on return on capital figures quoted in company accounts, as they're unlikely to be comparable.

To illustrate the range of definitions used for the return on capital employed percentages published in the accounts, I'll tell you about how BT, Tesco's and IMI define their return on capital employed:

– BT uses profit before tax, and net finance expense. It then compares this with its average capital employed. It defines capital employed as total assets less current liabilities excluding corporation tax, current borrowings, derivative financial instruments and finance lease creditors, less deferred tax assets, cash and cash equivalents, derivative financial instruments and investments.

– Tesco's uses profit before interest less tax, and divides it by average capital employed which it defines as net assets plus net debt less net assets held for sale.

– IMI defines it as operating profit before acquired intangible amortisation and impairment as a percentage of closing net assets (equity).

It's clear that there's little agreement about how to calculate the return on capital employed, you just have to choose an appropriate, comparable definition. I've suggested that it's useful to have two returns on capital – an adjusted return on total capital and an adjusted return on operating capital. You may decide just to keep it simple, using the equity and debt as the capital employed.

If a company wants to improve its return on capital it has to either improve its profitability or its asset utilisation. The return on capital employed is a multiplication of the profit margin and the asset turn, or asset turnover.

■ **The profit margin** – This expresses the profit used in the return on capital employed calculation as a percentage of the company's revenue. Improving the profit margin is a combination of increasing the company's gross margin and decreasing its overhead cost ratio.

■ **The asset turn or the asset turnover** – This tells you how many pounds of sales the company generates for every pound of capital invested in the business. If the number increases, a company is usually using its assets more effectively. Improving the asset turn is a combination of improving the property, plant and equipment turn and reducing the working capital ratio.

■ **The gross margin** – This tells you the profit percentage after deducting the company's cost of sales. It isn't always a comparable measure, as there isn't a standard definition of cost of sales.

■ **The overhead cost ratio** – This expresses the administration and distribution expenses as a percentage of revenue. As there aren't standard definitions for either administration or distribution expenses, you should be wary of using this ratio when you're comparing companies that have different definitions of cost of sales.

■ **The property, plant and equipment turn** – This tells you how many pounds of sales a company generates for every pound invested in property, plant and equipment. If the number increases, the company is using its property, plant and equipment more effectively, although it may be not replacing them.

■ **The working capital ratio** – This expresses the inventories, trade receivables, and trade payables as a percentage of sales. It tells you how many pence the company needs to have tied up in the working capital to fund a pound of sales.

■ **Inventory turn** – This divides cost of sales, or revenue, by inventories and shows you how many times in the period a company converts its stock into sales. If the number increases it usually means that the company is improving its stock control. However a reduction in the work in progress could mean that the company has had a fall in orders.

- **Inventory days** – This gives an approximation to the number of days' stock the company is carrying. You calculate this ratio by dividing inventories by cost of sales, or sales, and multiplying by the number of days in the period. If the number decreases it usually means that the company is improving its stock control (with the proviso above about work in progress).

- **Receivable days or the collection period** – This tells you how many days' credit the company is giving. You calculate this ratio by dividing trade receivables by revenue, and multiplying by the number of days in the period. If the number decreases it usually means that the company is improving its credit control.

- **Payable days or the payment period** – This gives an approximation to the number of days' credit the company is taking. You calculate this ratio by dividing trade payables by cost of sales, or sales, and multiplying by the number of days in the period.

Small changes in the subsidiary ratios can have a large effect on the return on capital employed, because of the multiplier effect of the profit margin and the asset turn.

IMI's profitability ratios in 2008

I'd now like to show you how to calculate these ratios from published accounts, and it's time to find out a little more about IMI. You know that it's solvent – but is it profitable? And if so, is it profitable enough? What drives its profitability? Let's see if we can find out.

Return on capital employed

I'll calculate the two return on capital employed ratios I introduced earlier – the return on total capital employed and the return on operating capital employed, which I'll use to work through the profitability hierarchy.

Return on total capital employed

Firstly I have to determine the profit and need some extracts from their 2008 income statement, and their note on financial income.

Operating profit – Exceptional items + Interest receivable and similar income

Adjusted shareholders' equity + Minority interests + Total debt + Provisions +
Net deferred tax – Associates and joint ventures –
Net assets of businesses held for sale

Income statement extract

	2008
	£m
Revenue (i)	1,900.6
Cost of sales (ii)	(1,144.1)
Gross profit	756.5
Selling and distribution costs (iii)	(228.0)
Administrative expenses (iv)	(318.7)
Other income (v)	–
Operating profit	209.8

i)   includes £3.8m economic hedge contracts net gain
ii)   includes £3.6m restructuring costs and £1.2m economic hedge contracts net loss
iii) includes £2.2m restructuring costs
iv)   includes £13.8m restructuring costs, £26.3m Severe Service investigation costs and
      fines and £13.2m of acquired intangible amortisation and impairment

Now you can see that it has exceptional costs, which are restructuring costs, Severe Service investigation costs and fines, amortisation and impairment of acquired intangibles.

	As published	Net of exceptional items
	2008	2008
	£m	£m
Revenue	1,900.6	1,900.6
Cost of sales	(1,144.1)	(1,140.5)
Gross profit	756.5	760.1
Selling and distribution costs	(228.0)	(225.8)
Administrative expenses	(318.7)	(265.4)
Operating profit	209.8	268.9

Extract from the note on financial income

| | | 2008 | | |
	Interest	Financial instruments	Other	Total
Recognised in the income statement	£m	£m	£m	£m
Interest income on bank deposits	10.2			10.2
Financial instruments at fair value through profit or loss:				
Designated hedges		3.1		3.1
Other economic hedges				
– future year transactions		–		–
Income from investments			0.7	0.7
Expected return on defined benefit pension plan assets			71.6	71.6
Financial income	10.2	3.1	72.3	85.6

The profit used in the return on total capital employed is:

Operating profit – Exceptional items + Interest receivable and similar income

IMI's operating profit before exceptional items is £268.9 million, it has £10.2 million interest received and 0.7 million income from investments. Consequently the profit used in the return on total capital employed is £279.8 million. Now I need to identify the appropriate figure for the capital employed based on the following formula.

Adjusted shareholders' equity + Minority interests + Total debt + Provisions + Net deferred tax – Associates and joint ventures – Net assets of businesses held for sale

Firstly let's adjust its equity:

IMI's equity in 2008 was £461.7 million:

Equity

Share capital	84.7
Share premium	165.1
Other reserves	71.1
Retained earnings	131.5
Total equity attributable to equity shareholders of the Company	452.4
Minority interest	9.3
Total equity	461.7

To adjust the equity I need to add back provisions, net deferred tax and goodwill.

Its provisions are £65.9 million:

Current provisions	29.4
Non current provisions	36.5
Total provisions	65.9

And their net deferred tax is minus £37.8 million:

Deferred tax liabilities	16.9
Less deferred tax assets	(54.7)
Net deferred tax	(37.8)

The last adjustment is to add back £364 million goodwill that was written off through retained earnings. Its adjusted equity is £825.7 million:

Reported total equity	461.7
Total provisions	65.9
Net deferred tax	(37.8)
Goodwill written off against retained earnings	364.0
Adjusted equity	853.8

Its total debt is £422.6 million:

Bank overdraft	4.6
Current interest-bearing loans and borrowings	46.5
Non current interest-bearing loans and borrowings	371.5
Total debt	422.6

This means that their adjusted capital employed is £1,276.4 million:

Adjusted total equity	853.8
Total debt	422.6
Adjusted total capital employed	1,276.4

IMI's return on total capital is 21.9%:

$$\frac{\text{Adjusted profit}}{\text{Adjusted capital employed}} = \frac{279.8}{1,276.4} = \textbf{21.92\%}$$

Profit margin

IMI's profit margin is 14.72%:

$$\frac{\text{Adjusted profit}}{\text{Revenue}} = \frac{279.8}{1,900.6} = \textbf{14.72\%}$$

Asset turn

$$\frac{\text{Revenue}}{\text{Total capital employed}} = \frac{1,900.6}{1,276.4} = \textbf{1.49 times}$$

This means that every pound invested in the business generates £1.49 revenue. Another way of looking at this is that every 1% improvement in the operating margin improves IMI's return on capital by 1.49%, as the return on capital is the multiplication of its profit margin and its asset turn.

Return on operating capital employed and subsequent ratios

This shows you the return that IMI is making from the assets that its managers control. It excludes the return from any investments and expresses the operating profit before exceptional items as a percentage of the operating capital employed. IMI's operating profit before exceptional items is £268.9 million, and its operating capital employed is £723.6:

Property, plant and equipment	266.4
Inventories	333.5
Trade receivables	347.3
Trade payables	(223.6)
Working capital	457.2
Operating capital employed	723.6

Its return on operating capital employed is 37.2%:

$$\frac{\text{Operating profit before exceptional items}}{\text{Operating capital employed}} = \frac{268.9}{723.6} = \textbf{37.16\%}$$

Improving return on operating capital employed

I'll now work through the profitability hierarchy to show you how to calculate the subsidiary ratios from published companies' accounts.

The return on operating capital is a multiplication of the operating margin and the asset turn. Both the operating margin and the asset turn use revenue, which was £1,900.6 million in 2008 for IMI.

Operating profit margin

IMI's operating margin is 14.15%:

$$\frac{\text{Operating profit before exceptional items}}{\text{Revenue}} = \frac{268.9}{1,900.6} = \textbf{14.15\%}$$

Asset turn

$$\frac{\text{Revenue}}{\text{Operating capital employed}} = \frac{1,900.6}{723.6} = \textbf{2.63 times}$$

This means that every pound invested in IMI's operating capital generates £2.63 revenue, making 14.15% profit. Or another way of looking at it is that a 1% change in its operating margin, changes its return on operating capital by 2.63%. So if its asset turn stays the same and IMI achieves its objective of a 15% operating margin, its return on capital would increase to 39.4%.

I can now check my return on operating capital by multiplying the operating margin of 14.15% by the asset turn of 2.63 times = 37.2%. (You'll find a small rounding error if you do the arithmetic!)

Improving profitability

This is a combination of improving the gross margin and the overhead cost ratio so let's work them out.

Gross profit margin

In 2008 IMI's gross profit margin is almost 40%:

$$\frac{\text{Gross profit before exceptional items}}{\text{Revenue}} = \frac{760.1}{1,900.6} = \textbf{39.99\%}$$

Overhead cost ratio

IMI's overheads are £491.2 million (selling and distribution costs of £225.8 million plus administrative expenses of £265.4 million) and were 25.84% of revenue in 2008:

$$\frac{\text{Overheads before exceptional items}}{\text{Revenue}} = \frac{491.2}{1,900.6} = \textbf{25.84\%}$$

Now let's see if the model is working; the gross margin less the overhead cost ratio should equal the operating profit margin:

$$39.99\% - 25.84\% = 14.15\% \quad \text{It works!}$$

Improving the asset utilisation

The arithmetical simplicity of the profitability hierarchy now starts to break down, as the assets are compared with revenue and only those assets and liabilities that relate to revenue are included.

IMI can improve its asset utilisation by utilising its property, plant and equipment and working capital more effectively. As it's not a brand business, its intangible asset turn is less relevant, but I have still calculated it. I've taken the property, plant and equipment and inventories straight from the balance sheet, but had to get the trade receivables' and trade payables' numbers from the notes to the accounts.

The intangible asset turn

Although I haven't included intangible assets in IMI's operating capital, as it's largely goodwill (£342.8 million), I thought I'd show you the calculation. IMI's intangible asset turn is 4.75 times:

$$\frac{\text{Revenue}}{\text{Intangible assets}} = \frac{1{,}900.6}{399.8} = \textbf{4.75 times}$$

The property, plant and equipment turn:

$$\frac{\text{Revenue}}{\text{Property, plant and equipment}} = \frac{1{,}900.6}{266.4} = \textbf{7.13 times}$$

This means that every pound it invests in property, plant and equipment generates £7.13 sales.

The working capital ratio

IMI's working capital ratio is 0.241 or, to be more precise, 24.06%:

$$\frac{\text{Working capital}}{\text{Revenue}} = \frac{457.2}{1{,}900.6} = \textbf{0.241}$$

This means that, at their current levels of working capital, it needs to find 24.06 pence in cash to fund every pound's worth of sales it makes. This ratio can be very useful if the company you're analysing is planning to expand, as you can use this to see if the company has enough cash to finance its expansion programme at current levels of working capital. (This will be important when the economy starts to grow, particularly if banks and investors are still restricting their corporate lending.) I'll show you how to do this, by using IMI's cash balance and its committed undrawn borrowing facilities. At the end of 2008 it had £123.9 million in cash and cash equivalents and committed undrawn borrowing facilities of £154 million, This means that it had 277.9 million available funds, and this would be enough to support increased sales of £1,153.1 million (277.9 ÷ 0.241). Its available cash balances at the end of 2008 would support a 60.7% increase in sales. You may recall that after the year end it also had another £25 million available. It's unlikely to need this to finance its working capital in 2009, so perhaps it has other plans for the money.

This is just as useful if the company's sales are declining, as you can work out how much cash would be generated from a fall in sales. So if IMI's sales fell by 10%, at its current levels of working capital, it would generate just over £45.8 million cash (190.06 × 0.241) from the reduction in its working capital.

You now know IMI's overall working capital ratio; let's look at its subsidiary ratios by analysing the components of working capital.

Stock control

You've seen that there are two different ways of analysing stocks – the inventory turn and inventory days. You can also analyse stocks using cost of sales, or revenue, as a comparable measure for companies with similar profit margins. I'll show you how to calculate all four possible combinations, although you'd only ever use one in a financial analysis. The choice is yours!

Inventory turn

This shows you how many times in a year the company converts its inventory into sales. The higher the number, the more effectively the company is managing its stocks. As I'll also be using cost of sales in some of the ratios, you need to know that IMI's cost of sales before exceptional items in 2008 was £1,140.5 million.

Revenue based:

$$\frac{\text{Revenue}}{\text{Inventories}} = \frac{1,900.6}{333.5} = \textbf{5.70 times}$$

Cost of sales based:

$$\frac{\text{Cost of sales}}{\text{Inventories}} = \frac{1,140.5}{333.5} = \textbf{3.42 times}$$

There's quite a difference between using revenue and cost of sales. Remember that using cost of sales is more accurate, but using revenue may be more comparable.

Now let's have a look at the alternative way of measuring stock control – inventory days.

Inventory days

This shows you how many days' stock the business is carrying. A low number usually indicates efficient stock control.

Revenue based:

$$\frac{\text{Inventories}}{\text{Revenue}} \times 365 = \frac{333.5}{1,900.6} \times 365 = \textbf{64.05 days}$$

Cost of sales based:

$$\frac{\text{Inventories}}{\text{Cost of sales}} \times 365 = \frac{333.5}{1,140.5} \times 365 = \textbf{106.73 days}$$

I can analyse the inventories into their component parts by extracting the information from the inventory note:

Raw materials	115.0
Work in progress	105.8
Finished goods	112.7

As I'm not comparing IMI with other companies I'll use cost of sales to calculate the ratios:

$$\frac{\text{Raw materials}}{\text{Cost of sales}} \times 365 = \frac{115.0}{1,140.5} \times 365 = \textbf{36.80 days}$$

$$\frac{\text{Work in progress}}{\text{Cost of sales}} \times 365 = \frac{105.8}{1,140.5} \times 365 = \textbf{33.86 days}$$

$$\frac{\text{Finished goods}}{\text{Cost of sales}} \times 365 = \frac{112.7}{1,140.5} \times 365 = \textbf{36.07 days}$$

Receivable days or the collection period

This shows you that IMI's customers take almost 67 days to pay.

$$\frac{\text{Trade receivables}}{\text{Revenue}} \times 365 = \frac{347.3}{1,900.6} \times 365 = \textbf{66.70 days}$$

Payable days or the payment period

This gives an indication of how long IMI takes to pay its suppliers, which I also calculated in the last chapter. The payable days' calculation can use either revenue or cost of sales, and I'll show you both.

Revenue based:

$$\frac{\text{Trade payables}}{\text{Revenue}} \times 365 = \frac{223.6}{1,900.6} \times 365 = \textbf{42.94 days}$$

Cost of sales based:

$$\frac{\text{Trade payables}}{\text{Revenue}} \times 365 = \frac{223.6}{1,140.5} \times 365 = \textbf{71.56 days}$$

Using EBITDA

Here's IMI's published and adjusted EBITDAs:

	As published	Net of exceptional items
Operating profit	209.8	268.9
Depreciation	43.1	43.1
Amortisation	16.4	3.2
EBITDA	269.3	315.2

Once again, I am only adding back the amortisation charged to operating profit, so the charge is less in the profit before exceptional items as the amortisation of acquired intangible assets is an exceptional item that has not been charged to profit before exceptional items. I shall use the adjusted EBITDA to calculate an adjusted return on total capital employed, a return on operating capital employed and an EBITDA margin.

The return on total adjusted capital employed is 25.6%:

$$\frac{\text{EBITDA} + \text{Interest receivable and similar income}}{\text{Capital employed}} = \frac{315.2 + 10.9 + 0.7}{1,276.4} = \textbf{25.6\%}$$

The return on operating capital employed is 43.6%:

$$\frac{\text{EBITDA}}{\text{Operating capital employed}} = \frac{315.2}{723.6} = \textbf{43.6\%}$$

The EBITDA margin is 16.6%:

$$\frac{\text{EBITDA}}{\text{Revenue}} = \frac{315.2}{1,900.6} = \mathbf{16.6\%}$$

What have we learned?

To be honest, not much more than we knew already, having looked at IMI's financial statements. Its return on operating capital employed, 45.4%, is greater than its return on total capital employed, 21.9% – but that's not surprising as it excludes intangible assets and other non operating assets and liabilities. Its return on capital is driven by both operating margins and asset utilisation. Again, not unusual in a manufacturing business.

Profitability ratios have to be viewed over a number of years. You really want to know if IMI is more, or less, profitable than it was and why its profitability is changing. I'm afraid you'll have to wait until Chapter 13 to discover the trend.

11

Cash management

Introduction

There's a close relationship between cash management and solvency, as a company that manages its cash resources effectively is unlikely to have any solvency problems. Consequently, the way that a company manages its cash is crucial to its long-term survival. It has to fund the business in the most efficient way and optimise its use of cash resources. If you want to understand a company's financial performance, its opportunities and its threats you must be able to analyse the way that it is managing cash. To do this you have to look at its:

- operating and financial reviews;
- cash flow statement;
- working capital ratios;
- loan profile.

The operating and financial reviews

These give you useful insights into a company, its opportunities, problems and cash management:

■ You've seen that the operating review identifies the main factors affecting the business's performance and gives a full discussion on the operating results. Because it analyses the business's dynamics and identifies the main risks and uncertainties facing the business, it gives useful insights that are not found elsewhere in the accounts.

■ You saw, in Chapter 6, that IMI's financial review talked you through the financial statements and identified the main factors for the changes in the business's financial performance. It also talked about some of the risks facing the company and the way that they're managed. There's a lot of information about the company's cash flow management including:

– specific information about its operational cash flows and the factors affecting them;

– its current liquidity, any seasonal borrowing requirements, and the maturity profile of its borrowings. More detail is given in the extensive note on financial risk management.

The cash flow statement

Once you have an overview of the company's cash management, you can start to analyse its cash flow during the year in more detail. The cash flow statement shows the year's cash inflows and outflows, and was discussed in detail in Chapter 4. The cash flows are categorised in a way that makes the business's cash movement during the year easy to understand.

I'll use the cash flow statement in my example to illustrate the analysis of a cash flow statement.

Cash flow statement

Cash flows from operating activities

Operating profit	10,000
Depreciation	1,000
Increase in inventories	(2,000)
Increase in receivables	(5,000)
Increase in payables	3,000
Cash generated from operations	7,000
Tax paid	(1,500)
Net cash from operating activities	5,500

Cash flows from investing activities

Purchase of property, plant and equipment	(15,000)
Disposal of property, plant and equipment	2,000
Interest received	1,000
Net cash from investing activities	(12,000)

Cash flows from financing activities

Issue of ordinary share capital	5,000
Additional loan	5,000
Interest paid	(7,000)
Dividends paid	(1,000)
Net cash from financing activities	2,000

Decrease in cash and cash equivalents	(4,500)
Cash and cash equivalents at the start of the year	9,500
Cash and cash equivalents at the end of the year	5,000

If you're analysing a cash flow statement it's useful to consider:

▦ How vulnerable is the company's operational cash flow to a fall in cash receipts?

▦ What is the cash interest cover?

▦ What proportion of the investment in fixed assets is being generated from internal sources?

▦ Is the company matching long-term sources of funds to long-term applications?

The operational cash flow

In my example I've haven't shown the presentation of the operating cash flows that uses the period's cash receipts and payments for operating items, as you'll rarely find it in published cash flow statement. I've also started with operating profit, whilst many companies (particularly overseas) start their cash flow statement with the profit for the year. This isn't a problem; it just means that they have to make more adjustments to arrive at their operating cash flow whereas I wanted to make it easier for you to follow.

Now let's see how vulnerable a company is to a fall in its receipts, a serious potential problem in a recession.

Firstly let's look at the cash generated from operations. The current year's trading *will* generate 11,000 in cash. This is EBITDA, the profit plus the depreciation and amortisation charges. However, the company has only managed to generate 7,000 from its operations because an additional net 4,000 has had to be tied up in the working capital. The increase in inventories (2,000) has been more than covered by the increase in payables (3,000), suggesting that the company may be taking longer to pay its suppliers. The company would either be taking longer to pay its suppliers or has had an increase in its other payables. Now let me replicate the information you would normally have – two year's figures. I'll just give you some relevant information.

	This year	Last year
Revenue	100,000	110,000
Balance sheet extracts:		
Inventories	10,000	8,000
Trade receivables	25,000	20,000
Trade payables	15,000	12,000
Other payables	3,000	3,000

The big movement in the working capital has come from receivables, which have increased by 5,000, when revenue has fallen. This could arise if:

■ its customers are taking longer to pay the company. This could be because they can't pay, or they won't pay;

■ it's changed its credit terms;

■ it delivered an unusually large order at the end of the financial year and this has distorted the numbers.

So the cash generated from operations tells you that the largest increase in working capital has come from the receivables. Now let me show you how to calculate the cash receipts from the data we have.

At the start of the year the company was owed 20,000 by its customers. During the year its sales were 100,000 and at the end of the year it was owed 25,000 by its customers. This means that its cash receipts were 95,000 during the year:

Opening receivables	20,000
Plus revenue in the year	100,000
Less closing receivables	(25,000)
Cash received in the year	95,000

The company appears to be vulnerable to a fall in receipts, as it would only take a fall in receipts of 7.4% (7,000 ÷ 95,000) for the company to lose its cash generated from operations. Whether this was likely to happen depends on the trends in receivable days. So you know the percentage, but what does this mean in days?

The working capital ratios

I calculated these in the last chapter, using information from the income statement and the balance sheet. These ratios always give you some useful information. The cash flow statement identifies that the additional 4,000 invested in the working capital reduced the company's operating cash flow, and that this has contributed to its cash flow problems. The working capital ratios tell you whether this was because increased business required more working capital, or the management is less efficient in controlling its working capital.

Firstly let's quantify the apparent inefficiency in controlling receivables, then I'll find out whether the 7.4% fall in cash receipts is likely to happen.

The receivable days:

This year:

$$\frac{\text{Trade receivables}}{\text{Revenue}} \times 365 = \frac{25,000}{100,000} \times 365 = \textbf{91.3 days}$$

Last year:

$$\frac{\text{Trade receivables}}{\text{Revenue}} \times 365 = \frac{20,000}{110,000} \times 365 = \textbf{66.4 days}$$

Wow! Receivable days have increased by a massive 25 days! Unfortunately, whilst I can quantify what has happened, I don't know why it has happened. You'll find that often analysing accounts doesn't give you answers, just better questions. You now know that something significant has happened in the company's business.

This year the company's revenue was 100,000, so on average it sold around 274 every day (100,000 ÷ 365 = 273.97). Now I've worked out, using the cash receipts, that a 7.4% reduction in the cash receipts eliminates the operating cash flow of 7,000. Now I can turn this into receivable days. The receivable days would have to increase by over 25 days to lose 7,000 (7,000 ÷ 273.97 = 25.55). Looking at last year, this increase is possible but probably unlikely as they ought to be focusing on improving their credit control.

Interest cover

This can be worked out from the cash flow statement, as well as the income statement. You can see that in my example the company is just covering its interest paid with its cash generated from operations and the interest received. Whilst you can see that the company may be close to having difficulties with its bank, you can't draw any conclusions from one year's cash flows.

Cash available for investment

This is a useful measure that shows if the company's capital expenditure and acquisitions could be funded from the cash generated during the year. You can identify this from the following cash flows:

Net cash from operating activities	5,500
Interest received	1,000
Interest paid	(7,000)
Dividends paid	(1,000)
Cash available for investment	(1,500)

As the company's operational cash flow doesn't cover its cash flows from net interest, it is unable to fund any capital expenditure from the current year's cash flow. This means that any further investment in its business has to be financed from existing cash balances, external sources or disposals.

Matching funds to applications

It is important that a company acquires its long-term assets with long-term funds – buying property, plant and equipment with bank overdrafts is risky. The bank can demand repayment at any time, whereas the payback from property, plant and equipment is long term. On the other hand, funding seasonal working capital requirements with overdrafts is a reasonable option. The general rule is that long-term assets should be funded with long-term sources of funds.

The company in my example spent 13,000, net, on its property, plant and equipment purchases, and raised 5,000 from a share issue and 5,000 from long-term loans. The balance of 3,000 was partly funded by using 500 from its cash balance, with the remainder coming from bank overdrafts. This means that 10,500 came from long-term sources and there's a 2,500 'mismatch'. On its own it doesn't appear serious, but it could indicate poor cash management.

The loan profile

Looking at the types of borrowing that a company has can tell you a lot about the way it manages its cash. You'll find information about:

■ the types of loans it has;

■ when the loans have to be repaid;

■ its current maximum agreed level of borrowings;

■ its exposure to interest rate movements and how it manages this exposure.

You've seen that this information is disclosed in the notes to the accounts.

The types of loans

Loans can be secured or unsecured. Whilst it is common for small private companies to have secured borrowings, in the UK it is unusual for large listed companies to have secured loans. When you look at some multinational companies' accounts you'll probably find that only a small proportion of their borrowings is secured. This tends to be in their overseas subsidiaries, as in some countries there is a legal requirement that all loans are secured. Consequently, if you are looking at a large company's accounts and find that previously all loans were unsecured but are now secured, you have an indication of their bank's level of confidence, or rather lack of confidence, in the company.

It is worth remembering that not all loans have to be repaid. There is an increasing number of convertible loans, usually in the form of bonds. These loans give the lender the option, usually on maturity, to receive cash when the loan is repaid, or to convert into shares at a price that was fixed when the bond was issued. If the option price is below the share's current market price, the bondholders would be better off converting into ordinary shares, and then selling the share if they want the cash. In that situation, it is unlikely that the bondholders would exercise the cash option. But it all hinges on the company's current share price. So if the company has convertible bonds you need to compare the current market price, and its trend, with the option price, as this will give you an indication of whether the company is likely to have to repay the loan.

The terms and debt repayment schedule

You may remember that I showed you the importance of the terms and debt repayment schedule in Chapter 9 when discussing solvency.

You've already seen that the company in my example would have difficulties repaying its loans in the short term – there's insufficient cash being generated in the business to cover its tax and interest bill let alone repay any loans. But it doesn't have to repay its loans now; all we know at the moment is that it will have to repay them at some time in the future. *When* they have to be repaid is obviously important, and that's why you need to look at the terms and debt repayment schedule. If it isn't generating sufficient cash to repay them, when they fall due there will be only three alternatives:

- Have a share issue to repay its loans – but this is unlikely to be possible in the short term, as it's just had a share issue.
- Repay its existing loans with new loans – again unlikely because of its poor interest cover and cash generation.
- Sell some assets or businesses.

IMI's cash management

Now you've already discovered that IMI is solvent, and you'd expect it to manage its cash well. Let's see if it does.

There's a copy of IMI's cash flow statement on the next page, so that I can review its cash management in 2008. Its operating cash flow increased by 81% in 2008, largely from increasing EBITDA by £47.8 million, turning working capital from an outflow of £10.7 million in 2007 to an inflow of £1.2 million in 2008, and the increase in their provisions and employee benefits.

In 2008 its investing cash flow fell, as it made no acquisitions, and in both years it had a surplus before financing, although in 2007 it wasn't sufficient to pay interest and dividends.

CONSOLIDATED STATEMENT OF CASH FLOWS

FOR THE YEAR ENDED 31 DECEMBER 2008

	2008	2007
	£m	£m
Cash flows from operating activities		
Profit for the period	116.0	119.9
Adjustments for:		
Depreciation	43.1	35.9
Amortisation	16.4	13.9
(Profit)/losses from discontinued operations (net of tax)	–	(1.9)
Other income – disposal of business	–	(1.7)
Gain on sale of property, plant and equipment	(0.2)	(0.1)
Financial income	(85.6)	(81.1)
Financial expense	119.4	81.8
Equity-settled share-based payment expenses	3.9	3.1
Income tax expense	60.0	53.0
Decrease/(increase) in trade and other receivables	17.6	(12.6)
Increase in inventories	(9.2)	(18.6)
Increase in trade and other payables	(7.2)	20.5
(Decrease)/increase in provisions and employee benefits	14.4	(6.6)
Cash generated from the operations	288.6	205.5
Income taxes paid	(54.4)	(37.1)
	234.2	168.4
Additional pension scheme funding	(16.8)	(15.6)
European commission fine	–	(32.8)
Net cash from operating activities	217.4	120.0

▶

Cash flows from investing activities

Interest received	12.4	7.2
Proceeds from the sale of property, plant and equipment (including £1m from discontinued operations in 2007)	3.1	8.3
Sale of investments	0.1	0.1
Purchase of investments	(0.8)	(1.2)
Income from investments	0.7	
Acquisition of subsidiaries, net of cash required	–	(52.2)
Disposal of businesses (net of cash disposed)	–	2.0
Acquisition of property, plant and equipment	(47.6)	(49.9)
Capitalised development expenditure	(5.1)	(3.2)
Net cash from investing activities	(37.2)	(88.9)
Cash flows from financing activities		
Interest paid	(29.0)	(19.9)
Purchase of own shares	(16.7)	(93.3)
Proceeds from the issue of share capital for employee share schemes	1.9	8.7
(Repayment)/drawdown of borrowings	(45.5)	110.7
Dividends paid to minority interest	(2.4)	(2.4)
Dividends paid	(66.2)	(63.9)
Net cash from financing activities	(157.9)	(60.1)
Net increase/(decrease) in cash and cash equivalents	22.3	(29.0)
Cash and cash equivalents at the start of the year	77.4	103.6
Effects of exchange rate fluctuations on cash held	19.6	2.8
Cash and cash equivalents at the end of the year*	119.3	77.4

* Net of bank overdrafts
Notes to the cash flow appear in note 24.

Now let's consider IMI's cash management in more detail.

Vulnerability to a fall in receipts

In 2008 IMI's revenue was £1.900.6 million, this means that if its customers took an extra day to pay them it would lose just over £5.2 million cash

$(1,900.6 \div 365 = 5.2071)$. As its cash flow from operations was before the additional pension contribution was £288.6 million, its customers would have to take over 55 more days to pay them before the operational cash flow is eliminated. Even if I use the operating cash flow of £217.4 million its customers would have to take almost 42 more days to pay before the operating cash was eliminated. As they're currently paying in 66.7 days, their payment terms would have to increase by over 62% and it is highly unlikely that this would happen. So I think it's fair to say that IMI is not vulnerable to a fall in receipts.

Cash interest cover

You may recall from Chapter 9 that IMI has no problems affording its interest, as its interest cover is over 16 times. The cash based interest cover uses cash of £271.8 million (the cash generated from operations of £288.6 million less the additional pension contribution of £16.8 million).

$$\frac{\text{Operational cash flow}}{\text{Net interest paid}} = \frac{271.8}{16.6} = 16.4 \text{ times}$$

Matching funds to applications

If you look at IMI's cash flow statement, you can group its cash flows into those that are associated with 'revenue' items, reinvestment and capital restructuring:

Some of its operating cash flow has to be used to pay interest tax and dividends. I've classified these cash flows as 'revenue' items:

Net cash from operating activities	217.4
Interest received	12.4
Interest paid	(29.0)
Dividends paid to minority interest	(2.4)
Dividends paid	(66.2)
Trading cash flow available for reinvestment	132.2

So, having taken account of financing costs and tax, IMI has £132.2 million of its 2008 trading cash flow available to reinvest in its business. I'll consider the reinvestment in its existing business first. It spent a net £44.5 million on property, plant and equipment and £5.1 million on capitalised development expenditure and spent a net £0.7 million on the sale of investments. So all of its long-term expenditure was funded by the current year's cash flow.

So you can see that IMI matched its long-term sources of funds with its long-term expenditure and had no need to use its large cash balances to fund part of the expenditure.

IMI's terms and debt repayment schedule

You saw this in Chapter 9 and discovered that IMI has more than enough cash to pay the contractual cash flows on its debt in 2009, and could pay over 80% of 2010's contractual debt cash flows. When you look back at this note you'll see that most of its loans have to be repaid after 2011, so it's not going to have to refinance its business in the middle of a recession.

You know that it has additional borrowing facilities in place. At the end of December 2008 it had £154 million undrawn committed borrowing facilities, and in its financial review it disclosed that:

- a further £25 million facility was agreed in January 2009;

and

- it has received indicative offers, of additional funding facilities and confirmation of the lenders' intention to agree to the renewal of a number of existing facilities.

What have we learned?

IMI can afford to support higher levels of borrowing and if expansion, or acquisition, opportunities arise it has additional borrowing facilities in place. In 2008 it managed its cash in a prudent way, matching funds to applications.

12

The investors' perspective

Introduction

You already know why people invest in shares – they want to make money! No one would invest in a company unless they thought they were going to make money, and preferably more money than they can get from a building society. There are two ways to make money from shares – either the price rises and you have a capital gain on your investment that you realise when you sell the shares, or you receive dividends. Some shares attract investors looking for growth (capital gain), and others attract those looking for income (dividend payments). You'll find this reflected in some of the ratios that analyse the company's performance from the investors' point of view.

Investors are interested in:

■ The return on their investment, and this can be expressed in two different ways:

– the overall return, the return on equity;

– the annual return, dividends.

■ The stock market's view of the future return on their investment:

– the price earnings, also called the PE, ratio.

Analysts also use other measures based on assets, sales, cash flow, market value and shareholder value. Institutional investors use a combination of these to identify whether the share represents a good investment, considering the company's ratios with other companies in its sector.

In this chapter I'll look at a company from the investor's perspective showing you how to calculate these investment ratios, and tell you what they reveal about the company's performance.

The investment ratios

I'm going to start by introducing you to two other ratios that are published in company accounts – earnings per share and dividends per share, as they are used in some of the other investment ratios.

Earnings per share (eps)

The earnings per share figure is shown at the bottom of listed companies' income statement (I didn't include it in IMI's income statement in Chapter 2, as I hadn't told you what it was.) It's an important ratio for all investors, and institutional investors are always attracted to companies showing earnings per share growth. In principle it's fairly easy to calculate, as it's the profit attributable to the company's ordinary shareholders divided by the number of shares in issue. So if this profit was £2,000 and there were 10,000 shares in issue, the earnings per share would be 20 pence. If you only had one share in this company, 20 pence of the profit would be yours! You are unlikely to receive all of this as dividends, so the immediate cash benefit is likely to be less. The retained earnings affect the share price, as long as the market believes that the additional investment will generate increased profits in the future. So the earnings per share encapsulates the two possible returns for investors, as, if the earnings per share grow, the dividends and the share price will probably increase as well.

All listed companies have to publish their earnings per share in the accounts underneath their income statement. It is simply calculated by using the following formula:

$$\frac{\text{Profit attributable to ordinary shareholders}}{\text{Number of ordinary shares in issue}}$$

Let's work out the earnings per share in my example – the relevant extracts from their financial statements are shown below.

Extracts from the income statement and the notes:

Income statement:
Profit for the year   2,000
Notes:
Dividend proposed and paid for the year   1,000

> This is the profit attributable to the company's ordinary shareholders.

(You'll recall that my example is a simple one, as there's no minority interests or preference shares.)

Balance sheet extract:

Shareholders' equity:
  Share capital (nominal value 1.00 each)   20,000
  Retained earnings   30,000
                                                   50,000

> There are 20,000 shares in issue at their year end.

Cash flow statement extract:

Financing:
  Issue of ordinary share capital   5,000
  Additional loan   5,000
  Net cash inflow from financing   10,000

> It's had a share issue during the year.

My company has had a share issue during the year, so the number of issued shares has changed. Companies don't use the year end number of shares in the earnings per share calculation, they usually use the weighted average number of shares. The only exceptions to this arise when the number of shares has changed, but there's no corresponding change in resources. For example this could happen in:

▪ A share consolidation, share split or a bonus issue – The company's capital structure changes because there are more shares, but there's no additional cash in the business. In this case, the company has to base *all* the earnings per share figures shown in the accounts on the new number of shares.

▪ A rights issue – This is slightly more complicated, as cash does come into the business. But there's a discount element in the price, representing a bonus to shareholders, which has to be excluded.

I'll assume that my company had the share issue three months before its year end, so the weighted average number of shares in issue would be 16,250 [(20,000 × 0.25) + (15,000 × 0.75)]. In this case its earnings per share would be:

$$\frac{2{,}000}{16{,}250} = 0.123$$

(If the company's reporting currency was sterling, this would be expressed as 12.3 pence.)

There's usually more than one earnings per share

Unfortunately the calculation of earnings per share is not always this simple, as it's often complicated by:

▪ **Amortisation of acquired intangible assets and exceptional items** – These can distort the trends, consequently most companies also show an *adjusted* earnings per share eliminating the effect of amortisation of acquired intangibles and exceptional items. (You'll see that IMI's adjusted earnings per share also excludes gains and losses on most financial instruments (it does include economic hedge gains and losses) because of the volatility of these instruments in the second half of 2008, when the losses reached £22.3 million.)

▪ **Share options** – The exercise of share options and warrants can reduce the earnings per share in the future, if the number of shares increases without a corresponding improvement in profits. This is referred to as *earnings dilution*. The accounting standard IAS 33 (*Earnings per share*) requires all companies having outstanding share options to also publish a *diluted earnings per share*, including all the outstanding options in the number of shares.

This means that usually you'll find that companies publish a number of earnings per share figures, reflecting different profit figures and numbers of shares. The three earnings per share figures you'll usually find at the bottom of companies' income statements are:

- A *basic* earnings per share figure, calculated by dividing the profit attributable to ordinary shareholders by the weighted average number of shares in issue.

- A *diluted* earnings per share figure, calculated by dividing the profit attributable to ordinary shareholders by the weighted average number of shares in issue plus any outstanding share options.

- An *adjusted* earnings per share figure. Companies can show other earnings per share figures, and many show one that is calculated by dividing the profit before exceptional items and amortisation of acquired intangible assets attributable to ordinary shareholders by the weighted average number of shares in issue. This gives you an understanding of the underlying earnings per share and is similar to the earnings figure used by the financial press (see below) to calculate the published ratios.

  Companies may show two adjusted figures – an adjusted basic earnings per share, and an adjusted diluted earnings per share.

You'll see even more earnings per share figures if the business has discontinued operations, as both the basic and diluted earnings per share also have to be shown using the profit from continuing operations. This will give you a measure of sustainable earnings.

And the financial press and analysts use yet another earnings calculation

You now know that companies show a number of earnings per share figures in their accounts. Whilst presenting multiple earnings per share figures represents a more realistic view of the company's performance, it is a problem for analysts and businesses such as the *Financial Times* whose readers would find it confusing to be confronted by a number of different ratios. Consequently analysts and the financial press use a definition of earnings originally developed by the Institute of Investment Management Research, now part of the CFA Society of the UK (it's the analysts' professional body). This adjusts for some, but not all, exceptional items, and provides an internationally more comparable basis for measuring a company's performance that focuses on its trading activities.

Dividends per share

I know it's unusual in accounting, but this is just what it says it is! It's the dividend that is paid on each of the company's shares. It's usually disclosed in the accounts, but can be simply calculated by dividing the total dividend by the number of shares receiving the dividend.

In my example the company proposes to pay 1,000 in dividends, and had 20,000 shares in issue. (The dividend shown in the notes is the final proposed dividend – you can see in the cash flow statement that there haven't been any dividends paid during the year.) The dividend per share is calculated by dividing the total dividend by the number of shares receiving the dividend, so the dividend per share is 0.05:

$$\frac{1,000}{20,000} = 0.05$$

You now understand the two ratios that are published in the financial statements, and I'll now show you how they're used in other investment ratios. You know that the shareholder will receive 0. 05 as a dividend – but is the company being generous, or mean? To find out you look at its *dividend cover*, or the *payout ratio*.

Dividend cover

This is similar to interest cover, and measures how many times the dividend could be paid from the available profits.

$$\frac{\text{Profit attributable to ordinary shareholders}}{\text{Dividends}} = \frac{2,000}{1,000} = 2 \text{ times}$$

The payout ratio

This expresses the dividend cover in a different way, identifying the percentage of the available profit that is paid out as dividends:

$$\frac{\text{Dividends}}{\text{Profit attributable to ordinary shareholders}} \times 100 = \frac{1,000}{2,000} = 50\%$$

The company is paying out half of the available profit as dividends. The more the company gives to its shareholders the less it has available to reinvest in the business. Determining the size of the dividend is a fine balancing act for most companies. They want to pay sufficient to maintain a stable share price, but they need to retain funds for reinvestment. Dividend cover at two times may appear imprudent, but it hasn't been unusual for a UK company to give half its profits to shareholders as dividends. However, the credit crunch has reduced many companies' ability to pay dividends. And, just like salary increases for staff, the decision is largely determined by people's expectations, and what everyone else is paying. If other companies are cutting salaries, or dividends, you can too!

Dividend yield

The dividend yield tells you the percentage cash return on the investment, and can be directly compared with interest rates and other investment opportunities. It expresses the dividend per share as a percentage of the current share price. The dividend yield is calculated using the following formula:

$$\frac{\text{Dividend per share}}{\text{Today's share price}} \times 100$$

To calculate the dividend yield for my example, I have to know the market price and it's 2.46. This means that the dividend yield is 2.03%:

$$\frac{0.05}{2.46} = 2.03\%$$

So if you buy the share at the current price, and dividends remain the same, you'd receive a cash return of 2.03% on your investment. I've used the current share price in my example, but if you use the ratios published in the financial press, the share price isn't the same as the cash you would receive if you sold the share, or the price you'd have to pay to buy the share. It is the average of the buy price and the sell price – the 'mid' market price. The dividend yield published in financial press is updated for any subsequent interim results.

The share offers a poor dividend return – if I shopped around I'd probably be better off keeping my money in a bank. However, it may offer some scope for capital gain. This depends on the company's ability to deliver future profit growth, relative to its sector, and to see the market's view of the share's potential I have to look at another ratio, the *price earnings* ratio.

The price earnings (PE) ratio/the multiple

There are different names for the same thing. The *Financial Times* publishes listed companies' PE ratios, but often talks about their multiples in its articles. It updates PE ratios for interim results, but remember it doesn't use the same earnings per share figure shown in the accounts as it tries to normalise companies' earnings.

The price earnings ratio compares the company's current share price to its reported earnings per share, and I'll assume that my earnings per share is the same as the normalised earnings:

$$\frac{\text{Today's share price}}{\text{Earnings per share}}$$

Using a share price of 2.46 for the company in my example, it has a PE ratio of 20.

$$\frac{2.46}{0.123} = 20$$

You now know how to calculate the PE ratio, but what does it tell you? The company's share price is 20 times its current earnings. This means that if you buy the shares at today's price of 2.46, and profits remain constant, it will take you 20 years to get your money back and still hold the share. (You'll get your money back from the dividends paid and the capital gain. Both are reflected in the earnings calculation. Dividends are paid out of after tax profits, and relative retained profits should improve the share price if they're reinvested wisely.)

Although people criticise the stock market for its short termism, there are very few of us who would be prepared to wait 20 years to get our money back! Most investors are looking for a payback in five to seven years, depending on the risk profile of the investment. So if someone is prepared to pay 20 times current earnings, but expects to get their money back in five to seven years, they're expecting profits to rise significantly in the next few years. You're taking a *current* figure, the share price, and comparing it with a *historical* figure, the latest earnings per share. A high PE ratio usually indicates that the market *expects* profits to grow (although it might just be that the share is expensive). A low PE usually means that the market *expects* profits to fall. You'll notice that I've italicised the word expects – a high PE ratio isn't necessarily 'good'; neither is a low PE a bad sign. It's about the market's expectation, which may or may not be realised.

If the market believes that earnings will grow, and a company issues a profits warning, its share price will fall steeply. A share with a high PE is often volatile, small pieces of good news (supporting the market's view) will cause the price to jump. However any small item of bad news (contradicting the market's view) and the price plummets.

Now here's another way of looking at PE ratios.

Prospective PEs

As the share price reflects expectations of *future* earnings it is often more appropriate to compare the price with the expected earnings, especially towards the end of the financial year and in the months after the financial year end before the results are published. This is called the *prospective PE*. This uses the estimated earnings per share for the next year, rather than the latest published earnings per share. The prospective PE matches the anticipated future earnings with the current price. So if the earnings in my company were expected to double from the reported 0.123 to 0.246, the prospective PE would be half the PE published in the financial press – 10 times earnings (2.46 ÷ 0.246). You can see that this is probably a more useful measure, particularly if you're close to the company's year end. The market has already built the anticipated profit growth into the current price. The company may have had a bad year last year and is now expected to recover. This example illustrates that a high PE doesn't necessarily mean that the company is a growth stock; it may simply reflect that a company has had a temporary fall in its profits, or its share is overvalued.

As the prospective PE is based on an individual analyst's view of future earnings, a company's prospective PE will vary from analyst to analyst as they'll have different earnings forecasts (although you can get consensus earnings forecasts as you'll discover later). In practice the historic earnings are also likely to be adjusted, as analysts don't necessarily rely on the published figures. There's sometimes a tendency for reported earnings per share figures to be 'managed' – after all directors' bonuses and reported ratios depend on it!

PE relatives

A company's PE ratio should be considered in context, relative to the market and the company's sector. Share prices move with:

- the market as a whole;
- the relative attractiveness of the sector;
- the company's position within the sector;
- the market's view of the company's performance.

The *Financial Times* publishes sector averages in the Actuaries share indices, and some ratios for the sector. Consequently, it's possible to look at the company's performance relative to its sector by using the following calculation:

$$\frac{\text{PE ratio of the company}}{\text{PE ratio of the sector}}$$

Looking at the company's relative performance within the sector gives you an indication of the market's view of the company's relative attractiveness. A company with a PE of 20 looks to have a lot of potential for profit growth, but if the sector average PE is 25, the market believes that this company offers less potential for growth than most other companies in its sector.

So PE ratios reflect the market's view of the company's profit growth over the next few years, now let me introduce you to another way of looking at growth – the PEG ratio.

PEGs

The PEG ratio was developed some years ago by the investment guru Jim Slater. It is another earnings-based measure that compares the price earnings ratio with the forecasted earnings growth, hence the name PEG (*price earnings to growth*). In my example the prospective price earnings ratio is 10 and the forecasted earnings growth is 100%, as the earnings per share are expected to double from 0.123 to 0.246. This means that the PEG would be 0.1 (10 ÷ 100). A good investment is supposed to have a PEG less than one, as this means that the expected earnings growth hasn't been fully reflected in the share price. So at last there is something positive to say about the company in my example!

PE ratios are used in the PEG ratio, but there's another way of comparing the price to the earnings – the *earnings yield*.

The earnings yield

The earnings yield is the reciprocal of the PE ratio, and is calculated in the same way as the dividend yield:

$$\frac{\text{Earnings per share}}{\text{Today's share price}}$$

In my example the current share price is 2.46 and the company's earnings per share is 0.123, so the earnings yield is 5% (0.123 ÷ 2.46). This means that if you buy the share at the current price, and profits stay the same, you can expect to earn 5% on your money.

The PE ratio and the earnings yield look at the relationship between profit and the current share price. However there is another important relationship: the relationship between the profit for the year and the capital that the shareholders invested in the company – the *return on equity*.

The return on equity

This is an overall measure of the return on the shareholders' investment, looking at the investment in the context of the company's book value. It takes the profit attributable to ordinary shareholders and divides it by the company's shareholders' equity (also referred to as the company's *sharehold-ers' funds* or *equity*):

$$\frac{\text{Profit for the year attributable to ordinary shareholders}}{\text{Shareholders' equity}}$$

In my example the shareholders' equity is 50,000 and the profit attribut-able to ordinary shareholders is the profit after tax of 2,000, so the return on equity is 4% (2,000 ÷ 50,000). It doesn't sound like a good return on invest-ment, but you would really need to know more information before you could take a view. You would need to know:

■ What the returns on equity had been in the past, as the market expects profits to grow in the future.

- How its return on equity compares with its competitors' returns on equity.

- The components of the shareholders' equity, and how, and if, they've changed. A revaluation of assets has a detrimental effect on the return on equity, as would a share issue towards the end of the financial year (the additional profits arising from the cash injection wouldn't have had time to be fully reflected in increased profit). Whereas fair value losses on financial instruments, pension deficits and past goodwill write offs improve the return on equity.

As you can see, the return on equity suffers from the same problems as net worth and the return on capital. However it is a popular measure, particularly in the US and Asia, and can be useful if the shareholders' equity is more comparable. The shareholders' equity also affects the next ratio.

Book value, or net asset value, per share

This tells you the value of the net assets attributable to each share, and is calculated by dividing the shareholders' equity by the number of shares in issue:

$$\frac{\text{Shareholders' equity}}{\text{Number of shares in issue}}$$

In my example this would be 2.50 (50,000 ÷ 20,000). This is often described as indicative of the company's break up value, but is totally dependant on the accuracy of the asset valuations. However, it does give some indication of how much of the share price is underpinned by the company's asset value and how much by its growth prospects. This relationship between the book value and the current price is measured in the *price to book ratio*.

Price to book ratio

This compares the book value, or net asset value, per share with the current share price. If you felt that the book value reflected an accurate asset value, this ratio would provide you with an indication of the inherent security of the share. If the net asset value is higher than the market value, shareholders might get their money back if the company is liquidated.

$$\frac{\text{Today's share price}}{\text{Net asset value per share}}$$

In my example the current share price is 2.46 and the company's book value per share is 2.50, giving a price to book ratio of 0.984. This means that the market values the company almost 2% below its net book value. Another way to calculate this ratio is to compare the company's value on the stock market (called its *market capitalisation*) with its value to its ordinary shareholders in the accounts. The market capitalisation in my example is 49,200 (20,000 shares in issue x the current share price of 2.46). If I divide it by the 50,000 shareholders' equity, I get the same price to book ratio of 0.984. This implies that the share price is underpinned by the company's asset value rather than its growth potential. You may find that a company's asset value is much greater than its current share price, which could suggest that it's a good buy. Be warned – that's unlikely. This usually happens when its return on capital is less than its cost of capital, and I'll tell you more about this later.

Price to sales

To calculate a price to sales ratio, you have to calculate the sales per share. In my example the revenue is 100,000, and the weighted average number of shares in issue is 16,250. (You use the weighted average number of shares in this ratio, as the revenue is earned over the year, so the share price is divided by the average number of shares in the year.) This gives sales per share of 6.15 (100,000 ÷ 16,250). As the current share price is 2.46, the price to sales ratio is 0.40 (2.46 ÷ 6.15).

Like all price based ratios. It's more meaningful if considered relative to the company's sector and you'll find that it's usually quoted as price to sales relative, in the same way as you see PE relatives. They offer a different perspective to earnings and cash flow based valuations, and are particularly useful in valuing cyclical stocks. Industries with high fixed costs and high breakeven points are often cyclical stocks, and small changes in their sales can have a dramatic effect on their earnings.

They can also be useful in other situations. Just think about a company adopting a long-term strategy and growing its market share to strengthen its future position. This strategy could have a detrimental effect on its earnings and cash flow in the short term. But this strategy would be evident in its sales per share ratio.

Price to sales should always be considered in the light of at least one other variable – the company's operating margins. A company could have a high price to sales relative to its sector because it has the highest operating margin in the sector. This should then work through to enhanced earnings, dividends, and cash flow.

In industries where companies have to have a high investment in research and development, such as pharmaceuticals, just comparing operating margins wouldn't help explain differences in the price to sales ratios. There is a number of different ways that you can resolve this problem:

- The charge for research and development could be added back to operating profit.
- The price could be compared with research and development expenditure.
- The price should be considered relative to other businesses in the sector.

Price to sales ratios have a number of advantages:

- Sales are the same in every country, making it a useful measure for cross-border comparisons.
- Sales are easier to predict than earnings and cash flow, as they are more stable and have fewer determining variables.
- They are a very good basis for valuing cyclical businesses, which often have high fixed costs and big earnings swings through the economic cycle.

Cash flow

Cash flow measures are generally thought to be better measures than earnings, as they can't be manipulated in the same way. There are two approaches to cash flow used in valuation:

- cash flow per share;
- discounted cash flow.

Cash flow per share

There is a number of different ways of calculating the cash flow per share, and I'll introduce you to:

▧ a cash flow per share used on most financial websites;

▧ free cash flow.

A cash flow per share used on financial websites

This is commonly used in the US and Asia, and is also the definition used by FT.com and Reuters on their websites. It is like an after tax version of EBITDA as it's the profit after tax plus depreciation, amortisation and impairment. In my example I only have to add back depreciation:

Profit for the year	2,000
Depreciation	1,000
Cash flow	3,000

This is then divided by the weighted average number of shares in issue, which gives my company a cash flow per share of 0.185 (3,000 ÷ 16,250), or if it's based in the UK 18.5 pence.

Free cash flow

I have some really bad news – some companies talk about free cash flow in their accounts, but different companies have different definitions. Analysts do however have a standard definition that they use in company valuation models, and I'll start by explaining and illustrating the 'valuation free cash flow'.

Analysts define free cash flow as the operating cash flow that is available to the providers of capital, so it's after any reinvestment in the existing business. So it includes changes in working capital, capital expenditures, other operating assets (such as intangible assets and goodwill) and liabilities. It excludes cash flows from non operating items such as exceptional cash flows, cash flows from discontinued operations and income from investments in unrelated businesses. (These are included in a company's valuation but not in free cash flow as they're not part of the company's underlying operating cash flow.)

Consequently it includes acquisitions, although analysts usually calculate free cash flow both before and after acquisitions in acquisitive businesses to see the underlying trends. This means that it's the operating cash flow less the investing cash flow. This is the definition of free cash flow I'll use, as it's the one that you'll come across in analysts' reports. It's also the definition used in the discounted cash flow valuations discussed later in this chapter.

Companies often refer to free cash flow in their annual report, but they have different definitions that are broadly similar. You may recall that IMI in its financial review referred to 'free cash flow before corporate activity' that was a revised operating cash flow (it also deducted net capital expenditure) less net interest. The corporate activity covered acquisitions and disposals, share buy backs, dividend payments and debt. MacDonald's also talks about free cash flow in its financial statements and defines it as the cash flow from operations less capital expenditures, which is a commonly used definition in the US. The difference between this definition and IMI's is that it doesn't deduct net interest.

This means that analysts define free cash flow as the cash flow that's available for the providers of capital, and companies define it as the cash flow available for acquisitions, dividends (and in the US interest payments) and capital restructuring. Now I really don't think you could get much further apart! If anyone talks to you about a company's free cash flow, the first thing you need to ask them is how they've defined it!

I'll use the analyst's definition to calculate the free cash flow per share, and here's the relevant extracts from the cash flow statement.

Net cash from operating activities	5,500
Purchase of property, plant and equipment	(15,000)
Disposal of property, plant and equipment	2,000
	(7,500)

The free cash flow is (7,500), and the free cash flow per share is (0.462). (The total free cash flow of (7,500) ÷ 16,250 weighted average shares in issue.) This means that the large capital expenditure prevented the company from being able to fund its obligations to its providers of capital from the cash it generated during the year.

Price to cash flow

This ratio compares the price of the share with the cash flow per share. Different analysts use different cash flows for this ratio, so I'll show you how to calculate it using both the simple cash flow and the free cash flow. You'll see that the company in my example has negative figures, as both its cash flow per share figures are negative.

Based on the simple cash flow

If the company's current share price is 2.46, and the cash flow per share is 0.185, the price to cash flow is 13.3.

Based on the free cash flow

If the company's current share price is 2.46, and the free cash flow per share is (0.462), the price to cash flow is (5.32).

Discounted cash flow

Discounted cash flow takes a future value and identifies the original amount you would have had to invest to receive that amount in the future. The best way to show you what I mean is answer the question 'How much would I need to invest today to receive 105, in a years time, if interest rates were 5%?' It's easy to work out:

$$\frac{105}{1.05} = 100$$

If you wanted to know how much you needed to invest to have 110.25, in two years time and interest rates are at 5% the answer is the same, as you're getting another year's interest:

$$\frac{110.25}{1.05^2} = 100$$

This 100 is referred to as the *present value* of 110.25 using a *discount rate* of 5%.

This technique is applied to all sorts of investment decisions, and ideally the present value of an investment's cash flows should exceed the original investment. So if you were offered an investment opportunity, with the same risk as putting money on deposit, that guaranteed you 110.25 in two years time but you were only asked to invest 95, you have a bargain! You are making 5 more than the alternative opportunity. This 5 is referred to as the *net present value*, and is the difference between the present value and the amount you're being asked to invest. As long as the present value is positive, you're doing better than putting the money in a bank, if it's negative you'd be better off investing in the bank.

So a positive net present value indicates a good investment. However, whether an investment shows a positive net present value depends on two things:

- the accuracy of the predicted future cash flows;
- the discount rate used.

Discounted cash flow is a commonly used way of valuing a company. Theoretically, the value of a company is the present value of its free cash flows in perpetuity. Think about it – this means you have to estimate the company's free cash flows in perpetuity! In practice, however, the company's free cash flows are usually just estimated for a short period, three to five years, and the subsequent cash flows are determined using the growing perpetuity formula:

$$\frac{\text{Free cash flow in the first year after the forecast period}}{\text{Weighted average cost of capital} - \text{Anticipated growth in future cash flows}}$$

Let me explain the formula by sharing a little secret with you – I'm going to live forever! And I think I'm going to need 100,000 a year to support my extravagant lifestyle. I'm trying to work out how much I'd need to invest to guarantee this annual income if interest rates are at 5%. Calculating this is fairly simple:

$$\frac{\text{Required income}}{\text{Interest rate}} = \frac{100,000}{5\%} = 2,000,000$$

So I need to have two million to support my lifestyle in perpetuity – or do I need a little more? I've heard a nasty rumour about something called inflation. Now if inflation's running at 3%, my real return is only 2% so I think I'd need five million:

$$\frac{\text{Required income}}{\text{Interest rate} - \text{Inflation}} = \frac{100,000}{5\% - 3\%} = 5,000,000$$

Now it's just a case of substitution ...The free cash flow replaces my required income, the weighted average cost of capital replaces the interest rate and the anticipated growth replaces inflation!

A small word of caution about the growing perpetuity formula

Whilst everyone uses the growing perpetuity formula, it does have some worrying underlying assumptions:

■ Profit margins and asset turns are constant in perpetuity.

■ Therefore returns on capital are constant.

■ The marginal return on capital is the same as the return on capital.

■ Cash growth is constant.

The weighted average cost of capital

Now the formula referred to the weighted average cost of capital – what is it? The weighted average cost of capital (the *WACC*) simply reflects the cost of financing the company's funds. However, the cost of equity that is used in the WACC isn't the cost of dividends – although this is the cash cost to the business of funding the equity. If you're a shareholder what really matters is the opportunity cost of having money tied up in the business. This opportunity cost comprises three elements:

■ The return you expect to get from a risk free investment, such as government bonds.

■ The risk of investing in the stock market. (You expect a bigger return from the stock market than a building society.)

■ The risk of investing in a specific company. This is measured by the volatility in its share price. (This is reflected in the company's *beta*, which measures the movement in the company's shares when the market as a whole moves by 1%. So if the company's shares move by 3%, the beta would be three. If a company's beta is less than one the share is less volatile, and therefore less risky, than the market as a whole. If its beta is more than one, its share is more volatile and riskier than the market. You can find company's betas on the web, and when you look you'll find they're not always the same. This is because different organisations use

different time periods, and the current market volatility has a significant effect on betas using short time periods.)

These three elements are brought together in a model, called *the capital asset pricing model*, which calculates the cost of equity as:

The risk free·rate + (The market risk premium × The company's beta)

Over time the returns on shares have been around 6% higher than the return on long term government bonds. (I'm ignoring the late 1990s when, to support companies' market values, there didn't appear to be any risk premium for investing in the stock market. Investors seemed to think the stock market was a one way bet!) In the UK long-term government bond rates have averaged around 5%, although they're currently around 4%, so an average cost of equity is between 10–11%. Most companies also borrow, so the WACC is just the weighted average cost of the two. To calculate the WACC, the cost of each component of the company's capital employed is weighted by its proportion of the total. But it's not as simple as it looks, as when you're calculating the WACC you have to use the *market value*, rather than the book value and you have to adjust the interest to reflect its *cost after tax*. Most analysts use the capital asset pricing model to calculate the WACC and value companies, so let's see how to calculate a WACC.

Calculating the weighted average cost of capital

The WACC is the discount rate that is used in discounted cash flow valuations. I'll show you how to calculate it by using the company in my example. Firstly, here's the relevant extracts from the company's balance sheet showing you its loans:

Bank overdraft	10,000
Loan (at 10% interest)	60,000

As these are conventional bank loans, the book value of 70,000 is used. The company's market capitalisation is 49,200 (20,000 shares in issue × the current share price of 2.46). Consequently, the total market value of the capital employed is 119,200. (This is almost the same as the *enterprise value*, which I'll discuss later in this chapter.) Of the capital, 41.28% is equity and 58.72% is debt. Now I'll calculate the cost of equity assuming that the company has a beta of 1.2, the return on long-term government bonds is 5%, and the market risk premium is 6%. Using the capital asset pricing model, the cost of equity is 12.2%:

> The risk free rate + (The market risk premium × Beta)
> 5% + (6% × 1.2) = 12.2%

I'll assume that the cost of financing all of the debt is 10%, and corporation tax is 30%. Why have I introduced tax rates? It's to make the interest cost comparable with the shareholders' return, which is after tax. The after tax cost of interest is 7% (10% less the tax benefit of 30%). You'll notice that loans are cheaper than equity, and this isn't just in my example. Loans are cheaper to finance when corporate interest rates are low.

I can now calculate the company's weighted average cost of capital:

$$\begin{array}{ccc} (41.28\% \times 12.2\%) & + & (58.72\% \times 7\%) \\ = \quad 5.04\% & + & 4.11\% \quad = 9.15\% \end{array}$$

You read in IMI's financial review that its WACC is 8%, and this was calculated similarly using net debt, rather than total debt, and excluding the pension deficit.

Using discounted cash flow valuations

So you now know that the company's free cash flows are estimated for a short period, and the subsequent cash flows are derived from the growing perpetuity model. These are then discounted by the company's cost of capital. A positive net present value shows that the company is achieving a better return than its cost of capital. If the present value of the free cash flows is greater than the market value less the debt, the company is seen as a 'buy'. If the present value is less than the market value less the debt it is rated as a 'sell'.

Unfortunately, discounted cash flow valuations can only be prepared within a company, or by analysts, as they'll usually have far more information about the company than is publicly available. They are likely to be the only people who will have access to the detailed information you need to be able to forecast the cash flows. But don't forget – although discounted cash flows appear more precise than other valuation methods, they are equally subjective and just as inaccurate. They are reliant on the accuracy, and timing, of the forecasted cash flows and the growth rates used in the growing perpetuity formula.

EBITDA and enterprise value

If you read the financial press, you'll find they often refer to EBITDA and enterprise value, so I'd like to remind you what they are and show you how they're used. Firstly, I'll tell you about EBITDA.

EBITDA

You know that EBITDA is an acronym for *e*arnings *b*efore *i*nterest, *t*ax, *d*epreciation and *a*mortisation. Although the word 'earnings' is used, it's operating profit that is used to calculate EBITDA. EBITDA is a profit measure that is especially useful when making international comparisons, as the depreciation and amortisation rules vary from one country to another. As depreciation and amortisation are the largest non cash charges made to operating profit, EBITDA is a cash related measure indicative of the underlying cash flow from the company's operations. Some analysts also add back provisions, the other major non cash charge, to more closely align EBITDA with the cash flow.

Some companies, such as IMI, disclose it in their accounts but it's easy to calculate it yourself, as it's just the operating profit plus depreciation and amortisation. I calculated EBITDA for my example in earlier chapters, and it was 11,000.

Now you let me tell you more about enterprise value.

Enterprise value

I've already discussed the return on equity and the return on capital employed. Both of these ratios are based on the *original* investment in the company. Enterprise value represents the *market* value of the company's capital employed, using net debt in the calculation. Some analysts also include minority interests, which are difficult to value, and preference shares.

You have seen, in the price to book ratio, that the shareholders' equity is rarely the same as a company's market capitalisation. In my example, the market capitalisation is 49,200 (20,000 shares in issue × the current share price of 2.46). This is less than the shareholders' equity of 50,000, as you've already seen that it has a price to book ratio of less than one.

The company also has a bank loan of 60,000, a bank overdraft of 10,000, and cash of 5,000. The net debt is 65,000 and the market capitalisation is

49,200, so the company's enterprise value is 114,200. (If the company's debt is quoted, for example it may have bonds rather than a bank loan, the debt's market value would be used in the calculation.)

You now know how to calculate it, but why is it useful? It's regarded as a theoretical takeover price; because this is the minimum price a company would have to pay: the company's current market value. It acquires the equity but also has to take on, and repay, the debt but would be able to pocket the cash.

Enterprise value is rarely used in isolation, and is usually compared with sales and EBITDA. This means that you might have to adjust the enterprise value to exclude associates and joint ventures, as they're not included in either sales or EBITDA. Consequently, most analysts make an adjustment that eliminates investments from the company's enterprise value.

Fortunately, the company in my example is simple and has the following ratios.

Enterprise value to sales

The company's revenue is 100,000 and consequently its enterprise value to sales ratio is 1.142.

$$\frac{114,200}{100,000} = 1.142$$

My example currently has a market value of £1.14 for every pound of sales it makes. This is an alternative to the price to sales ratio.

Enterprise value to EBITDA

This is the commonest enterprise value ratio, as it's used to measure out how many years it would take to pay back the investment if you acquire the company at its current market value. With EBITDA of 21,000, the enterprise value to EBITDA is 5.44:

$$\frac{114,200}{21,000} = 5.438$$

The company's value is 5.44 times its EBITDA, and it would take 5.4 years to repay the investment if you could buy the company at its enterprise value. This is really the reciprocal of a market based return on capital employed,

EBITDA to enterprise value, which is cash rate of return on investment. In my example it's 18.4%.

Shareholder value

The business cliché of the 1990s was shareholder value. Most people have no idea what this means. Is it measured by profits, earnings, return on capital – or something completely different? Shareholders want the best total return – dividends and capital growth. However, no one seems to know what drives a company's long-term value and what destroys it. The attempt to determine the drivers of shareholder value has become a modern holy grail. A number of different consulting companies think that they have found it. They have developed different 'packages', broadly offering the same solutions.

In 1990 some consultants from McKinsey & Company, Inc. wrote a book called *Valuation*, which introduced the concept of *value based management* (*VBM*). It started from the premise that a company must generate a better return than its cost of capital, and a company only adds value for its shareholders when it achieves this. (This makes sense, as you'd expect a business to earn more than its financing costs, because you wouldn't borrow money at 10% and invest it at 8% and think you were making money.) They call the difference between the return on capital and the cost of capital *economic profit*, and the value of a business is the original capital invested plus the present value of the economic profit. (You may recall that IMI referred to this in its financial review, as it's one of its financial KPI's.)

This approach is reflected in the work of another firm of consultants called Stern Stewart. Their research showed that if a company wants to increase its market value, it has to generate a return greater than its cost of capital. They call the difference between the return on capital and the cost of capital *economic value added*, or *EVA*. The difference between the capital originally invested in a business and its current market value is called the *market value added*, or *MVA*. Both EVA and MVA can be positive or negative, depending on whether the company is adding or destroying value. The link between the two is that a company's market value added is the net present value of all the future EVAs.

Both approaches are based on the view that the conventional accounting definitions of profit and capital employed are inadequate measures, as they don't reflect the underlying profitability and capital invested in the business. Whilst their approach is broadly similar, both their jargon and adjustments are different. This sometimes makes it difficult to appreciate the underlying similarities.

Value based management is a *process* enabling companies to develop an understanding of how to grow value by developing the systems and structures that enable value growth. It shows companies how to identify the most important elements of growing shareholder value in their organisation (the *value drivers*) and how to calculate the value that is being generated by the business. The financial value drivers are:

- Revenue growth.
- Operating profit margin.
- Required reinvestment:
  - working capital;
  - capital expenditure.
- Cost of capital.
- Adjusted cash tax charge (they ignore deferred taxation and the effect of interest on the tax charge).

You'll notice that the tax is included in the value drivers, but wouldn't affect a conventional return on capital calculation. That's because shareholder value models don't use a conventional return on capital calculation! They're ultimately concerned with the return to *investors*, which is always after tax. The return on capital is a very different figure from the one you're used to seeing. Firstly the profit figure is not the same as the reported one. Any amortisation of goodwill is always added back. But, after that, different models make different adjustments.

Stern Stewart argues that accounting conventions force companies to charge as costs many things that are in reality investments in the business's future, such as research and development and staff training. These should be capitalised and amortised over a three-year period, as they're an investment in future earnings and shouldn't be charged to the income statement in one year. (In practice, analysts only capitalise research and development, as training costs are rarely disclosed.) Operating leases are also capitalised.

I've summarised the differences in the following table.

McKinsey model	Stern Stewart model
Profit is called NOPLAT (an acronym for net operating profit less adjusted taxes)	*Profit is called NOPAT* ((an acronym for net operating profit after tax).
NOPLAT adjustments:	NOPAT adjustments:
• Tax on operating profit	• Tax on operating profit
• Goodwill amortisation	• Goodwill amortisation
	• Unspent provisions
	• Research and development (but there is a charge for the amortisation of research and development)
	• Operating leases
Invested capital is …	Invested capital is:
• Operating non current assets	• Operating non current assets
• Operating current assets (excluding investments)	• Operating current assets (excluding investments)
• Current liabilities (excluding financing elements – debt and dividends)	• Current liabilities (excluding financing elements – debt and dividends)
	• Provisions
	• Research and development (net of amortisation)
	• Operating leases

As the definitions are different, the two models will have different surpluses over the cost of capital (usually called the *spread*) and different valuations. However the principles are essentially the same. Both models are a clever combination, and repackaging, of some old ideas – the profitability hierarchy and discounted cash flow. The profitability hierarchy provides the value drivers, and discounted cash flow the ultimate valuation.

What is common in both models is that different numbers are used for both profit and capital employed than in those used in a conventional return on capital employed calculation. Consequently, to differentiate between the return on capital employed, many companies refer to this as the return on invested capital, or its acronym ROIC.

As time has progressed, analysts have used a combination of both models in their valuation, and you'll find that the terms economic profit and EVA have become synonymous. Analysts use shareholder value models to value companies. This means that if you want to improve your company's value you need to improve the spread between your return on capital and the cost of capital. You've already seen how companies improve their return on capital, so now let's consider the cost of capital. Before the credit crunch, large listed companies paid on average 6% interest on their loans. After tax, the cost of borrowing dropped to around 4% (if tax rates are 30%, it's 4.2%). A company with a beta of 1 had a cost of equity of 11%. So one way of improving your share price was to swap equity for debt, and analysts encouraged businesses to do this as it gave them a more 'efficient capital structure'. This is why many large companies bought back shares and increased their debt. This was fine when the global economy was growing, but now it's shrinking many companies are finding themselves in breach of banking covenants. It's like all performance measures: there are different ways of achieving them, and the companies who focused on reducing their cost of capital rather than increasing their return on capital are now paying the price.

You'll find most listed companies refer to shareholder value in their financial review, either referring to return on invested capital, EVA, or economic profit. Economic value added is one of IMI's key performance indicators. It defines it as 'the net operating profit after tax on continuing operations before restructuring costs less a capital charge' (the capital charge is its WACC times its average net assets).

Summary

I've covered many different ways of looking at a business from the investors' point of view, and I'd now like to categorise and summarise them and tell you about some of their advantages and disadvantages.

Earnings based

Ratios that use earnings per share are:

▨ not internationally comparable;

▨ improved if the company buys back its shares.

These ratios include:

- **Earnings per share** – This takes the profit available for the ordinary shareholders and divides it by the number of shares in issue. You'll usually find a number of earnings figures in a company's accounts. The *basic* earnings per share divides the profit available for ordinary shareholders by the weighted average number of shares in issue. The *diluted* earnings per share divides the profit available for ordinary shareholders by the weighted average number of shares that would have been in issue if all the share options had been exercised. The *adjusted* earnings per share uses the profit before exceptional items.

- **Price earnings ratios** – There is no need to calculate these as they are published in the financial press. The price earnings ratio is a payback measure telling you how many years it would take you to get your money back if profits remain constant. A high PE ratio may mean that the share is expensive, but usually indicates that the market expects profits to rise. A low PE may mean that the share is cheap, but it usually means that the market expects profits to fall. *Prospective* PEs use the expected earnings per share in the following year, rather than historical earnings per share. A PE *relative* compares the company's PE ratio with the average for its sector.

- **Earnings yield** – This is a different way of looking at the PE ratio, expressing the earnings per share as a percentage of the current share price.

- **PEG** – This compares the prospective price earnings ratio with the expected rate of growth in earnings over the same period. If the PEG is less than one the share may be a good one to buy, as the expected earnings' growth has not been fully reflected in the share price.

- **Return on equity** – This expresses the profit attributable to ordinary shareholders as a percentage of the shareholders' equity.

Dividend based

The ratios using dividends are:

- **Dividend per share** – This is the dividend that is paid on each share and is calculated by dividing the total dividend by the number of shares receiving a dividend.

▨ **Dividend yield** – This tells you the percentage dividend return if you buy the share at the current price and dividends are the same as the current dividend per share. The dividend yield can be compared with interest rates.

▨ **Dividend cover** – This tells you how many times the dividend could be paid from the available profit, and is calculated by dividing the profit available to ordinary shareholders by the ordinary dividend. Another way of looking at this is the *payout ratio;* this expresses the dividend as a percentage of the profit available to ordinary shareholders.

Asset based

The main problem with asset based ratios is that they are based on the book values, which can be very different from the market values. As depreciation, asset valuations and accounting for goodwill differ from one country to another, they are not internationally comparable.

The ratios using assets are:

▨ **Book value, or net asset, per share** – This tells you the value of each share's investment in the company's net assets, and is calculated by dividing the shareholders' equity by the number of shares in issue.

▨ **Price to book ratio** – This compares the company's share price with the share's book value, and gives an indication of the inherent security of the share. If the price to book ratio is less than one, if you bought the share at the current price you should receive some money if the business is liquidated assuming that someone is prepared to buy the assets at their book value. (Although often a price to book of less than one is indicative that the company's return on capital is less than its cost of capital.)

Sales based

Sales based valuations are useful when making international comparisons, and for valuing cyclical businesses. The following ratios use sales:

▨ **Sales per share** – This divides the revenue by the weighted average number of shares in issue during the year.

▨ **Price to sales** – This compares the current share price to the sales per share and, like all price based ratios, is more informative when compared to the sector as a *price to sales relative*. Operating margins should be taken into account when looking at relative price to sales ratios, as investors will be prepared to pay a higher price if the company's operating margins are higher than the sector average.

■ **Enterprise value to sales** – This compares the company's market value with its sales.

Cash based

There is a number of different definitions of cash that can be used, the commonest being:

■ **A simple cash flow measure** – This adds back depreciation and amortisation to the profit for the financial year, to more closely align the profit to the cash flow. It is used on many financial websites.

■ **Free cash flow** – Companies often use a different definition to that used by analysts:

– Companies define free cash flow as the cash flow after interest, tax, dividends and capital expenditure. This is the cash that is available for acquisitions and capital restructuring.

– Analysts define free cash flow as the cash that is available for the providers of capital, so it is the cash after taxation and reinvestment in the business. This definition of free cash flow is used in discounted cash flow valuations.

Cash is a 'clean' measure of performance, it can't be created and is internationally comparable. The ratios using cash are:

■ **Cash flow per share** – This takes the chosen cash definition and divides it by the weighted average number of shares in issue during the year.

■ **Price to cash flow** – This compares the current share price with the cash flow per share, telling you how many year's cash flow are needed to payback the current price.

EBITDA

This is an internationally comparable measure that is closely aligned to a company's cash flow. It is calculated by adding the depreciation and amortisation charges back to the company's *operating* profit. EBITDA is used in the following ratios:

▓ **EBITDA to sales** – This is a more internationally comparable version of the operating profit margin. Some analysts use the reciprocal of this – sales to EBITDA.

▓ **Enterprise value to EBITDA** – This compares the company's net market value with EBITDA, telling you how many years' EBITDA are needed to support the company's current value. It can be a useful comparative measure, as it's unaffected by a company's capital structure. However, its calculation is complicated by the valuation of minority interests and there's no standard way to adjust for them.

Enterprise value

This is the company's market capitalisation and its net debt. The debt is shown at market value if it is traded; otherwise its book value is used. Enterprise value is used in the following ratios:

▓ **Enterprise value to EBITDA**.

▓ **Enterprise value to sales** – This compares the enterprise value with revenue, and tells you how many years' sales are reflected in the company's market value.

Discounted cash flow

In theory, the value of a company is the present value of its free cash flows in perpetuity, using the company's weighted average cost of capital as the discount rate. This means that theoretically the company's free cash flows should be estimated in perpetuity. However, in practice the company's free cash flows are usually only estimated for a short period, three to five years, and the subsequent cash flows are determined using the growing perpetuity formula. Unfortunately this means that the majority of the company's value is derived from the growing perpetuity formula, and the formula's underlying assumptions are questionable.

Shareholder value, VBM and EVA

These are all variants of the same underlying principle – a company's value only differs from the value of the original capital invested to the extent of the present value of the difference between its return on capital and its cost of capital. These models represent a process for understanding and growing value and are a combination of net present value and the hierarchy of profitability.

The return on capital used in shareholder value models is different from that used in conventional financial analysis, and is usually referred to as the return on invested capital. The profit will be after adjusted *cash* taxes, and before goodwill amortisation. EVA valuations also add back any provisions that have been charged to profit but not spent, operating leases, and research and development. Operating leases are depreciated in the same way as property, plant and equipment, and research and development is amortised over three years. The invested capital is the operating capital employed with EVA valuations also including operating leased assets (net of depreciation), research and development (net of amortisation) and provisions. This means that different models will give different business values.

IMI's investment ratios in 2008

I'd now like to show you how to calculate most of these ratios for a real company, and it's time to find out a little more about IMI. You know that it's solvent and profitable – but is this reflected in their investment ratios? Let's see if we can find out!

Earnings based ratios

Earnings per share

I'll start with its earnings per share, as you don't have to work it out – it's always shown at the bottom of the income statement. IMI shows four earnings per share figures underneath its income statement, disclosing the earnings per share for continuing operations for comparative purposes, as in 2007 it had a £1.9 million after tax gain from discontinued operations:

	Notes	2008
Earnings per ordinary share	10	
Basic earnings per share		35.4p
Diluted earnings per share		35.1p
Basic earnings per share (continuing operations)		35.4p
Diluted earnings per share (continuing operations)		35.1p

In the five-year summary it also shows an adjusted basic earnings per share of 54.1 pence, and in the notes to the accounts report an adjusted diluted earnings per share of 53.7 pence. This is its underlying earnings per share and to calculate this it has added back the after tax costs of restructuring, the Severe Service investigation costs and fines, acquired intangible amortisation and impairment, other income, and the losses on its financial instruments excluding economic hedges. You can see that its exceptional items had a significant effect on its earnings per share and if all its share options had been exercised, the earnings per share would have fallen slightly.

Neither of these earnings per share figures are used in the calculation of the published PE ratio, as the earnings figure used in the financial press uses a 'normalised' earnings per share developed by the CFA Society of the UK. It's impossible to work this out yourself, as you have to consider the tax effect of the exceptional items, so you may as well use the published data. I'll also use the adjusted earnings per share to show you how to calculate IMI's PE ratio and its earnings yield.

Price earnings ratio

Because the share price used in this ratio is a 'current' one, I'll be using IMI's share price when I started to write this chapter – 326.5 pence. I'll calculate it firstly using the diluted earnings per share, as this is the earnings per share used on most financial websites. Using this, IMI's PE ratio is 9.3:

$$\frac{\text{Current share price}}{\text{Diluted earnings per share}} = \frac{326.5}{35.1} = 9.3$$

You know that there's a lot of exceptional items in 2008, so if you're trying to look at IMI's performance over a number of years you'll need to use its adjusted earnings per share of 53.7p:

$$\frac{\text{Current share price}}{\text{Adjusted diluted earnings per share}} = \frac{326.5}{53.7} = 6.1$$

Prospective PE

You can find consensus earnings figures on the FT.com website, and the average expectation for IMI's diluted adjusted earnings per share for the year ending December 2009 is currently 34.5 pence, with a high estimate of 39.1 pence and a low estimate of 26.5 pence. This means that analysts expect IMI's earnings to fall, hardly surprising considering the probable effect of the recession on its markets. But just look at the difference between the high estimate and the low estimate – it's 12.6 pence. So there's not much agreement between the analysts, with the bulls predicting earnings 47.5% higher than the bears!

I'll use the average estimate to calculate the prospective PE:

$$\frac{\text{Current share price}}{\text{Forecast adjusted diluted earnings per share}} = \frac{326.5}{34.5} = 9.5$$

PE relative

The sector average PE for industrial engineering is 8.48, so IMI is seen as having slightly more potential for profit growth than other companies in its sector and has a PE relative of 1.10:

$$\frac{\text{Company's PE ratio}}{\text{Sector's PE ratio}} = \frac{9.30}{8.48} = 1.10$$

This implies that IMI is expected to have 10% more earnings growth than the sector as a whole.

Earnings yield

This is the reciprocal of the PE ratio, expressing earnings as a percentage of the current price. I'll calculate this for the diluted earnings per share, and the adjusted earnings per share. The yield using the diluted earnings per share is 10.8%:

$$\frac{\text{Diluted earnings per share}}{\text{Current share price}} = \frac{35.1}{326.5} = 10.8\%$$

IMI's reported earnings are 10.8% of its current share price, but if you're looking at the underlying earnings this increases to 16.5%:

$$\frac{\text{Adjusted diluted earnings per share}}{\text{Current share price}} = \frac{53.7}{326.5} = 16.4\%$$

PEG ratio

As the market expects IMI's earnings to fall in 2009, this is not a relevant ratio.

Return on equity

This shows the return on the shareholders' equity. Now you've learnt by now that, if you want to make comparisons, you have to adjust the shareholders' equity for any goodwill previously written off through reserves, provisions and, if appropriate, revaluation. The published shareholders' equity is £452.4 million, as when you're looking for the return on the investment of IMI's shareholders you ignore the minority interests:

Shareholders' equity	
Called up share capital	84.7
Share premium	165.1
Other reserves	71.1
Retained earnings	131.5
Total equity attributable to equity shareholders of the Company	452.4
Minority interest	9.3
Total equity	461.7

However, its retained earnings has been reduced by:

■ £28.1 million total unspent provisions less the net deferred tax asset. This cash has not left the business, and you've seen that different countries have different rules about provisions and deferred tax.

■ £364 million goodwill has been written off for businesses it acquired before December 1998. This is money that has been invested in the business, and most countries have always shown goodwill as an intangible asset.

It hasn't revalued their properties, so their adjusted shareholders' equity is £844.5 million (£452.4 million + £28.1 million + £364 million). If the company you're analysing has revalued, you'll also have to exclude the revaluation reserve if you're comparing it with companies who haven't revalued their assets.

As there were so many exceptional items in 2008, it seems appropriate to calculate an adjusted return on equity figure. You can find the adjusted profit in the note on earnings per share:

From continuing operations	2008	2007
		Restated
	£m	£m
Profit for the year	116.0	118.0
Minority interest	(3.1)	(2.9)
	112.9	115.1
Charges/(credits) included in profit for the year:		
Restructuring costs	19.6	22.0
Severe Service investigation costs and fines	26.3	4.9
Acquired intangible amortisation and impairment	13.2	10.9
Other income	–	(1.7)
Financial instruments excluding economic hedge contract gains and losses	19.6	(1.6)
Taxation on charges/(credits) included in profit before tax	(19.0)	(11.0)
Earnings for adjusted EPS	172.6	138.6

Its profit attributable to shareholders before exceptional items was £172.6 million, after exceptional items it fell to £112.9 million. I'll work out four return on equity figures using profit attributable to its shareholders before and after exceptional items, and its published and adjusted equity figures. (You'd normally only calculate one return on equity ratio, but I want to show you how to calculate the four possibilities.)

$$\frac{\text{Profit attributable to shareholders}}{\text{Shareholders' equity}} = \frac{112.9}{452.4} = 25.0\%$$

$$\frac{\text{Attributable profit before exceptional items}}{\text{Shareholders' equity}} = \frac{172.6}{452.4} = 38.2\%$$

$$\frac{\text{Profit attributable to shareholders}}{\text{Adjusted shareholders' equity}} = \frac{112.9}{844.5} = 13.4\%$$

$$\frac{\text{Attributable profit before exceptional items}}{\text{Adjusted shareholders' equity}} = \frac{172.6}{844.5} = 20.4\%$$

The last return on equity, using profit before exceptional items and adjusted shareholders' equity, is a comparable measure showing IMI's underlying return on equity.

Dividend based ratios

Dividend yield

If you bought IMI's shares at their current price, and the dividend per share doesn't change, you would receive 6.34% of your investment as dividends:

$$\frac{\text{Dividend per share}}{\text{Current share price}} = \frac{20.7}{326.5} = 6.34\%$$

Dividend cover

IMI's declared dividends during the year were £65.9 million, and it could pay its dividend 2.6 times out of the profit after exceptional items:

Before exceptional items:

$$\frac{\text{Profit attributable to ordinary shareholders}}{\text{Dividends}} = \frac{172.6}{65.9} = 2.6 \text{ times}$$

After exceptional items:

$$\frac{\text{Profit attributable to ordinary shareholders}}{\text{Dividends}} = \frac{112.9}{65.9} = 1.7 \text{ times}$$

Asset based ratios

Unless the asset values are kept up to date, these have limited relevance. However, I'll show you how to work them out.

Book value, or net asset, per share

Excluding the 20.6 million shares that are IMI holds as treasury shares, there were 318.3 million shares in issue at the end of December 2008. (For this ratio you use the shares in issue at the end of the year, as you're comparing it with the shareholders' equity at the end of the year.) You'll find that the book values per share published on websites use the reported equity, and with IMI's goodwill write off, that makes them pretty useless for comparative purposes. But here's how they calculate it:

$$\frac{\text{Shareholders' equity}}{\text{Number of shares in issue}} = \frac{452.4}{318.3} = 1.42$$

This means most websites would report that each share has an asset value of £1.42, whereas its underlying asset value is almost twice that:

$$\frac{\text{Adjusted shareholders' equity}}{\text{Number of shares in issue}} = \frac{844.5}{318.3} = 2.65$$

Price to book ratio

This shows you that its share is trading at 2.3 times its book value, and 1.28 times its adjusted book value:

$$\frac{\text{Current share price}}{\text{Net asset value per share}} = \frac{326.5}{142.1} = 2.30$$

$$\frac{\text{Current share price}}{\text{Net asset value per share}} = \frac{326.5}{265.3} = 1.23$$

This may reflect that its assets are undervalued on the books, which they are, and/or that the share price is largely underpinned by an expectation of profit growth, and you've seen that the market does not expect its profits to grow next year, although they do expect profits to grow in future years as the global economy improves.

Sales based ratios

IMI's 2008 revenue was £1,900.6 million.

Sales per share

During 2008 the weighted average number of shares in issue was 319.3 million. (This is used to calculate the sales per share, as the revenue is generated throughout the year.) Consequently IMI had £5.95 sales per share.

$$\frac{\text{Revenue}}{\text{Number of shares}} = \frac{1,900.6}{319.3} = \text{£5.95 or 595 pence}$$

Price to sales

$$\frac{\text{Current share price}}{\text{Sales per share}} = \frac{326.5}{595.2} = 0.55$$

The current share price reflects 55% of IMI's sales.

Cash based ratios

Simple cash flow

This is the depreciation and amortisation charge added back to the profit attributable to IMI's shareholders. Once again I'm going to calculate an adjusted cash per share as well. (This is particularly important, as most of its exceptional items don't involve cash flows.) Firstly, let's follow the standard definition:

Profit for the year	112.9
Depreciation	43.1
Amortisation and impairment	16.4
Cash flow	172.4

$$\frac{\text{Cash flow}}{\text{Number of shares}} = \frac{172.4}{319.3} = £0.54$$

If you use the reported figure each share has 54 pence cash generated in the year. However, when you look at the underlying cash flow things look better:

Adjusted profit for the year	172.6	This is included in the amortisation charge.
Less amortisation of acquired intangibles and impairment	(13.2)	
Depreciation	43.1	
Amortisation and impairment	16.4	
Cash flow	218.9	

$$\frac{\text{Adjusted cash flow}}{\text{Number of shares}} = \frac{218.9}{319.3} = £0.69$$

Free cash flow

I'll use the definition of free cash flow that you'll find in analysts' reports. This is the cash flow that's available for the providers of capital, so it's the operating cash flow less capital expenditure and acquisitions and disposals. Here are the relevant extracts from IMI's cash flow statement:

Net cash from operating activities	217.4
Proceeds from the sale of property plant and equipment	3.1
Acquisition of property, plant and equipment	(47.6)
Capitalised development expenditure	(5.1)
Free cash flow	167.8

$$\frac{\text{Free cash flow}}{\text{Number of shares}} = \frac{167.8}{319.3} = £0.53$$

Price to cash flow

This doesn't usually use the free cash flow, so I'll base it on the simple cash flow.

$$\frac{\text{Current share price}}{\text{Cash flow per share}} = \frac{326.5}{54.0} = 6.05$$

IMI's share is trading at 6.05 times its cash flow, and 4.76 times its adjusted cash flow:

$$\frac{\text{Current share price}}{\text{Adjusted cash flow per share}} = \frac{326.5}{68.6} = 4.76$$

EBITDA

This is usually based on operating profit before exceptional items, as analysts are concerned about a company's underlying profitability. IMI's operating profit before exceptional items was £268.9 million in 2008. Its depreciation and amortisation charged to profit before exceptional items was £46.3 million, so its 2008 EBITDA is £315.2 million:

	£ million
Operating profit before exceptional items	268.9
Depreciation	43.1
Amortisation charged to profit	3.2
EBITDA	315.2

This is used in a number of ratios, including EBITDA to sales.

EBITDA to sales

IMI's 2008 revenue was £1,900.6 million, and its EBITDA to sales ratio was 16.58%.

$$\frac{\text{EBITDA}}{\text{Revenue}} = \frac{315.2}{1,900.6} = 16.58\%$$

The unadjusted EBITDA was £269.3 million, giving an EBITDA to sales margin of 14.17%.

Sales to EBITDA

You'll often see this in analyst's reports, and it's simple to calculate, as it's the reciprocal of EBITDA to sales.

$$\frac{\text{Revenue}}{\text{EBITDA}} = \frac{1,900.6}{315.2} = 6.03$$

IMI converted its adjusted EBITDA into sales 6.03 times in 2008.

Enterprise value

This is IMI's market capitalisation, its net debt, and minority interests. Theoretically the debt and minority interests should be shown at their market value, which is not freely available and so I'll use their book value. Their market capitalisation was £1,042.5 million, their net debt was £298.7 million and their minority interest was £9.3 million giving an enterprise value of £1,350.5 million.

Enterprise value to EBITDA

I shall use the adjusted EBITDA in this calculation, as if someone was interested in acquiring IMI they'd be looking at their underlying cash flow.

$$\frac{\text{Enterprise value}}{\text{EBITDA}} = \frac{1{,}350.5}{315.2} = 4.28$$

IMI's enterprise value is 4.28 times its EBITDA, so in the unlikely event that someone could acquire IMI for its enterprise value it would take them 4.28 years to recover the cost assuming EBITDA stayed the same.

Enterprise value to sales

$$\frac{\text{Enterprise value}}{\text{Revenue}} = \frac{1{,}350.5}{1{,}900.6} = 0.71$$

IMI's market value is 0.71 times its revenue.

What have we learned?

As I've just looked at 2008, we've only learned a limited amount about how investors see IMI. But we have discovered that in 2008 it's probably more an income share than a growth share, as its dividend yield is relatively high. The market expects its profit to grow slightly faster than the sector average, which is currently depressed by the state of the global economy.

IMI

Introduction

I'm now going to analyse IMI's performance over the last four years. Normally I prefer to analyse companies over five years, but I've shortened the analysis period as IMI's business changed in 2005 when it sold its building products business, Polypipe, in September. This was a material disposal, as it comprised 15% of the group's revenue and 11% of its operating profit in 2005. Although the income statement was analysed between continuing and discontinued operations on a line by line basis for 2005 and 2004, only the total operating and investing cash flows were disclosed making it impossible to adjust all the other financial statements.

Starting the analysis

I always start a financial analysis in the same way, by understanding where the company has come from. It's even more important when you're analysing over a relatively short period, such as four years. So I start with its financial summary, and IMI's shows its financial performance over five years.

Once I have this context, I'll read through its financial and operating reviews as this gives me more information about its divisional performance and the risks and opportunities currently facing their business. I then read through the rest of its accounts to get some more information about its business, and follow up any questions I may have. Once I've done this I can decide what I want to analyse, and have identified the ratios I'll need to calculate. (I know I've shown you how to do all of them in the earlier chapters, but I never use them all.)

Consequently in this chapter you'll find:

- *IMI's five-year summary;*

- *its operating review (its financial review is shown in full in Chapter 6);*

- *a summary of its accounts for its financial years 2005–2008;*

- *the ratios I plan to use, and why I plan to use them;*

- *ratio analysis and commentary for its financial years 2005–2008.*

IMI's five-year summary

When you look at IMI's five-year summary on the following pages you'll see that its:

- Revenue, profit and EBITDA have grown in the last five years, but don't forget that these are influenced by exchange rates, particularly in 2008. (In the financial review IMI disclosed that in 2008 weakening sterling had a significant effect on its reported profitability increasing revenue by £179 million (10.4%) and its underlying profit before tax by £27 million (11.6%).)

- Underlying earnings per share have increased significantly over the period and dividends per share grew in real terms until 2008 when growth dropped to 2% following the onset of the recession.

- The group's net borrowings and gearing were low until 2007, when it increased its debt. However, borrowings still only reflect 1.1 times 2008's EBITDA and are very affordable.

IMI FIVE YEAR SUMMARY

Continuing operations

Revenue £m

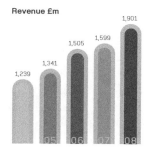

Profit before tax* £m

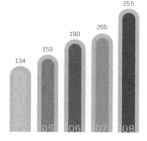

	2004 £m	2005 £m	2006 £m	2007 £m	2008 £m
Income statement					
Revenue	1,239	1,341	1,505	1,599	**1,901**
Adjusted profit before tax*	134.4	159.2	190.2	205.5	**254.7**
Restructuring costs	(2.9)	(4.2)	(19.7)	(22.0)	**(19.6)**
Investigation costs and fines	–	–	–	(4.9)	**(26.3)**
Acquired intangible amortisation and impairment	(4.2)	(3.3)	(14.6)	(10.9)	**(13.2)**
Other income	–	–	–	1.7	**–**
Financial instruments and economic hedge contracts	0.8	(0.6)	2.3	1.6	**(19.6)**
Profit before tax	128.1	151.1	158.2	171.0	**176.0**
EBITDA†	175	198	211	220	**269**

* before restructuring, investigation costs and fines, acquired intangible amortisation and impairment, other income and financial instruments excluding economic hedge contract gains and losses.

† earnings before interest, tax, depreciation, amortisation and impairment and other income.

2008 Sales by geographical destination**

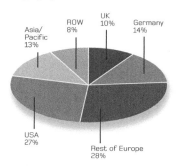

ROW 8%
UK 10%
Germany 14%
Asia/Pacific 13%
USA 27%
Rest of Europe 28%

** before economic hedge contract gains and losses.

Group sales by destination

	2004 £m	2005 £m	2006 £m	2007 £m	2008 £m
UK	164	164	173	188	**183**
Germany	178	179	194	209	**266**
Rest of Europe	300	324	376	423	**533**
USA	431	466	490	460	**517**
Asia/Pacific	107	141	183	202	**249**
Rest of World	59	67	89	117	**149**
	1,239	1,341	1,505	1,599	**1,897**
Economic hedge contract gains and losses	–	–	–	–	**4**
	1,239	1,341	1,505	1,599	**1,901**

Earnings and dividends

	2004	2005	2006	2007	**2008**
Adjusted earnings per share (pre-restructuring)			37.8p	41.9p	**54.1p**
Adjusted earnings per share (post-restructuring)	29.5p	33.4p			
Earnings per share	19.1p	3.9p	21.4p	35.4p	**35.4p**
Ordinary dividend per share	16.5p	17.5p	18.7p	20.2p	**20.7p**

Balance sheet

	2004 £m	2005 £m	2006 £m	2007 £m	**2008 £m**
Net operating assets including intangible assets	698	578	690	771	**973**
Other non-operating liabilities (excluding borrowings)	(67)	(146)	(193)	(125)	**(212)**
Net borrowings	(76)	(11)	(80)	(233)	**(299)**
Net assets	555	421	417	413	**462**

Statistics

	2004	2005	2006	2007	**2008**
Segmental operating profit as a percentage of segmental revenue	11.2%	12.0%	12.6%	13.0%	**14.0%**
Segmental operating profit as a percentage of segmental net assets	27.7%	28.0%	27.4%	27.0%	**27.4%**
Net assets per share (excluding treasury shares)	156.4p	123.3p	123.7p	128.1p	**144.4p**
Net borrowings as a percentage of shareholders' funds	13.7%	2.5%	19.5%	57.3%	**66.0%**
Net debt: EBITDA	0.3	–	0.4	1.1	**1.1**
EBITDA: Interest	19	24	28	17	**17**

IMI's operating review

When you read IMI's operating review you'll discover:

That 2008 was largely a successful year for IMI with revenues increasing by 19%, overall organic sales growth (growth in revenue from its existing businesses) of 5%, and 14% of its revenues coming from new products launched in the last three years. This enabled it to increase its adjusted earnings per share by 29%. However the recession had already started to affect some of its businesses.

■ The Fluid Controls division had organic sales growth of 5% and increased its operating margins from 14.4% to 15.7%, but within the division the performance was mixed:

– Severe Service had organic revenue growth, excluding exchange rate movements, of 9% increasing to 15% in the second half of the year. Its operating margin increased from 15.4% in 2007 to 18.4% in 2008. Severe Service still has a positive outlook for 2009 although there has been some slowing of order intake in some of its markets.

– The Fluid Power business had 3% organic revenue growth, and operating margins increased from 13.2% to 13.7%. However it was particularly affected by the onset of the recession, as its customers cut back on their capital expenditure in the second half of the year, particularly in November and December. Most Fluid Power markets are expected to be 'extremely challenging' during 2009 and in the three months to the end of February were 30% down on the previous year.

– Indoor Climate's organic revenue growth was 6%, and its operating margins increased from 15.7% to 16.1% with stronger margins in the second half of the year. Indoor Climate expects the commercial construction markets to be 'challenging', and is shifting its focus towards government infrastructure projects, where it hopes to benefit from its energy efficient products.

■ The Retail Dispense division had organic sales growth of 3% and its operating margin was maintained at 9.6%.

– However organic revenue declined by 1% in Beverage Dispense where revenues were down 6% in the second half of the year following a sharp reduction in demand in a number of its markets.

– Merchandising showed strong organic growth of 11% and the operating margin fell from 11% in 2007 to 10.3% in 2008 largely following increases in steel costs in the first half of the year. Margins improved in the second half.

For the three months to the end of February, like for like revenues are 15% lower than the equivalent period in the previous year and since late November trading conditions have deteriorated in:

- automotive and commercial vehicles;
- factory automation;
- commercial construction markets.

However, energy markets are still buoyant and there is increased government investment in infrastructure projects.

It has taken steps to mitigate the effect of the recession by:

- Only allocating resources to growth areas.
- 'Right-sizing' its business by closing factories and reducing staff.
- Maintaining margins by managing mix, differentiating products and reducing costs.
- Focusing on optimising cash. Its cash conversion ratio is expected to be more than 90%. You may remember this from the financial review. It's similar to free cash flow, but excludes tax, as it expresses EBITDA less working capital requirements and net capital expenditure (including capitalised development costs as percentage of segmental operating profit less restructuring costs. This means that there are three drivers of their cash conversion ratio:
  - EBITDA (which will fall in a recession, but the fall should be matched in the denominator, segmental operating profit).
  - Working capital requirements (which should decrease, as volumes fall).
  - Capital expenditure (which, apart from capitalised development expenditure will probably reduce as part of their 'right-sizing' activities).

OUR GOALS AND HOW WE ARE ACHIEVING THEM

We aim to deliver sustainable organic growth in excess of GDP growth and over time to reach operating margins of 15%.

We have a clear strategy that is relevant and appropriate for a successful engineering solutions business in the 21st century and we continue to pursue it vigorously. We are focused on growth with industry or sector leading customers in niche markets which are themselves growing. Adding value to such customers and improving their performance is the route to sustainable profit growth for our shareholders. We operate in markets where we already hold or can achieve a market leadership position where we can clearly differentiate ourselves from our competitors with end-user insight and the application of innovative technology. Key account management and project management are important disciplines for the effective delivery of bespoke solutions to our leading customers. We also provide aftermarket support in the form of service and spares to our customers' installed product base.

Our five business platforms share this common philosophy. The Severe Service, Fluid Power and Indoor Climate business platforms serve Fluid Controls markets, where our customers are plant operators and original equipment manufacturers.

The Beverage Dispense and Merchandising businesses operate in Retail Dispense markets, where our customers are brand owners and retailers.

Our strategic growth drivers are understood by all the senior management in IMI and embedded throughout our businesses.

Accelerating our key account focus

Highly talented, customer-focused, entrepreneurial-minded teams of people in IMI add long-term value for both customers and ourselves. Developing these skills, understanding the drivers of our customers' businesses, and our own, and ensuring that we work with the best customer partners, are critical components of our business model. Recognising where value can be added for both parties is a fundamental part of our approach. A centrally-based 'Key Account Academy' helps to train our people and ensure that best practice is shared across the Group.

Increasing our creative abilities

We invest in techniques that improve market and customer insight, frequently working with academics and other partners who can aid our understanding. We then apply our acquired knowledge and our engineering capabilities to the issues faced by our customers. The result is relevant, new, value-adding technologies and products that strengthen our customer relationships.

▶

Seizing the initiative in emerging economies

We continue to invest in the emerging markets of Eastern Europe, the Middle East and Asia, particularly China which have been growing rapidly. In recent years we have significantly increased our ability to generate sales, manufacturing and procurement opportunities in these territories through the development of regional and local teams with relevant local industry knowledge and experience. Focused investment of this sort enables us to support our customers as they enter new markets, whilst also helping to drive value for our customers in established markets. A high-profile advisory board supports our commitment to current and future activities in China.

Balance sheet management

Strategic acquisitions that support our existing businesses help us to develop new markets further. Acquisitions must align with our strategy and should bring technology, talent, market sector or key account relationships with the ability to create significant differentiation, so strengthening further our leadership positions in our well-defined niche markets. They must also be supportive of our growth and margin targets.

In addition to our acquisition programme, we continue to invest organically in our existing businesses where we see potential to promote organic growth. All potential acquisitions and all major investment proposals must be able to demonstrate positive economic value added on a cumulative basis within three years. The Group also aims to maintain cash conversion levels at no less than 80%.

Business performance is evaluated regularly by the Board of IMI using a variety of tools. Five of the most important key performance indicators (KPIs) are shown here.

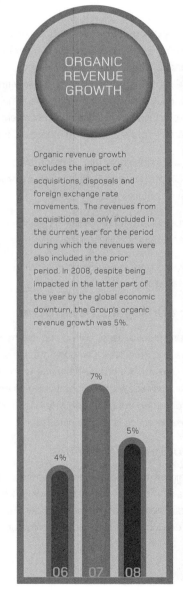

ORGANIC REVENUE GROWTH

Organic revenue growth excludes the impact of acquisitions, disposals and foreign exchange rate movements. The revenues from acquisitions are only included in the current year for the period during which the revenues were also included in the prior period. In 2008, despite being impacted in the latter part of the year by the global economic downturn, the Group's organic revenue growth was 5%.

4% 7% 5%
06 07 08

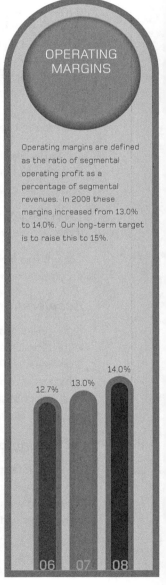

OPERATING MARGINS

Operating margins are defined as the ratio of segmental operating profit as a percentage of segmental revenues. In 2008 these margins increased from 13.0% to 14.0%. Our long-term target is to raise this to 15%.

12.7% 13.0% 14.0%
06 07 08

Each business unit of IMI participates in an annual round of planning meetings with the Executive Committee of the Board, during which future plans for that business are reviewed and updated. These plans include specific local, regional and sector targets and KPIs which reflect and measure business performance.

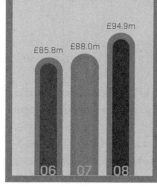

ECONOMIC VALUE ADDED

Economic value added (EVA) is defined as the net operating profit after tax on continuing operations before restructuring costs less a capital charge. The capital charge is arrived at by applying the after tax weighted average cost of capital to the average invested capital (net assets plus net debt, but net debt excludes the IAS19 pension deficit). For the sixth year running, IMI delivered positive EVA. The 2008 EVA was £94.9m which is an increase of 8% over 2007.

£94.9m
£85.8m £88.0m

06 07 08

LOST TIME ACCIDENT RATES

The Group takes seriously its responsibility for the safety of all our employees. Our lost time accident (LTA) rate again improved in 2008 to 0.47 accidents per 100,000 hours worked from 0.49 in 2007. We recognise the need for further improvement and significantly raised the profile of health & safety in 2008. We have introduced a corporate target to reduce this by 25% over the next 3 years to no more than 0.35.

0.50 0.49 0.47

06 07 08

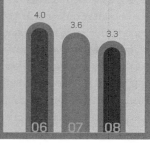

CO$_2$ EMISSIONS

Our CO$_2$ emissions in 2008 amounted to 101,000 tonnes (2007: 106,000 tonnes). Normalised against hours worked, our performance improved by 8% to 3.3 CO$_2$ tonnes/1,000 hours worked. In light of the recent volatility in exchange rates, it was considered appropriate to revise the KPI to be relative to working hours and not to sales. In the absence of this change, the 2008 CO$_2$ emissions normalised against sales would have shown a 20% reduction. Given the difficult economic environment and a proportion of our energy consumption not being directly linked to hours worked, it will be more challenging to make progress in 2009.

4.0
3.6
3.3

06 07 08

In addition, each business has its own regular business reviews from weekly updates to formal quarterly reviews. This process enables the Board to review performance against tactical and strategic milestones and allows informed decisions to be taken at each level of the organisation.

Regional markets

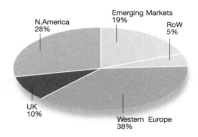

N.America 28%
Emerging Markets 19%
RoW 5%
UK 10%
Western Europe 38%

End markets

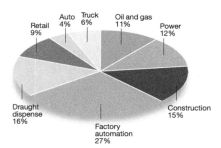

Auto 4%
Truck 6%
Oil and gas 11%
Power 12%
Retail 9%
Draught dispense 16%
Factory automation 27%
Construction 15%

We are pleased to report another good set of results for the group in 2008, with encouraging progress in most areas of the business. However the global economic downturn presents the group with significant challenges in 2009 and beyond. Consequently we are taking early and decisive actions to position the Group to meet these challenges and mitigate against the financial impact.

Performance in 2008

In 2008 revenue, operating profit, operating margin and adjusted earnings per share again all showed significant progress over the prior year. Organic sales growth for the Group as a whole was 5%. Segmental operating profit increased by 28% and the segmental operating margin improved from 13.0% to 14.0%.

Adjusted earnings per share increased by 29% to 54.1p. The Board is recommending a final dividend of 12.7p, maintained at last year's level. We recognise the importance of the dividend to our shareholders but at the same time need to be mindful of the more challenging markets that we face in 2009. This makes the total dividend for the year 20.7p, an increase of 2% over last year's 20.2p. Maintenance of the dividend will be a core objective through the economic downturn.

During 2008 we made further good progress against our well defined operational strategies in each of our businesses. We made further investment in emerging markets during the year where our businesses continued to grow with revenues up by 19%. We have now completed our 3 year restructuring programme to move a greater proportion of our manufacturing capacity to low cost economies, and the benefits are being delivered as expected. We continue to build on our new product development capabilities and the percentage of revenues derived from new products launched in the prior three years was 14%. New product introductions during 2008 included: the launch of new Drag wellhead gas production chokes in our Severe Service business, aimed at developing share in the upstream gas market; several new valve systems in the important life sciences sector by Norgren, our Fluid Power business; and 'Viper', a frozen beverage dispenser with high performance output and the ability to serve a broader range than traditional equipment.

Our Fluid Controls businesses again delivered strong results, with organic sales growth of 5% and an increase in operating margins from 14.4% to 15.7%. The Severe Service, Fluid Power and Indoor Climate businesses all performed well benefiting from relatively buoyant end markets particularly in the first half.

Organic sales for the year in our Retail Dispense businesses grew by 3% and the operating margin was maintained at 9.6%. Merchandising performed well benefiting from strong shipments in the second half to a major US supermarket company. Under the terms of the original purchase agreement we acquired the remaining 19.1% minority interest in Display Technologies in January 2009. Based on the contracted pricing mechanism the cash consideration is expected to be around £20m. Beverage Dispense after a satisfactory first six months faced more challenging market conditions in the second half.

Focus for 2009

The Group highlighted in its interim management statement in November 2008 that it had seen some evidence of a slow down in certain of its markets since the summer as a result of the global economic downturn. This included the in-plant automotive and European commercial vehicle sectors in Fluid Power and the demand from major soft drinks bottlers in both North America and Europe in Beverage Dispense.

Since late November trading conditions have deteriorated across many of our end markets. Sectors such as automotive and commercial vehicles have suffered a sharp contraction, as has investment in factory automation as businesses seek to reign back capital expenditure in the face of balance sheet concerns and poor forward visibility. Construction markets, particularly within the once fast growing regions of Eastern Europe and Dubai, have also contracted sharply, as access to credit has evaporated.

Whilst pockets of resilience do exist, with energy markets remaining buoyant for our Severe Service business; increased Government investment in infrastructure providing new opportunities for our Fluid Power and Indoor Climate businesses; and the customer focus on value and comfort purchases presenting new project opportunities for both the Beverage Dispense and Merchandising businesses; the prevailing picture is one of significant retrenchment. For the three months to the end of February, like for like revenues for the Group are around 15% lower than the equivalent period last year, reflecting sharply lower activity in the Fluid Power business, down nearly 30% on last year, partly offset by continued growth in Severe Service.

We took significant and decisive management action early to respond to these challenges, and this has been and continues to be focused in four key areas:

1. Resource Allocation:

We are focusing our resources on sectors providing greater resilience such as energy, infrastructure, life sciences, and value retailing, as well as sectors benefiting from increased legislation such as energy efficiency. Opportunities affording certainty and speed are receiving the highest priority.

▶

2. Capacity Alignment:

We have taken rapid action to right size the business to the lower activity levels, with 10% of the global workforce having been released since December, and short-time working arrangements having been implemented wherever practicable. Further releases are planned and we expect to be fully reconciled to the current levels of activity by the end of June. As part of this sizing initiative we have also taken the opportunity to bring forward some of our longer range plans to transfer more of our manufacturing capacity from North America and Europe to the lower cost areas of China, Czech Republic and India. The combination of these two activities will incur rationalisation costs of around £25m in 2009, and £10m in 2010. The savings arising from the right sizing initiatives will be around £15m in 2009, with an additional £10m per year savings generated from the moves to lower cost operating environments from 2011 onwards.

3. Product Margins:

We are firmly focused on product margins, robustly defending our pricing and value positions around a product portfolio which is well differentiated and highly customised, whilst at the same time extracting maximum benefit from a sharp fall in commodity prices over the last few months. Coupled with an austere approach to wage and salary inflation, with wage freezes for large parts of our organisation, we expect these various initiatives to cushion the profit impact of lower revenues in 2009 by at least £30m.

4. Cash Optimisation:

We are focused on our balance sheet, and the implementation of even tighter controls around cash conversion which have always been a key feature of our business. We anticipate cash conversion for 2009 in excess of 90% which, coupled with lower capital expenditure this year, will ensure we retain a strong balance sheet.

Severe Service investigation

We expect to reach final agreement in the near future on a settlement with the US Department of Justice in respect of certain irregular payments by our US subsidiary Control Components Inc (CCI) that violated the US Foreign Corrupt Practices Act. An investigation has also been completed into possible incidental breaches of US trade law by CCI. Legal costs incurred in 2008, together with a provision for the expected fines and certain related legal costs, totalling £26.3m has been separately disclosed in the 2008 accounts due to its one off nature and quantum. We will also have to deal with a number of collateral issues in other jurisdictions outside the US.

IMI people

Bob Stack joined the Board as a non-executive director in June 2008. Bob brings with him extensive international experience from a number of blue chip companies including 18 years at Cadbury plc. Lance Browne, who had been a non-executive director since 2005, retired from the Board at the end of 2008. Lance will remain as Chairman of the IMI China Advisory Board. We would like to thank Lance for his considerable contribution to the IMI Board.

David Nicholas, executive director, has confirmed that he plans to retire in December this year at age 60, stepping down from the Board on 1 September. With the onset of more difficult trading conditions, the Company has decided to make a number of management changes with immediate effect. Roy Twite, executive director, is appointed President of the Fluid Power business, taking full responsibility for day to day activities. During his career with IMI, Roy has held a number of senior management positions in Fluid Power and this experience will be invaluable in leading the business through the current challenging markets. David Nicholas retains his responsibility for the Indoor Climate business and in addition now leads the Group Supply and Mergers & Acquisitions teams. The Severe Service, Beverage Dispense and Merchandising businesses now report directly to Martin Lamb, Chief Executive.

Our success in 2008 is fundamentally linked to the skills, energy, initiative and commitment of our people across our worldwide operations.

We are again grateful for their continued hard work and enthusiasm which will assist us in facing the challenges in 2009.

Outlook

As a result of the global economic downturn many of our end markets are extremely challenging. However, we have taken decisive management actions to right size the business for the current lower activity levels.

The Group retains a healthy balance sheet and good cash generation. The repositioning of the Group over the last few years with a focus on higher added value products and more resilient end markets, together with lower operating costs resulting from our restructuring programme will help the Group to face the challenges in 2009. In the longer term as economic conditions improve we will be well placed with strengthened market positions, a lower cost base and the ability to scale up capacity quickly to respond to growth opportunities.

Norman B M Askew Chairman
4 March 2009

Martin J Lamb Chief Executive
4 March 2009

OUR FIVE
PLATFORM BUSINESSES ...

IMI plc is the ultimate holding company of the Goup and has been listed on the London Stock Exchange since 1966. At 31 December 2008 it had a market value fo £921m and shareholders' funds of £452.4m. The Company's headquarters is at Lakeside, Birmingham Business Park, England. The trading activities of the IMI Group are conducted through subsidiary companies.

Severe Service

The Severe Service business continued to trade very well through the year with revenues up 22% and organic revenue growth, excluding exchange rate movements, at 9%. The second half performance was particularly strong with organic revenue growth of 15%. As previously indicated, routes to market are now fully reopened following the disruption caused by the CCI investigation and order intake progressed well during the year.

Project activity in the oil and gas and power markets remained healthy during the year. In power all three major regions of Americas, Europe/Middle East and Asia showed improvements in order intake. Interest in new nuclear applications is continuing to grow and we made good progress in securing the required industry certifications. Nuclear sales performance was broadly flat but with a strong improvement in margins which helped to improve the overall operating margin for Severe Service to 18.4% from 15.4% last year.

The outlook for the Severe Service business remains positive although an extended period of lower oil prices could impact future order intake. Whilst we have not seen any significant project deferrals or cancellations, we have seen some recent slowing of order intake in the North American power market and lower activity levels in Japan.

Fluid Power

Overall organic revenue growth in Fluid Power was 3% for the full year. However, this represented a small decline in the second half after organic growth of 7% in the first half with November and December being particularly difficult.

Our sector business targets niche markets with major customers in the commercial vehicle, in-plant automotive, life science, rail, print, packaging and PET/beverage markets. After a strong first half, the sector business suffered a significant reversal late in the year, with the in-plant automotive, European commercial vehicles, and print markets sharply lower. Performance in the rail, packaging and life science sectors mitigated to a degree, containing the year on year second half organic revenue decline to 5%, and leaving the sector business as a whole recording a 2% organic revenue growth for the full year.

The remainder of the Fluid Power business provides general pneumatic and fluid control solutions for a broad range of industrial users. Overall revenue in this area showed organic growth of 3%. This reflected a weaker second half, particularly in Western Europe and North America, after a strong first half performance. Germany and Asia Pacific continued to grow in the second half.

Operating margins overall for the year increased from 13.2% to 13.7%. As anticipated most Fluid Power markets have continued to be extremely challenging at the start of 2009. Since the onset of the economic downturn in the autumn the Fluid Power business has moved quickly to reduce costs to help mitigate the impact of lower volumes. This has included a 13% headcount reduction from peak levels in 2008, as well as aggressive procurement initiatives and other cost saving measures.

Indoor Climate

The Indoor Climate organic revenue growth was 6%. This represents a consistent strong performance throughout most of the year and is a reflection of both volume gains and the successful implementation of price increases across the business. However, certain markets did slow in November and December.

Sales of balancing valves maintained momentum in Western European construction markets for most of the year, although the market became more challenging in the last quarter as the new construction sector slowed sharply. Heimeier, our thermostatic radiator valve business, performed well in Germany benefiting from increased refurbishment activity helped by recent legislation in respect of energy efficiency.

Pneumatex continued to perform well in the second half of 2008. Integration of the business is progressing and the Indoor Climate Group is successfully using its existing sales infrastructure to broaden the geographic presence of the Pneumatex range of water conditioning equipment.

Operating profit for Indoor Climate increased by 39% to £45.2m. The operating margin increased from 15.7% to 16.1% with stronger margins being delivered in the second half, in part as a result of the anticipated seasonality of the Pneumatex business.

2009 is expected to be challenging as the commercial construction market continues to weaken in most geographies. However, the business should benefit from a shift in focus towards Government infrastructure projects, further growth of Pneumatex products in new markets and the fact that the thermostatic radiator valve business is more dependent on replacement and maintenance activity which continues to hold up reasonably well. The business has also taken actions to lower costs by reducing headcount and by seeking to benefit from lower materials costs.

Beverage Dispense

The organic revenue decline for the year was 1% in Beverage Dispense. This reflected particularly difficult market conditions in the second half after a satisfactory performance in the first half.

As previously reported the Beverage Dispense business experienced a sharp reduction in demand from the major soft drinks bottlers in North America. Second half revenues were down 6% on an organic basis

▶

on the corresponding period last year. The UK beer market continued to be very challenging with the capital budgets of major brewers being further tightened. Revenue in our UK business, which is focused on this market, declined by over 20% in the year. Sales in Asia Pacific benefited from a significant rollout for a fast food chain in Australia.

Our new product agenda continues to make good progress with several new launches addressing the changes in consumer tastes as well as the demand for more energy efficient equipment. We remain confident of the medium term opportunities in the health and indulgence drinks categories such as water, juices, dairy, smoothies and frozen drinks.

Operating profit for the year was £27.6m, an increase of 11% from 2007, representing a small increase in operating margin to 9.0%. Markets continue to be challenging in most areas and, accordingly, we are actively reducing the cost base through headcount reductions and further procurement and operating savings.

Merchandising

The organic growth for the year was 11% with stronger growth in the second half of 12%. Revenues in the second half benefited from strong shipments to a major US supermarket chain. The strongest sector performance in 2008 was in consumer electronics which made excellent progress over 2007 levels. The food and cosmetics sectors maintained good momentum for most of the year although there was some weakness evident in the last quarter. The automotive sector was significantly below last year's levels.

The operating margin was 10.3%, slightly down from 11.0% last year. As previously reported in the Interim Results, margins were impacted in the first half by the rapid increase in steel costs. Second half operating margins recovered to 11.9% as a result of management actions to improve the supply chain and to consolidate manufacturing with the closure of a factory in California.

The general economic environment means that the market in 2009 is challenging, particularly in sectors such as automotive. However, there are other sectors such as cosmetics, value retailers and grocery where there continue to be good opportunities to win new business.

The global drive towards greener power production and more energy efficient products impacts all areas of our business

The consequences of unrestrained growth in global energy demand is a concern for all countries. One of the biggest challenges is how to meet this energy demand, whilst still reducing the growth of emissions of greenhouse gases.

Concerns about current global energy consumption, which is predicted to grow by approximately 50% by 2030, and the environmental impact have put a renewed emphasis on innovation to make all things more energy-efficient.

Market trends

As a result, governments have been encouraging investment in 'clean' renewable energy sources. For example, $80 billion of the current economic stimulus package agreed in the US is directed towards the construction of a new, national clean energy infrastructure. There has also been a resurgence in nuclear power with over 200 new nuclear plants currently expected to commence commercial operations by 2020. Nuclear power reduces the reliance on the limited reserves of oil and gas and reduces emissions of greenhouse gases.

As well as a shift towards greener energy generation, demand is also increasing for more energy efficient buildings, manufacturing equipment, transport and other consumer products. Increased government regulation in this area, as well as consumer demands for more cost effective solutions, is already encouraging manufacturers to develop more energy efficient products.

How we contribute

The global drive towards greener power production and more energy efficient products impacts all areas of our businesses and is a key driver of our research and development activity. In Severe Service our valve, actuation and control solutions make a significant contribution to meeting the world's energy demands efficiently and effectively. Our valves are utilised in greener power generation in areas such as thermo solar energy and we expect to have a significant role in the next generation of nuclear power stations which are being planned and built. Balancing systems and thermostatic radiator valves supplied by our Indoor Climate businesses help our customers to meet local and international regulatory obligations, significantly reduce energy consumption and deliver personal comfort in both commercial and domestic buildings.

CCI's steam-conditioning turbine bypass valves ensure continuous and efficient operation at a thermo solar energy plant in Spain.

In Beverage Dispense we have focused on developing more energy efficient products. For example, our new Energize cooler for carbonated beverage dispense reduces energy consumption by up to 40% in comparison with traditional models. This is important in helping our key customers meet their public commitments to reduce carbon emissions. For similar reasons, in Merchandising we have developed new LED lighting systems for our customers which reduce energy consumption significantly compared to traditional fluorescent lighting.

Investment in infrastructure provides a significant long-term opportunity for IMI

A common initiative amongst governments of major economies facing the economic downturn has been to commit to increase or accelerate investment in major infrastructure projects.

▶

Governments are aiming to provide an immediate boost to their economies by creating employment and demand for other locally produced products and services. This boost in investment has improved an area of the market which was already seeing positive trends, particularly from the developing economies such as China, India and Brazil.

Market trends

A number of countries have already announced significant increases in investment. The new US administration will make the largest investment in the nation's infrastructure since the 1950s to 'save or create' around 4m jobs. China plans to invest almost 600 billion US dollars to boost the economy and will largely focus this on infrastructure. Mexico is planning the largest infrastructure budget in its history, equivalent to 6.5% of GDP. The UK Government is investing significantly in upgrading London's rail transportation systems and in delivering the 2012 Olympics.

In the longer term, countries with strong growth rates such as China will have to continue investing heavily to maintain growth. In addition, some developed countries have been neglecting their infrastructure needs for many years. As a consequence, The CIBC World Bank has estimated that between 25 and 30 trillion US dollars will be injected into global infrastructure over the next 20 years. This represents a significant long-term opportunity for engineering businesses such as IMI which focus on infrastructure as one of their core strategies.

How we contribute

To take advantage of this, IMI will increasingly focus a number of its activities in this market during 2009. The Severe Service business will continue to supply its bespoke valve, actuation and control solutions to power generation and other infrastructure markets. Our knowledge of plants includes a dedicated customer service network which supports our installed base of high-performance valves for the life of each plant. Norgren's rail business grew strongly in 2008 and good opportunities in this sector are expected to continue.

Our Indoor Climate business is tailoring its successful seminar programme towards infrastructure customers to take advantage of new opportunities as they arise. We have already been successful in securing orders for the main 2012 Olympic Stadium in London. Strong balancing system design, experience, commissioning and project management skills are essential to ensure that projects such as hospitals, airports and other facilities enjoy indoor environments that optimise the comfort for employees and customers, whilst also being energy efficient.

We engineer advantage by enabling our customers to operate faster, more efficiently, with greater flexibility and more cost effectively

Automation plays an increasingly important role in the global economy. Significant growth in the power and use of computers over the last 50 years has enabled a massive increase in automation across most industries.

Engineers are striving to combine automated devices with control mechanisms to create complex systems for a rapidly expanding range of applications and human activities.

Market trends

Automation continues to have asignificant impact in a wide range of highly visible manufacturing and non-manufacturing industries. For many manufacturing companies the aim of automation has shifted beyond simply increasing productivity and reducing costs to broader issues, such as increasing quality and flexibility in the manufacturing process. A major shift has been the move towards flexibility and convertibility where manufacturers increasingly need the flexibility to switch between the manufacture of different products, without having to completely rebuild the production line.

In the current economic environment most capital budgets are constrained. However, investment in greater automation will still be a significant factor across many industries in delivering necessary cost savings, particularly where the pay back is relatively short.

How we contribute

A large proportion of the valves and actuator products supplied by our Fluid Power business help to deliver increased automation for our customers. We engineer advantage for them by enabling them to operate faster, more efficiently, with greater flexibility and more cost effectively. This is particularly true in our targeted market sectors which include commercial vehicles, rail, life sciences, in-plant automotive, printing and PET bottling applications.

Our Retail Dispense businesses are delivering automation to our customers, enabling them to operate with fewer employees. For example, in Merchandising, our Visi-Slide™ and other sliding shelving systems ensure that products are always prominently displayed to the consumer without the need to constantly restack shelves. In the 'drive thru' section of a major restaurant chain, Cornelius has successfully introduced its Automated Beverage System for carbonated soft drinks which is reducing staffing requirements.

Retailers will only gain market share if they are clearly differentiated from competitors, have strong brand equity, innovate to maintain differentiation and offer an experience that excites customers

Over the long-term the retail sector has offered strong growth opportunities, but along with many industries, the current economic downturn is likely to present significant challenges to consumer-facing markets. In this testing environment a focus on the customer experience will be key to gaining a competitive advantage.

Our Retail Dispense businesses focus on delivering products and solutions that give key customers a sales uplift on their higher margin products.

▶

Market trends

Market trends in the retail sector will be driven by the difficult economic environment throughout 2009. Companies that do succeed will offer either lower prices or focus on managing their brands and consumers' experience of it. There is already evidence that consumers are likely to be intensely value-orientated, even more so than in recent history. Retailers will only gain market share if they are clearly differentiated from competitors, have srong brand equity, innovate to maintain differentiation and offer an experience that excites customers. These factors will privide retailers with some pricing power and effective merchandising will be key to delviering this.

Despite the economic downturn some market areas are expected to perform well, notabley discount retailers of both food and general merchandise.

Resources need to be skewed towards these most resilient areas. Elsewhere some specific higher-value sectors, for instance cosmetics, can also perform well in recessions. Other sectors, such as the automotive trade are likely to be much more challenging. Similarly amongst restaurants, quick-service chains are expected to perform well relative to higher end and middle market competitors. Major global quick-service chains have continued to demonstrate solid sales growth over recent months.

In the longer term, beyond 2009, the push towards retail globalisation is expected to continue with developing economies like China, India and Brazil viewed as some of the most lucrative markets to invest in.

How we contribute

Our Merchandising businesses are focused on niche areas where they can drive impulse purchases on products which generate high margins for both brand owner and retailer. They create and deliver display equipment specifically designed to achieve our customers' sales and marketing objectives. In the current market the key will be to focus on those retail sectors which are expected to be more resilient. In cosmetics, which is a high margin and volume sector, we use retail intelligence and creative new product development to produce merchandising solutions that give our key customrs a sales uplift.

Our objective in Beverage Dispense is to drive growth for our customers, the world's leading beverage brand owners and major retailers. Our new product development programme is driven by customer needs and changing consumer tastes such as 'health and indulgence' beverages and sustainability initiatives.

IMI's financial statements

Now it's time to look at IMI's financial statements for the last four years. Although you've seen an overview of IMI's financial performance in the five-year summary, the financial statements are more detailed. However you'll find that they're not presented in the same way that you've seen in the published accounts.

■ In the income statement (Table 13.1) I've shown underlying operating profit, operating profit before and after exceptional items, separated the elements of financial income and expense, and shown the loss from discontinued operations as a single figure. This enables you to see the trends in the business's underlying profitability over the period. (In 2005 IMI spent £4.2 million restructuring the business, however it did not disclose them, as they were not material. Whilst they subsequently disclosed them, they did not disclose where they had been charged. Consequently I have had to ignore them in the analysis.)

■ You'll find that there's more information on the balance sheets (Table 13.2) than is presented in their accounts, as I've extracted more details from the notes to their accounts.

■ The cash flow statements (Table 13.3) also has a number of sub-totals, which I find useful, that you won't find in the published statements.

Table 13.1　Income statements

	2005 £m	2006 £m	2007 £m	2008 £m
Profit before tax	151.1	158.2	171.0	176.0
Revenue	1,341.0	1,504.9	1,599.2	1,900.6
Cost of sales	(800.5)	(896.4)	(959.2)	(1,140.5)
Gross profit	540.5	608.5	640.0	760.1
Selling and distribution costs	(197.3)	(202.5)	(197.4)	(225.8)
Administration expenses	(187.1)	(218.6)	(234.8)	(265.4)
Underlying operating profit	156.1	187.4	207.8	268.9
Other income	1.1	0.8	1.7	
Operating profit before exceptional costs	157.2	188.2	209.5	268.9
Restructuring costs		(18.5)	(22.0)	(19.6)
Investigation costs			(4.9)	(26.3)
Amortisation and impairment of acquired intangibles	(3.3)	(14.6)	(10.9)	(13.2)
Operating profit after exceptional items	153.9	155.1	171.7	209.8
Interest income	6.9	5.5	7.4	10.2
Income from investments				0.7
Interest expense	(15.1)	(13.0)	(20.2)	(26.3)
Net return on pensions	6.0	8.3	10.5	3.8

	2005	2006	2007	2008
Financial instruments	(0.6)	2.3	1.6	(22.2)
	2005	*2006*	*2007*	*2008*
	£m	*£m*	*£m*	*£m*
Tax	(48.4)	(49.0)	(53.0)	(60.0)
Profit after tax	102.7	109.2	118.0	116.0
Discontinued operations	(86.5)	(33.5)	1.9	
Total profit for the period	16.2	75.7	119.9	116.0
Attributable to:				
Equity shareholders of the parent	13.5	72.7	117.0	112.9
Minority interests	2.7	3.0	2.9	3.1
	16.2	75.7	119.9	116.0
Basic earnings per share	3.9	21.4	35.4	35.4
Diluted earnings per share	3.8	21.3	35.3	35.1
Continuing basic earnings per share	28.6	31.3	34.8	35.4
Continuing diluted earnings per share	28.4	31.1	34.7	35.1
Adjusted earnings per share	33.4	37.8	41.9	54.1
Dividend per share	17.5	18.7	20.2	20.7

Table 13.2   **Balance sheets**

	2005	*2006*	*2007*	*2008*
	£m	*£m*	*£m*	*£m*
Assets				
Intangible assets	185.8	286.8	314.7	399.8
Property, plant and equipment	192.1	190.3	207.9	266.4
Employee benefit assets	–	0.7	1.3	2.4
Deferred tax assets	75.5	55.8	37.2	54.7
Total non current assets	**453.4**	**533.6**	**561.1**	**723.3**
Inventories	205.6	217.4	252.0	333.5
Trade receivables	230.9	262.3	286.7	347.3
Other receivables	66.6	29.1	41.3	51.2
Receivables falling due after a year	4.3	3.8	4.6	10.0

	2005 £m	2006 £m	2007 £m	2008 £m
Current tax	18.6	8.7	1.9	4.7
Investments	13.0	15.0	14.4	17.8
Cash and cash equivalents	188.9	107.2	106.5	123.9
Total current assets	**727.9**	**643.5**	**707.4**	**888.4**
Total assets	**1,181.3**	**1,177.1**	**1,268.5**	**1,611.7**
Liabilities				
Bank overdraft	(6.9)	(3.6)	(29.1)	(4.6)
Interest bearing loans and borrowings	(44.4)	(43.3)	(5.0)	(46.5)
Trade payables	(144.2)	(171.8)	(185.2)	(223.6)
Other payables	(157.7)	(150.2)	(164.8)	(224.6)
Exceptional payables		(33.5)		
Provisions	(1.1)	(6.2)	(6.9)	(29.4)
Current tax	(27.1)	(18.2)	(21.0)	(26.6)
Total current liabilities	**(381.4)**	**(426.8)**	**(412.0)**	**(555.3)**
Interest bearing loans and borrowings	(148.2)	(140.7)	(305.5)	(371.5)
Employee benefits	(172.8)	(121.3)	(64.9)	(139.5)
Other payables	(20.4)	(21.9)	(20.4)	(30.3)
Provisions	(33.0)	(34.3)	(34.0)	(36.5)
Deferred tax liabilities	(4.4)	(15.5)	(18.8)	(16.9)
Total non current liabilities	**(378.8)**	**(333.7)**	**(443.6)**	**(594.7)**
Total liabilities	**(760.2)**	**(760.5)**	**(855.6)**	**(1,150.0)**
Net assets	**421.1**	**416.6**	**412.9**	**461.7**
Equity				
Issued capital	89.6	90.3	84.6	84.7
Share premium	149.4	155.2	163.3	165.1
Reserves	7.3	(0.4)	6.8	71.1
Retained earnings	171.3	167.6	151.8	131.5
Total equity attributable to equity holders of the parent	**417.6**	**412.7**	**406.5**	**452.4**
Minority interest	3.5	3.9	6.4	9.3
Total equity	**421.1**	**416.6**	**412.9**	**461.7**

Table 13.3   Statements of cash flows

	2005 £m	2006 £m	2007 £m	2008 £m
Profit/(loss) for the period	16.2	75.7	119.9	116.0
Adjustments for:				
Depreciation	38.4	38.7	35.9	43.1
Amortisation	5.6	17.0	13.9	16.4
Discontinued operations (profit)/loss	86.5	33.5	(1.9)	-
Other income – disposal of business			(1.7)	-
Profit on sale of property, plant and equipment		(2.0)	(0.1)	(0.2)
Financial income	(67.0)	(73.8)	(81.1)	(85.6)
Financial expense	69.8	70.7	81.8	119.4
Equity settled share based payment expense	2.0	2.9	3.1	3.9
Income tax expense	48.4	49.0	53.0	60.0
EBITDA before changes in working capital and provisions and exceptional items	**199.9**	**211.7**	**222.8**	**273.0**
Decrease/(increase) in inventories	5.7	(14.8)	(18.6)	(9.2)
Decrease/(increase) in trade and other receivables	(8.9)	(30.9)	(12.6)	17.6
Increase/(decrease) in trade and other payables	24.6	19.0	20.5	(7.2)
Increase/(decrease) in provisions and employee benefits	(12.0)	1.3	(6.6)	14.4
Cash generated from operations	**209.3**	**186.3**	**205.5**	**288.6**
Income taxes paid	(54.2)	(40.0)	(37.1)	(54.4)
Net cash from operating activities before exceptional cash flows	**155.1**	**146.3**	**168.4**	**234.2**
Exceptional cash flow	(31.3)		(32.8)	
Additional pension funding	(15.6)	(15.6)	(15.6)	(16.8)
Net cash from operating activities	**108.2**	**130.7**	**120.0**	**217.4**
Cash flows from investing activities				
Interest received	10.0	8.4	7.2	12.4
Proceeds from sale of property, plant and equipment	5.6	7.7	8.3	3.1
(Purchase of)/proceeds from sale of investments	(1.1)	(2.5)	(1.1)	(0.7)
Income from investments				0.7
Acquisition of subsidiary, net of cash acquired	(63.6)	(118.4)	(52.2)	
Acquisition of property, plant and equipment	(41.9)	(39.7)	(49.9)	(47.6)
Disposal of subsidiary, net of cash	206.4		2.0	

	2005 £m	2006 £m	2007 £m	2008 £m
Redemption of Polypipe's vendor loan note		35.9		
Development expenditure	(5.2)	(4.4)	(3.2)	(5.1)
Net cash flow from investing activities	**110.2**	**(113.0)**	**(88.9)**	**(37.2)**
Cash flows from financing activities				
Interest paid	(18.2)	(17.0)	(19.9)	(29.0)
Proceeds from the issue of share capital	10.4	6.5	8.7	1.9
Purchase of own shares	(72.6)	(42.4)	(93.3)	(16.7)
Drawdown/(repayment) of borrowings	(14.0)	7.4	110.7	(45.5)
Dividends paid to minorities	(1.6)	(2.1)	(2.4)	(2.4)
Dividends paid	(59.4)	(60.7)	(63.9)	(66.2)
Net cash flow from financing activities	**(155.4)**	**(108.3)**	**(60.1)**	**(157.9)**
Net (decrease)/increase in cash and cash equivalents	63.0	(90.6)	(29.0)	22.3
Cash and cash equivalents at the start of the year	115.4	182.0	103.6	77.4
Effect of exchange rate fluctuations on cash held	3.6	12.2	2.8	19.6
Cash and cash equivalents at the end of the year	**182.0**	**103.6**	**77.4**	**119.3**

Initial observations on the four year's financial statements

The income statements show that revenue and operating profits have grown significantly in the last four years, but have been affected by currency translation. In the financial review IMI discloses the effect of currency translation, and even when this is excluded there is significant year on year revenue and profit growth:

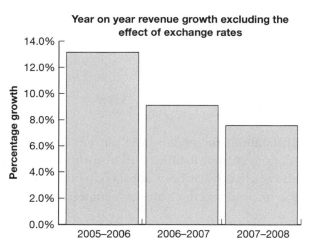

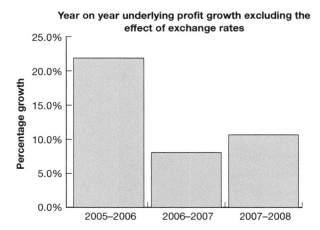

Year on year underlying profit growth excluding the effect of exchange rates

In the period IMI has spent over £60 million in restructuring costs to move more of its manufacturing to low cost manufacturing sites. This restructuring programme has now finished and should help maintain its margins in the recession. (However you know that it's currently in the middle of another restructuring programme to 'right size' it business, and this is likely to cost £25 million in 2009, and £10 million in 2010.) You can see that the interest is affordable.

On the balance sheet you can see that intangible assets have increased significantly. If you looked at the details found in the notes you find that it's acquisition driven with the majority of the intangible assets being goodwill, followed by acquired intangible assets:

	2005 £m	2006 £m	2007 £m	2008 £m
Goodwill	165.5	230.8	261.3	342.8
Capitalised development cost	11.0	12.3	12.8	18.3
Other acquired intangibles	9.3	43.7	40.6	38.7
Total intangible assets	185.8	286.8	314.7	399.8

Throughout the period IMI's current assets have been significantly greater than its current liabilities, indicating that the business is solvent. You can also see that it has been re-balancing its capital structure as the share capital has reduced and the loans have increased.

On the cash flow statement you can see that they have spent a total of £225 million over the last four years buying back their own shares. Whilst some would be needed for employee share schemes, the majority would be held in treasury or cancelled. The cash flow statement shows a business that generates enough cash from its operating activities to pay both interest and dividends, showing a surplus in all years.

Analysing IMI's financial performance 2005–2008

It's now time to start the analysis and the first question is – what do I want to analyse? You should now have a reasonable understanding of IMI's business. You've seen how it has changed over the last five years, identified the key drivers of its performance in its operating review, and looked at its financial statements for the last four years. When you analyse a business's performance you're interested in its:

■ **Solvency** – Can it repay the money it owes on time? This is normally the first place you start. Now you've looked at IMI's accounts, I think you already know the answer to that question … it's a resounding 'YES'. You don't have to work out any ratios to know that its business would have to undergo a fundamental change (like the transition from GEC to Marconi) before it would experience difficulties repaying on time. This means that doing ratios proving this would largely be a waste of time. If you're like me you'll have a spreadsheet that does them automatically, but it's pointless calculating them unless they're going to tell you anything. However, many of the companies you'll analyse will not have IMI's financial strength and you'll undoubtedly have to calculate these ratios. You only have to calculate ratios if they tell you something about a business – please don't calculate every ratio in the book!

■ **Cash management** – This links with solvency, as it explores how the company is managing its cash. You've already seen its cash flow statements and know that it manages cash effectively. Measuring this would give you no additional information.

■ **Profitability** – Is the business profitable? Is its profitability improving or declining? Why is it changing?

■ **Attractiveness to investors** – Does IMI represent a good investment? Are investors' expectations unrealistic?

As solvency and cash management aren't an issue in IMI, I'll start by looking at its profitability. Firstly I'll look at the return on capital employed ratios. This means that I have to identify the profit and the capital employed I'm going to use. So let's look at its profit. I'm analysing the business over four years, so if I want to look at its underlying profitability I'll have to use profit before exceptional items and other income. For the return on operating capital employed I'll use its underlying operating profit and for the overall return on capital employed I'll add the income from its investments to this figure.

	2005 £m	2006 £m	2007 £m	2008 £m
Underlying operating profit	156.1	187.4	207.8	268.9
Interest income	6.9	5.5	7.4	10.2
Income from investments				0.7
Underlying profit	163.0	192.9	215.2	279.8

Now let's identify the capital employed – I'm going to use an adjusted capital employed including provisions, deferred tax, and goodwill written off through retained earnings.

	2005 £m	2006 £m	2007 £m	2008 £m
Total reported equity	421.1	416.6	412.9	461.7
Goodwill charged to retained earnings	364.0	364.0	364.0	364.0
Deferred tax asset	(75.5)	(55.8)	(37.2)	(54.7)
Short-term provisions	1.1	6.2	6.9	29.4
Long-term provisions	33.0	34.3	34.0	36.5
Deferred tax liabilities	4.4	15.5	18.8	16.9
Adjusted equity	748.1	780.8	799.4	853.8
Short-term debt	51.3	46.9	34.1	51.1
Long-term debt	148.2	140.7	305.5	371.5
Adjusted capital employed	947.6	968.4	1,139.0	1,276.4

I can now calculate the return on total capital employed, the profit margin and the asset turn.

Return on total capital employed ratios

Return on total capital employed

You can see that the return on capital employed improved between 2005 and 2006, then reduced in 2007 as the increase in profit of 11.6% was less than the 17.6% increase in the capital employed. In 2008, it increased significantly and the return on capital had increased to almost 22%.

	2005	2006	2007	2008
Underlying profit	163.0	192.9	215.2	279.8
Adjusted capital employed	947.6	968.4	1,139.0	1,276.4
Return on total capital employed	17.20%	19.92%	18.89%	21.92%

Profit margin

You can see that the profit margin has steadily increased over the period:

	2005	2006	2007	2008
Underlying profit	163.0	192.9	215.2	279.8
Revenue	1,341.0	1,504.9	1,599.2	1,900.6
Profit margin	12.16%	12.82%	13.46%	14.72%

Asset turn

IMI's asset turn has not been consistent over the period:

	2005	2006	2007	2008
Revenue	1,341.0	1,504.9	1,599.2	1,900.6
Adjusted capital employed	947.6	968.4	1,139.0	1,276.4
Asset turn	1.42	1.55	1.40	1.49

The best asset turn was in 2006, when the increase in revenue, 12.22%, easily outpaced the increase in capital employed of 2.2%.

You can now see that the driver of the improvement in the return on total capital employed has been the profit margin. Now let's look at the return on operating capital employed and see what has been influencing the changes in the business's operating profitability.

Return on operating capital employed and subsequent ratios

The next step is to calculate the operating capital employed:

	2005 £m	2006 £m	2007 £m	2008 £m
Property, plant and equipment	192.1	190.3	207.9	266.4
Inventories	205.6	217.4	252.0	333.5
Trade receivables	230.9	262.3	286.7	347.3
Trade payables	(144.2)	(171.8)	(185.2)	(223.6)
Operating capital employed	484.4	498.2	561.4	723.6

You can see that the operating capital employed increased significantly in 2007 and 2008, so now let's see its effect on the return on operating capital employed:

	2005	2006	2007	2008
Underlying operating profit	156.1	187.4	207.8	268.9
Operating capital employed	484.4	498.2	561.4	723.6
Return on operating capital employed	32.23%	37.62%	37.01%	37.16%

You can see that this follows the same trend as the return on total capital employed, but the variation between the years is smaller. Now I need to find out why the return on operating capital employed has changed. I think it's largely because of improved profitability, but let's see if I'm right. You know that the return on operating capital employed is the driver of the return on total capital and can be analysed in detail through the operating profitability hierarchy of ratios, which identifies why it has changed.

Operating margin

	2005	2006	2007	2008
Underlying operating profit	156.1	187.4	207.8	268.9
Revenue	1,341.0	1,504.9	1,599.2	1,900.6
Operating margin	11.64%	12.45%	12.99%	14.15%

You've already seen that IMI's operating margin improved over three years, now you know that it has consistently improved throughout the period. They have a long-term target to improve this to 15%, and this looks achievable in the next few years, as long as the recession isn't lengthy.

Asset turn

	2005	2006	2007	2008
Revenue	1,341.0	1,504.9	1,599.2	1,900.6
Operating capital employed	484.4	498.2	561.4	723.6
Asset turn	2.77	3.02	2.85	2.63

Here you can see the effect of the increase in the operating capital in 2007 and 2008. In 2007 revenue increased by 6.3%, whereas the operating capital increased by 12.7%. In 2008 revenue increased by 18.9%, whereas the operating capital increased by 28.9%.

So now you know that IMI's operating margin has consistently improved in the period, and its asset turn has been erratic as the increases in operating capital have sometimes been greater than increases in revenue. This would not be unusual if the changes arose from property, plant and equipment, as these move in the same way as fixed costs. When a company reaches maximum capacity it needs to buy more equipment that can often support higher levels of sales. Working capital, on the other hand, is more closely aligned to revenue. If you double your sales you wouldn't be surprised to see that your stocks, receivables and payables double as well.

Let's start by looking at IMI's gross margin and overhead cost ratios to see which has been the largest contributor to the margin improvement.

Gross margin

You can see that the gross margin has been around 40% throughout the period. It improved in 2006 and has been falling slightly since then.

	2005	2006	2007	2008
Gross profit	540.5	608.5	640.0	760.1
Revenue	1,341.0	1,504.9	1,599.2	1,900.6
Gross margin	40.31%	40.43%	40.02%	39.99%

Overhead cost ratio

Firstly, I'll need to calculate the overheads. You can see that selling and distribution costs fell in 2007, and increased by over 14% in 2008:

	2005 £m	2006 £m	2007 £m	2008 £m
Selling and distribution costs	197.3	202.5	197.4	225.8
Administration expenses	187.1	218.6	234.8	265.4
Overheads	384.4	421.1	432.2	491.2

The real improvement in the operating margin has come from controlling overheads, which have fallen as a percentage of revenue.

	2005	2006	2007	2008
Overheads	384.4	421.1	432.2	491.2
Revenue	1,341.0	1,504.9	1,599.2	1,900.6
Overhead cost ratio	28.67%	27.98%	27.03%	25.84%

This isn't surprising, as most overheads are fixed costs, which move in 'steps' rather than directly with volumes.

I've now analysed IMI's operating profitability, so let's analyse its asset utilisation starting with the property, plant and equipment turn.

Property, plant and equipment turn

The property, plant and equipment turn fell in 2008:

	2005	2006	2007	2008
Revenue	1,341.0	1,504.9	1,599.2	1,900.6
Property, plant and equipment	192.1	190.3	207.9	266.4
Property, plant and equipment turn	6.98	7.91	7.69	7.13

You can see that property, plant and equipment increased significantly in 2008. I wonder why? Perhaps it bought more? Well it did buy some more, £48.9 million, and sold some with a book value of £2.9 million. But that doesn't explain the difference, as it's much greater than the difference you can see between the two years, as most of the assets would have depreciated. IMI's a global business, with factories all over the world, and exchange adjustments added £55.6 million to the value of its property, plant and equipment! If 2008's property, plant and equipment had been shown at 2007's exchange rates it would have been £210.8 million (266.4 – 55.6). If I exclude the effect of exchange rates on the group's revenue it would have been £1,721.6 million. This gives a property, plant and equipment turn that would have increased to 8.17, as exchange rates increased revenue by 10.4% and the value of property, plant and equipment by 26.4%. What can I say? Sterling's collapse during 2008 makes it a difficult year for financial analysis. Exchange rates have always had a slight effect on ratios, but I've never known it this severe.

Now let's move on to the working capital ratio.

Working capital ratio

Firstly, I need to calculate IMI's working capital:

	2005 £m	2006 £m	2007 £m	2008 £m
Inventories	205.6	217.4	252.0	333.5
Trade receivables	230.9	262.3	286.7	347.3
Trade payables	(144.2)	(171.8)	(185.2)	(223.6)
Working capital	292.3	307.9	353.5	457.2

Now I can calculate the working capital ratio:

	2005	2006	2007	2008
Working capital	292.3	307.9	353.5	457.2
Revenue	1,341.0	1,504.9	1,599.2	1,900.6
Working capital ratio	21.80%	20.46%	22.10%	24.06%

You can see that the working capital ratio has increased significantly over the last two years, so let's see if we can discover why.

Inventory turn and inventory days

As I'm not comparing IMI with other companies, I'll use cost of sales for calculating the inventory ratios:

	2005	2006	2007	2008
Inventories	205.6	217.4	252.0	333.5
Cost of sales	800.5	896.4	959.2	1,140.5
Inventory turn	3.9	4.1	3.8	3.4
Inventory days	93.7	88.5	95.9	106.7

You can see that in 2006 inventory days were at their lowest in the period, but they have increased significantly in the last two years. Unfortunately we don't know *why* they've increased, as poor stock control may be only part of the answer. Exchange rates could have affected the inventory's value if it's being held overseas. The other factor that could have affected stock levels is the move to low cost manufacturing. I mentioned in Chapter 8 that it isn't unusual if you're manufacturing in China for stock to increase, as the goods can spend a month on a ship before they arrive at the warehouse. So here's the frustration of financial analysis: you don't necessarily have answers, but you do have better questions! However, I can analyse the stock into its component parts to see where the increase occurred and see if that gives any clues as to why stock has increased. I've extracted the relevant information from the notes to the accounts:

	2005	2006	2007	2008
Raw materials	75.2	85.8	89.5	115.0
Work in progress	61.8	78.0	85.6	105.8
Finished goods	68.6	53.6	76.9	112.7
Cost of sales	800.5	896.4	959.2	1,140.5
Raw materials days	34.3	34.9	34.1	36.8
Work in progress days	28.2	31.8	32.6	33.9
Finished goods days	31.3	21.8	29.3	36.1

You can see that raw materials' inventory days were fairly stable until 2008 when it increased by 2.7 days. This probably reflected the onset of the economic down turn.

Work in progress increased significantly in 2006, and then grew steadily throughout the period. This reflects orders being manufactured at the end of the year and is indicative of activity and lead times. It's possible that the increase in 2008 reflected earlier orders being manufactured (you may remember that most of its businesses were growing until November and December).

You can see that finished goods' inventory days fell in 2006, and then increased in the last three years when IMI was restructuring its business to move 35% of its manufacturing to low cost countries. The increase to 36.1 days' stock in 2008 may also reflect the economic downturn, where customers stopped 'calling off' orders.

So although I've analysed the components of inventory, I still don't know why inventories increased, I just know why they *might* have increased. I know that the value of stock held overseas may have increased in 2008 because of exchange rates. I know that work in progress increases if the business's activity level is increasing, as it reflects future revenue. This may even be true in 2008, when all businesses except Beverage Dispense had increased levels of activity until the end of the year. The increase in finished good in 2008 could be explained by a combination of the move to low cost manufacturing and translation differences.

Now let's look at receivables.

Receivable days

	2005	2006	2007	2008
Trade receivables	230.9	262.3	286.7	347.3
Revenue	1,341.0	1,504.9	1,599.2	1,900.6
Receivable days	62.85	63.62	65.44	66.70

This time 2005 is the best year, and receivable days have steadily risen over the period. Had receivable remained at 2005 levels the trade receivables would have been over £20 million lower (£1,900.6 ÷ 365 = £5.207 per day × 3.85 days = £20.047 million)!

The final ratio in the return on operating capital hierarchy is payable days, which I'll calculate using cost of sales as I'm only analysing one company.

Payable days

You can see that payable days have steadily increased over the period, and are possibly being used to offset the increases in inventories and receivables:

	2005	2006	2007	2008
Trade payables	144.2	171.8	185.2	223.6
Cost of sales	800.5	896.4	959.2	1,140.5
Payable days	65.8	70.0	70.5	71.6

Now you know that the improvement in the return on operating capital has been driven by improving operating margins. All aspects of the asset turn, apart from payable days, have deteriorated since 2006. Exchange rates explain the deterioration in the property, plant and equipment turn and may have affected the working capital ratios. If you think back to Chapter 8, I showed you that the three commonest reasons for changes in profitability were changes in price, mix and volumes. In its operating review IMI told us that some of its businesses, mainly in the Fluid Power and Beverage Dispense, had challenging markets. Some of its businesses were experiencing falling volumes, and some were growth businesses. Operating profits can fall in a growth business in the short term when the business moves up a fixed cost 'step', but the analysis suggests that overheads are under control. So that would only leave higher manufacturing costs and material prices (which you know affected their Merchandising business) or changes in the product or business mix. There's no information about product mix in the financial statements, only business mix in the segmental analysis. So let's see what this tells us.

Segmental analysis

I've used the note shown in Chapter 6 and its equivalent in the previous accounts to look at how the business mix has changed in the period. Firstly I'll show you how the balance of revenue in its various businesses has changed. I've used horizontal stripes for the Fluid Controls division and solid blocks for Retail Dispense, to help you assess the division's contributions. You can see that the contribution from Fluid Controls has steadily increased in the period, and in 2008 it represented 73.3% of IMI's revenue.

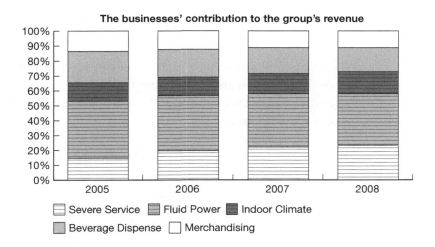

Fluid Control's revenue growth has been considerable over the period, particularly in Severe Service:

Segmental revenue growth

	2004–2005	2005–2006	2006–2007	2007–2008
Fluid Controls				
Severe Service	20.3%	40.8%	20.7%	22.4%
Fluid Power	12.1%	13.2%	2.5%	16.6%
Indoor Climate	2.4%	8.1%	11.3%	35.7%
Total	11.9%	18.9%	9.3%	21.9%
Retail Dispense				
Beverage Dispense	4.1%	1.4%	1.1%	7.0%
Merchandising	−1.1%	−3.2%	−3.3%	16.1%
Total	2.0%	−0.4%	−0.6%	10.5%
Group total	**8.2%**	**12.2%**	**6.2%**	**18.6%**

The large increase in 2006's Severe Service revenue is largely explained by the acquisition of Truflo, a specialist valve manufacturer. The underlying revenue growth in 2008 isn't as large as that shown in the segmental analysis, as it includes the effects of currency translation which represented 59% of the total revenue increase. However, you'll recall from the operating review that some businesses still had real revenue growth; Severe Service's organic revenue growth was 9% before exchange rate movements

When you look at the next chart, you can see that for the last two years just over half of the group's revenue has been in Europe, revenue in the US has declined over the period and Asia/Pacific and the Rest of the World has become more important.

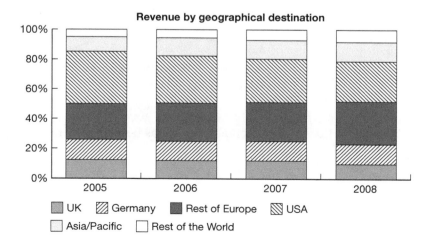

Revenue by geographical destination

Key: UK, Germany, Rest of Europe, USA, Asia/Pacific, Rest of the World

Now lets' look at IMI's profitability and I've prepared a graph looking at the businesses' contribution to the group's underlying profitability. However the numbers prior to 2007 exclude all intangible amortisation, whereas those in 2007 and 2008 only exclude the amortisation of acquired intangible assets. The amortisation of capitalised development costs was £2.3 million in 2005 and £2.4 million in 2006, so it's unlikely to have a material effect on the comparative business performance.

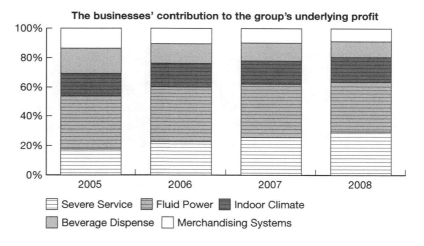

Again you can see the Fluid Control's businesses' predominance, contributing almost 82% of the group's profits in 2008. Here's the analysis of segmental operating profit before exceptional items and the economic hedge gain of £2.6 million in 2008:

	2005 £m	2006 £m	2007 £m	2008 £m
Fluid Controls				
Severe Service	28.3	45.1	55.9	81.3
Fluid Power	60.0	72.4	75.4	91.3
Indoor Climate	25.6	29.5	32.5	45.2
Total	**113.9**	**147.0**	**163.8**	**217.8**
Retail Dispense				
Beverage Dispense	28.4	25.4	24.8	27.6
Merchandising	21.4	19.4	19.2	20.9
Total	**49.8**	**44.8**	**44.0**	**48.5**
Total adjusted operating profit	**163.7**	**191.8**	**207.8**	**266.3**

So you've seen that IMI's mix of business has changed in the last four years. Now let's look at the business's operating margins, where you'll find that Fluid Control's margins are higher than those found in Retail Dispense and have improved consistently over the period. In 2008 the Severe Service business and the Indoor Climate business had already beaten the group's long-term profit margin target of 15%, having operating margins of 18.4% and 16.1% respectively.

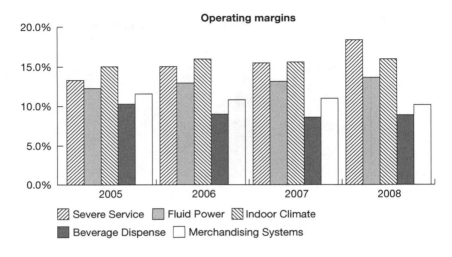

You've seen that the segmental information discloses the segmental operating assets and liabilities, and from these I have calculated the segmental net assets and return on operating capital employed.

Firstly here's the segmental net assets.

Segmental net assets

	2005 £m	2006 £m	2007 £m	2008 £m
Fluid Controls				
Severe Service	81.3	174.4	187.9	238.9
Fluid Power	243.7	261.9	309.7	407.5
Indoor Climate	59.9	58.4	87.0	96.6
Total	**384.9**	**494.7**	**584.6**	**743.0**
Retail Dispense				
Beverage Dispense	81.5	83.1	88.8	119.4
Merchandising	110.8	103.8	97.2	110.3
Total	**192.3**	**186.9**	**186.0**	**229.7**
Total segment net assets	**577.2**	**681.6**	**770.6**	**972.7**

The large increase in 2006's Severe Service net assets is largely explained by the acquisition of Truflo. The rest of the growth has largely arisen from the increased working capital needed to support revenue growth, as most of the group's capital expenditure has been in Fluid Power:

Capital expenditure

	2005 £m	2006 £m	2007 £m	2008 £m
Fluid Controls				
Severe Service	4.5	9.6	9.0	10.6
Fluid Power	18.7	21.4	26.0	25.1
Indoor Climate	5.3	4.9	6.1	8.8
Total	**28.5**	**35.9**	**41.1**	**44.5**
Retail Dispense				
Beverage Dispense	6.2	6.7	7.6	6.5
Merchandising	8.3	4.4	3.8	2.7
Total	**14.5**	**11.1**	**11.4**	**9.2**
Total capital expenditure	**43.0**	**47.0**	**52.5**	**53.7**
Discontinued and corporate	10.8	1.4	0.6	0.3
Total	**53.8**	**48.4**	**53.1**	**54.0**

When you look at the segmental return on operating capital employed all businesses have a return considerably greater than IMI's WACC of 8%. Indoor Climate has consistently delivered the best return, as it has a low net assets figure relative to its profits.

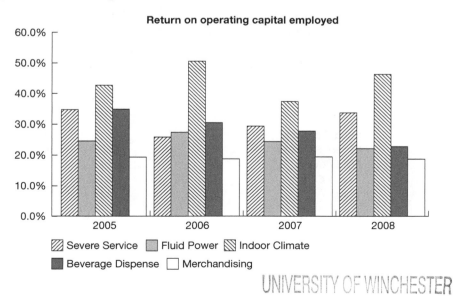

Return on operating capital employed

Legend: Severe Service, Fluid Power, Indoor Climate, Beverage Dispense, Merchandising

You've seen the businesses' operating margins and return on operating capital employed, now let's look at their asset turns.

Asset turn

	2005	2006	2007	2008
Fluid Controls				
Severe Service	2.62	1.72	1.93	1.85
Fluid Power	2.02	2.13	1.84	1.63
Indoor Climate	2.87	3.18	2.38	2.91
Total	2.28	2.11	1.95	1.87
Retail Dispense				
Beverage Dispense	3.41	3.39	3.21	2.55
Merchandising	1.68	1.73	1.79	1.83
Total	2.41	2.47	2.47	2.21

Until 2008, when its organic sales fell by 1% following the economic downturn, Beverage Dispense had the best asset turn, as its revenues were high in relation to its net assets. Severe Service's asset turn fell in 2006, as it acquired all of Truflo's assets, but only had its revenue for part of the year. (I wanted to specifically point this out to you, as it's a common occurrence after an acquisition.)

Cash generation – EBITDA

The segmental analysis gives little direct information about cash generation. However it does disclose depreciation and amortisation, excluding the impairment charge for Commtech (which is in Indoor Climate). A little arithmetic, and adding the impairment charge, and I can reconcile the segmental information with IMI's underlying EBITDA:

	2005 £m	2006 £m	2007 £m	2008 £m
Fluid Controls				
Severe Service	32.7	60.2	67.5	91.1
Fluid Power	79.5	94.3	97.1	114.2
Indoor Climate	31.9	35.8	38.8	58.4
Total	144.1	190.3	203.4	263.7

	2005 £m	2006 £m	2007 £m	2008 £m
Retail Dispense				
Beverage Dispense	34.6	33.1	29.2	34.4
Merchandising	27.5	23.5	24.3	27.0
Total	62.1	56.6	53.5	61.4
Discontinued and corporate	13.5	0.6	0.7	0.7
Total	219.7	247.5	257.6	325.8
Economic hedge gain				2.6
Group underlying EBITDA	219.7	247.5	257.6	328.4

Fluid Controls is the largest cash generator, providing over 80% of the group's underlying EBITDA, with Fluid Power the major cash contributing business.

Fluid Power's contribution to IMI's EBITDA

2005	2006	2007	2008
36.2%	38.1%	37.7%	34.8%

Now you may recall that Fluid Power consistently had the largest capital expenditure in the group, so some of the cash it raised had to be reinvested in the business. However, if you deduct capital expenditure from EBITDA to arrive at a net EBITDA, Fluid Power still represents 32.5% of the group's net EBITDA. This could affect the group's cash generation in 2009, as the Fluid Power business is one of the businesses that is most affected by the recession.

Profitability summary

Now let's summarise what we've discovered about their profitability.

Their best return on total capital employed was in 2008, whereas IMI had its best return on operating capital employed in 2006. The profit margins for both ratios have increased steadily over the last four years, but the asset turns for both ratios peaked in 2006. Gross margins have remained fairly constant throughout the period, with the growth in operating margins arising from the improved overhead cost ratio, as revenues grew faster than overheads. Whilst the property, plant and equipment turn appeared to peak in 2006, when it was adjusted for the effect of exchange rates 2008 showed the best utilisation of property, plant and equipment. There is some concern about the control of working capital, as the ratio was at its lowest in 2006. Since then inventory days have increased and receivable days have increased throughout the period, although the effect has been somewhat mitigated by a year on year increase in payable days. Whilst exchange rates could have affected the 2008 ratios, it would not have explained the deterioration in 2007, although the move to low cost manufacturing may have contributed to the increase in inventory days. Had working capital been maintained at the same level as 2006, 20.46% of revenue, IMI would have released over £68 million (revenue of £1,900.6 × 3.6% = £68.422 million). If you reduced their operating capital employed by this amount, its return on operating capital employed would have increased by almost 4% to 41.04%.

Now you understand the trends in IMI's profitability, let's look at its investment potential.

Investment potential

Any investors buying shares are hoping to make money. They're only going to do this if the share price rises and/or they receive some dividends. I've used IMI's closing share price at the end of its financial year to calculate its capital gain during the years and added this to the dividend payment:

	2005	2006	2007	2008
Closing share price	503.00p	507.00p	393.75p	271.75p
Capital gain/(loss)	109.25p	4.00p	(113.25p)	(122.00p)
Dividend	17.5p	18.7p	20.2p	20.7p
Total shareholder return per share	126.8p	22.7p	(93.1p)	(101.3p)

You can see that IMI's share price has fallen in the last two years, and the dividend has been insufficient to offset the capital loss. In its remuneration report IMI, like all UK listed companies, publishes a total shareholder return graph, comparing its performance with the total shareholder return of the FTSE All Share Index and the FTSE All Share Industrial Engineering Sector, both of which showed some growth in 2007. They disclose that 'Over the past five years the IMI share price has underperformed the FTSE All Share Industrial Engineering Sector by 33.93% and the FTSE All Share Index by 19.51%. Over the same period total shareholder return has underperformed the FTSE All Share Industrial Engineering Sector by 16.54% and the FTSE All Share Index by 2.12%.' This tells you that the share price has not increased at the same rate as its peers, implying a lower rate of anticipated growth. (Although you'll remember that its current PE relative suggests that it had better current growth prospects than its peers.) However, its dividend payments have been better than its peers. This suggests that IMI is an income share, rather than a growth share.

Now you've already learned that the current share price already incorporates the market's view about a company's *future* performance, which analysts will have extrapolated from its past performance using information they have gleaned about IMI's business plans. They're interested in identifying trends in:

▓ **Sales** – You know that this drives some costs and working capital, and consequently affects cash flow. Sales may also affect fixed costs and property, plant and equipment if the company is trading close to its capacity limit.

▓ **Operating profits** – This is the most important element in the income statement, as it's the only sustainable source of earnings.

▓ **EBITDA** – This just adjusts operating profit to make it more comparable across companies. It's also indicative of the cash that should be generated from the company's trading activities.

▓ **Dividends and dividend cover** – This affects both the investors' return and the retained profits. If a company has a low level of retained profit, it will have to raise funds to finance any planned expansion programme.

▓ **Cash flow** – Cash can be used to finance a business's expansion, or it could be returned to investors.

All of these drive the company's share price and consequently its enterprise value. In Chapter 12 I showed you the ratios analysts use to assess companies' investment potential. Most of these compare one of the elements I've listed above with the share price. The recent falls, and volatility, in the stock market make historical analysis of little value; consequently I'd like to adopt a slightly different approach in looking at IMI's investment potential. I'm going to look at:

▓ how these key factors have changed in the last four years;

▓ where analysts expect some of them to move in the next two years.

So let's see how IMI's ratios have changed over the last four years.

The last four years

I'll start by looking at sales, as this drives profits, EBITDA and cash flow.

	2005	2006	2007	2008
Revenue	1,341.0	1,504.9	1,599.2	1,900.6
Weighted average shares in issue	349.7	339.3	330.7	319.3
Sales per share	3.83	4.44	4.84	5.95

You can see that IMI has consistently increased its sales per share.

EBITDA and EBITDA to sales

This is usually based on operating profit before exceptional items, as analysts are concerned about a company's underlying profitability. You'll notice that I'm not adding back all the amortisation charges, as the amortisation of acquired intangible assets is one of the exceptional items and hasn't been charged to underlying operating profit.

	2005	2006	2007	2008
Underlying operating profit	156.1	187.4	207.8	268.9
Depreciation	38.4	38.7	35.9	43.1
Amortisation charged to underlying profit	2.3	2.4	3.0	3.2
EBITDA before exceptional items	196.8	228.5	246.7	315.2
EBITDA to sales	14.7%	15.2%	15.4%	16.6%

You can see that IMI's EBITDA has increased steadily over the period, as has EBITDA as a percentage of revenue.

This growth is reflected in the underlying earnings per share, as you'll see opposite.

Earnings per share (eps)

	2005 pence	2006 pence	2007 pence	2008 pence
Adjusted earnings per share	33.4	37.8	41.9	54.1
Adjusted eps growth	13%	13%	11%	29%
Basic earnings per share*	28.6	31.3	34.8	35.4
Basic eps growth	23%	9%	11%	2%
Diluted earnings per share*	28.4	31.1	34.7	35.1
Diluted eps growth	23%	10%	12%	1%

* Continuing business

Return on equity

	2005 £m	2006 £m	2007 £m	2008 £m
Reported total equity	417.6	412.7	406.5	452.4
Current provisions	1.1	6.2	6.9	29.4
Non current provisions	33.0	34.3	34.0	36.5
Deferred tax assets	(75.5)	(55.8)	(37.2)	(54.7)
Deferred tax liabilities	4.4	15.5	18.8	16.9
Goodwill written off against retained earnings	364.0	364.0	364.0	364.0
Adjusted equity	744.6	776.9	793.0	844.5

The underlying return on equity has grown consistently over the last four years:

	2005	2006	2007	2008
Adjusted continuing profit for the year	106.9	129.9	138.6	172.6
Adjusted equity	744.6	776.9	793.0	844.5
Adjusted return on equity	14.36%	16.72%	17.48%	20.44%

Cash flow and cash flow per share

Simple cash flow

I'll start by calculating the simple cash flow per share, firstly calculating the underlying after tax cash flow:

	2005 £m	2006 £m	2007 £m	2008 £m
Underlying after tax profit attributable to shareholders	106.9	129.9	138.6	172.6
Depreciation	38.4	38.7	35.9	43.1
Amortisation charged to underlying profit	2.3	2.4	3.0	3.2
Cash flow	147.6	171.0	177.5	218.9

You can see that the cash flow has grown over the period, and as IMI has been buying back shares it isn't surprising that the cash flow per share has increased significantly over the period:

	2005	2006	2007	2008
Underlying cash flow	147.6	171.0	177.5	218.9
Weighted average shares in issue	349.7	339.3	330.7	319.3
Cash flow per share	£0.42	£0.50	£0.54	£0.69

Free cash flow

I'll use the definition of free cash flow that you'll find in analysts' reports. This is the cash flow that's available for the providers of capital, so it's the operating cash flow less capital expenditure and acquisitions and disposals. As I'm looking at trends I'll exclude the exceptional cash flows, and here are the relevant extracts from IMI's cash flow statements:

	2005 £m	2006 £m	2007 £m	2008 £m
Net cash from operating activities	108.2	130.7	120.0	217.4
Plus exceptional cash flow	31.3		32.8	
Proceeds from sale of property plant and equipment	5.6	7.7	8.3	3.1
Acquisition of property, plant and equipment	(41.9)	(39.7)	(49.9)	(47.6)
Development expenditure	(5.2)	(4.4)	(3.2)	(5.1)
Free cash flow before acquisitions and disposals	98.0	94.3	108.0	167.8
Acquisitions	(63.6)	(118.4)	(52.2)	
Disposals	206.4		2.0	
Free cash flow after acquisitions and disposals	240.8	(24.1)	57.8	167.8

You can see that both free cash flows per share have increased since 2006:

	2005	2006	2007	2008
Free cash flow before acquisitions and disposals	98.0	94.3	108.0	167.8
Free cash flow after acquisitions and disposals	240.8	(24.1)	57.8	167.8
Weighted average shares in issue	349.7	339.3	330.7	319.3
Free cash flow per share before acquisitions and disposals	£0.28	£0.28	£0.33	£0.53
Free cash flow per share after acquisitions and disposals	£0.69	−£0.07	£0.17	£0.53

Dividends, dividend yield and dividend cover

IMI's dividends have grown throughout the period:

	2005	2006	2007	2008
Dividend per share	17.5	18.7	20.2	20.7
Dividend per share growth	6%	7%	8%	2%

Now let's look at the dividend yield, as IMI is paying better dividends than other companies in its sector and its shares may be being held for income.

Dividend yield

As IMI's share price has fallen, its yield has increased:

	2005	2006	2007	2008
Dividend per share	17.5	18.7	20.2	20.7
Year end share price	503.00	507.00	393.75	271.75
Dividend yield	3.48%	3.69%	5.13%	7.62%

Now let's see if the dividends are sustainable by looking at the dividend cover.

Dividend cover

I'll calculate two dividend covers, one based on the adjusted earnings per share, showing the underlying dividend cover, and the other showing the actual dividend cover using the basic earnings per share.

	2005 pence	2006 pence	2007 pence	2008 pence
Adjusted earnings per share	33.4	37.8	41.9	54.1
Dividend per share	17.5	18.7	20.2	20.7
Underlying dividend cover	1.91	2.02	2.07	2.61
Basic earnings per share	28.6	31.3	34.8	35.4
Dividend per share	17.5	18.7	20.2	20.7
Actual dividend cover	1.63	1.67	1.72	1.71

You can see that the underlying dividend cover has improved over the period, and the actual dividend cover has been at similar levels for the last two years.

You've discovered that over the period IMI has been growing revenues, EBITDA, cash flow and earnings per share. Before the recession they were also growing dividends in real terms, and wish to maintain dividends in the future. So now let's see what the analysts are predicting for the next two years.

And the next two years?

I'd like to show you the median analyst's view of IMI's performance in the next two years. The years 2005–2008 are IMI's reported numbers and the subsequent years (marked E) are the median estimates.

You may be surprised that IMI's revenue isn't expected to fall as much as you'd expect in the recession. The answer is simple – exchange rates. In its interim management statement, issued before their Annual General Meeting, it disclosed that 'if average exchange rates ruling in the first four months of 2009 were applied to 2008 full year results both revenues and segmental operating profits would have been approximately 16% higher'. In another part of its interim management statement it disclosed that 'group revenues for the four month period to the end of April are around 16% lower than the prior year, on a constant currency basis'. You'll also notice that analysts are expecting its revenue to rise slightly in 2010, although probably not in real terms.

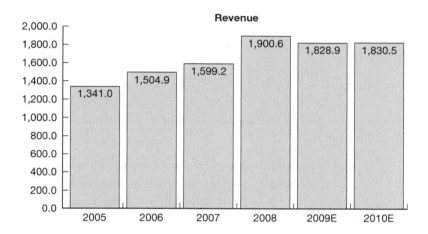

However, you can see that underlying EBITDA is expected to fall considerably in 2009, and rise slightly in 2010. If you think about it, EBITDA will be hit by:

▦ Falling revenues will hit profitability disproportionally, as whilst IMI is restructuring it won't be able to fully reduce its fixed costs to match the reduction in revenue. Plus, any fixed cost reductions are unlikely to work through until the second half of the year.

▦ Fluid Power is the biggest contributor to EBITDA, and its revenues and profits have been affected by the recession. In its interim management statement IMI discloses that its 'first half profits will be sharply down on last year, albeit this should improve appreciably in the second half as the full benefit of cost reduction measures taken earlier in the year accrues'.

In 2010 it should recover as the cost base reduces and the new 'low cost' factories become operational.

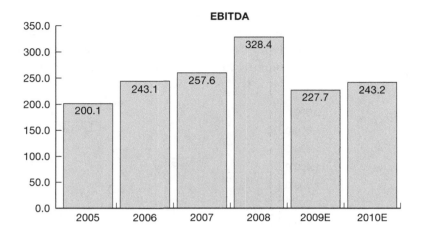

This is then reflected in the earnings and dividends per share. You can see that the adjusted earnings per share are expected to fall by 36% in 2009 and increase by 4% in 2010. Dividends are expected to increase slightly in 2009 and 2010.

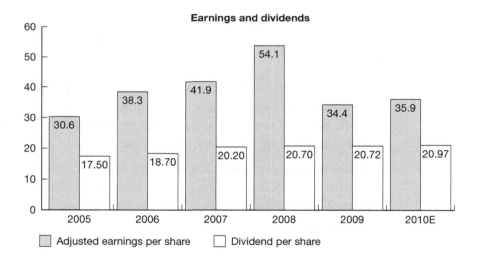

These are the estimates of IMI's future performance that are underpinning its current share price. As a number of its operations are vulnerable to the global recession, the share price is depressed because of the uncertainties about the duration and depth of the recession.

part 3

How can I use my analysis?

14

How can I use my analysis?

Introduction

In the first part of this book you learned about the information that you could find in the accounts, and in the second part you learned how to analyse and interpret the data. This final part of the book shows you how to use your analytical and interpretative skills. There are three main areas where you're most likely to use financial analysis:

- Analysing suppliers' accounts.
- Analysing customers' accounts.
- Analysing competitors' accounts.

It's also possible that you could be asked to help the group identify an acquisition prospect.

In this part of the book I'll show you how to do assess IMI's businesses, and how financial analysis can address your key concerns. Once you add financial understanding to your existing knowledge about your suppliers, customers and competitors, you'll have a comprehensive understanding of its companies' position in the marketplace. This section shows you how to undertake a financial analysis, and once you've acquired this important skill you'll have a real understanding of your company's strengths and weaknesses, and of the threats and opportunities facing it.

This section of the book shows you how to apply your knowledge. It looks at each application and identifies:

- the important questions you need to answer;
- the ratios that will help you answer these questions.

Each chapter shows you how to approach the analysis, and the most appropriate ratios to use.

15

Suppliers' accounts

Introduction

The viability of suppliers is essential for any company's long-term survival. No one wants to squeeze a good supplier so hard on price and payment terms that they risk losing them. This means that understanding your suppliers' financial performance is an integral part of the supply relationship. If you want to protect your own business, you have to understand your suppliers' businesses.

When you're analysing suppliers' accounts you're usually trying to answer a number of questions:

- *Will they be able to deliver the order if we give it to them?*

- *Have we got a good deal?*

- *What's the strength of our negotiating position?*

If you look at the first question, you'll see that there's two parts to it, and financial analysis can only help you with one of them:

- The first element concerns suppliers' manufacturing ability. It's asking the question 'Will they be able to deliver the right quality product, on time?' Unfortunately, no amount of financial analysis can answer this question.

■ The second part is concerned with the supplier's financial viability, and this is where financial analysis helps. You want your suppliers to be successful.

If you want to assess their financial viability, you can look at the three elements of the deal:

■ *The price* – Whilst you want your suppliers to be successful, you don't want their success to be at the expense of your business. It's a supply partnership where both parties should win. You have to reassure yourself that your suppliers aren't ripping you off, but are generating sufficient profits to continue in business. It's a balance, and your ability to influence your suppliers' business depends on how important you are to them and on the level of competition.

■ *Stock levels* – Your suppliers may have agreed to carry stock for you, or have agreed a consignment stock arrangement that will reduce your working capital requirements, with the effect of increasing theirs. Can they afford to do this?

■ *Credit terms* – Do you have the same credit terms as their other customers? If you're paying faster, have you got a better price?

The third concern raises the question of how important you are to them. You will have a completely different negotiating position if you are 1% of their business than if you are 20%. Your analysis could show you that they need your business much more than you need them!

In this chapter I'll address these concerns and show you the relevant ratios to use when assessing your suppliers' financial performance.

The first decision ... which accounts to use

You may find that your supplier is part of a large group. This means that you have to decide whether you want to use the individual company's accounts or the group accounts. If it's a very small part of a large group, you may feel that the group accounts would be inappropriate. If it is registered in the UK you will be able to get its accounts from Companies House, but if it is based overseas it will be more difficult, and in some countries impossible, to get a private company's accounts. There are two problems you'll have if you choose to use the individual company's accounts:

■ They'll be more out of date. Private companies in the UK must file their accounts within nine months of their year end; whereas public companies have to file them within six months of their year end. Most companies file their accounts on the last possible day, so private companies' accounts aren't as up to date as those available from listed companies.

■ They'll be less detailed, particularly if they're a smaller company. (If you want to know the information you'll find in smaller companies' accounts, I tell you about it in Chapter 19.)

But you may need to look at the individual company's accounts anyway, particularly if you have concerns about its solvency. Being part of a group doesn't necessarily mean that the group will extend financial support. In October 2002 the American power company TXU decided to protect the group's credit rating by selling its European business, TXU Europe. It cut off all financial support to its cash strapped European subsidiary, which was then unable to pay its suppliers in full. Fortunately at the eleventh hour, and in just five days, the British part of the business, supplying electricity to 5.25 million customers mainly in the old Eastern and Norweb regions, was sold to Powergen (owned by Germany's E.on).

The individual company's accounts may be out of date but more relevant. However, don't forget that the group accounts will give you some useful information about different businesses in the note on segmental information. The revenue, profit, operating assets, capital expenditure and depreciation are analysed between the different businesses in this note.

First steps

The first steps are always the same:

1 If the company is listed, go onto it's website and read (and possibly watch and hear) its latest presentation to the analysts. (Just go into the 'investors' section and you'll find 'analysts presentations'.) This shows you the 'spin' that the company is putting on its numbers and the more information about its future prospects. If you have time, you could look at the past presentations to see if it's delivered everything that it's promised.

2 Then look at its five-year summary, this shows you how it's performed over the last five years and should give you an instant feel for the business's performance.

3 Next go to the operating review, as this will explain how it's performed in the last year and the main threats and opportunities facing its businesses.

4 Then read the financial review – this will reiterate some of the information in the operating review, but will also disclose information about the risks facing the business, the way the business is funded, and its cash management.

5 By now you should understand where the business has come from, and how it performed last year. So the next step is to look at the financial statements, reading the notes for any extra information you need. It's always worth reading the segmental analysis note, as this shows you which part of the group has the best returns.

6 You should know what you want to measure and what ratios you'd like to use. The ratios I've detailed below are the ones you're most likely to want to calculate, but the ratios you use should really be determined by what you've found when you looked at the accounts.

So let's have a look at the ratios that will help you analyse your supplier's financial performance.

Relevant ratios

Most of the ratios have some relevance in the analysis of suppliers' accounts, but I've selected the ones that are particularly useful. I'll start by considering its solvency, as you're bound to be interested in whether it's likely to be around in the future.

Solvency

Your first concern is whether your suppliers can deliver the goods on time. You'll already have assessed their operational performance, now it's time to assess their financial performance. If they are going to deliver on time, they ought to be able pay their suppliers on time and to repay bank loans when they're due. The solvency ratios should be useful as they help you to identify whether your supplier has:

▓ current, or potential, problems with their suppliers and banks;

▓ the ability to absorb any increase in their working capital.

I'll start by showing you how to see if they may have potential problems with their suppliers, and then look at potential problems with their banks. You know that suppliers are always concerned with how long they have to wait to be paid, and this is measured by their payable days.

Payable days

You may find payable days in the directors' report, but you know that the information may be too general to be useful. The holding company's practice could be very different from the group as a whole, and the company you're analysing! So it's probably best to calculate it from the accounts. Payable days are calculated using the following formula:

$$\frac{\text{Trade payables}}{\text{Purchases/cost of sales}} \times 365$$

If you're calculating payable days, the first thing that you have to decide is whether to use revenue, purchases (if you have this) or cost of sales. As you're trying to assess the possible risk of dealing with a specific supplier, you can use purchases (if your supplier uses the presentation that discloses this income statement) or a cost of sales based calculation (if they use the most popular presentation). This calculation would show payable days that more closely reflected the actual payment period.

It's important to see if the company's experiencing difficulties paying its own suppliers. If your supplier is always 'on stop' it is unlikely to be able to meet your delivery deadlines, so payable days is a good indicator of its probable supplier relationships.

Now you can move on to consider their banking relationships.

Interest cover

I think that this is one of the most important ratios, as it identifies whether the company can afford its current level of debt. I usually start with the profit based measure, as this may be a banking covenant, using the following formula:

$$\frac{\text{Profit before interest}}{\text{Net interest payable}}$$

A company with a low interest cover, below three times, can't afford to have falls in profits or rising interest rates. It's also relying on future profit growth to repay its loans, and may be close to a loan covenant. A low interest cover also indicates that it's unlikely to be able to increase its working capital, as this would probably have to be financed and additional loan finance is unlikely to be available. Banks are reluctant to lend to companies with low interest cover, as the company has problems affording its existing debt, let alone any additional debt. On the other hand, a company with a high interest cover, over seven times, would find no difficulty supporting, and obtaining, additional loans.

You could double check the company's ability to afford its loans by calculating a cash based interest cover. You could use the information from the statement of cash flows:

$$\frac{\text{Cash generated from operations}}{\text{Net interest paid}}$$

or you could use EBITDA:

$$\frac{\text{EBITDA}}{\text{Net interest payable}}$$

Now if you felt that the company could be under pressure from suppliers, or asked to repay its loans immediately, it's worth checking its acid test.

The acid test

This looks at the relationship of the company's liquid assets, those it can rapidly convert into cash, to its current liabilities. So it tells you whether the company could repay all its payables if it's asked to do so. As usually companies don't have to repay their current liabilities immediately, it's only worth doing this ratio if you think that the company has a problem.

$$\frac{\text{Liquid assets}}{\text{Current liabilities}}$$

Before you calculate this ratio you have to identify the company's liquid assets. They're largely determined by the nature of the business, but in a manufacturing company they are likely to be receivables receivable within a year and cash and cash equivalents. You'll find that most companies are unable to repay all of their short-term liabilities out of liquid assets, as they're not expecting to have to repay them all immediately. The most important thing to identify is the trend. Is the business becoming more, or less, liquid and why? Could liquidity be a problem when they come to finance your order?

The current ratio

This ratio measures the company's ability to repay short-term liabilities with its short-term assets:

$$\frac{\text{Current assets}}{\text{Current liabilities}}$$

The size of the 'ideal' current ratio varies from one industry to another. It depends on the length of the company's 'conversion' cycle, and the frequency of the purchasing decision. The longer it takes the company to turn its raw materials back into cash the larger the current ratio. You've seen that businesses such as Tesco's don't have enough current assets to pay their short-term liabilities. The buying decision is made daily, and their customers pay them long before they have to pay their suppliers. Unfortunately your suppliers are rarely in the same position as grocers! If they have insufficient current assets to meet their short-term liabilities, they may have to sell property, plant and equipment to pay their suppliers. This means that the likelihood of the short-term liabilities having to be repaid is critical. So far you've looked at immediate and short-term solvency, but banking relationships will also depend on the company's ability to repay its loans on time, so it may be worth looking at the company's terms and debt repayment schedule, cash balance and cash generation.

The terms and debt repayment schedule

This shows you the future contracted cash outflows for the company's debt and *when* its loans have to be repaid. If the company has to repay its loans in the next two years, it's useful to look at the company's cash and cash generation to see if your supplier is likely to be able to repay them from its existing resources.

Cash and cash generation

The balance sheet shows you how much cash the business has at its year end, and the statement of cash flows shows you how much it generated during the year. It's useful to see how much cash the company could use from this year's cash flow to repay its loans. You can do this by totalling the following cash flows:

- cash flow from operating activities;
- net cash flow from investing activities excluding acquisitions and disposals;
- interest paid.

(I've selected these cash flows, as the company needs some cash to reinvest in its business, and has to pay tax and interest. Acquisitions and dividends are discretionary.)

The total of these cash flows is the amount the business could have repaid from the current year's cash flow. If you look at this over a number of years, you can calculate an average cash flow and see whether it is increasing, or decreasing.

You should now know how much cash the business has, how much it generates each year, and whether it's likely to be enough to repay its loans. If it isn't, the company may have difficulties repaying its loans unless it can:

- *Repay existing loans with new loans.* To determine this you'd need to ask yourself whether lenders would view the business as a good risk in the current environment. You should consider things such as its relative performance, market conditions and interest cover. You can also take into account any unused borrowing facilities.

- *Generate sufficient cash to repay the loans.* This doesn't have to come from its operations. Companies can generate cash by reducing their working capital, or selling some of their assets.

- *Have a share issue.* A number of major companies have managed to have a rights issue, getting more cash from their shareholders by highlighting the alternatives!

Can the supplier finance the order?

If you're giving a supplier a large order, you should check that it can find sufficient finance to be able to deliver the goods. If you're giving it a £1 million order it has to fund the working capital requirements. There are two ways of approximating the cash needed to fund the order:

▨ Use its working capital ratio.

▨ Calculate the order's specific working capital.

The working capital ratio

This is simply calculated:

$$\frac{\text{Inventories} + \text{Trade receivables} + \text{Trade payables}}{\text{Revenue}}$$

This tells you how many pence it will need to have tied up in the working capital to fund a pound's worth of sales, based on its current business mix. So if its working capital ratio was 0.3, it needs to have 30 pence in its working capital for every pound of sales. This means that if you give it the £1 million order it will either have to find £300,000 to fund the order, or reduce its working capital requirements. (If it reduced its inventory and receivables days and increased its payable days, it could use the same amount of working capital to finance the increased sales.) If it's listed, you could look at its undrawn committed borrowing facilities to see if it could raise the cash, and calculate the subsidiary working capital ratios to see if there's room for improvement. All of the working capital ratios are very useful as:

▨ They are a measure of management efficiency – an efficient management team minimises its investment in working capital.

▨ You can see if the company could fund an increase in its sales from its existing resources. If you add the cash shown on the balance sheet to the undrawn committed borrowing facilities, you have the total cash currently available to the company. If you divide this by the working capital ratio, you discover the sales that can be supported from the current available funds. So if a company has £0.2 million cash at its year end, and £1.4 million undrawn committed facilities, it has £1.6 million funds available. If it needed 20 pence invested in its working capital to fund a pound's sales, its available funds would support extra sales of £8 million (£1.6 million ÷ 0.2).

■ Inventory days and receivable days affect your supplier's relationships with its customers. If the supplier has been reducing its finished goods stocks and receivables, you may have difficulty convincing it to carry your inventory, or to offer you extended credit terms. You could find that its average receivable days are 72, and you pay in 45 days. You're paying faster than its average customer, so perhaps there's some scope for discussions on price.

So I think it's useful to use the following ratios:

Total inventory days (or you could calculate inventory turn if you prefer):

$$\frac{\text{Inventories}}{\text{Cost of sales (or revenue as appropriate)}} \times 365$$

Work in progress days, as this also gives you some idea of manufacturing times:

$$\frac{\text{Work in progress}}{\text{Cost of sales (or revenue as appropriate)}} \times 365$$

Finished goods inventory days, as this also indicates whether it's likely to be willing to carry your inventory:

$$\frac{\text{Finished goods inventories}}{\text{Cost of sales (or revenue as appropriate)}} \times 365$$

Receivable days:

$$\frac{\text{Trade receivables}}{\text{Revenue}} \times 365$$

Payable days:

$$\frac{\text{Trade payables}}{\text{Cost of sales (or purchases as appropriate)}} \times 365$$

The specific working capital requirements of the order

The working capital ratio is a good approximation for the order's working capital requirement if your order represents a similar product on the same terms as the rest of its business. If it isn't you may have to adjust the working capital accordingly. However, if you have the information, or are prepared to make some assumptions, you can work out how much cash the supplier will need to finance your order. You'd need to know, or assume, the:

▪ materials cost percentage;

▪ length of the production cycle (its lead time is a good approximation for this);

▪ labour cost percentage;

▪ overhead cost percentage;

▪ probable profit margin on the order.

If you have an 'open book' relationship with your suppliers (where they give you a breakdown of their costs and cost structure), you already have this information. Otherwise you will have to deduce this, and may decide that you have to make so many assumptions that the current working capital ratio would give you a good enough guide to the cash requirements. However, I'll show you how to calculate the working capital requirements using the following example.

Example

A supplier is offered an order for £1 million, with payment 60 days after delivery. The lead time for delivery is two months. The supplier has told you that its cost, and profit, structure is:

▪ materials are 50% of the total cost;

▪ labour is 30% of the total cost;

▪ overheads are 20% of the total cost;

▪ the profit margin is 5% of sales.

You have calculated the following ratios from the company's accounts:

▪ raw materials inventory days – 30 days;

▪ finished goods inventory days – 15 days;

▪ payable days – 50 days.

This means that the profit and loss account for the order would be:

Revenue	1,000,000
Material costs	475,000
Staff costs	285,000
Overheads	190,000
Profit	50,000

To complete the order the supplier has to fund the working capital. It has to hold the stock, wait the agreed credit period, and this would be offset by the credit it receives from its own suppliers. So let's work out how much it need.

Inventories

The supplier has to fund the three components of stock: raw materials, work in progress, and finished goods. You just use a variant of the inventory days formula to find out how much it has to finance:

Cash required to fund raw materials inventories, based on 30 days' inventory:

$$\frac{30}{365} \times 475,000 = 39,041$$

I'm only including the materials costs at this stage, as the other costs are only incurred once it starts to manufacture the product.

Cash required to fund its work in progress, based on the two months' lead time for delivery:

$$\frac{60}{365} \times 950,000 = 156,164$$

(I've assumed that all of the costs begin to be incurred as the product is manufactured, and consequently I've based this calculation on the total costs, rather than the materials cost.)

Cash required to fund its finished goods inventories – based on 15 days' inventory:

$$\frac{15}{365} \times 950,000 = 39,041$$

The total cash that will be tied up in inventories is £234,246.

Receivables and payables

The cash required to finance the receivables on the agreed credit terms will be:

$$\frac{60}{365} \times 950,000 = 156,164$$

(I've used the costs in this calculation, not the sales, as the company doesn't have to fund the profit, only the costs.)

This will be offset by the credit that the supplier is able to get from its suppliers:

Materials' suppliers:

$$\frac{50}{365} \times 475{,}000 = 65{,}068$$

I've assumed that the company will be able to get 30 days' credit from staff and overhead suppliers:

$$\frac{30}{365} \times 475{,}000 = 39{,}041$$

This means that it's likely that the company's payables will be £104,109.

Total working capital requirement

The supplier will have to finance £260,273:

£234,246 (inventories) + £156,164 (receivables) − £104,109 (payables)

= £286,301

You know the company's cash position, and its unused borrowing facilities. Could it raise another £290,000 to satisfy your order? If not, could it reduce its working capital requirements for the rest of its business? The last thing you would want to do is to give a supplier an order that would cripple its business!

Profitability

Companies always have a dilemma when dealing with their suppliers ... they want them to be profitable, as in the long run they'll only survive if they're profitable. But you don't want them to be too profitable, as that might mean that they are ripping you off! When you're looking at suppliers' accounts you're interested in the trends in both the operating profit margin and the return on capital employed.

Operating profit margin or return on sales

You want your suppliers to have an acceptable operating profit margin, but you don't want them to be too profitable at your expense! This means that you need to calculate their profit margin over a number of years to see if it has changed and, if it has, why it has changed. The operating margin is simple to calculate:

$$\frac{\text{Operating profit}}{\text{Revenue}}$$

If their margin has changed, you should think about what may have caused it to change. I discussed the possible reasons in detail in Chapter 8, but the changes in profit margins usually arise from changes in:

- Volumes – Once the company's sales are above breakeven, anything above variable costs is pure profit. Small changes in sales can lead to a large change in profits, and therefore profit margins.

- Price – This is both the selling price and the price that the company pays for its costs. You're particularly interested if cost reduction has improved profits. It could have used different, cheaper materials, or perhaps its staff costs or overheads have reduced. You should be able to see this by looking at its costs, and don't forget staff numbers and total staff costs are always disclosed in the notes to the accounts. If your supplier has improved its overall profitability through cost reduction, perhaps you'd like a share of the improvement and there's some scope for a price reduction?

- Mix – This could be product mix, business mix or market mix.

Your supplier should give you some clues about the reason for the change in its operational review and the note on segmental information.

Return on operating capital employed

If you think about it, customers can have a large impact on their suppliers' return on operating capital. The price you negotiate affects their profitability; your stockholding requirements and credit terms affect their asset utilisation. You know that to add 'shareholder value' they need a return on capital that's greater than their cost of capital. So you're interested in their return on capital and why it's changed. The return on operating capital employed is calculated using the following formula:

$$\frac{\text{Operating profit}}{\text{Operating capital employed}}$$

If return on capital has changed over the period, why has it changed? You've already looked at their operating profit margin ... if that doesn't explain the difference, the explanation lies in their asset utilisation.

Asset utilisation

This is reflected in the asset turn ratio:

$$\frac{\text{Revenue}}{\text{Operating capital employed}}$$

You know that this is a combination of two things, their utilisation of property, plant and equipment combined with their control of working capital. You've already looked at their working capital, so that only leaves their property, plant and equipment turn. You calculate it using the formula below:

$$\frac{\text{Revenue}}{\text{Property, plant and equipment}}$$

There are three reasons why you can have changes in property, plant and equipment turns:

▩ The assets are being used more, or less, effectively. Perhaps they're now used continuously, instead of on two shifts – or vice versa.

▩ The composition of property, plant and equipment could have changed. Perhaps they now rent properties, whereas they previously owned them. This will be disclosed in the notes.

▩ The asset's value has changed following an acquisition, or a major capital expenditure programme, or disposals. This would be shown in the cash flow statement and disclosed in the note on property, plant and equipment.

You've already calculated the working capital ratios when you've considered the supplier's ability to finance the order, so you should now understand what has driven any changes in its working capital.

The importance of your order

If you want to know the strength of your negotiating position you have to know how important your business is to your suppliers. What percentage is your business of their total revenue? (It's at this point that it's useful to have the individual company's accounts. Your order may be totally irrelevant to the group, but could be 30% of the individual company's business.) If you are a large customer you have a strong negotiating position, but often can't afford to drive too hard a bargain, as you could determine the company's future. If you negotiate price reductions and extended credit terms you affect both their profitability and solvency. You could be responsible for the company being liquidated – or force the group's parent to close, or sell, your supplier. If you have a key supplier in financial difficulties, and you're one of their key customers, you have a strategic dilemma. Should you continue to negotiate hard, or should you structure the negotiation to help the supplier? It's often cheaper to pay a better price, than to find an alternative supplier. Being a large customer is a two-edged sword, with power comes responsibilities!

Summary

Financial analysis is an integral part of the sourcing decision. Before you place a large order, you should ascertain the financial viability of the supplier and how your order will affect its business. Sometimes companies are liquidated because they are its too fast. They have no difficulty getting the orders, but they just can't get the cash to fund them!

Financial analysis is not just important in vetting suppliers; it can also play a useful role in the negotiating process. It helps you to identify your best negotiating position, and use it effectively.

16

Customers' accounts

Introduction

If you want to develop a close relationship with your customers it is essential that you understand their business. You have to appreciate their businesses' strengths and weaknesses if you would like to understand the opportunities and threats facing your business. Clients' accounts are a useful addition to your normal market intelligence as they will quantify the success, or otherwise, of their marketing activities, and clarify some of the threats and opportunities facing their, and consequently your, business.

When you're looking at your clients' businesses you're usually interested in discovering:

- *Will they be able to pay us on time?*

- *Will they be in business next year?*

- *Is there any potential for increasing our sales?*

- *What is the best way to structure the sales negotiation?*

Financial analysis helps you address some of these concerns, and gives you useful information for your sales negotiations. If you read through your customers' accounts, and analyse them, you'll understand:

- Where they sell their products:
  - the sales in each division;
  - the sales in different countries and regions.
- Which parts of their business have the potential for real sales growth
- Where they're making their profits:
  - the profits of each division;
  - the profits made in different countries and regions.
- Where their profits have grown, or fallen.
- Their cost structure.
- Where they make the best return on their operating assets.
- The other companies in the group, as they could represent sales opportunities.
- The parts of the business they intend to develop in the future.

The accounts don't just contain financial information; the operating and financial reviews, or the business review in the directors' report in smaller companies' accounts, also disclose the key factors influencing their businesses' performance. It should disclose the factors, and the trends, underlying the company's performance, and any factors that are expected to impact on the company's future performance. It will tell you about any industrial, or environmental changes, expected to affect the companys' results. This includes new product developments, acquisitions, disposals, changes in their market conditions, and market share. The financial review discusses the businesses' risks and how they manage them, the effect of exchange rates, their revenue and margins. Reading the accounts will give you an understanding of how your clients see their performance and their focus for the future. It often provides you with a starting point for a more detailed discussion with your clients. For example, if you are selling capital equipment, you will be able to see their current level of capital expenditure and some indication of their likely future spend.

The first decision ... which accounts to use

You may find that your customer is part of a large group. This means that you have to decide whether you want to use its individual company's accounts or the group accounts. If it's a very small part of a large group, you may feel that the group accounts would be inappropriate. If it is registered in the UK you will be able to get its accounts from Companies House, but if it is based overseas it will be its difficult, and in some countries impossible, to get a private company's accounts. There are two problems you'll have if you choose to use the individual company's accounts:

▨ They'll be more out of date. Private companies in the UK must file their accounts within nine months of their year end; whereas public companies have to file them within six months of their year end. Most companies file on the last possible day, so private companies' accounts aren't as up to date as those available from listed companies.

▨ They'll be less detailed, particularly if they're a smaller company. (If you want to know the information you'll find in smaller companies' accounts, I tell you about it in Chapter 19.)

But you may need to look at the individual company's accounts anyway, particularly if you have concerns about its solvency. Being part of a group doesn't necessarily mean that the group will extend financial support. (For example, in May 2009 the card company Clintons placed its loss-making subsidiary Birthdays into administration.)

The individual company's accounts may be out of date, but more relevant. However, don't forget that the group accounts will give you some useful information about different businesses in the note on segmental information. The sales, profit and operating assets are analysed between the different businesses in this note.

First steps

The first steps are always the same:

1 If they're listed, go onto their website and read (and possibly watch and hear) their latest presentation to the analysts. (Just go into the 'investors' section and you'll find 'analysts presentations'.) This shows you the 'spin' that the company is putting on its numbers and gives you more information about its future prospects. If you have time, you could look at the past presentations to see if they've delivered everything that they've promised. You may also be able to sign up for email news alerts.

2 Then look at their five-year summary, as this shows you how they've performed over the last five years and should give you an instant feel for the businesses' performance.

3 Next go to the operating review, as this will explain how they've performed in the last year and the main threats and opportunities facing their businesses.

4 Then read the financial review – this will reiterate some of the information in the operating review, but will also disclose information about the risks facing the business, the way the businesses are funded, and their cash management.

5 By now you should understand where each business has come from, and how it performed last year. So the next step is to look at the financial statements, reading the notes for any extra information you need. It's always worth reading the segmental analysis note, as this shows you which part of the group has the best returns.

6 You should know what you want to measure and the ratios you'd like to use. The ratios I've detailed below are the ones you're most likely to want to calculate, but the ratios you use should really be determined by what you've found when you read through the accounts.

So let's have a look at the ratios that will help you analyse your customer's financial performance.

Relevant ratios

I'll start by considering the company's solvency, as one of your first concerns is whether the company will be able to pay your invoices. So let's see if it can, and whether it's likely to continue trading in the future.

Solvency

The solvency ratios are useful as they help you to identify whether your customer has:

▦ current, or potential, problems with its other suppliers and banks;

▦ sufficient financial strength to grow its business.

I'll start with potential problems with suppliers, and then move on to consider problems with banks. Ideally you'd do this analysis *before* granting your customer credit, as it could be giving you the order because it's 'on stop' with its existing suppliers. You're concerned with how long you'll have to wait to be paid, and this is measured by payable days.

Payable days

Although you might find some information on payable days in the directors' report, you've seen that it's not always useful. If it isn't adequately disclosed there, you'll have to calculate it from the accounts. Payable days is calculated using the following formula:

$$\frac{\text{Trade payables}}{\text{Revenue/cost of sales}} \times 365$$

If you're calculating payable days, the first thing that you have to decide is whether to use revenue, purchases (if you have this) or cost of sales. As you're trying to assess the possible risk of dealing with a specific customer, you should use purchases (if your customer shows this in its income statement) or, if that's not available, a cost of sales based calculation. Using cost of sales shows payable days that more closely reflects its actual payment period. This can be a useful ratio for existing clients, as well as new ones. It tells you their average payment period, and you can compare this with the time it's taking to pay you.

Now you can move on to consider its banking relationships.

Interest cover

You know that banks sometimes withdraw their support, and force a company into receivership. The last thing that you'd want is to be an unsecured creditor in a business that's in receivership – you're right towards the end of the payment queue and the chances of being paid are remote. This is why interest cover is important; it's a common banking covenant that identifies whether the company can afford its current level of debt. It's quickly calculated by using the following formula:

$$\frac{\text{Profit before interest}}{\text{Net interest payable}}$$

A company with a low interest cover, below three times, is exposed to falls in profits and rising interest rates. It's also relying on future profit growth to repay its loans, and may be close to breaching a loan covenant. Banking relationships become increasingly difficult as the interest cover approaches three, and if it falls to two and a half times your client may be asked to repay its loans.

Now you could double check the company's ability to afford its loans by calculating a cash based interest cover either using information from the cash flow statement:

$$\frac{\text{Cash generated from operations}}{\text{Net interest paid}}$$

or you could use EBITDA:

$$\frac{\text{EBITDA}}{\text{Net interest payable}}$$

There's another clue about banking relationships – the company's *committed undrawn borrowing facility*, disclosed in the notes to listed companies' accounts. If banks are prepared to commit themselves to give the company additional funds, they are confident in the company and its future.

Now if you felt that the company could be under pressure from suppliers, or asked to repay its loans immediately, it's worth checking its acid test.

The acid test

Customers will try to extend payment terms if they have a liquidity problem, so the acid test is a useful ratio. It looks at the relationship of the customers' liquid assets, those it can rapidly convert into cash, to its current liabilities. So it tells you whether the company could repay all their creditors if it's asked to do so. As companies usually don't have to repay their current liabilities immediately, it's only worth doing this ratio if you think that the company could have a problem.

$$\frac{\text{Liquid assets}}{\text{Current liabilities}}$$

Before you calculate this ratio you'll need to identify the company's liquid assets. They're largely determined by the nature of its business, but they are likely to comprise current receivables and cash and cash equivalents. You'll find that most companies are unable to repay all of their short-term liabilities out of liquid assets, as they're not expecting to have to repay them all immediately.

The current ratio

I'd use this ratio, rather than the acid test, if you felt that it's unlikely that your customer is going to have to repay all its short-term liabilities immediately. It measures the company's ability to repay short-term liabilities with its short-term assets:

$$\frac{\text{Current assets}}{\text{Current liabilities}}$$

The size of the 'ideal' current ratio varies from one industry to another. It depends on the length of the company's 'conversion' cycle, and the frequency of the purchasing decision. The longer it takes the company to turn its raw materials back into cash the larger the current ratio. You've seen that businesses such as Tesco's don't have enough current assets to pay their short-term creditors. The buying decision is made daily, and their customers pay them long before they have to pay their suppliers. So if you're selling to retailers you'll probably find relatively low current ratios.

So far you've looked at immediate and short-term solvency, but banking relationships will also depend on the company's ability to repay loans on time, so it may be worth looking at the company's loan repayment schedule, cash balance and cash generation.

The terms and debt repayment schedule

This shows the contractual cash flows arising from the company's existing debt and tells you *when* its loans have to be repaid. If your customer has to repay its loans in the next two years, it's useful to look at the company's cash and cash generation to see if it is likely to be able to repay them from its existing resources.

Cash and cash generation

The balance sheet shows you how much cash the business has at its year end, and the cash flow statement shows you how much it generated during the year. It's useful to see how much cash the company could use from this year's cash flow to repay its loans. You can do this by totalling the following cash flows:

- cash flow from operating activities;
- net cash flow from investing activities excluding acquisitions and disposals;
- interest paid.

(I've selected these cash flows, as the company needs some cash to reinvest in its business, and has to pay tax and interest. Acquisitions and dividends are discretionary.)

The total of these cash flows is the amount the business could have repaid from the current year's cash flow. If you look at this over a number of years, you can calculate an average cash flow and see whether it is increasing, or decreasing.

You should now know how much cash the business has, how much it generates each year, and whether it's likely to be enough to repay its loans. If it isn't, your customer may have difficulties repaying its loans unless it can:

- *Repay existing loans with new loans.* To determine this you'd need to ask yourself whether lenders would view the business as a good risk. You should consider things such as its relative performance, its market conditions and its interest cover. You can also take into account its unused borrowing facilities.

▨ *Generate sufficient cash to repay the loans.* This doesn't have to come from their operations. Companies can generate cash by reducing their working capital, or selling some of their assets.

▨ *Have a share issue.* A number of major companies have recently managed to have a rights issue, getting more cash from their shareholders by highlighting the alternatives!

Profitability

You've looked at your customer's solvency, now let's look at its profitability. Does it have any growth potential? Are its sales increasing or decreasing? If you look at its income statement you'll see the trends in their revenue and profits.

Operating profit margin, or return on sales

The operating margin is simple to calculate:

$$\frac{\text{Operating profit}}{\text{Revenue}}$$

If its margin has changed, you should think about what may have caused it to change. I discussed the possible reasons in detail in Chapter 8, but the changes in profit margins usually arise from changes in:

▨ Volumes – Once the company's sales are above breakeven, anything above variable costs is pure profit. Small changes in sales can lead to a large change in profits, and therefore profit margins.

▨ Price – This covers both its selling price and the price your customer pays for its own costs.

▨ Mix – This could be product mix, business mix, or market mix.

Your customer's accounts should give you some clues about the reason for any changes in the operational review and the note on segmental analysis.

If your client is focusing on improving its operating profitability, and you are selling it revenue items it'll probably be looking for price reductions in the next negotiation. (This would be particularly relevant if your product was one of its major costs. If it can negotiate a 5% reduction on something that is 40% of the total cost, it'll have a significant improvement in its profits!)

If your customer is part of a large group, you may only be selling to a specific part of its business. In this case you'll find that the segmental information, usually the first note in the accounts, is a useful part of your analysis.

Segmental information

This shows you what's happening in the part of the business you're selling to, and how this compares with the rest of the group's results. Groups tend to focus their investment and energies on the part of their business that is generating the best return, or with the best prospects. You can work out the operating margin, and the return on capital for the group's various businesses. Any division that is under performing is likely to be sold, or closed down unless it generates a lot of cash. Whereas any division that is performing well will be developed and strengthened. You can also see which parts of the group are receiving most of the investment (their operating assets will be increasing), and those that are being used as cash cows (their operating assets will be decreasing and their capital expenditure will be less than the depreciation charge).

Return on operating capital employed

Every business has to have an acceptable return on its capital. If it wants to add value for its shareholders, it has to have a return on capital that's greater than its cost of capital. So you're interested in its return on capital and why it's changed. The return on operating capital employed is calculated using the following formula:

$$\frac{\text{Operating profit}}{\text{Operating capital employed}}$$

If the return on operating capital has changed over the period, why has it changed? You've already looked at its operating profit margin ... if that doesn't explain the difference, the explanation lies in its asset utilisation.

Asset utilisation

This is reflected in the asset turn ratio:

$$\frac{\text{Revenue}}{\text{Operating capital employed}}$$

You know that this is a combination of two things: its utilisation of property, plant and equipment, and control of working capital. Let's consider its property, plant and equipment turn first. You calculate it using the formula below:

$$\frac{\text{Revenue}}{\text{Property, plant and equipment}}$$

There are three reasons why the property, plant and equipment turn may have changed:

▪ The assets are being used more, or less, effectively. Perhaps they're now used continuously, instead of on one or two shifts – or vice versa.

▪ The composition of property, plant and equipment could have changed. Perhaps it now rents properties, whereas it previously owned them. This will be disclosed in the notes.

▪ An asset's value has changed following an acquisition, or a major capital expenditure programme, or disposals. This would be shown in the cash flow statement and disclosed in the note on property, plant and equipment.

The property, plant and equipment turn is particularly interesting if you're selling it capital items. If your customer is trying to use its property, plant and equipment more effectively, you could have a sales opportunity. Perhaps you have a machine, or tooling, that can extend its asset life, or speed up production.

The next thing to consider is its working capital, starting with the working capital ratio:

$$\frac{\text{Working capital}}{\text{Revenue}}$$

All of the working capital ratios are very useful as:

▪ They measure management efficiency – an efficient management team minimises its investment in working capital.

▪ You can see if the company could fund an increase in its sales from its existing resources. If you add the cash shown on the balance sheet to the undrawn committed borrowing facilities, you have the total cash currently available to the company. If you divide this by the working capital ratio, you discover the sales that can be supported from the current available funds. So if a company has £0.2 million cash at its year end, and £1.4 million undrawn committed facilities, it has £1.6 million funds available. If it needed 20 pence invested in its working capital to fund a pound's sales, its available funds would support extra sales of £8 million (£1.6 million ÷ 0.2).

▓ You can use the inventory days and payable days to prepare for your negotiation with a client. If you found that your customer's payable days were longer than your current payment terms, your customer is paying you faster than its other suppliers. The company's buyer will probably try to extend your payment terms in the negotiation, unless you're prepared to offer a prompt payment discount. If it's trying to reduce its inventories, it will be looking for an improvement in lead times and may be asking you to carry part of its inventory. Perhaps you should consider a consignment stock arrangement?

So I think it's useful to use the following ratios:

Total inventory days (or you could calculate inventory turn if you prefer):

$$\frac{\text{Inventories}}{\text{Cost of sales (or revenue as appropriate)}} \times 365$$

Receivable days:

$$\frac{\text{Trade receivables}}{\text{Revenue}} \times 365$$

Payable days:

$$\frac{\text{Trade payables}}{\text{Cost of sales (or revenue as appropriate)}} \times 365$$

Summary

Financial analysis is a useful tool for anyone involved in sales. It gives you a wealth of additional information and can be used as a guide to future negotiations. If you use financial analysis in conjunction with your market intelligence you should be able to turn your customer's threats into your business opportunities!

17

Competitors' accounts

Introduction

Curiosity is a human trait. We are always intrigued by our competitors' financial performance and want to know whether they're performing better, or worse, than we are. We see their marketing activities, have some idea about their commercial strategies, and want to know how this translates into their financial performance. Are their marketing activities more, or less, successful than ours? This will be reflected in their profitability and the way investors feel about their business.

If you're looking at your competitors you're usually interested in three things:

- *Solvency* – You're concerned with the answers to questions such as ... Will they be able to continue trading? Do they have enough cash to support an aggressive discounting policy?

- *Relative profitability* – You're interested in identifying the most profitable company in the sector and why it's the most profitable.

- *Relative investment potential* – You're interested in how the stock market views the company and whether its share price indicates that the market feels that it has better, or worse, profit growth prospects.

Financial analysis helps you address these concerns. It shows you whether their marketing activities are successful, whether they are likely to survive, and their perceived investment potential.

The first decision ... which accounts to use

You may find that you only compete with the company in one of its markets, or you only compete with one company in a large group. This means that you have to decide whether you want to use the individual company's accounts or the group accounts. If the competing company is a very small part of a large group, you may feel that the group accounts would be inappropriate. If it is registered in the UK you can to get its accounts from Companies House, but if it is based overseas it will be more difficult, and in some countries impossible, to get a private company's accounts. There are two problems you'll have if you choose to use the individual company's accounts:

- They'll be more out of date. Private companies in the UK must file their accounts within nine months of their year end; whereas public companies have to file them within six months of their year end. Most companies file on the last possible day, so private companies' accounts aren't as up to date as those available from listed companies.

- They'll be less detailed, particularly if they're a smaller company. (If you want to know the information you'll find in smaller companies' accounts, I tell you about it in Chapter 19.)

But you may need to look at the individual company's accounts anyway, particularly if you have concerns about its solvency. Being part of a group doesn't necessarily mean that the group will extend financial support. You may remember that in October 2002 the American power company TXU decided to protect the group's credit rating by selling the British part of its European business, TXU Europe. It cut off all financial support to its cash strapped European subsidiary, which was then unable to pay its suppliers in full. Fortunately at the eleventh hour, and in just five days, the British part of the business, supplying electricity to 5.25 million customers mainly in the old Eastern and Norweb regions, was sold to Powergen (owned by Germany's E.on).

The individual company's accounts may be out of date, but more relevant. However, don't forget that the group accounts will give you some useful information about different businesses in the note on segmental information. The sales, profit and operating assets are analysed between the different businesses in this note.

First steps

The first steps are always the same:

1 If they're listed, go onto their website and read (and possibly watch and hear) their latest presentation to the analysts. (Just go into the 'investors' section and you'll find 'analysts presentations'.) This shows you the 'spin' that the company is putting on its numbers and gives you more information about its future prospects. If you have time, you could look at the past presentations to see if they've delivered everything that they've promised. You may also be able to sign up for email news alerts.

2 Then look at their five-year summary, this shows you how they've performed over the last five years and should give you an instant feel for the businesses' performance.

3 Next go to the operating review, as this will explain how they've performed in the last year and the main threats and opportunities facing their businesses.

4 Then read the financial review – this will reiterate some of the information in the operating review, but will also disclose information about the risks facing the business, the way the businesses are funded, and their cash management.

5 By now you should understand where each business has come from, and how it performed last year. So the next step is to look at the financial statements, reading the notes for any extra information you need. It's always worth reading the segmental analysis note, as this shows you which part of the group has the best returns.

6 You should know what you want to measure and what ratios you'd like to use. The ratios I've detailed below are the ones you're most likely to want to calculate, but the ratios you use should really be determined by what you've found when you looked at the accounts.

So let's have a look at the ratios that will help you compare your competitors' financial performance with your own.

Relevant ratios

I'll start by considering their solvency, as you're bound to be interested in whether they're likely to continue trading in the future.

Solvency

The solvency ratios should be useful as they help you to identify whether the company has:

- Current, or potential problems with its suppliers and banks.

- Sufficient financial strength to support a price led market penetration programme. You know that any reduction in price requires a disproportionate increase in volume to maintain profits at current levels and, unless the product is very price sensitive, reducing prices usually leads to falling profits. This means that any company engaging in marketing activities driving prices down needs a strong balance sheet to survive and realise the future benefits of increased market share.

- The ability to absorb an increase in the working capital. Many manufacturers are under pressure to carry their customers' stock and extend receivable days. If the company has solvency problems, it is unlikely to be able to respond to these requests.

I'll start with potential problems with suppliers, and then move on to consider problems with banks. You know that suppliers are concerned with how long they have to wait to be paid, and this is measured by payable days.

Payable days

You may find payable days in the directors' report, but if it isn't disclosed adequately there, you'll have to calculate it from the accounts. Payable days is calculated using the following formula

$$\frac{\text{Trade payables}}{\text{Revenue/cost of sales}} \times 365$$

If you're calculating payable days the first thing that you have to decide is whether to use revenue or cost of sales. Generally revenue is a more comparable basis if the companies' definitions of cost of sales are different. However, it's only comparable if the companies have similar operating margins. As long as there is no real difference in profitability, revenue is an acceptable base – at least you'd be consistently wrong!

It's important to see if the company's experiencing difficulties paying its suppliers. If it's always 'on stop' it is unlikely to be able to meet delivery deadlines, so payable days is a good measure of likely supplier relationships.

Now you can move on to consider their banking relationships.

Interest cover

I always look at interest cover, as it identifies if the company can afford its current level of debt. I usually start with the profit based measure, as this may be a banking covenant. It's quickly calculated by using the following formula:

$$\frac{\text{Profit before interest}}{\text{Net interest payable}}$$

A company with a low interest cover, below three times, is exposed to falls in profits and rising interest rates. It's also relying on future profit growth to repay its loans, and may be close to a loan covenant. This means that it's unlikely to want to reduce its prices, as it needs profits to increase, not fall. A low interest cover also indicates that it's unlikely to be able to increase its working capital, as this would have to be financed and loan finance is unlikely to be available. Banks are reluctant to lend to companies with low interest cover, as the company has problems affording its existing debt, let alone any additional debt. On the other hand, a company with a high interest cover, over seven times, would find no difficulty supporting, and obtaining, additional loans.

Now you could double check the company's ability to afford its loans by calculating cash based interest cover. You could use the information from the statement of cash flows:

$$\frac{\text{Cash generated from operations}}{\text{Net interest paid}}$$

or you could use EBITDA:

$$\frac{\text{EBITDA}}{\text{Net interest payable}}$$

There's another clue about banking relationships – the company's *committed undrawn borrowing facilities*, disclosed in the notes to the accounts. If banks are prepared to commit themselves to give the company additional funds they must be confident in the company and its future. If the company is close to its agreed borrowing level, it will be reluctant to carry customers' stock, or give them extended credit terms. The note on financial risk management should also give you some information about the company's banking covenants and whether it's complying with them.

Now if you felt that the company could be under pressure from suppliers, or asked to repay its loans immediately, it's worth checking its acid test.

The acid test

This looks at the relationship of the company's liquid assets, those it can rapidly convert into cash, to its current liabilities. So it tells you whether the company could repay all its creditors if it's asked to do so. As usually it doesn't have to repay its current liabilities immediately, it's only worth doing this ratio if you think that the company has a problem.

$$\frac{\text{Liquid assets}}{\text{Current liabilities}}$$

Before you calculate this ratio you have to determine the company's liquid assets. They're largely determined by the nature of the business, but in a manufacturing company they are likely to be current receivables and cash and cash equivalents. You'll find that most companies aren't able to repay all of their short-term liabilities out of liquid assets, as they're not expecting to have to repay them all immediately.

So far you've looked at immediate solvency, but banking relationships will also depend on the company's ability to repay loans on time, so it may be worth looking at the company's terms and debt repayment schedule, cash balance and cash generation.

The terms and debt repayment schedule

This shows you the future contracted cash outflows for the company's debt and *when* its loans have to be repaid. If the company has to repay its loans in the next two years, it's useful to look at the company's cash and cash generation.

Cash and cash generation

The balance sheet shows you how much cash the business has at its year end, and the cash flow statement shows you how much it generated during the year. It's useful to see how much cash the company could use from this year's cash flow to repay its loans. You can do this by totalling the following cash flows:

■ cash flow from operating activities;

■ net cash flow from investing activities excluding acquisitions and disposals;

■ interest paid.

(I've selected these cash flows, as the company needs some cash to reinvest in its business, and has to pay tax and interest. Acquisitions and dividends are discretionary.)

The total of these cash flows is the amount the business could have repaid from the current year's cash flow. If you look at this over a number of years you can calculate an average cash flow and see whether it is increasing, or decreasing. You should now know how much cash the business has, how much it generates each year and whether it is enough. If it isn't, the company may have difficulties repaying its loans unless it can:

■ *Repay existing loans with new loans.* To determine this you'd need to ask yourself whether lenders would view the business as a good risk taking into account things such as its relative performance, its market conditions and its interest cover. You can also take into account its unused borrowing facilities.

■ *Generate sufficient cash to repay the loans.* This doesn't have to come from its operations. Companies can generate cash by reducing their working capital, or by selling some of their assets.

■ *Have a share issue.* A number of major companies have managed to have a rights issue, getting more cash from their shareholders by highlighting the alternatives!

Profitability

You're probably familiar with your competitors' prices, and have a fair idea of their service levels. Now let's find out how this translates into profitability. Are they more, or less, profitable than your company? To answer this you need to look at the two measures of profitability: operating profit margins and the return on capital.

Operating margins, or return on sales

Are their operating margins similar to yours? It's simple enough to find out, as all you have to do is to calculate the operating margin:

$$\frac{\text{Operating profit}}{\text{Revenue}}$$

If their operating margin is different, why is it different? I usually expect, over a period of time, to find similar operating margins within the same industry. There is a number of reasons why the margins may be different. Perhaps patented new products allow one company to charge higher prices, or one company has a larger market share. (If you want to review how this affects profitability, you'll need to read Chapter 8 and the discussion of fixed and variable costs and breakeven analysis.) Its costs could be different, maybe it's manufacturing abroad. The notes to the income statement will tell you how many people it employs and its total staff costs. (However you'll need to read these carefully if there's a lot of part-time staff, as some companies disclose total employees whereas others disclose full-time equivalents.)

If a similar competitor in the same market has a very different operating margin it may have:

- Identified a new market – this only gives it a short-term advantage, as competitors rapidly enter a new profitable market.

- Developed a new manufacturing process, or a different method of distribution – again this only gives a short-term advantage, as competitors will copy it unless its been patent protected.

- Engaged in creative accounting – I've a very simple rule – *If it looks too good to be true, it probably is!*

You'd be really concerned about the first two, although it's difficult to keep new developments secret for very long so you may have already heard about them. Careful reading of the notes to the accounts would help to verify, or eliminate, the creative accounting option. And if your competitor is engaged in creative accounting, *why* are they doing it. You don't fool any one for long, as cash soon runs out.

If its margin is different, you should think about why it's different. I discussed the reasons in detail in Chapter 8, but the difference usually arises from differences in:

▨ Volumes – Once the company's sales are above breakeven, anything above variable costs is pure profit.

▨ Price – This is both their selling price and the price that your competitor pays for its own costs.

▨ Mix – This could be product mix, business mix, or market mix.

Return on capital employed

You know that this is important, as it also affects 'shareholder value' and the investors' perception of the company. It's probably worth working through the main ratios in the profitability hierarchy, as some of the subsidiary ratios can give you some useful insights into your competitors' business.

When looking at competitors' accounts, I'm interested in looking at the return on operating capital employed, as this is where you'll find the effects of their sales and marketing activities. Is their return on capital better, or worse, than other companies in the industry? To find out you need to use the following formula:

$$\frac{\text{Operating profit}}{\text{Operating capital employed}}$$

If it's different, why is it different? You've already looked at their operating profit margin ... if that doesn't explain the difference, the explanation lies in their asset utilisation.

Asset utilisation

This is reflected in the asset turn ratio:

$$\frac{\text{Revenue}}{\text{Operating capital employed}}$$

You know that this is a combination of two things: their utilisation of property, plant and equipment and control of working capital. Let's consider their property, plant and equipment first. You calculate it using the formula below:

$$\frac{\text{Revenue}}{\text{Property, plant and equipment}}$$

Differences in property, plant and equipment turns could arise for three reasons:

- The assets are being used more effectively, perhaps they're used continuously, instead of on one or two shifts.

- The composition of the property, plant and equipment could be different. Perhaps one company rents properties and the other owns them – the assets will be analysed in the notes.

- The assets' value is very low. This could happen if they're very old (check the note on property, plant and equipment), or if the assets are leased on operating leases (check the note on operating leases).

The next thing to consider is their working capital, starting with the working capital ratio:

$$\frac{\text{Working capital}}{\text{Revenue}}$$

All of the working capital ratios are very useful as:

- They measure management efficiency – an efficient management team would be minimising its investment in working capital.

- You can see if the company could fund an increase in its sales from its existing resources. If you add the cash shown on the balance sheet to the undrawn committed borrowing facilities, you have the total cash currently available to the company. If you divide this by the working capital ratio, you discover the sales that can be supported from the current available funds. So if a company has £0.2 million cash at its year end, and £1.4 million undrawn committed facilities, it has £1.6 million funds available. If it needed 20 pence invested in its working capital to fund a pound's sales, its available funds would support extra sales of £8 million (£1.6 million ÷ 0.2).

▧ Inventory days and receivable days affect your competitors' relationships with their customers. And I'd like to suggest that it would be useful if you calculated a few more ratios. It's useful to analyse stock in its component parts, working out stock days for raw material stock, work in progress and finished goods stock. If your competitors are carrying more raw materials' stock, they may be in a better position to cope with rush orders and shorter delivery times. A difference in the work in progress may reflect a difference in manufacturing times, which will work through into lead times. A difference in finished goods stock may reflect their willingness, or otherwise, to carry stocks for their customers. Receivable days gives an indication of their credit terms with customers, in the same way that payable days does with their suppliers.

So I think it's useful to use the following ratios:

Total inventory days (or you could calculate stock turn if you prefer):

$$\frac{\text{Inventories}}{\text{Cost of sales (or revenue as appropriate)}} \times 365$$

Raw material inventory days:

$$\frac{\text{Raw materials}}{\text{Cost of sales (or revenue as appropriate)}} \times 365$$

Work in progress days:

$$\frac{\text{Work in progress}}{\text{Cost of sales (or revenue as appropriate)}} \times 365$$

Finished goods inventory days:

$$\frac{\text{Finished goods inventories}}{\text{Cost of sales (or revenue as appropriate)}} \times 365$$

Receivable days:

$$\frac{\text{Trade receivables}}{\text{Revenue}} \times 365$$

Payable days:

$$\frac{\text{Trade payables}}{\text{Cost of sales (or revenue as appropriate)}} \times 365$$

The investor's perspective

You may be surprised to find this is important when you're analysing a competitor's business, and it's really only worth doing if the competitor is listed. I've included it because if your competitor is listed, the market has a view about its future profitability, and this view is reflected in its current share price. You can go onto the financial websites and see the analysts' views and their estimates for the next two year's revenue and profits. These will already be reflected in the company's market capitalisation (the number of shares in issue x the current share price), which represents the market's view of a company's *future* profitability. You can also see this in the price earnings ratio.

PE ratio

This is published in the financial press and is calculated by dividing the current share price by the earnings per share. A PE ratio between five and seven usually indicates that the market expects no real growth in the company's earnings. These shares tend to have relatively high dividend yields, approximating to interest rates. (As this would be the alternative opportunity if you felt that there was no opportunity for a capital gain.) A high PE either indicates that the markets believe that profits will grow, or the share is expensive. You're really interested in your competitor's PE ratio relative to your own, and the rest of your sector. A higher PE relative indicates that the stock market believes that its profits will grow faster than other companies in the same industry.

The market's view is indicative, but it's not perfect. It's possible that a company's growth prospects aren't fairly reflected in its PE ratio, as share prices are influenced by all sort of extraneous factors. The market prefers some chief executives to others. The board's presentation of its future plans may have been unconvincing, after all the stock market is the same as any other market – it's full of people! Personal relationships are crucial. A company's shares can under perform the market, in the short term, because some leading analysts don't like, or trust, the board. The market is not always right – remember that every time a share changes hands both parties think they have made the right decision!

Other things can affect the share price, such as the company's gearing. This affects the company's share price, and its return on equity, in different ways at different stages in the economic cycle. In a highly geared company, shareholders will fare badly in a recession and well in a recovery. Interest has to be paid regardless of profits, whereas dividends can be reduced. When sales and profits increase, a highly geared company can reward its shareholders, as the increased profit is spread amongst relatively fewer shares.

Thinking about the investors' perception of the company is useful, as they're the other funding option available to the company. Loans aren't the only form of finance.

Financial websites

If your competitor's listed, you can also access information on financial websites about the analysts' opinion and estimates (usually of profits and revenue). And some of the websites allow you to set up alerts, so that if there's any news about your competitor you'll receive it before it's in the press.

Summary

Financial analysis can give you some useful insights into your competitors' business. You can measure the success of their marketing, identify potential problems facing their business, and see how they could respond to their customers. It gives you a rounded view of your competitors' performance.

18

Identifying a company's acquisition potential

Introduction

Acquisitive companies usually want to enhance their profitability, and they can achieve this in a number of different ways. An acquisition could:

- improve their market share;
- give economies of scale;
- improve their product range;
- improve their cash position and cash flow.

If you're acquiring companies in the same industry you tend to benefit from economies of scale and increased market share. It may be the cheapest way to improve your product range and improve your technology. (Companies that have a technological advantage and better products are often takeover targets, particularly if their processes and products are patent protected. Although if the stock market has already recognised their potential, they may be too expensive to acquire.)

Other companies become acquisitive because they want to diversify, particularly if they're a single product company that is vulnerable to market changes. They may want to move out of declining industries into expanding ones, or feel that a diverse company offers better protection against the vagaries of the economic cycle.

This all sounds simple and very obvious, but many companies are less profitable after an acquisition than they were before. So what makes some companies more successful with acquisitions than others? The successful predators all seem to have similar criteria, and there appear to be five 'golden rules'.

- *Firstly, they buy businesses they understand.* They avoid glamorous acquisitions. They often either stay within their own sector, or integrate vertically – buying into suppliers or customers. Any diversification outside of their existing business is in a mature established market producing everyday products. They don't buy companies with sophisticated technologies operating in emerging markets – the risks are too great and are often unquantifiable.

- *Secondly, the business must have the potential to be cash generative.* Most successful predators like an acquisition to generate significant amounts of cash in the first year. The cash could be generated in a variety of ways:

  - The business could be inherently cash generating, allowing the predator to use it as a 'cash cow' – stripping cash from the subsidiary through dividend payments.

  - The company may have subsidiaries that could be sold off to generate cash. You'll often find that this leaves the remaining business more profitable without its subsidiaries than it was with them. Five minus two can equal seven!

  - The company may have under-utilised assets that could be sold. If the acquired company has prime commercial property that is undervalued in its accounts and not reflected in its share price, it is vulnerable to 'asset stripping'. This tends to be more common when property prices are rising and there are shortages of good commercial property.

  - The company could be badly managed. If it has more cash tied up in working capital than other companies in the industry, the introduction of proper stock and credit control procedures would rapidly generate cash.

- *Thirdly, the acquired company is 'asset backed'.* In other words, its asset value is greater than its market value. This means that the predator is less exposed to losing money on the acquisition, as long as he can realise the asset values.

▦ *Fourthly, the company is often performing relatively poorly.* Companies that are performing well are always be more expensive to buy. The ideal take over target is one that's performing badly at the moment, and has already started to rationalise its business, but it's too early for the effects of their rationalisation programme to show in its financial statements. If the market's uncertain whether its strategy is working, it'll still be relatively cheap and the predator will appear to turn the company around. Once the predator has improved its profits, it could even be sold at a later date. A poorly performing business with good asset backing is always attractive, as it provides a number of options for the future.

▦ *And finally they are pessimists, not optimists.* They always look at what can go wrong, rather than what may go right.

In summary, successful predators are risk averse. They tend to buy companies that are undervalued by the market because of their current poor performance, and always avoid exposure to technical risks. Their acquisitions are cash generative, or at worst potentially cash generative once the business's underlying performance has improved. Their asset backing gives them greater security, as any under utilised assets can always be sold to generate cash.

If you're a manager, you're unlikely to be involved in identifying acquisitions for diversification programmes. But you may become involved in acquiring competitors, particularly smaller competitors who are niche players in your market place. They may, or may not, be looking to sell their business. You use your market information in conjunction with some financial analysis to identify a company's acquisition potential. If you take a leaf out of the successful predator's book, you're looking for companies that have:

▦ relatively poor financial performance;

▦ the potential to generate cash;

▦ an asset value greater than their market value.

In this chapter I'll show you how you can use financial analysis to identify a company's acquisition potential, and ensure that it will meet the above criteria. I'll show you the ratios to use, and introduce you to the way that your company will eventually determine the price it's prepared to pay to acquire the business.

Relevant ratios

You can see that you're looking for a business where there is scope to improve the profitability, so the profitability ratios are the obvious place for the analysis to start. The company's return on capital employed is crucial, as it gives an indication of both the underlying profitability and the company's future cash generation potential.

Return on capital employed

This is the only application where you're interested in the overall return on capital employed as well as the return on operating capital employed. There could be two reasons why the company may be under performing its sector:

- Its investments could be a larger proportion of its capital employed and are yielding a poorer return.

- Its return on operating capital employed is lower than the rest of its sector's.

You should start by looking at the company's overall return on capital employed, seeing how it has changed over the period and how it compares with your own. It's calculated using the following formula:

$$\frac{\text{Operating profit} - \text{Exceptional items} + \text{The share of associates' and joint ventures' operating profit} + \text{Interest receivable and similar income}}{\text{Adjusted shareholders' equity} + \text{Minority interests} + \text{Total debt} + \text{Provisions and deferred tax}}$$

(If you're unsure about which numbers to include, and why, I discuss this in detail in Chapter 10.)

You can then compare this with its return on operating capital employed:

$$\frac{\text{Operating profit} - \text{Exceptional items}}{\text{Intangible assets} + \text{Property, plant and equipment} + \text{Inventories} + \text{Trade receivables} - \text{Trade payables}}$$

Now you're usually primarily interested in the company's trading performance, so you need to look at the hierarchy of profitability ratios to see what is driving the company's return on operating capital employed. Any changes, or differences, in its return on operating capital employed will have arisen from either its profitability, or asset utilisation. I'll start by looking at the operating margin.

Operating profit margin, or return on sales

The operating margin is simple to calculate:

$$\frac{\text{Operating profit}}{\text{Revenue}}$$

You'll probably want to look at this before exceptional items to understand the underlying trend in operating margins. If their margin has changed, or is different from your own, you should think about what may cause this. I discussed the possible reasons in detail in Chapter 8, but profit margins are usually affected by differences in:

▪ Volumes – Once the company's sales are above breakeven, any revenue above variable costs is pure profit. Small changes in sales can lead to large changes in profits, and consequently its profit margins.

▪ Price – This is both the selling price and the price that the company pays for its costs. You may already know about its relative selling prices, so your prime interest is likely to be differences in costs, to see if there's any scope for improving its profitability by reducing costs. You should be able to see this by looking at its costs on the profit and loss account, and don't forget staff numbers and total staff costs are always disclosed in the notes to the accounts. The note on segmental analysis often discloses any central costs that aren't attributable to any business. (These are the costs that are likely to disappear after you've bought the business.)

▪ Mix – This could be product mix, business mix, or market mix. The segmental information note could be useful here, as it analyses profits between different businesses and also geographically. This is useful information, as it could be that it's strong in markets where you are weak, or vice versa. It also shows you whether the target company would be a good fit with your own.

You should also find some clues about the reason for any changes in the margins in its operational review. Then you'll be able to make some informed guesses about why its margin has changed and why it's different from your own.

If its operating margins don't explain any changes, or differences, in its return on operating capital, the explanation lies in its asset utilisation.

Asset utilisation

This is reflected in their asset turn ratio:

$$\frac{\text{Revenue}}{\text{Operating capital employed}}$$

If this has changed you need to know why it's changed. You know that this is a combination of two things, their utilisation of property, plant and equipment and their control of working capital. The asset turn is probably less important than its two constituent ratios: the property, plant and equipment turn and the working capital ratios. I'll start with their property, plant and equipment turn, and you calculate it using the formula below:

$$\frac{\text{Revenue}}{\text{Property, plant and equipment}}$$

This is a useful measure that helps you identify if the company's assets are being used effectively. If they used to generate £5.00 of sales for every pound invested in property, plant and equipment and are now only managing to generate £3.00, they may have excess capacity. You could either use this capacity, or you could sell off the assets and generate cash. If their property, plant and equipment turn has changed in the period, or is different from your own, you need to think about why and there are three possible reasons:

- The assets are being used more, or less, effectively. Perhaps they're used continuously, instead of on one or two shifts – or vice versa.

- The composition of property, plant and equipment could have changed. Perhaps they now rent properties, whereas they previously owned them. This will be disclosed in the notes.

- Their assets' value could have changed following an acquisition, or a major capital expenditure programme, or disposals. This would be shown in the cash flow statement and disclosed in the note on property, plant and equipment.

You're also interested in the condition of their assets, as this would influence whether you could sell them and how much you'd realise. Unfortunately you only have a few clues about the state of the assets in the accounts. The cash flow statement shows you their capital expenditure in recent years. As a general rule you would expect a company to be investing at a rate greater than the depreciation charge. Depreciation is based on historical costs and historical technologies. Whilst this does vary from one industry to another, you would expect a company's expenditure to have to exceed the depreciation charge just to stand still. If the company's spending less than its depreciation charge, the business has been run as a cash cow. You can find an indication of the age of the assets by looking at the note on property, plant and equipment in the accounts. This will show the cost, the depreciation to date and the book value. If the book value is 20% of the cost, and the assets are 80% through their lives, they're probably old. The note on depreciation in the accounting policies will disclose the asset lives, so you may get a feel for how old. But you're never going to get an accurate view on their asset's lives, as you'll face two big problems:

■ The calculation is distorted by recent capital expenditure, and even if you take this into account your analysis won't be accurate.

■ The bands given for the asset lives may be so broad (for example, three to 20 years) that it is impossible to calculate the age of the assets.

The next thing to consider is their control of working capital, starting with the working capital ratio:

$$\frac{\text{Working capital}}{\text{Revenue}}$$

All of the working capital ratios are very useful as they:

■ measure management efficiency, as an efficient management team would be minimising its investment in working capital;

■ identify if there's an opportunity to generate cash by reducing their investment in working capital;

■ identify whether their return on operating capital could be improved, as reducing working capital will also improve this ratio.

As you're likely to be looking at a potential acquisition in a similar business, you can compare their working capital ratios to your own company's to see if they're more, or less, efficient. It's then useful to analyse the components of their working capital using the following ratios:

Total inventory days (or you could calculate inventory turn if you prefer):

$$\frac{\text{Inventories}}{\text{Cost of sales (or revenue as appropriate)}} \times 365$$

Work in progress days, as this also gives you some idea of manufacturing times and you will be interested in whether they take longer to produce the goods than your company:

$$\frac{\text{Work in progress}}{\text{Cost of sales (or revenue as appropriate)}} \times 365$$

Finished goods stock days:

$$\frac{\text{Finished goods}}{\text{Cost of sales (or revenue as appropriate)}} \times 365$$

(But you need to remember that high finished goods stock isn't necessarily indicative of poor stock control. It may reflect their trading relationships, as they could be holding stocks for their customers.)

Receivable days:

$$\frac{\text{Trade receivables}}{\text{Revenue}} \times 365$$

Payable days:

$$\frac{\text{Trade payables}}{\text{Cost of sales (or revenue as appropriate)}} \times 365$$

Receivable and payable days will be important as they may reflect, in part, their relationships with their customers and suppliers.

Once you've worked out their ratios, and compared them with your own and with other companies in the sector you can then start to see their acquisition potential.

Post-acquisition profitability

You've identified their relative profitability over the past few years, now it's time to think about their likely profitability if you owned them.

Only operating profit offers long-term sustainable profits, and this is the place to start. You would expect operating profits to improve after the acquisition. The company will be absorbed into your infrastructure, and its costs should reduce as many of the central costs disappear. If you have spare capacity, you may be able to close some of their offices and factories and relocate the business to your sites. As a larger business you'll have more purchasing power, and many of your external costs should reduce. But it won't all be good news. You can't expect to maintain all their sales after you've acquired them. They'll probably have some customers who prefer to do business with them because they don't want to do business with your company! You should expect to lose a proportion of their sales. If you know the marketplace, and the customer base, you should be able to make a reasonable estimate of a post-acquisition revenue.

Once you've considered all of these factors you should be able to use the current level of profit to extrapolate a post-acquisition profit, taking into account any likely cost savings that should arise following the acquisition.

Next you move on to look at the likely capital employed. If the target company had industry average property, plant and equipment turns, what is the likely value of its property, plant and equipment? And what would be the effect of amalgamating some of its facilities with your own? If it had similar working capital ratios to your own, or the industry average, how much would it have tied up in its working capital? You could run through a number of different scenarios to develop a likely operating capital employed figure.

You then have to do some sensitivity analysis, remembering that successful predators are risk averse, and what can go wrong usually does. What would be the effect on profitability of losing another 10% of the sales, or of only achieving 50% of the planned cost reduction, or only 50% of the planned reduction in working capital? You'll have to generate a number of profit projections, giving each a probability of occurrence.

Cash management and the statement of cash flows

The cash flow statement is an important document as it reveals the company's potential to generate cash. However, if you're considering a small private company you would have to prepare a cash flow statement yourself, as it doesn't have to publish one.

Cash generated from operations

You should start by looking at the cash generated from operations, as it's the most important cash flow in any business. You can divide it into two parts: the cash flows that will arise from their sales during the year and the cash flows from working capital. Why the split? You want to be able to eliminate the effect of any changes in the business's working capital, as this could arise from management inefficiencies. You've discovered in earlier chapters that if you take the operating profit, add back depreciation and amortisation, losses on sale of assets, deduct any profits on sale of assets and the utilisation of provisions, you identify the cash flow from sales. This is unlikely to be the same as the cash flow from operations, as the operating cash flow is also affected by changes in working capital requirements. Ideally you're looking for a company with a strong cash flow from sales, reduced by an increasing investment in working capital. This could arise from either poor management or expansion; either way it would only be a short-term problem, and the company offers opportunities for future cash generation. Once you've made this 'split' between the two types of operating cash flows you could then identify its future cash flow by using your revised probable profit and working capital requirements.

Interest payments

So far I've focused on the importance of the company's profits to the acquisition decision. Unfortunately you don't just buy profits and cash flow, you also buy assets and liabilities. If the company has a lot of debt, you're acquiring it too. You may even have to repay the loans as soon as you acquire the company, as loans often have a covenant requiring immediate repayment if the company is acquired. If you buy the company you take over their debts, and consequently you'll be interested in its ability to service its debts out of its current cash flow. Cash based interest cover is important, as if it's having difficulties with its bank it may be more likely to accept a low offer. You'll also need to look at a future cash interest cover – you may well acquire the company by increasing your loans (particularly at the moment when it's a cheap form of finance). Will the acquired company make a cash contribution to your business after it's paid the interest on its own loans and your acquisition finance?

Taxation

If you're successful in improving the company's profitability, you'll have to pay more tax on the increased profits.

Capital expenditure

Ideally the business should be self funding, with its cash flow after tax, interest and dividends covering any capital expenditure. You'd really need some idea of the state of its current property, plant and equipment before you could see if this was likely, but you've already seen that it's difficult to get this information from the accounts. The only way to be certain is to see them, and you're only likely to see them once the negotiations have started and if it's a friendly bid.

Dividends paid

You're not just interested in the company's ability to pay interest; you'll also want to receive some dividends from it if you acquire it.

Cash flow before investing activities

Ideally you would want the company to have a positive cash flow, or at least a potentially positive cash flow, before investing activities. You'd hope that this, when combined with its existing cash balance, would be enough to repay its loans when they fall due.

You have seen how the cash flow statement can help you to identify the company's ability to generate cash. Before I move on to look at company valuation I'd like to remind you about the valuation free cash flow I discussed in Chapter 12.

Free cash flow

This is the cash flow that is usually used in company valuations, as it's the cash flow that is available to the providers of capital, after any reinvestment in the existing business. So it's the operating cash flow less taxation, capital expenditure, and acquisitions and disposals. This tells you how much cash is available for servicing and repaying the company's debt, and for the company's investors.

You've now considered the potential acquisition's profitability and its cash generation; I'd now like to look at how the company might be valued, and consequently how an offer price is determined.

Company valuation

It's probably unlikely that you'll be involved in determining the acquisition's price, but if you've helped to identify the acquisition's potential, you're bound to be interested in how the final price is determined. Companies use a combination of five different bases for valuing potential investments:

- assets;
- profits;
- cash;
- dividends.

The first three are appropriate for valuing acquisitions; a valuation based on dividends is only relevant when you have a small stake in a company. (It's useful when you are looking at the potential return on your investment and comparing it with the price of the share.)

Asset based valuation

This looks at the net worth of the company and is a useful starting point in company valuation. You know that the net worth is the bottom line of a typical UK balance sheet, and tells you the value of the company's net assets based on its current accounting policies. Many UK companies don't revalue their assets, so the assets' book value may be much lower than their market value. You may remember that IMI showed its properties at depreciated historical cost, and consequently the net worth shown on its balance sheet understates the value of its properties. If you wanted to know what the company's assets are really worth you would have to find answers to the following questions:

- *Land and buildings:*

    - Are they owned or leased?
    - How long does the lease have to run?
    - Have they been revalued? When?

▦ *Plant and machinery:*

- – Has the company been replacing its machinery?
- – How old is the equipment?

▦ *Other elements of property, plant and equipment:*

- – What are they?
- – How have they been valued?

▦ *Inventories:*

- – What is it?
- – Are the inventory days higher than the industry average? (This could be a sign of inefficiency, or perhaps they have obsolete stock that has not been written off, or their trading relationships with their customers require them to offer consignment stock.)

▦ *Receivables:*

- – What is included?

  ... trade receivables

  ... other receivables

  ... prepayments

  ... receivables due in more than a year

- – Are their receivable days higher than the industry average? (This could be a reflection of management inefficiency, or it may be that they have not been writing off their bad debts, or their trading relationships with their customers require them to offer longer payment terms.)

▦ *Payables:*

- – What is included?
- – How much is debt?
- – Is it secured?
- – On what?
- – What is the repayment schedule?

You won't be able to find the answers to all of these in the accounts, so you'd probably have to guess some of them. This means that you'd have your view of what the company's assets are worth, but someone else may well have a different view. However, all you've discovered is what the business's assets are worth – not what the *company* is worth. Remember you're buying assets, profits and cash.

Profit based valuations

There are two different ways of approaching a valuation based on profits:

■ return on capital;

■ price earnings ratio.

Return on capital

Every company wants to improve its return on capital employed; so the last thing that it would want is to make an acquisition that reduces it. This means that the return on capital is likely to be one of the key acquisition criteria, and it can also be used to value a company. When I've talked about the return on capital in other parts of the book I've always used a pre tax profit, as I've used it as a comparative measure. However, if you're considering buying another company you would normally look at its after tax profits, as you're also concerned about the tax effect of the acquisition and how it will affect your earnings line.

This means that most companies use an after tax return on capital employed, applying a target return on capital percentage to the profits of the potential acquisition to determine a price band. I'll illustrate this approach in the following example.

A company expects all its businesses to have a post-tax return on capital of 10%. It is considering acquiring a company that is currently averaging £500,000 after tax profits. However, its analysis has indicated that profits can be increased to £600,000 following the acquisition. The return on capital can be used to value the company based on both its current and anticipated profits:

Based on current profits:

$$\frac{£500,000}{10\%} = £5,000,000$$

This would form the basis for the original offer.

Based on anticipated future profits:

$$\frac{£600,000}{10\%} = £6,000,000$$

This would be the maximum price that the company is prepared to pay.

The PE ratio

This is the other profit based valuation method. It uses the PE ratios of quoted companies and applies them to the potential acquisition. It is often a useful guide to the price that the business's current owners expect to receive from the sale of the company.

Using the PE ratio also involves judgement, as you have to identify similar companies with similar growth prospects to provide the benchmark. (The growth prospects are important, as these are reflected in the price and therefore the PE ratio.)

Continuing with my earlier example, if a similar company had a PE ratio of 14 the owners might expect to receive at least 14 times current earnings, i.e. £7,000,000. However, this exceeds the maximum amount suggested by the return on capital criterion. This means that the company's owners may well expect to receive more for the business than your company is prepared to pay.

Discounted free cash flow valuation

You know that, theoretically, the value of any company is the present value of its 'valuation' free cash flows in perpetuity. If you want to value a business using discounted cash flow, you estimate its free cash flows for a short period, three to five years, and discount them by your weighted average cost of capital. You then have to calculate its value in the subsequent years (called its terminal, or continuing, value) and this is calculated using the growing perpetuity formula:

$$\frac{\text{Free cash flow in the first year after the forecast period}}{\text{Weighted average cost of capital} - \text{Anticipated growth in future cash flows}}$$

Whilst discounted cash flow valuations appear precise, they're no more accurate than any other valuation method, as they're based on the same forecasts. The terminal value usually represents most of the company's value, and the growing perpetuity formula is based on some unrealistic assumptions.

Enterprise value to EBITDA

This is an important ratio to use when you're considering an acquisition, as it's a quasi payback measure telling you how many years it would take you to repay the investment if you bought the company at its *current* market value. Enterprise value is the company's market capitalisation, if it's listed, plus its net debt.

$$\frac{\text{Enterprise value}}{\text{EBITDA}}$$

Summary

Companies attempt to buy other companies for a variety of reasons that usually have more to do with long-term strategic gains than short-term profit enhancement.

However, irrespective of the reason for the acquisition, a structured analysis of a company's past and current financial performance provides valuable information for both the selection and negotiation process. Whilst many of the ratios are the same as those used in other contexts, they enable you to assess a company's acquisition potential. A company's net worth, its ability to generate cash and profits, will be reflected in the price that someone is prepared to pay. There are three main valuation techniques, and in practice they are all used to produce a range of prices based on different assumptions.

19

The availability of accounts

Where can I find a company's accounts?

In the UK accounts are readily available for all companies. Suppliers and customers will normally give you their accounts, but often the accounts they provide aren't the ones you'd like to see. If they're part of a large group they'll usually give you the group accounts. However, you may prefer to analyse the individual company's accounts, rather than the group accounts, as the group's accounts may not reflect the same risks as those facing the company you're interested in. It's possible that the subsidiary company you're dealing with is viable, but the group has financial difficulties. Alternatively the group may be viable and the subsidiary isn't and will shortly be sold, or closed. By looking at the two you would have a greater understanding of the company and its commercial opportunities and threats.

Accounts are available from three sources:

- **The company itself** – Most listed and large companies have their accounts on their websites. Try the 'investors' tab on listed companies' websites and 'about us' on other companies' websites. Listed companies will usually send potential investors a copy of their accounts.

- **FT.com Free Annual Report Service** – This free service, provided by Precision IR, offers the annual reports of a number of major companies. You can access this through FT.com or directly using FT.com.ar.wilink. com. A similar service is provided by www.OrderAnnualReports.com

- **Companies House** – All companies must file their accounts at Companies House who have offices in Cardiff, Edinburgh and London. Their internet address is www.companies-house.co.gov.uk, and you can download the company's accounts (currently costing £1.00) and/or the company's annual return (also £1.00). A company's annual return includes:

  - the address of its registered office;

  - details of its company secretary and directors;

  - a summary of its share capital;

  - a list of members and any changes in members since its last annual return.

  You can also contact them at one of their offices, or by telephone (+44 (0)30 31 23 45 00).

- **Financial websites** – There's lots of financial information on the internet, including how the analysts view listed companies, including IMI. Websites such as Digital Look, FT.com, Reuters, and Yahoo finance currently offer this information for free. Some of the websites give you all the financial statements for the last few years and the ratios (usually unadjusted and they all have slightly different definitions). However, I must sound a word of warning about some of the financial data, as they're not always inputted correctly and so the answers they provide are inaccurate. One website shows IMI's EBITDA the same as operating profit, with an n/a inserted for depreciation and amortisation and another shows that IMI had a gross profit the same as its revenue in the interim financial statements! They disclose the analysts' sentiment (whether they think the share is a 'buy', whether it will 'outperform', you should hold the share, whether it'll 'underperform', or whether they think you should sell the share) and some of their estimates for the next two years. I can't replicate the tables in the book, as they're covered by copyright, but I can tell you that the consensus for IMI is 'outperform', with 38% of analysts rating the share as a 'buy', 15% as 'outperform', 38% as a 'hold', and 8% as an underperform.

The format of the small and medium-sized private companies' accounts filed at Companies House

The accounts that are filed at Companies House may not be as detailed as the ones I've shown you earlier. Small and medium-sized private companies can opt to file *modified* accounts, whereas large private companies and public companies must file their full accounts. The modified accounts filed by smaller companies are a summarised version of the accounts prepared for their shareholders. (This is designed to help them by ensuring that smaller companies don't have to show the general public information that could be harmful to their business.) These modified accounts don't allow you to do a full financial analysis, as you don't have any information about small companies' profitability.

In the first chapter, I told you about the changing accounting requirements for smaller companies, and the emergence of two sets of accounting practice. Large companies have to comply with increasingly detailed accounting rules and disclosure requirements. Whereas smaller private companies comply with a shorter, restricted set of rules that reduce the disclosures in their accounts. This is reflected in the accounts filed at Companies House for small and medium-sized private companies (I gave you a definition of these in Chapter 1). In its full accounts a small private company can choose to use a shorter format for the balance sheet, combining many items that are shown separately by larger companies. They can then file an even shorter version of this balance sheet, reducing even further the detail in the disclosures.

Small private companies' accounts

A small company must file:

■ **A modified balance sheet** – There's an example on the next page where you'll see that it only shows the totals for each balance sheet category. This is less detailed than the balance sheet prepared for its shareholders, which you may be able to get from the company, but usually only if it's one of your customers or suppliers.

- Notes to the accounts disclosing:
    - accounting policies;
    - any debtors falling due in more than a year;
    - authorised and allotted share capital;
    - details of any shares allotted during the year;
    - analysis of the cost and depreciation of fixed assets (only for the major categories that are disclosed in the abbreviated balance sheet);
    - details of its indebtedness;
    - the basis of converting foreign exchange into sterling;
    - comparative numbers for the previous year.

The presentation of a small company's modified balance sheet filed at Companies House

Fixed assets
   Intangible assets
   Tangible assets
   Investments

Current assets
   Stocks

   Debtors
   Investments
   Cash at bank and in hand

Creditors: amounts falling due within a year

Net current assets

Total assets less current liabilities

Creditors: amounts falling due after more than a year

Provisions for liabilities and charges

Accruals and deferred income

Capital and reserves
   Called up share capital
   Share premium account
   Revaluation reserve
   Other reserves
   Profit and loss account

You can see that whilst small companies disclose some information about their assets they give you very little information about their liabilities.

Medium-sized private companies' accounts

There are fewer exemptions for medium-sized companies, who have to file:

■ a directors' report;

■ a full balance sheet;

■ a modified profit and loss account, which starts with gross profit, and consequently it doesn't disclose the company's turnover or cost of sales.

Index

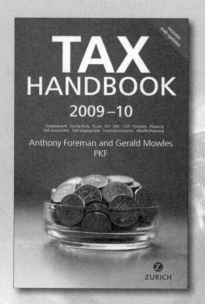

UNIVERSITY OF WINCHESTER
LIBRARY